IELTS

雅思听力词汇
强化训练手册

◎ 大学生英语学习研究团队　编著

中国水利水电出版社
www.waterpub.com.cn

内 容 提 要

　　本书专门为参加雅思英语考试的考生编写。编者基于"practice makes perfect 熟能生巧"的学习原则，精选了在雅思英语听力考试中最常见的 210 句及大量核心词汇，通过循环听力练习，加深记忆。本书在每个常用句型的词汇详解之后，都配有单词和句子的听写练习。以 10 周为学习进度安排，让学习者切实感受到自己的进步。

　　为了方便读者学习，本书的所有例句和大部分词汇详解内容都配有外籍专家的朗读录音，学习者可以登录中国水利水电出版社网站 http：//www. waterpub. com. cn/softdown/ 免费下载。

图书在版编目（ＣＩＰ）数据

雅思听力词汇强化训练手册 / 大学生英语学习研究团队编著. -- 北京：中国水利水电出版社，2014.1
ISBN 978-7-5170-1531-4

Ⅰ．①雅… Ⅱ．①大… Ⅲ．①IELTS－听说教学－自学参考资料②IELTS－词汇－自学参考资料 Ⅳ．①H310.41

中国版本图书馆CIP数据核字(2013)第309439号

书　　　名	**雅思听力词汇强化训练手册**	
作　　　者	大学生英语学习研究团队　编著	
出 版 发 行	中国水利水电出版社	
	（北京市海淀区玉渊潭南路 1 号 D 座　　100038）	
	网址：www. waterpub. com. cn	
	E-mail：sales@waterpub. com. cn	
	电话：（010）68367658（发行部）	
经　　　售	北京科水图书销售中心（零售）	
	电话：（010）88383994、63202643、68545874	
	全国各地新华书店和相关出版物销售网点	
排　　　版	北京捷龙创易图文设计中心	
印　　　刷	北京鑫瑞兴印刷有限公司	
规　　　格	170mm×230mm　16 开本　25.5 印张　435 千字	
版　　　次	2014 年 1 月第 1 版　2014 年 1 月第 1 次印刷	
印　　　数	0001—5000 册	
定　　　价	**49. 80 元**	

编写委员会

主编：洪韦韦

编委：傅南林　　郭　妹　　黄汉德

　　　黄立华　　黄亚君　　蒋人祥

　　　李金桂　　刘　燕　　卢彩华

　　　卢　飞　　莫丽艳　　莫小鹏

　　　唐朝连　　韦凤秋　　周婀娜

　　　郑国智

本书特色

听力考试从来是中国考生的弱项，因为周围的语言环境都是中文（除了学习者刻意创造一个英语的环境），所以大部分考生在听力考试这一部分都是五分靠猜测、五分靠真实的听力能力。

经过多年雅思实践教学经验，编者认为要想提高雅思英语听力水平，必须提高耳朵对雅思英语听力常用词汇和句子的敏感度，如此才能把握所听内容的要点、重点，准确回答所提的问题。换言之，捕捉听力内容的重点必须要以"听懂"为前提，而"听懂"必须依赖于耳朵对英语的敏感度，所以提高听力能力归结为一点——熟悉听力常用词汇和句子。

本书正是基于此项学习要求而编写，编写的特色如下：

 循环练习，加深记忆

本书编写是基于"practice makes perfect 熟能生巧"的学习原则，精选了在雅思英语听力考试中最常见的 210 句及大量核心词汇，考生在不断重复地聆听常用句型和词汇详解之后，对这些重点的句子和词汇则会产生深刻的记忆。

 听写训练，快速提高

本书的另一大特色是在每个常用句型的词汇详解之后，都有相关的单词听写练习和句子听写练习。听写的步骤如下：

1. 在掌握了核心词汇的用法后，先听一遍录音；

2. 在词汇听写部分，听完一遍录音后，则可以依次写下所给单词；

3. 在句子听写部分，先听一遍录音，如果在听完第二遍后能够把整个句子都写下来，是最理想的；如果写不出整个句子，则先写句子的主干，在听第三遍时，把剩下的"枝叶"添加上去；

4. 听完后核对答案，检查对错，核对自己写下的内容与听力原文，分析错误原因。为加强记忆，建议全都重新听两遍，确保自己牢记这个句型和句中的核心词汇。

10 周为限，效果显著

本书以 10 周为时间安排期限，每周 7 天，每天 3 个句子（内含约 12～15 个核心词汇），内容安排合理、科学。经过 10 周的强化训练，读者肯定能够在短期内切实感受到自己的进步。

本书适合的读者对象

- 英语听力水平一般的初三和高中学生；
- 想要在短期内提高雅思英语听力考试水平的学习者；
- 想要掌握雅思英语常用词汇和句子的学习者；
- 有一定英语基础但是多年未练习英语听力的学习者；
- 英语听力水平有待提高的学习者；
- 将出国留学或生活想要提高英语听力能力的学习者。

编者

2013.10

目 录

第 1 周

1. If you want to move into a homestay family, I'll need to get some particulars from you and I also need to know what kind of accommodation you'd like, so I can get you something suitable.

如果你想搬到寄宿家庭，我需要知道你的一些详细情况。并且，我还需要知道你想要什么样的住宿条件，这样，我才能替你找到合适的家庭。

homestay [ˈhəumstei] *n.* （在国外的访者）在当地居民家居住

【例】If you want to move into a **homestay** family, I'll need to get some particulars from you and I also need to know what kind of accommodation you'd like, so I can get you something suitable.

如果你想搬到**寄宿**家庭，我需要知道你的一些详细情况。并且，我还需要知道你想要什么样的住宿条件，这样，我才能替你找到合适的家庭。

【记】homogeneous *a.* 同性质的，同类的；由相同（或同类型）事物（或人）组成的

honest *a.* 诚实的；坦诚的；老实的

homely *a.* 〈尤英〉家常的；平凡的；〈美〉（人）不好看的；相貌平庸的

particular [pəˈtikjulə] *a.* 特别的；详细的；独有的；挑剔的　*n.* 详细说明；个别项目

【变】particulars

【例】If you want to move into a homestay family, I'll need to get some **particulars** from you and I also need to know what kind of accommodation you'd like, so I can get you something suitable.

如果你想搬到寄宿家庭，我需要知道你的一些**详细情况**。并且，我还需要知道你想要什么样的住宿条件，这样，我才能替你找到合适的家庭。

【搭】particular case 特定情况　particular about 对⋯⋯特别讲究

【记】particularly *ad.* 特别；尤其；异乎寻常地

1

partition *n.* 划分，分开；分割；隔离物；隔墙 *v.* 分开，隔开；区分；分割

participate *v.* 参加某事；分享某事

accommodation [əkɔmə'deiʃn] *n.* **住处，膳宿；调节；和解；预订铺位**

【变】accommodations

【例】If you want to move into a homestay family, I'll need to get some particulars from you and I also need to know what kind of **accommodation** you'd like, so I can get you something suitable.

　　如果你想搬到寄宿家庭，我需要知道你的一些详细情况。并且，我还需要知道你想要什么样的**住宿**条件，这样，我才能替你找到合适的家庭。

【搭】accommodation bill 通融汇票　accommodation bridge 专用桥梁

【记】accompany *v.* 陪伴；补充；与⋯⋯共存；为⋯⋯伴奏 *v.* 伴奏

accomplish *v.* 完成；达到（目的）；走完（路程、距离等）；使完

accord *n.* 一致；[音乐]（音调的）谐和；（色彩的）协调 *v.* 给予；使和谐一致；使适合

suitable ['sjuːtəbl] *a.* **适当的；相配的**

【变】more suitable　most suitable

【例】If you want to move into a homestay family, I'll need to get some particulars from you and I also need to know what kind of accommodation you'd like, so I can get you something **suitable**.

　　如果你想搬到寄宿家庭，我需要知道你的一些详细情况。并且，我还需要知道你想要什么样的住宿条件，这样，我才能替你找到**合适的**家庭。

【记】suitcase *n.* 手提箱；衣箱

suit *n.* 一套外衣；套装；诉讼；恳求 *v.* 适合于（某人）；尤指服装、颜色等相配；合身；适宜

sullen *a.* 愠怒的，不高兴的；（天气）阴沉的；悲哀的；行动缓慢的

词汇听写

1. _____　　2. _____　　3. _____

句子听写

2. Your <u>rent</u> will be ＄160 per week. You'll have to pay me ＄320 as a <u>deposit</u> before you move in. The deposit is as <u>insurance</u>, <u>in case</u> you break something.

　　你的租金是每周 160 美元，在你搬进之前，你要给我 320 美元的保证金，这个保证金是一种保险费，在你打破东西的情况下进行赔付。

---

rent ［rent］ *n.* 租金 *v.* 出租；租用；租借

【变】rented　rented　renting　rents

【例】Your **rent** will be ＄160 per week. You'll have to pay me ＄320 as a deposit before you move in. The deposit is as insurance, in case you break something.

　　　你的**租金**是每周 160 美元，在你搬进之前，你要给我 320 美元的保证金，这个保证金是一种保险费，在你打破东西的情况下进行赔付。

【搭】rent account 租金账　rent charge 租费

【记】retire *v. & n.* 退休；撤退；后退，退却

　　repair *v. & n.* 修理；纠正；恢复；弥补

　　repay *v.* 偿还；付还；报答；酬报

---

deposit ［di'pɔzit］ *n.* 存款；保证金；沉淀物　*v.* 使沉积；存放

【变】deposited　deposited　depositing

【例】Your rent will be ＄160 per week. You'll have to pay me ＄320 as a **deposit** before you move in. The deposit is as insurance, in case you break something.

　　　你的租金是每周 160 美元，在你搬进之前，你要给我 320 美元的**保证金**，这个保证金是一种保险费，在你打破东西的情况下进行赔付。

【搭】deposit account 有息存款，储蓄存款　deposit book 存折

【记】deposition *n.* 沉积（物）；［法］（在法庭上的）宣誓作证，证词；免职，革职

　　depress *v.* 压下，压低；使沮丧；使萧条；使跌价

　　deprive *v.* 剥夺，夺去，使丧失

---

insurance ［in'ʃuərns］ *n.* 保险；保险费；保险契约；赔偿金

【例】Your rent will be ＄160 per week. You'll have to pay me ＄320 as a deposit before you move in. The deposit is as **insurance**, in case you break something.

你的租金是每周 160 美元，在你搬进之前，你要给我 320 美元的保证金，这个保证金是一种**保险费**，在你打破东西的情况下进行赔付。

【搭】insurance accounting 保险会计　insurance act 保险条例

【记】insure v. 保证；确保；为……保险；投保

assurance n. 保证，担保

ensure v. 确保；担保获得（避免）；使（某人）获得；使安全

in case *conj.* 万一；假使

【例】Your rent will be ＄160 per week. You'll have to pay me ＄320 as a deposit before you move in. The deposit is as insurance, **in case** you break something.

你的租金是每周 160 美元，在你搬进之前，你要给我 320 美元的保证金，这个保证金是一种保险费，**在你打破东西的情况**下进行赔付。

词汇听写

1. ＿＿＿＿＿＿＿　2. ＿＿＿＿＿＿＿　3. ＿＿＿＿＿＿＿

句子听写

3. The programme has sensational theatre, dance, circuses and also a large number of art exhibitions, but the thing the Festival is most famous for is its great street music.

该计划包含了精彩的戏剧、舞蹈、马戏表演，还有大量的艺术展览，但这个节日最有名的是非常棒的街头音乐。

sensational [sen'seiʃnl] *a.* 轰动的；耸人听闻的；非常好的；使人感动的

【例】The programme has **sensational** theatre, dance, circuses and also a large number of art exhibitions, but the thing the Festival is most famous for is its great street music.

该计划包含了**精彩的**戏剧、舞蹈、马戏表演，还有大量的艺术展览，但这个节日最有名的是非常棒的街头音乐。

【记】progress *n. & v.* 进步；前进；[生] 进化；（向更高方向）增长　program *n.* 程序；节目，节目单；计划 *v.* [计] 给……编写程序；为……制定计划

programmer *n.* [计] 程序设计者；程序设计器；节目编排者

circus ['sə:kəs] *n.* 马戏；马戏团；闹剧，闹哄哄的场面

【变】circuses

【例】The programme has sensational theatre, dance, **circuses** and also a large number of art exhibitions, but the thing the Festival is most famous for is its great street music.

该计划包含了精彩的戏剧、舞蹈、**马戏表演**，还有大量的艺术展览，但这个节日最有名的是非常棒的街头音乐。

【搭】circus performer 马戏团演员　a media circus 媒体的一场闹剧

【记】circuit *n.* 电路，线路；巡回；环形道；[电] 电流 *v.* 巡回，周游
circular *a.* 圆形的；环行的 *n.* 通告；印制的广告，传单

exhibition [eksi'biʃn] *n.* 展览，显示；展览会；展览品

【变】exhibitions

【例】The programme has sensational theatre, dance, circuses and also a large number of art **exhibitions**, but the thing the Festival is most famous for is its great street music.

该计划包含了精彩的戏剧、舞蹈、马戏表演，还有大量的艺术**展览**，但这个节日最有名的是非常棒的街头音乐。

【搭】exhibition aerobatics 表演性特技
make an exhibition of oneself 出洋相；当众出丑

【记】exhibit *v. & n.* 陈列，展览；呈现；证明
exposition *n.* 博览会；展览会；阐述
inhibition *n.* 抑制；压抑；禁止

festival ['festivl] *n.* 节日；庆祝，纪念活动；欢乐　*a.* 节日的，喜庆的；快乐的

【例】The programme has sensational theatre, dance, circuses and also a large number of art exhibitions，but the thing the **Festival** is most famous for is its great street music.

　　该计划包含了精彩的戏剧、舞蹈、马戏表演，还有大量的艺术展览，但这个节日最有名的是非常棒的街头音乐。

【搭】Festival of Lanterns 元宵节，灯节

【记】fetch *v.* 接来（某人）；吸引 *n.* 拿取，拿来

　　fete *n.* 游乐会，游园会；盛大节日 *v.* 宴请（某人），款待；向……致敬

　　festive *a.* 节日的，过节似的；喜庆的；欢乐的

词汇听写

1.	2.	3.

句子听写

Tuesday ·· ≪≪

1. This is a traveling circus which follows a long tradition by <u>perform</u>ing in a
<u>marquee</u> — which is really like a canvas <u>portable</u> building, usually <u>put up</u> in a
green or car park.

　　这是一个巡回表演的马戏团，一直以来，在一个大帐篷里进行表演，
这个帐篷就像是帆布便携式建筑，经常停在绿地或停车场。

perform [pəˈfɔːm] v. 执行；完成；演奏；机器运转

【变】performed　performed　performing　performs

【例】This is a traveling circus which follows a long tradition by **perform**ing in a
marquee — which is really like a canvas portable building, usually put up
in a green or car park.

　　这是一个巡回表演的马戏团，一直以来，在一个大帐篷里进行**表演**，
这个帐篷就像是帆布便携式建筑，经常停在绿地或停车场。

【搭】perform a ceremony 举行仪式　　perform an experiment in 做……实验，
对……做实验

【记】performance n. 履行；性能；表现；演出

　　repeat v. 复述，背诵；重复

marquee [mɑːˈkiː] n. 选取框；大天幕；华盖

【变】marquees

【例】This is a traveling circus which follows a long tradition by performing in a
marquee — which is really like a canvas portable building, usually put up
in a green or car park.

　　这是一个巡回表演的马戏团，一直以来，在一个**大帐篷**里进行表演，
这个帐篷就像是帆布便携式建筑，经常停在绿地或停车场。

【记】queen n. 女王；王后；重要的事物 v. 立……为王后（或女王）；使……
成为国王的妻子

　　marriage n. 结婚；婚姻生活；密切结合

　　marble n. 大理石；大理石制品 a. 大理石的；冷酷无情的

portable [ˈpɔːtəbl] *a.* 手提的，便携式的；轻便的　*n.* 手提式打字机

【变】portables

【例】This is a traveling circus which follows a long tradition by performing in a marquee — which is really like a canvas **portable** building, usually put up in a green or car park.

　　这是一个巡回表演的马戏团，一直以来，在一个大帐篷里进行表演，这个帐篷就像是帆布**便携式**建筑，经常停在绿地或停车场。

【搭】portable automatic hand 轻便型遥控把柄

　　portable appliance 手提（式）仪表

【记】porter *n.* 门童；搬运工人；（医院里护送病人的）护工

　　port *n.* 港口

　　portion *n.* 一部分；一份遗产（或赠与的财产）*v.* 把……分成份额；分配

put up 提供；建造；举起，推举，提名；供给……住宿

【变】put　put　putting　puts

【例】This is a traveling circus which follows a long tradition by performing in a marquee — which is really like a canvas portable building, usually **put up** in a green or car park.

　　这是一个巡回表演的马戏团，一直以来，在一个大帐篷里进行表演，这个帐篷就像是帆布便携式建筑，经常**停在**绿地或停车场。

【搭】put away 抛弃　put his hope in her efforts 把他的希望寄托在她的努力上

　　put more emphasis on 更加重视　put about 宣称；散布　put down 放下；记下

【记】deputy *n.* 代理人 *a.* 副的

　　input *v. & n.* 输入

　　compute *n.* 计算，估计

词汇听写

1. ＿＿＿＿＿＿＿　　2. ＿＿＿＿＿＿＿　　3. ＿＿＿＿＿＿＿

句子听写

2. There are just very <u>talented</u> clowning and <u>acrobatic</u> <u>routines</u>. The show has a lot of very funny moments, especially at the beginning, but the best part is the <u>magical</u> music and lighting.

团里有非常有才华的小丑和杂技表演。这个节目有很多非常有趣的地方，特别是在刚开始的时候，但最棒的地方是奇妙的音乐和灯光。

talent ['tælənt] *n.* 才能；天才；天资

【变】more talented　most talented

【例】There are just very **talented** clowning and acrobatic routines. The show has a lot of very funny moments, especially at the beginning, but the best part is the magical music and lighting.

团里有非常有**才华**的小丑和杂技表演。这个节目有很多非常有趣的地方，特别是在刚开始的时候，但最棒的地方是奇妙的音乐和灯光。

【记】untalented *a.* 没有天赋的，缺乏才能的，不聪明的

tangle *n.* 纠纷；慌乱；争论 *v.* （使）缠结，（使）乱作一团

tale *n.* 故事，传说

tail *n.* 尾巴；末尾

tablet *n.* 药片；碑，匾

acrobatic [ækrə'bætik] *a.* 杂技的；特技的

【例】There are just very talented clowning and **acrobatic** routines. The show has a lot of very funny moments, especially at the beginning, but the best part is the magical music and lighting.

团里有非常有才华的小丑和**杂技**表演。这个节目有很多非常有趣的地方，特别是在刚开始的时候，但最棒的地方是奇妙的音乐和灯光。

【搭】acrobatic aircraft 特技飞机　acrobatic dive 跳水动作

【记】across *prep.* 穿过；横穿，横过 *ad.* 横过，越过；在对面

athletic *a.* 运动员的；运动的；体格健壮的

routine [ru:'ti:n] *n.* [计]程序；日常工作；例行公事　*a.* 日常的；例行的

【变】routines

【例】There are just very talented clowning and acrobatic **routines.** The show has a lot of very funny moments, especially at the beginning, but the best

9

part is the magical music and lighting.

团里有非常有才华的小丑和杂技**表演**。这个节目有很多非常有趣的地方，特别是在刚开始的时候，但最棒的地方是奇妙的音乐和灯光。

【搭】routine adjustment 定期调整　routine medical examination 例行的体检

【记】route n. 航线；渠道 v. 按某路线发送；给……规定路线

rough a. 粗糙的，崎岖不平的；粗鲁的；未经加工的

rouse v. 惊醒；鼓舞；使发脾气

magical ['mædʒikl] a. 魔术的；有魔力的

【例】There are just very talented clowning and acrobatic routines. The show has a lot of very funny moments, especially at the beginning, but the best part is the **magical** music and lighting.

团里有非常有才华的小丑和杂技表演。这个节目有很多非常有趣的地方，特别是在刚开始的时候，但最棒的地方是**奇妙的**音乐和灯光。

【记】magnet n. 磁铁，磁石；有吸引力的人或物

magnetic a. 有磁性的，有吸引力的；有魅力的

magician n. 魔术师；巫师；变戏法的人

词汇听写

1. ＿＿＿＿＿＿＿　2. ＿＿＿＿＿＿＿　3. ＿＿＿＿＿＿＿

句子听写

3. This is a fantastic show and the best moment comes at the end — seeing the puppeteers. When the troupe walks up out of the water, you get this amazing feeling.

这是一个梦幻般的表演，最精彩的时刻是表演临近结束时——操纵木偶剧团出来了，当剧团从水里走出来时，你会有不可思议的奇妙感觉。

fantastic [fæn'tæstik] a. 奇异的；空想的；极好的，极出色的；不可思议的　n. 古怪的人

【例】This is a **fantastic** show and the best moment comes at the end — seeing the puppeteers. When the troupe walks up out of the water, you get this amazing feeling.

这是一个**梦幻般的**表演，最精彩的时刻是表演临近结束时 — 操纵木偶剧团出来了，当剧团从水里走出来时，你会有不可思议的奇妙感觉。

【记】fascinate v. 使着迷；使神魂颠倒

fan n. 扇子，风扇；迷，粉丝 v. 扇动；吹拂，扬去

fashion n. 时尚；时尚界；方式 v. 制作，塑造；使适应

puppeteer [ˌpʌpiˈtiə] n. 操纵木偶的人；操纵傀儡 v. 操纵

【变】puppeteers

【例】This is a fantastic show and the best moment comes at the end — seeing the **puppeteers**. When the troupe walks up out of the water, you get this amazing feeling.

这是一个梦幻般的表演，最精彩的时刻是表演临近结束时 — **操纵木偶剧团**出来了，当剧团从水里走出来时，你会有不可思议的奇妙感觉。

【记】puppy n. 小狗，幼犬；浅薄自负的年轻男子

purchase v. & n. 购买；采购

purpose n. 意志；目的（进行中的）行动 v. 有意；打算

puppet n. 木偶；傀儡；受他人操纵的人

troupe [truːp] n. 剧团；一班；一团 v. 巡回演出

【变】trouped trouped trouping troupes

【例】This is a fantastic show and the best moment comes at the end — seeing the puppeteers. When the **troupe** walks up out of the water, you get this amazing feeling.

这是一个梦幻般的表演，最精彩的时刻是表演临近结束时 — 操纵木偶剧团出来了，当**剧团**从水里走出来时，你会有不可思议的奇妙感觉。

【记】trousers n. 裤子

truck n. 货车；（行李）搬运车 v. 用卡车装运

amaze [əˈmeiz] v. 使大为吃惊，使惊奇 n. 吃惊，好奇

【变】amazed amazed amazing amazes

【例】This is a fantastic show and the best moment comes at the end — seeing the puppeteers. When the troupe walks up out of the water, you get this **amazing** feeling.

　　这是一个梦幻般的表演，最精彩的时刻是表演临近结束时 — 操纵木偶剧团出来了，当剧团从水里走出来时，你会有**不可思议的奇妙**感觉。

【记】ambassador *n.* 大使，使节；（派驻联合国等国际组织的）代表

blaze *n.* 火光；光亮 *v.* 燃烧

dramatic *a.* 戏剧的，戏剧性的

amateur *a.* 业余的 *n.* 业余爱好者

词汇听写

1. _____	2. _____	3. _____

句子听写

Wednesday ·· ≪

1. I've been referred to you because I'm enquiring about the refresher courses that you run. I'd like to find out a bit more about them.

別人让我来跟您咨询，因为我在打听您举办的进修课程，我想更多地了解这些课程。

---

refer to 参考；涉及；指的是；适用于

【变】referred   referred   referring   refers

【例】I've been **referred to** you because I'm enquiring about the refresher courses that you run. I'd like to find out a bit more about them.

别人让我来跟您**咨询**，因为我在打听您举办的进修课程，我想更多地了解这些课程。

【记】refer v. 提到；针对；关系到；归因于……；查阅

refine v. 提炼；改善；使高雅

reference n. 参考；参考书；涉及；介绍人

---

enquire [inˈkwaiə] v. 询问；调查；问候（等于 inquire）

【例】I've been referred to you because I'm **enquiring** about the refresher courses that you run. I'd like to find out a bit more about them.

别人让我来跟您咨询，因为我在**打听**您举办的进修课程，我想更多地了解这些课程。

【记】enquirer n.（＝inquirer）询问的人，探究的人，调查者

refresher [riˈfreʃə] n. 可提神的人或物；补习课程；清凉饮料 a. 专业性复习进修的

【例】I've been referred to you because I'm enquiring about the **refresher** courses that you run. I'd like to find out a bit more about them.

别人让我来跟您咨询，因为我在打听您举办的**进修**课程，我想更多地了解这些课程。

【搭】a refresher course 进修课   refresh my memory 唤醒我的记忆   refresh

13

myself with a cup of tea 喝一杯茶让自己清醒下

【记】refreshment *n.* 提神，精神恢复；提神物；点心，茶点

recreation *n.* 消遣（方式）；娱乐（方式）；重建，重现

refusal *n.* 拒绝；优先取舍权

course [kɔːs] *n.* 科目；进程；课程；方针 *v.* 快速地流动；奔流；跑过；追逐

【变】courses

【例】I've been referred to you because I'm enquiring about the refresher **courses** that you run. I'd like to find out a bit more about them.

别人让我来跟您咨询，因为我在打听您举办的进修**课程**，我想更多地了解这些课程。

【搭】course angle 航向角 course data 航向数据

【记】court *n.* 法庭；天井；宫廷；网球场 *v.* 招致；设法获得；向……献殷勤；追求

courteous *a.* 有礼貌的；谦恭的；殷勤的；客气的

courtesy *n.* 谦恭有礼，礼貌，请安；有礼貌的举止

词汇听写

1. ＿＿＿＿＿＿　　2. ＿＿＿＿＿＿　　3. ＿＿＿＿＿＿

句子听写

2. It's aimed at students like you who are uncertain about what to expect at college, and looks at a fairly wide range of approaches to university learning, to motivate you to begin your study and build on your own learning strategies.

它的目标人群是像你这样的学生，不确定自己在大学里应做什么，它为大学学习提供了相当多的方法，以此激励你开始你的学习研究，并建立自己的学习策略。

fairly ['feəli] *ad.* 相当地；公平地；简直

【变】more fairly　most fairly

【例】It's aimed at students like you who are uncertain about what to expect at college，and looks at a **fairly** wide range of approaches to university learning，to motivate you to begin your study and build on your own learning strategies.

　　它的目标人群是像你这样的学生，不确定自己在大学里应做什么，它为大学学习提供了**相当多的方法**，以此激励你开始你的学习研究，并建立自己的学习策略。

【搭】fairly and squarely 光明正大地

【记】fair *a.* 公平的；合理的；晴朗的；美丽的 *n.* 集市，庙会；商品交易会

unfair *a.* 不公正的，不公平的；违反规则或准则的

faith *n.* 信用，信任；宗教信仰

affair *n.* 事，事情

repair *v. &n.* 补救，纠正

stair *n.*（*pl.*）楼梯

dairy *n.* 牛奶场，奶店

approach [ə'prəutʃ] *n.* **方法；途径；接近** *v.* **接近；着手处理**

【变】approached　approached　approaching　approaches

【例】It's aimed at students like you who are uncertain about what to expect at college，and looks at a fairly wide range of **approaches** to university learning，to motivate you to begin your study and build on your own learning strategies.

　　它的目标人群是像你这样的学生，不确定自己在大学里应做什么，它为大学学习提供了相当多的**方法**，以此激励你开始你的学习研究，并建立自己的学习策略。

【搭】approaching crisis 步步逼近的危机　different approaches 不同的方法

【记】appropriate *a.* 适当的；恰当的；合适的

approval *n.* 同意；批准；赞成

approximate *a.* 约莫的，大概的

motivate ['məutiveit] *v.* **刺激；使有动机；激发……的积极性**

【变】motivated　motivated　motivating　motivates

【例】It's aimed at students like you who are uncertain about what to expect at college, and looks at a fairly wide range of approaches to university learning, to **motivate** you to begin your study and build on your own learning strategies.

　　它的目标人群是像你这样的学生，不确定自己在大学里应做什么，它为大学学习提供了相当多的方法，以此**激励**你开始你的学习研究，并建立自己的学习策略。

【记】motive *n.* 动机；（艺术作品的）主题 *a.* 运动的；动机的；发动的 *v.* 促使

motivated *a.* 有动机的；有积极性的

emotion *n.* 情绪，情感

elevate *v.* 提高（思想）；抬高

strategy ['strætədʒi] *n.* 策略，战略（strategy 的复数形式）

【变】strategies

【例】It's aimed at students like you who are uncertain about what to expect at college, and looks at a fairly wide range of approaches to university learning, to motivate you to begin your study and build on your own learning **strategies**.

　　它的目标人群是像你这样的学生，不确定自己在大学里应做什么，它为大学学习提供了相当多的方法，以此激励你开始你的学习研究，并建立自己的学习**策略**。

【搭】strategy of control 管理策略　strategy space 策略空间

【记】straw *n.* 稻草；麦秆；吸管；毫无价值的东西 *a.* 稻草的；假的；无价值的

strawberry *n.* 草莓；草莓色

frustrate *v.* 挫败；使无效

词汇听写

1. _____　2. _____　3. _____

句子听写

3. We do some motivational exercises to help the students feel <u>positive</u> and <u>enthusiastic</u> about their study. The process of learning and <u>exploring</u> a subject can <u>lead</u> to a whole new way of looking at the world.

我们做一些励志的训练，帮助学生培养学习的积极性和热情。学习和探索一门学科的过程能够使人产生一种新的世界观。

positive [ˈpɔzətiv] *a.* 积极的；确实的，肯定的；[数] 正的；[医] 阳性的
n. 正面；正片；[语] 原级形容词；[数] 正量

【变】positives

【例】We do some motivational exercises to help the students feel **positive** and enthusiastic about their study. The process of learning and exploring a subject can lead to a whole new way of looking at the world.

我们做一些励志的训练，帮助学生培养学习的**积极**性和热情。学习和探索一门学科的过程能够使人产生一种新的世界观。

【搭】positive accommodation 正调节（视近调节）　　positive axis 正轴，正半轴

【记】positively *ad.* 明确地；断然地；肯定地

position *n.* 位置，方位；地位；态度；状态 *v.* 安置；把……放在适当位置

possess *v.* 拥有；掌握，懂得；主宰；缠住，迷住

enthusiastic [inˌθjuːziˈæstik] *a.* 热心的；热情的；热烈的；狂热的

【例】We do some motivational exercises to help the students feel positive and **enthusiastic** about their study. The process of learning and exploring a subject can lead to a whole new way of looking at the world.

我们做一些励志的训练，帮助学生培养学习的积极性和**热情**。学习和探索一门学科的过程能够使人产生一种新的世界观。

【记】enthusiasm *n.* 热情，热忱；热衷的事物；宗教的狂热

entire *a.* 全部的；整个的；全体的

enthusiastically *ad.* 热心地，满腔热情地；起劲地

explore [ikˈsplɔː] *v.* 勘查，探测，勘探；[医] 探查（伤处等），探索，研究

【变】explored　explored　exploring　explores

【例】We do some motivational exercises to help the students feel positive and enthusiastic about their study. The process of learning and **exploring** a subject can lead to a whole new way of looking at the world.

　　我们做一些励志的训练，帮助学生培养学习的积极性和热情。学习和**探索**一门学科的过程能够使人产生一种新的世界观。

【记】explosion *n.* 爆炸，炸裂；（感情，尤指愤怒的）突然爆发

explosion *n.* 探测，勘探，探险

explosive *a.* 爆炸的 *n.* 爆炸物，炸药

lead to 把……带到；领到；（道路）通向；导致

【变】led　led　leading　leads

【例】We do some motivational exercises to help the students feel positive and enthusiastic about their study. The process of learning and exploring a subject can **lead to** a whole new way of looking at the world.

　　我们做一些励志的训练，帮助学生培养学习的积极性和热情。学习和探索一门学科的过程能够使人产生一种新的世界观。

【记】leader *n.* 领袖，领导者

leading *a.* 重要的，主要的

plead *v.* 为……辩护

leaf *n.* 叶子

league *n.* 同盟，联盟

lean *v.* 使倾斜，屈身；倚 *a.* 瘦的；贫乏的

leap *v.* & *n.* 跳，跳跃

词汇听写

1. ＿＿＿＿＿＿　　2. ＿＿＿＿＿＿　　3. ＿＿＿＿＿＿

句子听写

Thursday ·· ⫷

1. Two of the key <u>components</u> of the course are time <u>management</u> and <u>overcoming procrastination</u>.

这门课程的两个重要组成部分是时间管理和克服拖沓的习惯。

---

component [kəm'pəunənt] *a.* **组成的，构成的** *n.* **成分；组件；[电子] 元件**

【变】components

【例】Two of the key **components** of the course are time management and overcoming procrastination.

这门课程的两个重要**组成部分**是时间管理和克服拖沓的习惯。

【搭】component building 组合造房　component cost 个别成本

【记】compose *v.* 组成，构成；创作（乐曲、诗歌等）；为……谱曲

composite *a.* 混合成的，综合成的 *n.* 合成物，混合物

composer *n.* （尤指古典音乐）作曲家；调停人

---

management ['mænidʒmnt] *n.* **管理；管理人员；管理部门；操纵；经营 手段**

【变】managements

【例】Two of the key components of the course are time **management** and overcoming procrastination.

这门课程的两个重要组成部分是时间**管理**和克服拖沓的习惯。

【搭】management cycle 管理周期　management forms 经营状态

【记】manager *n.* 处理者，经理，管理人

manifest *v.* 显示，使显现 *a.* 明白的，明显的

manipulate *v.* 操作，处理；操纵

---

overcome [əuvə'kʌm] *v.* **克服；胜过**

【变】overcame　overcome　overcoming　overcomes

【例】Two of the key components of the course are time management and **overcoming** procrastination.

19

这门课程的两个重要组成部分是时间管理和**克服**拖沓的习惯。

【搭】overcome friction 克服摩擦力

【记】overestimate *v. &n.* 对（数量）估计过高，对……作过高的评价

overflow *v.* 溢出，淹没 *n.* 泛滥，溢出物 *a.* 溢出的，满出的

overwhelm *v.* 淹没；压倒

procrastination [prə(u)ˌkræsti'neiʃn] *n.* 耽搁，拖延

【例】Two of the key components of the course are time management and overcoming **procrastination**.

这门课程的两个重要组成部分是时间管理和克服**拖沓**的习惯。

【记】produce *v.* 生产；产生；制作；创作 *n.* 产品；产量

profession *n.* 专业；同行；宣称；信仰

proficiency *n.* 熟练，精通，娴熟

词汇听写

1. _____ 2. _____ 3. _____

句子听写

2. It's essential that you book well ahead of time. In fact, the Course Convenor tells me that there are only five places left.

重要的是你要提前预订。事实上，课程组织者告诉我，现在只剩五个名额。

essential [it'senʃl] *a.* **基本的；必要的；本质的；精华的** *n.* **本质；要素；要点；必需品**

【变】essentials

【例】It's **essential** that you book well ahead of time. In fact, the Course Convenor tells me that there are only five places left.

重要的是你要提前预订。事实上，课程组织者告诉我，现在只剩五个名额。

【搭】essential character 本质特征　　essential goods 必需品，主要货物

【记】essence *n.* 本质，实质；精髓；香精

establish *v.* 建立，创建；确立或使安全；使被安排好；使成为

estimate *n.* & *v.* 估计，预测；报价，预算书；评价，判断

book [buk] *n.* 书籍；卷；账簿；名册；工作簿　*v.* 预订；登记

【变】booked booked booking books

【例】It's essential that you **book** well ahead of time. In fact，the Course Convenor tells me that there are only five places left.

重要的是你要提前**预订**。事实上，课程组织者告诉我，现在只剩五个名额。

【搭】be fully booked 全被预订　　book cloth 封面布

【记】boot *n.* 长靴，皮靴；防护罩；[多用于英国] 行李箱 *v.* 穿（靴）；踢

booth *n.* 售货棚，摊位；公用电话亭；隔开的小间；（选举）投票站

bore *v.* 令人厌烦；钻孔 *n.* 使人讨厌的人

ahead of 在……之前

【例】It's essential that you book well **ahead of** time. In fact，the Course Convenor tells me that there are only five places left.

重要的是你要**提前**预订。事实上，课程组织者告诉我，现在只剩五个名额。

convenor [kən'viːnə] *n.* 会议召集人

【变】conveners

【例】It's essential that you book well ahead of time. In fact，the Course **Convener** tells me that there are only five places left.

重要的是你要提前预订。事实上，课程**组织者**告诉我，现在只剩五个名额。

【记】convention *n.* 会议；全体与会者；国际公约；惯例，规矩

conventional *a.* 传统的；习用的，平常的；依照惯例的；约定的

conversation *n.* 交谈，会话；交往，交际；会谈；（人与计算机的）人机对话

词汇听写

1. _____ 2. _____ 3. _____

句子听写

3. This course is more <u>in line with</u> your situation. Let me just get out a <u>registration</u> form and <u>take down</u> your details.

　　这门课程更符合你的情况。我拿一下登记表，写下您的详细信息。

in line with 符合；与……一致

【例】This course is more **in line with** your situation. Let me just get out a registration form and take down your details.

　　这门课程更**符合**你的情况。我拿一下登记表，写下您的详细信息。

【搭】in line with our general line 和我们总的原则一致　out of line with reality 不切实际　be lined with bushes 长满了灌木丛

【记】streamline *n.* 流线；流线型

underline *v.* 着重

decline *v.* 下倾；偏斜；衰退

registration [redʒit'streiʃn] *n.* 登记；注册；挂号

【变】registrations

【例】This course is more in line with your situation. Let me just get out a **registration** form and take down your details.

　　这门课程更符合你的情况。我拿一下**登记表**，写下您的详细信息。

【搭】registration from 登记表　registration fire 试射

【记】regret *v.* & *n.* 后悔，悔恨；遗憾，抱歉

register *n.* 登记，注册；登记簿 *v.* 登记，注册

regime *n.* 政治制度，政体；方法

take down 记下；拿下；拆卸；病倒

【变】took　taken　taking　takes

【例】This course is more in line with your situation. Let me just get out a registration form and **take down** your details.

　　这门课程更符合你的情况。我拿一下登记表，**写下**您的详细信息。

【搭】take sth. down in shorthand 用速记记录某事　　take down your umbrella 收起你的伞　　take down the barricades 拆掉路障

【记】take up 开始从事；接受（提议）；占用

　　take off 脱掉；起飞；突然成功

　　intake *n.* 吸入；输入能量

　　overtake *v.* 追上，超过

词汇听写

1. _____ 2. _____ 3. _____

句子听写

Friday ·· «

1. We're very <u>grateful</u> that the Committee has agreed that a <u>representative</u> for the Students' Union can <u>present</u> student's suggestions about the design for the <u>proposed</u> new Union building.

  对委员会同意由一名学生会代表呈述学生的建议，我们表示感谢，学生代表将对拟议的新联盟大厦的设计提出建议。

---

grateful ['greitful] *a.* 感谢的；令人愉快的，宜人的

【例】We're very **grateful** that the Committee has agreed that a representative for the Students' Union can present student's suggestions about the design for the proposed new Union building.

  对委员会同意由一名学生会代表呈述学生的建议，我们表示**感谢**，学生代表将对拟议的新联盟大厦的设计提出建议。

【搭】be grateful to him 对他很感激　be grateful for the man's advice 感激这个人的建议

【记】gratitude *n.* 感激，感谢；感激的样子；恩义

　　gravel *n.* 沙砾，碎石；砾石；[医] 结石

　　grate *v.* 磨碎，压碎 *n.* 炉格，刺耳的声音

---

representative [ˌrepri'zentətiv] *n.* 代表；继任者；议员　*a.* 典型的；有代表性的；代议制的；类似的

【变】representatives　more representative　most representative

【例】We're very grateful that the Committee has agreed that a **representative** for the Students' Union can present student's suggestions tions about the design for the proposed new Union building.

  对委员会同意由一名学生会代表呈述学生的建议，我们表示感谢，学生代表将对拟议的新联盟大厦的设计提出建议。

【搭】representative cost 代表成本　a representative of the UN 联合国代表

【记】representation *n.* 表现；表现……的事物

　　represent *v.* 象征；代表，代理；扮演；作为示范

reproach *v.* 责骂；使丢脸；损伤……的体面 *n.* 责骂；污辱；谴责

present [priˈzent] *v.* 提出；介绍；呈现；赠送 [ˈpreznt] *a.* 现在的；出席的 *n.* 现在；礼物

【变】presented presented presenting presents

【例】We're very grateful that the Committee has agreed that a representative for the Students' Union can **present** student's suggestions tions about the design for the proposed new Union building.

对委员会同意由一名学生会代表**呈述**学生的建议，我们表示感谢，学生代表将对拟议的新联盟大厦的设计提出建议。

【搭】present arms 举枪致敬　present ice 现代冰川

【记】presentation *n.* 陈述；报告；介绍；赠送

presently *ad.* 目前；不久；马上

presence *n.* 出席；仪表

propose [prəˈpəuz] *v.* 建议；打算，计划；求婚

【变】proposed proposed proposing proposes

【例】We're very grateful that the Committee has agreed that a representative for the Students' Union can present student's suggestions about the design for the **proposed** new Union building.

对委员会同意由一名学生会代表呈述学生的建议，我们表示感谢，学生代表将对**拟议的**新联盟大厦的设计提出建议。

【记】proposition *n.* & *v.* 命题；建议；主张

proposal *n.* 提议；建议；求婚；〈美〉投标

composer *n.* 作曲家；调停人

impose *v.* 利用；欺骗

词汇听写

1. _____　2. _____　3. _____

句子听写

2. We appreciate that some of our ideas may not be feasible in the circumstances, but we do feel that it is important that the ultimate beneficiaries of the facilities should have some say in its design.

我们知道我们的一些想法在此情况下可能是不可行的，但我们觉得让这些设备的最终受益者在它的设计上有一定的发言权，这点是很重要的。

appreciate [əˈpriːʃieit] *v.* 欣赏；感激；领会；鉴别

【变】appreciated　appreciated　appreciating　appreciates

【例】We **appreciate** that some of our ideas may not be feasible in the circumstances，but we do feel that it is important that the ultimate beneficiaries of the facilities should have some say in its design.

我们**知道**我们的一些想法在此情况下可能是不可行的，但我们觉得让这些设备的最终受益者在它的设计上有一定的发言权，这点是很重要的。

【记】appreciation *n.* 欣赏，鉴赏；感谢；评价；（尤指土地或财产的）增值

approach *v.* 接近，走近，靠近

appropriate *a.* 适当的；恰当的；合适的

feasible [ˈfiːzəbl] *a.* 可行的；可用的；可实行的；可能的

【例】We appreciate that some of our ideas may not be **feasible** in the circumstances，but we do feel that it is important that the ultimate beneficiaries of the·facilities should have some say in its design.

我们知道我们的一些想法在此情况下可能是不**可行的**，但我们觉得让这些设备的最终受益者在它的设计上有一定的发言权，这点是很重要的。

【搭】feasible solution 可行的解释　feasible problem 可以解决的问题

【记】feast *n.* 盛会；宴会；宗教节日

feature *n.* 特征，特点；面貌；（期刊的）特辑

feather *n.* 羽毛；翎毛；状态，心情；种类

ultimate [ˈʌltimət] *a.* 最终的；极限的；最大的　*n.* 终极；根本；基本原则

【变】ultimates

【例】We appreciate that some of our ideas may not be feasible in the circumstances，but we do feel that it is important that the **ultimate** beneficiaries of the facilities should have some say in its design.

　　我们知道我们的一些想法在此情况下可能是不可行的，但我们觉得让这些设备的**最终**受益者在它的设计上有一定的发言权，这点是很重要的。

【搭】ultimate analysis 最后分析　　ultimate weapon 杀手锏

【记】ultimately *ad.* 最后，最终；基本上；根本

　　ultrasonic *a.* ［声］超声的；超音波的，超音速的

　　ultraviolet *a.* 紫外的；紫外线的；产生紫外线的

beneficiary [beni'fiʃri] *n.* ［金融］受益人，受惠者；封臣　　*a.* 拥有封地的；受圣俸的

【变】beneficiaries

【例】We appreciate that some of our ideas may not be feasible in the circumstances，but we do feel that it is important that the ultimate **beneficiaries** of the facilities should have some say in its design.

　　我们知道我们的一些想法在此情况下可能是不可行的，但我们觉得让这些设备的最终**受益者**在它的设计上有一定的发言权，这点是很重要的。

【搭】beneficiary certificate 受益人证词　　beneficiary party 受益方

【记】benefit *n.* 利益，好处；救济金；恩惠

　　beneficial *a.* 有利的，有益的

　　berry *n.* 浆果；干果仁

词汇听写

1. _____　2. _____　3. _____

句子听写

3. The consensus was as follows. Firstly, regarding the crucial matter of the site, we presented the three options that you have proposed.

达成的共识如下。首先，关于地点这项重要的提议，我们选择了三个您所提供的选项。

consensus [kən'sensəs] *n.* 一致；舆论；合意

【变】consensuses

【例】The **consensus** was as follows. Firstly, regarding the crucial matter of the site, we presented the three options that you have proposed.

达成的**共识**如下。首先，关于地点这项重要的提议，我们选择了三个您所提供的选项。

【搭】consensus sequence 共有序列

【记】consent *n.* 准许，赞同；同意；（意见等的）一致

consequence *n.* 结果，成果；［逻］结论；重要性；推论

consequent *a.* 随之发生的；必然的，合乎逻辑的；继起的；［地］顺向的

regarding [ri'gɑːdiŋ] *prep.* 关于，至于

【例】The consensus was as follows. Firstly, **regarding** the crucial matter of the site, we presented the three options that you have proposed.

达成的共识如下。首先，**关于**地点这项重要的提议，我们选择了三个您所提供的选项。

【搭】regard as 把……认做；当做；看成；看做 regard with great detestation 非常讨厌；视如蛇蝎

【记】regardless *ad.* 不顾后果地；不管怎样，无论如何；不惜费用地

regenerative *a.* 恢复的；新生的；再生的；回热的

regard *v.* 关系；注意；（尤指以某种方式）注视；尊敬

crucial ['kruːʃl] *a.* 重要的；决定性的；定局的；决断的

【变】more crucial most crucial

【例】The consensus was as follows. Firstly, regarding the **crucial** matter of the site, we presented the three options that you have proposed.

达成的共识如下。首先，关于地点这项**重要的**提议，我们选择了三个您所提供的选项。

【搭】crucial element 关键零件 crucial use of variable 变项的严格运用

【记】crude *a.* 粗糙的；粗鲁的；天然的，未加工的；简陋的

　　cruel *a.* 残酷的；使人痛苦的，严酷的

　　cruise *v.* 巡游；漫游；巡航

option [ˈɔpʃn] *n.* ［计］选项；选择权；买卖的特权　*v.* 选择

【变】optioned　optioned　optioning　options

【例】The consensus was as follows. Firstly, regarding the crucial matter of the site，we presented the three **options** that you have proposed.

　　达成的共识如下。首先，关于地点这项重要的提议，我们选择了三个您所提供的**选项**。

【搭】option group 选项组　　option table 选择表

【记】optional *a.* 可选择的；随意的，任意的；非强制的；选修科目的

　　optical *a.* 视觉的，视力的；眼睛的；光学的

　　optimism *n.* 乐观；乐观主义

词汇听写

1. _____　2. _____　3. _____

句子听写

Saturday ·· ◀◀◀

1. There are three options: one, in the city centre, near the <u>Faculty</u> of Education; two, on the <u>outskirts</u> of the city, near the park, and three, out of town, near the halls of <u>residence</u>. Students are asked to <u>cite</u> reasons for and against these sites.

有三种选择：一是在城市中心，教育系附近；二是城市的郊区，公园附近；三是城外，在学生宿舍楼附近。学生无论是赞成或者反对这些地点都要陈述原因。

faculty [ˈfæklti] *n.* 科，系；能力；全体教员

【变】faculties

【例】There are three options: one, in the city centre, near the **Faculty** of Education; two, on the outskirts of the city, near the park, and three, out of town, near the halls of residence. Students are asked to cite reasons for and against these sites.

有三种选择：一是在城市中心，教育**系**附近；二是城市的郊区，公园附近；三是城外，在学生宿舍楼附近。学生无论是赞成或者反对这些地点都要陈述原因。

【搭】faculty adviser（美）（大学）指导教师　faculty club 教授俱乐部

【记】fade *v.* 褪去；逐渐消逝；凋谢，衰老

facilitate *v.* 促进，助长；使容易；帮助

outskirt [ˈautskəːt] *n.* 郊区，市郊

【变】outskirts

【例】There are three options: one, in the city centre, near the Faculty of Education; two, on the **outskirts** of the city, near the park, and three, out of town, near the halls of residence. Students are asked to cite reasons for and against these sites.

有三种选择：一是在城市中心，教育系附近；二是城市的**郊区**，公

园附近；三是城外，在学生宿舍楼附近。学生无论是赞成或者反对这些地点都要陈述原因。

【记】outstanding *a.* 杰出的；显著的；凸出的；未完成的

outset *n.* 开始，开端

outside *ad.* 在外面；向外面；在户外；露天

residence [ˈrezidns] *n.* 住宅，住处；居住

【变】residences

【例】There are three options：one, in the city centre, near the Faculty of Education；two, on the outskirts of the city, near the park, and three, out of town, near the halls of **residence**. Students are asked to cite reasons for and against these sites.

有三种选择：一是在城市中心，教育系附近；二是城市的郊区，公园附近；三是城外，在学生**宿舍**楼附近。学生无论是赞成或者反对这些地点都要陈述原因。

【搭】residence country 居住国　　residence hall 学生宿舍

【记】reside *v.* 住，居住，驻在；（性质）存在

resident *a.* 定居的，常驻的；固有的，内在的

residual *a.* 残余的；残留的

cite [sait] *v.* 引用；传讯；想起；表彰

【变】cited　cited　citing　cites

【例】There are three options：one, in the city centre, near the Faculty of Education；two, on the outskirts of the city, near the park, and three, out of town, near the halls of residence. Students are asked to **cite** reasons for and against these sites.

有三种选择：一是在城市中心，教育系附近；二是城市的郊区，公园附近；三是城外，在学生宿舍楼附近。学生无论是赞成或者反对这些地点都要**陈述**原因。

【搭】cite chapter and verse for 注明引证的出处

【记】citizen *n.* 公民；国民；市民；平民

city *n.* 城市；全市居民

civil *a.* 公民的；文明的；民用的，国民间的；[法] 民事的，根据民法的

词汇听写

1. _____ 2. _____ 3. _____

句子听写

2. Just over 40% of the respondents were in favor, but a largish minority were strongly against it, claiming that it is elitist and a waste of funds.

　　超过 40% 的受访者赞成，但有一个人口相当大的少数民族对此强烈反对，声称这是精英主义，浪费资金。

respondent [rit'spɔndnt] *a.* 回答的；应答的　*n.* [法] 被告；应答者

【变】respondents

【例】Just over 40% of the **respondents** were in favor, but a largish minority were strongly against it, claiming that it is elitist and a waste of funds.

　　超过 40% 的**受访者**赞成，但有一个人口相当大的少数民族对此强烈反对，声称这是精英主义，浪费资金。

【记】respond *v.* 回答，响应

　　response *n.* 反应；回答，答复

　　responsibility *n.* 责任；职责；责任感；负责任

in favor 赞成；支持；有利于

【例】Just over 40% of the respondents were **in favor**, but a largish minority were strongly against it, claiming that it is elitist and a waste of funds.

　　超过 40% 的受访者**赞成**，但有一个人口相当大的少数民族对此强烈反对，声称这是精英主义，浪费资金。

【记】favor（＝favour）*n.* 帮助；恩惠；赞同；善行

　　favourable *a.* 顺利的，良好的；有利的；赞许的；给人好印象的

　　favourite *a.* 特别受喜爱的 *n.* 特别喜爱的人（或物）

largish ['lɑːdʒiʃ] *a.* 稍大的；相当大的

【例】Just over 40% of the respondents were in favor, but a **largish** minority were strongly against it, claiming that it is elitist and a waste of funds.

超过 40% 的受访者赞成，但有一个人口相当大的少数民族对此强烈反对，声称这是精英主义，浪费资金。

【记】waste *n.* 浪费，挥霍钱财；废料，废品，废物；荒地，荒芜；损耗

wasp *n.* 黄蜂；易动怒的人

elitist [eiˈliːtist] *n.* 优秀人材；杰出人物　*a.* 优秀人材的；杰出人材的

【变】elitists

【例】Just over 40% of the respondents were in favor, but a largish minority were strongly against it, claiming that it is **elitist** and a waste of funds.

超过 40% 的受访者赞成，但有一个人口相当大的少数民族对此强烈反对，声称这是**精英主义**，浪费资金。

【记】elliptical *a.* 椭圆的；像椭圆形的；省略的

else *ad.* 其他；否则；另外

embarrass *v.* （使）窘迫，（使）局促不安；（使）困难

wash *v.* 洗，清洗；浸湿；冲刷，冲击；洗去罪名

词汇听写

1. _____　2. _____　3. _____

句子听写

3. School organizes trips to different places of historical interest and also which offers a variety of shopping.

学校组织不同名胜古迹的短途旅游，也组织到提供各种购物的地方旅游。

organize [ˈɔːgənaiz] *v.* 组织；使有系统化；给予生机；组织成立工会等

【变】organized　organized　organizing　organizes

【例】School **organizes** trips to different places of historical interest and also which offers a variety of shopping.

　　学校**组织**不同名胜古迹的短途旅游，也组织到提供各种购物的地方旅游。

【记】orient *v.* 标定方向；使……向东方

oriental *a.* 东方的；东方人的；东方文化的

origin *n.* 起源，根源；出身；［数］原点；［解］（筋、神经的）起端

historical [hit'stɔrikl] *a.* **历史的；史学的；基于史实的**

【例】School organizes trips to different places of **historical** interest and also which offers a variety of shopping.

　　学校组织不同名胜**古**迹的短途旅游，也组织到提供各种购物的地方旅游。

【搭】historical archives 文史资料馆，历史文献档案馆　historical cost 过去成本；原始成本

【记】history *n.* 历史，历史学；发展史；履历，经历

historic *a.* 在历史上重要的，有历史影响的；历史的，历史上的

historian *n.* 历史学家，史学工作者

offer [ˈɔfə] *v.* **提供；出价；试图；求婚；献祭　*n.* 提议；出价；意图；录取通知书**

【变】offered　offered　offering　offers

【例】School organizes trips to different places of historical interest and also which **offers** a variety of shopping.

　　学校组织不同名胜古迹的短途旅游，也组织到**提供**各种购物的地方旅游。

【搭】offer a choice 自己挑选，听凭选择　offer to treat 提议自己出钱请人吃饭等

【记】office *n.* 办公室；公职；（政府部门的）部

official *n.* 行政官员；公务员；［体］裁判；高级职员

offset *v.* 抵消；补偿

variety [vəˈraiəti] *n.* **多样；种类；变化，多样化**

【变】varieties

【例】School organizes trips to different places of historical interest and also which offers a **variety** of shopping.

　　学校组织不同名胜古迹的短途旅游，也组织到提供**各种**购物的地方旅游。

【搭】variety of play 多变打法　variety shop 杂货铺

【记】various *a.* 各种各样的；多方面的；许多的；各个的，个别的

　　vary *v.* 变化；不同，偏离；［生］变异

词汇听写

1. ＿＿＿＿＿＿＿＿　2. ＿＿＿＿＿＿＿＿　3. ＿＿＿＿＿＿＿＿

句子听写

Sunday ·· ≪

1. To start your visit, I'm just going to give you a brief <u>account</u> of the history of their museum before letting you <u>roam</u> about <u>on your own</u>.

要开始您的观光旅程了，在自由观光之前，我将简单地介绍一下他们博物馆的历史。

brief [briːf] *a.* 简短的，简洁的；短暂的，草率的　*n.* 摘要，简报；概要，诉书　*v.* 简报，摘要；作……的提要

【变】briefed　briefed　briefing　briefs

【例】To start your visit, I'm just going to give you a **brief** account of the history of their museum before letting you roam about on your own.

要开始您的观光旅程了，在自由观光之前，我将**简单**地介绍一下他们博物馆的历史。

【搭】brief case 公文包　　brief abstract 简易文摘

【记】bright *a.* 明亮的；聪明的；辉煌的；活泼的

bribe *v.* 贿赂，行贿

brighten *v.* （使）发亮；（使）生色；（使）生辉；（使）快乐

account [əˈkaunt] *n.* 账户；解释；账目，账单；理由　*v.* 解释；导致；报账；认为；把……视为

【变】accounted　accounted　accounting　accounts

【例】To start your visit, I'm just going to give you a brief **account** of the history of their museum before letting you roam about on your own.

要开始您的观光旅程了，在自由观光之前，我将简单地**介绍**一下他们博物馆的历史。

【搭】account bill 账单　　take sth. into account 把某物纳入考虑范围

【记】accountant *n.* 会计人员，会计师

accumulate *v.* 堆积，积累

accuracy *n.* 精确（性），准确（性）

roam [rəum] *v.* &*n.* 漫游，漫步；流浪

【变】roamed　roamed　roaming　roams

【例】To start your visit, I'm just going to give you a brief account of the history of their museum before letting you **roam** about on your own.

　　要开始您的观光旅程了，在自由**观光**之前，我将简单地介绍一下他们博物馆的历史。

【搭】roam about 漫游；东流西窜；流浪

【记】roar *v.* 咆哮；喧闹；吼叫；混乱或吵闹

　　Roman *a.* 古罗马的；罗马人的；罗马基督教会的；天主教的

on your own 独立地，自愿地

【例】To start your visit, I'm just going to give you a brief account of the history of their museum before letting you roam about **on your own**.

　　要开始您的观光旅程了，在**自由**观光之前，我将简单地介绍一下他们博物馆的历史。

【记】once *ad.* 一次，一趟；一倍；曾经；一旦

词汇听写

1. _____　2. _____　3. _____

句子听写

2. The water and the availability of raw materials in the area, like minerals and iron ore, and also the abundance of local fuels, all made this site suitable for industry from a very early time.

　　这个地方的水资源和原材料，如矿物质和铁矿石，以及当地丰富的燃料，都使得这个地方从很早以前就成为发展工业的合适之选。

availability [əˌveiləˈbiləti] *n.* 可用性；有效性；实用性

【例】The water and the **availability** of raw materials in the area, like minerals

37

and iron ore, and also the abundance of local fuels, all made this site suitable for industry from a very early time.

　　这个地方的水资源和原材料，如矿物质和铁矿石，以及当地丰富的燃料，都使得这个地方从很早以前就成为发展工业的合适之选。

【搭】availability coefficient 可用系数　　availability factor 使用效率，运转因数

【记】available a. 可用的；有空的；可会见的；（戏票、车票等）有效的

avenue n. 林荫路；大街；途径，手段；（美）（南北向）街道

aviation n. 航空；飞行术，航空学；飞机制造业

raw [rɔː] a. 生的；未加工的；刺痛的；无经验的；（在艺术等方面）不成熟的　　n. 擦伤处　　v. 擦伤

【变】rawer　rawest

【例】The water and the availability of **raw** materials in the area, like minerals and iron ore, and also the abundance of local fuels, all made this site suitable for industry from a very early time.

　　这个地方的水资源和**原**材料，如矿物质和铁矿石，以及当地丰富的燃料，都使得这个地方从很早以前就成为发展工业的合适之选。

【搭】raw meat 生肉　　raw distillate 粗馏物，粗馏出油

【记】ray n. （热或其他能量的）射线；光束，光线

race n. 种，种族；（速度）比赛；（事件等的）进行；人种

racial a. 种族的；人种的；存在或发生于种族之间的

mineral ['minrl] n. 矿物；（英）矿泉水；无机物；苏打水（常用复数表示）　　a. 矿物的；矿质的

【变】minerals

【例】The water and the availability of raw materials in the area, like **minerals** and iron ore, and also the abundance of local fuels, all made this site suitable for industry from a very early time.

　　这个地方的水资源和**矿物**质和铁矿石，以及当地丰富的燃料，都使得这个地方从很早以前就成为发展工业的合适之选。

【搭】mineral water 矿泉水　　mineral colour 矿物颜料，无机颜料

【记】mingle v. 混合，混淆

miniature *a.* 小型的，微小的

minimize *v.* 把……减至最低数量；对（某事物）作最低估计，极力贬低（某事物）的价值；极度轻视

abundance [əˈbʌndns] *n.* 充裕，丰富

【例】The water and the availability of raw materials in the area, like minerals and iron ore, and also the **abundance** of local fuels, all made this site suitable for industry from a very early time.

这个地方的水资源和原材料，如矿物质和铁矿石，以及当地**丰富的**燃料，都使得这个地方从很早以前就成为发展工业的合适之选。

【搭】abundance class 多度级　　abundance ratio 丰度

【记】abundant *a.* 大量的，充足的；丰富的，富有的

abuse *n.* 滥用；恶习；侮辱；恶言

academic *a.* 学院的，大学的，学会的，（学术、文艺）协会的；学究的

词汇听写

1. ＿＿＿＿＿＿＿　2. ＿＿＿＿＿＿＿　3. ＿＿＿＿＿＿＿

句子听写

3. In the top right hand corner is the show room where samples of all the tools that were made through the ages were on display. In the top left corner is the grinding shop where the tools were sharpened and finished.

右上角是展览室，陈列了古老工具的样本。左上角是研磨车间，工具磨尖和其他制作工序都在那里完成。

sample [ˈsæmpl] *n.* 样品；采样；例子

【变】samples

【例】In the top right hand corner is the show room where **samples** of all the tools that were made through the ages were on display. In the top left corner is the grinding shop where the tools were sharpened and finished.

右上角是展览室，陈列了古老工具的**样本**。左上角是研磨车间，工具磨尖和其他制作工序都在那里完成。

【搭】sample check 样品检查　sample bulb 取样瓶，样品瓶

【记】sanction *n.* 制裁，处罚；批准；约束力；鼓励

example *n.* 例子；榜样；范例；先例

sand *n.* 沙；沙滩；沙色

on display 展览，公开展出

【例】In the top right hand corner is the show room where samples of all the tools that were made through the ages were **on display**. In the top left corner is the grinding shop where the tools were sharpened and finished.

右上角是展览室，**陈列**了古老工具的样本。左上角是研磨车间，工具磨尖和其他制作工序都在那里完成。

【记】display *n.* 展览，陈列；展览品；显示器

displacement *n.* 取代；免职；（船）排水量；〔化〕置换

displease *v.* 使生气，使不愉快；冒犯，触怒

grind [graind] *v.* 磨碎；磨快；折磨　*n.* 磨；苦工作

【变】ground　ground　grinding　grinds

【例】In the top right hand corner is the show room where samples of all the tools that were made through the ages were on display. In the top left corner is the **grinding** shop where the tools were sharpened and finished.

右上角是展览室，陈列了古老工具的样本。左上角是**研磨**车间，工具磨尖和其他制作工序都在那里完成。

【搭】grind into 把……磨成粉末；将……碾进　grind out 沙哑地讲；生产出；创作出；弹奏

【记】grin *v.* 露齿而笑

grief *n.* 悲伤；悲痛；悲伤的事

sharpen [ˈʃɑːpn] *v.* 削尖；磨快；使敏捷；加重

【例】In the top right hand corner is the show room where samples of all the tools that were made through the ages were on display. In the top left corner is the grinding shop where the tools were **sharpened** and finished.

右上角是展览室，陈列了古老工具的样本。左上角是研磨车间，工具**磨尖**和其他制作工序都在那里完成。

【搭】sharpen up（使）变得更好（或技术更高、更有效等）

【记】sharply *ad.* 严厉地；明确地；锋利地；突然地

shatter *v.* 使破碎，使碎裂，砸碎；使……成为泡影

词汇听写

1. _____ 2. _____ 3. _____

句子听写

第 2 周

1. I'm taking your course in population studies. I'm having a bit trouble with the second assignment and it's due in 12 days.

我选了您开设的人口研究课程。在完成第二次的作业中，我碰到了一些问题，而这项作业在 12 天后就得上交了。

population [pɔpjuˈleiʃn] *n.* 人口；[生物] 种群，[生物] 群体；全体居民

【变】populations

【例】I'm taking your course in **population** studies. I'm having a bit trouble with the second assignment and it's due in 12 days.

我选了您开设的人口研究课程。在完成第二次的作业中，我碰到了一些问题，而这项作业在 12 天后就得上交了。

【搭】population accounting 人口统计　population biology 群体生物学

【记】porcelain *n.* 瓷，瓷器

porch *n.* 门廊；游廊，走廊

pore *n.* 毛孔；气孔；细孔

have trouble with ⋯⋯有困难

【例】I'm taking your course in population studies. I'm having a bit **trouble with** the second assignment and it's due in 12 days.

我选了您开设的人口研究课程。在完成第二次的作业中，我碰到了一些问题，而这项作业在 12 天后就得上交了。

【记】troublesome *a.* 令人讨厌的；令人烦恼的；引起麻烦的；（孩子等）难管的

trousers *n.* 裤子

truck *n.* 货车；（铁路的）无盖货车；（行李）搬运车

assignment [ə'sainmnt] *n.* 分配；任务；作业；功课

【变】assignments

【例】I'm taking your course in population studies. I'm having a bit trouble with the second **assignment** and it's due in 12 days.

我选了您开设的人口研究课程。在完成第二次的**作业**中，我碰到了一些问题，而这项作业在 12 天后就得上交了。

【搭】assignment card 作业卡片　assignment fee 转让费

【记】assist *n.* 帮助；援助；机器助手；辅助装置

assistant *n.* 助手，助理；[化学]（染色的）助剂；辅助物；店员，伙计

associate *v.* （使）发生联系；（使）联合；结交；联想

due [dju:] *a.* 到期的；预期的；应付的；应得的　*n.* 应付款；应得之物

ad. 正（置于方位词前）

【变】dues

【例】I'm taking your course in population studies. I'm having a bit trouble with the second assignment and it's **due** in 12 days.

我选了您开设的人口研究课程。在完成第二次的作业中，我碰到了一些问题，而这项作业在 12 天后就**得上交**了。

【搭】due bank 收款银行　after due consideration 经过适当考虑

【记】duke *n.* 公爵；君主

dull *a.* 钝的；迟钝的；呆滞的；阴暗的

dumb *a.* 哑的，无说话能力的

词汇听写

1. _____　2. _____　3. _____

句子听写

2. Extensions are normally given only for medical or compassionate reasons. Otherwise, that's really a question of organizing your study and we don't like giving an extension to a student who simply didn't plan the work properly.

通常只有医疗或其他获得了老师同情的原因才能允许作业延期上交。否则，因为自己时间安排不当、计划不周，导致无法按时完成，我们是不会允许延期的。

extension [ik'stenʃn] *n.* 延长；延期；扩大；伸展；电话分机

【变】Extensions

【例】**Extensions** are normally given only for medical or compassionate reasons. Otherwise, that's really a question of organizing your study and we don't like giving an extension to a student who simply didn't plan the work properly.

通常只有医疗或其他获得了老师同情的原因才能允许作业**延期**上交。否则，因为自己时间安排不当、计划不周，导致无法按时完成，我们是不会允许延期的。

【搭】extension of term 学期的延长　extension bar （扳手等的）接长杆，伸出杆

【记】extensive *a.* 广阔的，广大的；范围广泛的；[物] 广延的；[逻] 外延的

extent *n.* 程度；长度；广大地域

exterior *n.* 外部，外面，表面，外观；外貌；（戏、影视）户外布景

normally ['nɔːmli] *ad.* 正常地；通常地，一般地

【例】Extensions are **normally** given only for medical or compassionate reasons. Otherwise, that's really a question of organizing your study and we don't like giving an extension to a student who simply didn't plan the work properly.

通常只有医疗或其他获得了老师同情的原因才能允许作业延期上交。否则，因为自己时间安排不当、计划不周，导致无法按时完成，我们是不会允许延期的。

【搭】normally closed circuit 正常闭合电路　normally closed contact 常闭触点

【记】normal *a.* 正常的；正规的，标准的；[数] 正交的；精神健全的

normalization *n.* 正常化；标准化；正态化

north *n.* 北方；北部；（美国南北战争时与南方作战的）北部各州；北方发达国家（尤指欧洲和北美各国）

compassionate [kəm'pæʃnət] *a.* 慈悲的；富于同情心的　*v.* 同情；怜悯

【变】compassionated　compassionated　compassionating　compassionates

【例】Extensions are normally given only for medical or **compassionate** reasons. Otherwise, that's really a question of organizing your study and we don't like giving an extension to a student who simply didn't plan the work properly.

通常只有医疗或其他获得了老师**同情**的原因才能允许作业延期上交。否则，因为自己时间安排不当、计划不周，导致无法按时完成，我们是不会允许延期的。

【搭】compassionate leave（因家人生病、去世或其他个人原因而准许的）事假

【记】compatible *a.* 兼容的，相容的；和谐的，协调的；[生]亲和的；可以并存的，能共处的

compel *v.* 强迫，迫使；强制发生，使不得不

compensate *v.* 补偿，赔偿；报酬；抵消

properly ['prɔpəli] *ad.* 适当地；正确地；恰当地

【变】more properly　most properly

【例】Extensions are normally given only for medical or compassionate reasons. Otherwise, that's really a question of organizing your study and we don't like giving an extension to a student who simply didn't plan the work **properly**.

通常只有医疗或其他获得了老师同情的原因才能允许作业延期上交。否则，因为自己时间安排**不当**、计划**不周**，导致无法按时完成，我们是不会允许延期的。

【搭】eat properly 饮食合理　properly speaking 确切地说

【记】proper *a.* 适当的，相当的，正当的，应该的

propeller *n.* 螺旋桨，推进器

property *n.* 特性，属性；财产，地产；[戏]道具；所有权

词汇听写

1. ＿＿＿＿＿＿＿＿　2. ＿＿＿＿＿＿＿＿　3. ＿＿＿＿＿＿＿＿

句子听写

3. You should <u>get hold of</u> some important <u>references</u> and <u>check out</u> the journal articles in the list which are really <u>worth</u> reading.

你应该找出一些重要的参考资料，查查列表中的期刊文章，这些都非常值得一读。

get hold of 把握；抓住；得到

【例】You should **get hold of** some important references and check out the journal articles in the list which are really worth reading.

你应该**找出**一些重要的参考资料，查查列表中的期刊文章，这些都非常值得一读。

【记】hold *v.* 拿住；保存；拘押；容纳

hole *n.* 洞，孔；洞穴；缺陷

get *v.* 得到；抓住；说服；受到（惩罚等）

reference [ˈrefrns] *n.* 参照；涉及，提及；参考书目；介绍信；证明书　　*v.* 引用

【变】references

【例】You should get hold of some important **references** and check out the journal articles in the list which are really worth reading.

你应该找出一些重要的**参考资料**，查查列表中的期刊文章，这些都非常值得一读。

【搭】reference number 编号　　reference book 参考书

【记】refine *v.* 提炼；改善；使高雅

refinery *n.* 精炼厂；精炼设备；提炼厂；冶炼厂

check out 检验；结账离开；通过考核；盖章

【变】checked　checked　checking　checks

【例】You should get hold of some important references and **check out** the journal articles in the list which are really worth reading.

你应该找出一些重要的参考资料，**查查**列表中的期刊文章，这些都非常值得一读。

【记】check *v.* 检查，核对；抑制；在……上打勾

check in 记录，登记签到；归还经登记借出的东西；把……留给其他人照看

checkup *n.* 检查，核对；体格检查

worth ［wəːθ］ *a.* 值……的 *n.* 价值；财产

【例】You should get hold of some important references and check out the journal articles in the list which are really **worth** reading.

你应该找出一些重要的参考资料，查查列表中的期刊文章，这些都非常**值得**一读。

【搭】worth it 值得化费时间（精力），值得一干，有必要 worth while 值得

【记】would *aux.* 将，将要；愿意；会，打算；大概 *v.* (will 的过去式，用于转述) 将

worthwhile *a.* 值得做的；值得花时间的；有价值的

worthy *a.* 应得某事物；值得做某事；可尊敬的；配得上的，相称的

词汇听写

1. _____ 2. _____ 3. _____

句子听写

Tuesday ···

1. I've been asked today to talk to you about the <u>urban</u> <u>landscape</u>. In my talk, I'll focus on how <u>vegetation</u> can have a significant <u>effect</u> on urban climate.

　　他们让我今天和你们谈谈城市景观。在我的讲话里，我将重点讨论植被是如何对城市气候产生重要的影响。

urban [ˈəːbn] a. 城市的；住在都市的

【例】I've been asked today to talk to you about the **urban** landscape. In my talk, I'll focus on how vegetation can have a significant effect on urban climate.

　　他们让我今天和你们谈谈**城市**景观。在我的讲话里，我将重点讨论植被是如何对城市气候产生重要的影响。

【搭】urban area 城市地区；城区　　urban land 市区用地

【记】urge v. 催促；推进，驱策；力劝，规劝；极力主张

usage n. 使用；用法；习惯；惯例

ban v. 禁止，下令禁止；剥夺权利

landscape [ˈlæn(d)skeip] n. 风景，景色；山水画　v. 美化……景观

【变】landscaped　landscaped　landscaping　landscapes

【例】I've been asked today to talk to you about the urban **landscape**. In my talk, I'll focus on how vegetation can have a significant effect on urban climate.

　　他们让我今天和你们谈谈城市**景观**。在我的讲话里，我将重点讨论植被是如何对城市气候产生重要的影响。

【搭】landscape painting 风景画　　landscape park 天然公园

【记】land n. 陆地；国家；地产；土地

lane n. 小路；航道，空中走廊，规定的单向行车道；车道

vegetation [ˌvedʒiˈteiʃn] n. 植被；植物，草木；呆板单调的生活

【例】I've been asked today to talk to you about the urban landscape. In my talk, I'll focus on how **vegetation** can have a significant effect on urban climate.

他们让我今天和你们谈谈城市景观。在我的讲话里，我将重点讨论**植被**是如何对城市气候产生重要的影响。

【搭】vegetation form 植被型　vegetation map 植被图

【记】vegetable *n.* 蔬菜；植物；生活呆板的人

vehicle *n.* 车辆；交通工具；传播媒介，媒介物

veil *n.* 面纱；掩饰；覆盖物；托词

vein *n.* 静脉；[地] 矿脉，岩脉；[植] 叶脉；气质，倾向

effect [i'fekt] *n.* **影响；效果；作用**　*v.* **产生；达到目的**

【变】effected　effected　effecting　effects

【例】I've been asked today to talk to you about the urban landscape. In my talk，I'll focus on how vegetation can have a significant **effect** on urban climate.

他们让我今天和你们谈谈城市景观。在我的讲话里，我将重点讨论植被是如何对城市气候产生重要的**影响**。

【搭】whole effect 整体效果　effect mixer 音响效果混合器

【记】effective *a.* 有效的；起作用的；实际的，实在的；给人深刻印象

efficiency *n.* 效率，效能；实力，能力；[物] 性能；功效

effort *n.* 努力，尝试；工作；成就；杰作

词汇听写

1. _____　2. _____　3. _____

句子听写

2. The main difference between a tree and a building is a tree has got an internal mechanism to keep the temperature regulated. It evaporates water through its leaves.

一棵树和一个建筑物之间的主要区别是树拥有内部机制，以调节温度。它通过它的叶子蒸发水分。

internal [in'təːnl] *a.* 内部的；内在的；国内的

【例】The main difference between a tree and a building is a tree has got an **internal** mechanism to keep the temperature regulated. It evaporates water through its leaves.

一棵树和一个建筑物之间的主要区别是树拥有**内部**机制，以调节温度。它通过它的叶子蒸发水分。

【搭】internal action 固有作用　internal area 内域

【记】international *a.* 国际的；两国（或以上）国家的；国际关系的

interpret *v.* 解释；理解；诠释，体现；口译

interrupt *v.* 打断（别人的话等）；阻止；截断

mechanism ['mekniz'm] *n.* 机制；原理，途径；进程；机械装置；技巧

【变】mechanisms

【例】The main difference between a tree and a building is a tree has got an internal **mechanism** to keep the temperature regulated. It evaporates water through its leaves.

一棵树和一个建筑物之间的主要区别是树拥有内部**机制**，以调节温度。它通过它的叶子蒸发水分。

【搭】mechanism case 机构箱　mechanism of hearing 听觉机制

【记】medal *n.* 奖章，奖牌；勋章；纪念章；证章

media *n.* 媒体；［解剖学］血管中层；［语音学］浊塞音；介质

medical *a.* 医学的；医药的；医疗的；内科的

regulate ['regjuleit] *v.* 调节，规定；控制；校准；有系统的管理

【变】regulated　regulated　regulating　regulates

【例】The main difference between a tree and a building is a tree has got an internal mechanism to keep the temperature **regulated**. It evaporates water through its leaves.

一棵树和一个建筑物之间的主要区别是树拥有内部机制，以**调节**温度。它通过它的叶子蒸发水分。

【搭】regulate a clock 校准时钟　regulate capital 控制资本

【记】rehearsal *n.* 排练，排演；彩排，演习；复述，详述

reign *v.* 当政，统治；占主导地位

evaporate [iˈvæpəreit] *v.* 使……蒸发；使……脱水；使……消失

【变】evaporated   evaporated   evaporating   evaporates

【例】The main difference between a tree and a building is a tree has got an internal mechanism to keep the temperature regulated. It **evaporates** water through its leaves.

一棵树和一个建筑物之间的主要区别是树拥有内部机制，以调节温度。它通过它的叶子**蒸发**水分。

【记】eve *n.* 前夕，前夜；重要事件的前夕；傍晚

eventually *ad.* 终于，最后；竟；总归；终究

ever *ad.* 永远；曾经，这以前；究竟，到底；可能

词汇听写

1. _____ 2. _____ 3. _____

句子听写

3. Trees remain cooler than buildings because they <u>sweat</u>. This means they can <u>humidify</u> the air and cool it, a <u>property</u> which can be <u>exploited</u> to improve the local climate.

树木仍比建筑物凉爽，因为他们会流汗。这意味着他们可以加湿、冷却空气，这种特性可以用于改善当地的气候。

sweat [swet] *v.* 流汗，渗出；发酵；做苦工；〈非〉烦恼，焦急 *n.* 汗水

【变】sweat/sweated   sweat/sweated   sweating   sweats

【例】Trees remain cooler than buildings because they **sweat.** This means they can humidify the air and cool it, a property which can be exploited to improve the local climate.

树木仍比建筑物凉爽，因为他们会**流汗**。这意味着他们可以加湿、冷却空气，这种特性可以用于改善当地的气候。

【搭】sweat-stained clothing 被汗水浸透的衣服　break out in a sweat 出一身汗

【记】swear *v.* 发誓，诅咒

　　sweet *a.* 甜蜜的；快乐的；温柔的，亲切的

humidify [hjuˈmidifai] *v.* 使潮湿；使湿润

【变】humidified　humidified　humidifying　humidifies

【例】Trees remain cooler than buildings because they sweat. This means they can **humidify** the air and cool it, a property which can be exploited to improve the local climate.

　　树木仍比建筑物凉爽，因为他们会"流汗"。这意味着他们可以**加湿**、冷却空气，这种特性可以用于改善当地的气候。

【记】humorous *a.* 幽默的；滑稽的；风趣的

　　hundred *num.* 一百；许多

　　humid *a.* 潮湿的；湿气重的；湿润的

property [ˈprɔpəti] *n.* 性质，性能；财产；所有权

【变】properties

【例】Trees remain cooler than buildings because they sweat. This means they can humidify the air and cool it, a **property** which can be exploited to improve the local climate.

　　树木仍比建筑物凉爽，因为他们会"流汗"。这意味着他们可以加湿、冷却空气，这种**特性**可以用于改善当地的气候。

【搭】property account 财产清查　property ledger 财产分类账

【记】prophecy *n.* 预言；预言能力；预言书

　　prophet *n.* 预言家，先知；倡导者，主张者

　　proportion *n.* 比，比率；[数学] 比例（法）；面积；相称，平衡

exploit [ikˈsplɔit] *v.* 开发，开拓；剥削；开采

【变】exploited　exploited　exploiting　exploits

【例】Trees remain cooler than buildings because they sweat. This means they can humidify the air and cool it, a property which can be **exploited** to improve the local climate.

　　树木仍比建筑物凉爽，因为他们会"流汗"。这意味着他们可以加

湿、冷却空气，这种特性可以**用于**改善当地的气候。

【记】exploration *n.* 探测，勘探，探险；搜索，研究；［医］探查术

　　explore *v.* 探测，勘探；［医］探查（伤处等），探索，研究

　　explosive *a.* 爆炸的；突增的；暴躁的

词汇听写

1. ＿＿＿＿＿＿＿　2. ＿＿＿＿＿＿＿　3. ＿＿＿＿＿＿＿

句子听写

Wednesday ·· «

1. I went to the bank to <u>cash</u> some traveler's <u>cheques</u>. But when I went to the teller, they told me that the computer system was <u>temporarily</u> down. So they couldn't do any <u>transaction</u>.

　　我去银行兑换一些旅行支票，但当我去柜台，他们告诉我说，电脑系统暂时关闭。所以，他们不能进行任何交易。

cash [kæʃ] *n.* 现款，现金　*v.* 将……兑现；支付现款

【变】cashed　cashed　cashing　cashes

【例】I went to the bank to **cash** some traveler's cheques. But when I went to the teller, they told me that the computer system was temporarily down. So they couldn't do any transaction.

　　我去银行**兑换**一些旅行支票，但当我去柜台，他们告诉我说，电脑系统暂时关闭。所以，他们不能进行任何交易。

【搭】cash account 现金账户　cash advance 现金垫款

【记】cashier *n.* 出纳员

　　cassette *n.* 盒式录音带；弹夹；珠宝箱

　　cast *v.* 铸造；投掷；投射；脱落

cheque [tʃek] *n.* 支票

【变】cheques

【例】I went to the bank to cash some traveler's **cheques**. But when I went to the teller, they told me that the computer system was temporarily down. So they couldn't do any transaction.

　　我去银行兑换一些旅行**支票**，但当我去柜台，他们告诉我说，电脑系统暂时关闭。所以，他们不能进行任何交易。

【记】cherish *v.* 珍爱；怀有；爱护；抚育

　　cherry *n.* 樱桃；樱桃树；樱桃色

temporarily [ˈtempr(ər)ili] *ad.* 临时地，临时

【例】I went to the bank to cash some traveler's cheques. But when I went to the teller, they told me that the computer system was **temporarily** down. So they couldn't do any transaction.

我去银行兑换一些旅行支票，但当我去柜台，他们告诉我说，电脑系统**暂时**关闭。所以，他们不能进行任何交易。

【搭】temporarily surplus fund 暂时剩余基金

【记】temporary *a.* 临时的，暂时的；短暂的

tempt *v.* 引诱，怂恿；吸引；冒……的风险；使感兴趣

temper *n.* 性情，脾气；特征；怒气

transaction [trænˈzækʃən] *n.* 交易；事务；办理；会报，学报

【变】transactions

【例】I went to the bank to cash some traveler's cheques. But when I went to the teller, they told me that the computer system was temporarily down. So they couldn't do any **transaction**.

我去银行兑换一些旅行支票，但当我去柜台，他们告诉我说，电脑系统暂时关闭。所以，他们不能进行任何**交易**。

【搭】transaction account 交易账户   transaction data 事务数据

【记】transfer *v.* 使转移；使调动；转让（权利等）；让与

transform *v.* 改变；改观；变换

transformation *n.* 变化；（核）转换；（语）转换；（电）变换

词汇听写

1. _____ 2. _____ 3. _____

句子听写

2. I really want to do with the Cathedral is climb the tower. The view is supposed to be spectacular.

我真的想爬上大教堂的塔，景色应该是非常壮观的。

Cathedral [kəˈθiːdrl] *n.* 大教堂

【变】cathedrals

【例】I really want to do with the **Cathedral** is climb the tower. The view is supposed to be spectacular.

我真的想爬上**大教堂**的塔，景色应该是非常壮观的。

【记】Catholic *a.* 天主教的

cattle *n.*（总称）牛，牲口

cause *n.* 原因；动机；（某种行为、感情等的）理由；缘故

view [vju] *n.* 观察；视野；意见；风景　*v.* 观察；考虑；查看

【变】viewed　viewed　viewing　views

【例】I really want to do with the Cathedral is climb the tower. The **view** is supposed to be spectacular.

我真的想爬上大教堂的塔，**景色**应该是非常壮观的。

【搭】view as 把……看做……，认为……是……　view factor 视角因数

【记】viewpoint *n.* 观点，意见，角度；视角；（物）视点

vigorous *a.* 有力的；精力充沛的；充满活力的；朝气蓬勃的

vigour *n.* 精力，活力；气势；强健

suppose [sə'pəuz] *v.* 假设；认为；让（虚拟语气）；推想　*v.* 猜想；料想

【变】supposed　supposed　supposing　supposes

【例】I really want to do with the Cathedral is climb the tower. The view is **supposed** to be spectacular.

我真的想爬上大教堂的塔，景色**应该**是非常壮观的。

【搭】suppose that 假如

【记】suppress *v.* 镇压；忍住；阻止……的生长（或发展）

supreme *a.* 最高的；至高的；最重要的

super *a.* 超级的，极度的，极好的

spectacular [spek'tækjulə] *a.* 壮观的，惊人的

【变】spectaculars

【例】I really want to do with the Cathedral is climb the tower. The view is supposed to be **spectacular.**

我真的想爬上大教堂的塔，景色应该是**非常壮观的**。

【记】spectator *n.* 观众，旁观者

spectrum *n.* ［物理学］谱，光谱辐射源，能谱；光谱相片；范围

speculate *v.* 思索，猜测，推测

词汇听写

1. ＿＿＿＿＿＿＿＿　2. ＿＿＿＿＿＿＿＿　3. ＿＿＿＿＿＿＿＿

句子听写

3. We can chase up your tutor if you're not getting proper feedback on how you will be getting on your subjects.

　　如果关于如何开始你的科目学习，你还没有得到适当的反馈，那我们可以和你的导师进行核查。

chase up 追上；核查，查证

【变】chased　chased　chasing　chases

【例】We can **chase up** your tutor if you're not getting proper feedback on how you will be getting on your subjects.

　　如果关于如何开始你的科目学习，你还没有得到适当的反馈，那我们可以和你的导师进行**核查**。

【记】chase *v.* 追捕；追求；追寻

　　chatter *v.* 唠叨，喋喋不休；（鸟等）鸣

　　cheap *a.* 便宜的，低劣的；小气的，可鄙的

tutor ［ˈtjuːtə］ *n.* 导师；家庭教师；助教　*v.* 辅导；约束；当家庭教师；（美）在家庭教师指导下学习

【变】tutored　tutored　tutoring　tutors

【例】We can chase up your **tutor** if you're not getting proper feedback on how you will be getting on your subjects.

　　如果关于如何开始你的科目学习，你还没有得到适当的反馈，那我们可以和你的**导师**进行核查。

【搭】tutor oneself 自我约束　　tutor organizer（兼管课程安排的）导师

【记】tub *n.* 澡盆；桶；矿车

tube *n.* 管，管状物；电子管；地铁；电视机

tuberculosis *n.* 肺结核；[医] 结核病；痨；痨病

feedback ['fiːdbæk] *n.* 反馈；成果，资料；回复

【变】feedbacks

【例】We can chase up your tutor if you're not getting proper **feedback** on how you will be getting on your subjects.

如果关于如何开始你的科目学习，你还没有得到适当的**反馈**，那我们可以和你的导师进行核查。

【搭】feedback amplifier 回输 放大器　feedback coil 反馈线圈，回授线圈

【记】feed *v.* 喂养；满足（欲望等）；向……提供；供……作食物

　　feeble *a.* 虚弱的；无效的，无意的；缺乏决心的

　　fee *n.*（加入组织或做某事付的）费；小费，赏钱

subject ['sʌbdʒekt] *n.* 主题；科目；[语] 主语；国民　*a.* 服从的；易患……的；受制于……的　*v.* [səb'dʒekt] 使……隶属；使屈从于

【变】subjects

【例】We can chase up your tutor if you're not getting proper feedback on how you will be getting on your **subjects**.

如果关于如何开始你的科目学习，你还没有得到适当的反馈，那我们可以和你的导师进行核查。

【搭】subject age 学科年龄　subject area 主题范围

【记】submarine *n.* 潜艇；海底生物

　　submerge *v.* 淹没；把……浸入；沉没，下潜；使沉浸

　　submit *v.* 顺从，服从；甘受，忍受

词汇听写

1. ＿＿＿＿＿＿＿　2. ＿＿＿＿＿＿＿　3. ＿＿＿＿＿＿＿

句子听写

Thursday ·· ≪

1. If you think you're already <u>under stress</u>, you'll have to start <u>adjusting</u> to teaching and learning methods as well as the <u>mounting</u> pressures that the <u>deadline</u> for the first assignment creates upon you.

如果你认为你已经有压力，你将不得不开始调整教学和学习的方法，以及调整首次任务的截止日期给你带来的越来越大的压力。

under stress 在受力时；在压力之下

【例】If you think you're already **under stress**，you'll have to start adjusting to teaching and learning methods as well as the mounting pressures that the deadline for the first assignment creates upon you.

如果你认为你已经**有压力**，你将不得不开始调整教学和学习的方法，以及调整首次任务的截止日期给你带来的越来越大的压力。

【记】stress *n.* 强调；重音；压力；重力

stressful *a.* 有压力

stretch *v.* 伸展；张开；充分利用；使紧张

adjust [ə'dʒʌst] *v.* 调整，使……适合；校准

【变】adjusted　adjusted　adjusting　adjusts

【例】If you think you're already under stress, you'll have to start **adjusting** to teaching and learning methods as well as the mounting pressures that the deadline for the first assignment creates upon you.

如果你认为你已经有压力，你将不得不开始**调整**教学和学习的方法，以及调整首次任务的截止日期给你带来的越来越大的压力。

【记】adjustable *a.* 可调整的，可调节的

adjustment *n.* 调解，调整；调节器；调停

administration *n.* 管理；实行；（政府）行政机关；（法律、处罚等的）施行

mount [maunt] *v.* 登上；骑上；增加；上升

【变】mounted　mounted　mounting　mounts

【例】If you think you're already under stress, you'll have to start adjusting to teaching and learning methods as well as the **mounting** pressures that the deadline for the first assignment creates upon you.

如果你认为你已经有压力，你将不得不开始调整教学和学习的方法，以及调整首次任务的截止日期给你带来的**越来越大**的压力。

【记】mourn *v.* 哀痛；服丧

mouse *n.* 老鼠；鼠标；羞怯（胆小）的人

deadline ['dedlain] *n.* 截止期限，最后期限

【变】deadlines

【例】If you think you're already under stress，you'll have to start adjusting to teaching and learning methods as well as the mounting pressures that the **deadline** for the first assignment creates upon you.

如果你认为你已经有压力，你将不得不开始调整教学和学习的方法，以及调整首次任务的**截止日期**给你带来的越来越大的压力。

【记】deadly *a.* 极端的，非常的；致命的；非常有效的

deaf *a.* 聋的；不愿听的

deafen *v.* 使聋；使隔音；淹没

词汇听写

1. _____ 2. _____ 3. _____

句子听写

2. You'll have to cope with all these without your usual social network. All of this causes anxiety. Studying overseas can trigger a personal crisis.

你将在没有你往常的社会人脉网络的情况下应对所有这些问题。所有这些都会导致焦虑，海外留学会引发个人危机。

cope with 处理，应付

【变】coped coped coping copes

【例】You'll have to **cope with** all these without your usual social network. All of this causes anxiety. Studying overseas can trigger a personal crisis.

　　你将在没有你往常的社会人脉网络的情况下**应对**所有这些问题。所有这些都会导致焦虑，海外留学会引发个人危机。

【记】cope *v.* 成功地应付，对付；对抗

copper *n.* 铜；铜币；紫铜色；警察

copy *n.* 复制品；一份；（报刊等的）稿件

anxiety [æŋ'zaiəti] *n.* 焦虑；渴望；挂念；令人焦虑的事

【变】anxieties

【例】You'll have to cope with all these without your usual social network. All of this causes **anxiety**. Studying overseas can trigger a personal crisis.

　　你将在没有你往常的社会人脉网络的情况下应对所有这些问题。所有这些都会导致**焦虑**，海外留学会引发个人危机。

【搭】anxiety disorder 焦虑性障碍　anxiety reaction 焦虑反应

【记】anxious *a.* 焦急的；渴望的；令人焦虑的；流露出忧虑的

analogy *n.* 类似，相似；比拟，类比；类推

trigger ['trigə] *v.* 引发，引起；触发　*n.* 扳机；[电子] 触发器；制滑机

【变】triggered　triggered　triggering　triggers

【例】You'll have to cope with all these without your usual social network. All of this causes anxiety. Studying overseas can **trigger** a personal crisis.

　　你将在没有你往常的社会人脉网络的情况下应对所有这些问题。所有这些都会导致焦虑，海外留学会**引发**个人危机。

【搭】trigger action 触发作用　trigger carrier 触发器座架

【记】trim *v.* 修剪；整理；装饰

triangle *n.* 三角形；三人一组；三角铁；三角板

tribe *n.* 部落，部族；一帮，一伙；大群

crisis ['kraisis] *n.* 危机；危难时刻；决定性时刻，紧要关头；转折点

【变】crises

【例】You'll have to cope with all these without your usual social network. All of this causes anxiety. Studying overseas can trigger a personal **crisis**.

　　你将在没有你往常的社会人脉网络的情况下应对所有这些问题。所

有这些都会导致焦虑，海外留学会引发个人**危机**。

【搭】crisis export 转嫁危机   crisis manager 危机处理负责人

【记】crisp *a.* 脆的；干冷的；易碎的；新鲜的，爽快的

　　criterion *n.* （批评、判断等的）标准，准则；规范

　　critic *n.* 批评家；评论员；批评者；挑剔的人

词汇听写

1. _____   2. _____   3. _____

句子听写

3. Our resident chapel can offer you spiritual guidance if that what you want.

　　我们的居民教堂可以为您提供精神指导，如果这是你想要的。

resident ['rezidnt] *a.* 居住的；住院医师；定居的　*n.* 居民

【变】residents

【例】Our **resident** chapel can offer you spiritual guidance if that what you want.

　　我们的**居民**教堂可以为您提供精神指导，如果这是你想要的。

【搭】resident auditor 常驻审计员   local resident 当地居民

【记】residence *n.* 住处，住宅；居住时间；公馆

　　residual *a.* 残余的；残留的

　　resign *v.* 辞职，放弃

chapel ['tʃæpl] *n.* 小礼拜堂，小教堂；礼拜　*a.* 非国教的

【变】chapels

【例】Our resident **chapel** can offer you spiritual guidance if that what you want.

　　我们的居民**教堂**可以为您提供精神指导，如果这是你想要的。

【搭】go to chapel 去教堂   a college chapel 学院的小教堂

【记】chapter *n.* 章，回；（俱乐部、协会等的）分会

　　character *n.* 性格，特征；品行；字母，符号；人物

　　characteristic *a.* 特有的；独特的；表示特性的；显示……的特征的

spiritual [ˈspiritʃuəl] *n.* 圣歌（尤指美国南部黑人的）　*a.* 精神的，心灵的

【变】spirituals

【例】Our resident chapel can offer you **spiritual** guidance if that what you want.
　　我们的居民教堂可以为您提供**精神**指导，如果这是你想要的。

【搭】spiritual court 宗教法庭　spiritual value 精神价值

【记】spit *v.* 吐，吐出

　　spider *n.* 蜘蛛；三脚架

guidance [ˈgaidns] *n.* 指导，引导；领导

【变】guidances

【例】Our resident chapel can offer you spiritual **guidance** if that what you want.
　　我们的居民教堂可以为您提供精神**指导**，如果这是你想要的。

【搭】guidance rod 导杆　guidance sensor 制导传感器

【记】guide *v.* 引路；指导；操纵；影响

　　guilt *n.* 有罪，犯罪行为，罪恶，[法律] 轻罪，过失；知罪；自责

　　guitar *n.* 吉他；六弦琴

词汇听写

1. ＿＿＿＿＿＿＿＿　2. ＿＿＿＿＿＿＿＿　3. ＿＿＿＿＿＿＿＿

句子听写

Friday   ·· 《《

1. There may be a huge amount of family <u>pressure</u> on you to succeed. And if you fail a subject or <u>drop off</u> a course because it's too difficult, then your <u>self-esteem</u> can <u>suffer</u>.

　　在你通往成功的路上，可能会遇上巨大的家庭压力。而且，如果因为课程太困难，你没有通过某一门课程或放弃了一门课程，那么你的自尊心都会受到影响。

---

pressure ['preʃə] *n.* 压力；压迫　　*v.* 迫使；密封；使……增压

【变】pressured　pressured　pressuring　pressures

【例】There may be a huge amount of family **pressure** on you to succeed. And if you fail a subject or drop off a course because it's too difficult, then your self-esteem can suffer.

　　在你通往成功的路上，可能会遇上巨大的家庭**压力**。而且，如果因为课程太困难，你没有通过某一门课程或放弃了一门课程，那么你的自尊心都会受到影响。

【搭】considerable pressure 相当大的压力　　intense pressure 沉重的压力

【记】prestige *n.* 威信，威望，声望；声誉

　　presumably *ad.* 据推测；大概；可能；想来

　　pretend *v.* 假装，伪装；假称；装扮

　　pretty *a.* 漂亮的；机灵的，聪明的

---

drop off 减少；让……下车；睡着

【变】dropped　dropped　dropping　drops

【例】There may be a huge amount of family pressure on you to succeed. And if you fail a subject or **drop off** a course because it's too difficult, then your self-esteem can suffer.

　　在你通往成功的路上，可能会遇上巨大的家庭压力。而且，如果因为课程太困难，你没有通过某一门课程或**放弃**了一门课程，那么你的自尊心都会受到影响。

【记】drought *n.* 干旱（时期），旱季；旱灾

drown *v.* 淹死；浸没

wardrobe *n.* 衣柜，衣橱

drown *v.* 淹死，淹没，浸泡

self-esteem [ˈselfisˈtiːm] *n.* 自尊；自负；自大

【例】There may be a huge amount of family pressure on you to succeed. And if you fail a subject or drop off a course because it's too difficult, then your **self-esteem** can suffer.

在你通往成功的路上，可能会遇上巨大的家庭压力。而且，如果因为课程太困难，你没有通过某一门课程或放弃了一门课程，那么你的**自尊心**都会受到影响。

【记】selfish *a.* 自私的，利己的

esteem *v.* 敬重；以为；考虑

deem *v.* 认为，相信

suffer [ˈsʌfə] *v.* 受痛苦，感到痛苦（或苦恼），受苦难；感到疼痛；患病

【变】suffered   suffered   suffering   suffers

【例】There may be a huge amount of family pressure on you to succeed. And if you fail a subject or drop off a course because it's too difficult, then your self-esteem can **suffer.**

在你通往成功的路上，可能会遇上巨大的家庭压力。而且，如果因为课程太困难，你没有通过某一门课程或放弃了一门课程，那么你的自尊心都会**受到影响**。

【搭】suffer a defeat 战败，遭受挫败   suffer losses 遭受损失

【记】suffice *v.* 足够；有能力

sufficiently *ad.* 足够地，充分地；十分，相当

sufficient *a.* 足够的，充足的

词汇听写

1. _____   2. _____   3. _____

句子听写

2. Remember full-time students can get a low <u>interest</u> <u>loan</u> of up to 600 dollars to buy books and for similar study <u>related</u> <u>expenses</u>.

记住，全日制学生可以得到高达 600 美元的低利率贷款，用于买书和类似的与学习相关的费用。

---

interest ['intrist] *n.* 兴趣，爱好；利息；趣味；同行　*v.* 使……感兴趣；引起……的关心；使……参与

【变】interested　interested　interesting　interests

【例】Remember full-time students can get a low **interest** loan of up to 600 dollars to buy books and for similar study related expenses.

记住，全日制学生可以得到高达 600 美元的低利率贷款，用于买书和类似的与学习相关的费用。

【搭】interest account 利息账户　interest note 利息单

【记】interact *v.* 相互作用；互相影响；互动

integral *a.* 完整的；积分的；必需的

---

loan [ləun] *n.* 贷款；借款　*v.* 借出

【变】loaned　loaned　loaning　loans

【例】Remember full-time students can get a low interest **loan** of up to 600 dollars to buy books and for similar study related expenses.

记住，全日制学生可以得到高达 600 美元的低利率**贷款**，用于买书和类似的与学习相关的费用。

【搭】loan account 贷款账户　loan collection 在展览会中借来的展览品

【记】load *n.* 负荷；负担；装载；工作量

loaf *n.* 一条（块）面包

lobby *n.* 门厅，大厅；休息室；游说团；投票厅

---

relate [ri'leit] *v.* 叙述；使……有联系；涉及；认同；符合；与……有某种联系

【例】Remember full-time students can get a low interest loan of up to 600 dollars to buy books and for similar study **related** expenses.

记住，全日制学生可以得到高达 600 美元的低利率贷款，用于买书

和类似的与学习**相关的**费用。

【搭】relate to 涉及；同……有关系；与……协调

　　　relate with 把……同……联系起来

【记】relation *n.* 关系，亲戚（关系）；说话，报告；比数

　　　relationship *n.* 关系；联系；浪漫关系；血缘关系

expense [ik'spens] *n.* **损失，代价；消费；开支**　*v.* **向……收取费用**

【变】expenses

【例】Remember full-time students can get a low interest loan of up to 600 dollars to buy books and for similar study related **expenses**.

　　　记住，全日制学生可以得到高达 600 美元的低利率贷款，用于买书和类似的与学习相关的**费用**。

【搭】expenses quota 经费限额　　expenses statement 费用表

【记】expensive *a.* 昂贵的，花钱多的；豪华的

　　　experience *n.* 经验，体验；经历，阅历

　　　experiment *n.* 实验，试验；尝试

词汇听写

1. ＿＿＿＿＿＿　　2. ＿＿＿＿＿＿　　3. ＿＿＿＿＿＿

句子听写

3. Last academic year in spite of staff cuts, we counseled 240 international students for a total of 2600 hours' counseling.

　　　上一个学年，尽管员工减少了，我们仍然为 240 个国际学生提供了 2600 小时的咨询。

academic [ˌækə'demik] *a.* **学术的；理论的；学院的**　*n.* **大学生，大学教师；学者**

【变】academics

【例】Last **academic** year in spite of staff cuts, we counseled 240 international students for a total of 2600 hours' counseling.

上一个**学年**，尽管员工减少了，我们仍然为 240 个国际学生提供了 2600 小时的咨询。

【搭】academic activity 学术活动　academic course 普通课程，学术课程

【记】academy *n.* 学院；一般的高等教育；私立学校，学术团体

accelerate *v.* （使）加快，（使）增速；加速；促进

acceleration *n.* 加速；（物）加速度；加速升级；（优秀学生的）跳级

in spite of 尽管；不管，不顾

【例】Last academic year **in spite of** staff cuts, we counseled 240 international students for a total of 2600 hours' counseling.

上一个学年，**尽管**员工减少了，我们仍然为 240 个国际学生提供了 2600 小时的咨询。

【记】spite *n.* 恶意；怨恨；恶事

splash *v.* 使（液体）溅起

splendid *a.* 壮观的，豪华的；闪亮的

staff [stɑːf] *n.* 职员；参谋；棒；支撑　*a.* 职员的；行政工作的　*v.* 供给人员；给……配备职员

【变】staffed　staffed　staffing　staffs

【例】Last academic year in spite of **staff** cuts, we counseled 240 international students for a total of 2600 hours' counseling.

上一个学年，尽管**员工**减少了，我们仍然为 240 个国际学生提供了 2600 小时的咨询。

【搭】staff cost 人事费用，职员费用　staff gauge 标尺，水位尺；水尺

【记】stage *n.* 阶段；舞台；戏剧；驿站

stagger *v.* 蹒跚；犹豫；动摇

stain *v.* 弄脏；污染；被玷污

counsel ['kaunsl] *n.* 法律顾问；忠告；商议；讨论；决策　*v.* 建议；劝告；商讨；提出忠告

【变】counseled　counseled　counseling　counsels

【例】Last academic year in spite of staff cuts, we **counseled** 240 international students for a total of 2600 hours' counseling.

上一个学年，尽管员工减少了，我们仍然为 240 个国际学生**提供**了 2600 小时的**咨询**。

【搭】counsel for the defence 辩护律师，被告律师

【记】count *n.* 计数；计算

counter *n.* 柜台；对立面；计数器

词汇听写

1. ＿＿＿＿＿＿＿ 2. ＿＿＿＿＿＿＿ 3. ＿＿＿＿＿＿＿

句子听写

Saturday .... 《《

1. I think we should do a questionnaire. That would be so much less time consuming than organizing interviews, I recommend.

我觉得我们应该做一个调查问卷。这将比组织面试所耗的时间要少得多，我建议调查问卷。

questionnaire [ˌkwestʃə'neə] *n.* 问卷；调查表

【变】questionnaires

【例】I think we should do a **questionnaire**. That would be so much less time consuming than organizing interviews, I recommend.

我觉得我们应该做一个**调查问卷**。这将比组织面试所耗的时间要少得多，我建议调查问卷。

【搭】questionnaire form 调查表，征求意见表

【记】question *n.* 问题；疑问；议题

quest *n.* 探索；追求

queen *n.* 女王；王后；重要的事物，女王般的人；皇后

consume [kən'sjuːm] *v.* 消耗，消费；使……着迷；挥霍

【变】consumed　consumed　consuming　consumes

【例】I think we should do a questionnaire. That would be so much less time **consuming** than organizing interviews, I recommend.

我觉得我们应该做一个调查问卷。这将比组织面试所**耗**的时间要少得多，我建议调查问卷。

【搭】consume away 毁掉，毁灭　be consumed with guilt 深感内疚

【记】consumption *n.* 消费；耗尽

consumer *n.* 消费者，顾客

consul *n.* 领事；（古罗马共和国时期）执政官

interview ['intəvjuː] *n.* & *v.* 接见，采访；面试，面谈

【变】interviewed　interviewed　interviewing　interviews

【例】I think we should do a questionnaire. That would be so much less time consuming than organizing **interviews**, I recommend.

我觉得我们应该做一个调查问卷。这将比组织**面试**所耗的时间要少得多，我建议调查问卷。

【搭】interview approach 访问手法　during the interview 面试时

【记】interval *n.* 间隔；幕间休息；（数学）区间

intervene *v.* 阻碍；出面；插嘴；介于……之间

interview *n.* 接见；采访；面试；会谈

recommend [ˌrekəˈmend] *v.* **推荐，介绍；劝告；使受欢迎；托付**

【变】recommended　recommended　recommending　recommends

【例】I think we should do a questionnaire. That would be so much less time consuming than organizing interviews，I **recommend**.

我觉得我们应该做一个调查问卷。这将比组织面试所耗的时间要少得多，我**建议**调查问卷。

【搭】recommend a hotel 推荐一家旅店

【记】commend *v.* 推荐；表扬

recommendation *n.* 推荐，推荐信；建议

reconcile *v.* 使和好；调停

recognition *n.* 认识；认可

词汇听写

1. _____　2. _____　3. _____

句子听写

2. So far, in these lectures, we've been looking at crimes like robbery and murder, both from historical point of view and also in contemporary society.

到目前为止，在这些讲座中，我们一直从历史的角度，还有现代社会的角度出发，讨论如抢劫和谋杀等罪行。

crime [kraim] *n.* 罪行，犯罪；罪恶；犯罪活动　*v.* 控告……违反纪律

【变】crimed　crimed　criming　crimes

【例】So far, in these lectures, we've been looking at **crimes** like robbery and murder, both from historical point of view and also in contemporary society.

到目前为止，在这些讲座中，我们一直从历史的角度，还有现代社会的角度出发，讨论如抢劫和谋杀等**罪行**。

【搭】crime sheet［法］处罚记载　increase in crime 犯罪活动增加

【记】criminal *n.* 罪犯，犯人　*a.* 刑事的；犯罪的

robbery ['rɔbri] *n.* 抢劫，盗窃；抢掠

【变】robberies

【例】So far, in these lectures, we've been looking at crimes like **robbery** and murder, both from historical point of view and also in contemporary society.

到目前为止，在这些讲座中，我们一直从历史的角度，还有现代社会的角度出发，讨论如**抢劫**和谋杀等罪行。

【搭】robbery insurance 盗劫保险　robbery suspect［法］抢劫嫌疑犯

【记】robber *n.* 强盗，盗贼

rob *v.* 抢劫；抢夺

probe *n.* 探针　*v.* 用探针探

acrobat *n.* 杂技演员

point of view 观点

【例】So far, in these lectures, we've been looking at crimes like robbery and murder, both from historical **point of view** and also in contemporary society.

到目前为止，在这些讲座中，我们一直从历史的角度，还有现代社会的**角度**出发，讨论如抢劫和谋杀等罪行。

【搭】from this point of view 从这个角度出发

【记】viewpoint *n.* 观点，意见；

view *v.* 看　*n.*［建筑学］视图；风景；意图

interview *v.* 接见，会见

review *v.*&*n.* 评论；复习

contemporary [kən'temprəri] *n.* 同时代的人；同时期的东西　*a.* 当代的；
同时代的；属于同一时期的

【变】contemporaries

【例】So far，in these lectures，we've been looking at crimes like robbery and murder，both from historical point of view and also in **contemporary** society.

　　到目前为止，在这些讲座中，我们一直从历史的角度，还有**现代**社会的角度出发，讨论如抢劫和谋杀等罪行。

【搭】contemporary imperialism 现代帝国主义

　　contemporary literature 现代文学

【记】contempt *n.* 轻视；轻蔑；不顾

　　contain *v.* 包含，容纳；克制

　　contact *n.* 接触；触点

词汇听写

1. _____　2. _____　3. _____

句子听写

3. Corporate crime is committed for the corporate organization. So crimes like theft by employees, embezzlement or fraud against one's actual employer are excluded.

　　公司犯罪是指为了法人组织的利益犯下的罪行。因此，像公司员工对雇主犯下的偷窃、贪污、欺诈等都不算是公司犯罪。

commit [kə'mit] *v.* 犯罪，做错事；把……交托给；指派……作战；使……
承担义务

【例】Corporate crime is **committed** for the corporate organization. So crimes like theft by employees, embezzlement or fraud against one's actual employer are excluded.

公司犯罪是指为了法人组织的利益**犯下**的罪行。因此，像公司员工对雇主犯下的偷窃、贪污、欺诈等都不算是公司犯罪。

【搭】commit a crime 犯罪　commit a sin 犯罪；造孽；作孽

【记】committee *n.* 委员会，全体委员；（为促进共同目标的实现而自发组织起来的）促进会

commit *v.* 犯罪，做错事；把……托付给

commission *n.* 委员会，委员；［商］佣金，手续费

embezzlement [em'bezlmnt] *n.* 侵占；挪用；盗用

【例】Corporate crime is committed for the corporate organization. So crimes like theft by employees, **embezzlement** or fraud against one's actual employer are excluded.

公司犯罪是指为了法人组织的利益犯下的罪行。因此，像公司员工对雇主犯下的偷窃、**贪污**、欺诈等都不算是公司犯罪。

【记】embody *v.* 表现，象征；包含，收录；使具体化

embarrass *v.*（使）窘迫，（使）局促不安；（使）困难

embassy *n.* 大使馆；大使馆全体成员；重任，差使

fraud [frɔːd] *n.* 欺骗；骗子；诡计

【变】frauds

【例】Corporate crime is committed for the corporate organization. So crimes like theft by employees, embezzlement or **fraud** against one's actual employer are excluded.

公司犯罪是指为了法人组织的利益犯下的罪行。因此，像公司员工对雇主犯下的偷窃、贪污、**欺诈**等都不算是公司犯罪。

【搭】fraud in fact ［法］事实上的欺诈

【记】freedom *n.* 自由，自主；直率；特权，特许；自由权

freeze *v.* 使结冰，使冻僵

fraction *n.* 分数

fracture *n.* 破裂；裂痕

fragile *a.* 脆的；体质弱的

exclude [ik's klu:d] *v.* **排除；排斥；拒绝接纳；逐出**

【变】excluded   excluded   excluding   excludes

【例】Corporate crime is committed for the corporate organization. So crimes like theft by employees, embezzlement or fraud against one's actual employer are **excluded.**

公司犯罪是指为了法人组织的利益犯下的罪行。因此，像公司员工对雇主犯下的偷窃、贪污、欺诈等都**不算**是公司犯罪。

【记】exclusive *a.* 专用的；高级的；排外的；单独的

excursion *n.* （尤指集体）远足；短途旅行，游览；离题

词汇听写

1. ＿＿＿＿＿＿＿   2. ＿＿＿＿＿＿＿   3. ＿＿＿＿＿＿＿

句子听写

Sunday ┈┈┈┈┈┈┈┈┈┈┈┈┈┈┈┈┈┈┈┈┈┈┈┈┈ ≪

1. Corporate crime tends to be underreported in comparison with conventional crime in news broadcasts and in crime series of films and so on.

　　与传统犯罪相比，公司犯罪在新闻广播片和犯罪电影、电视中都往往被忽视。

underreport [ˌʌndəriˈpɔːt] *v.* 低估；少报（收入等）

【例】Corporate crime tends to be **underreported** in comparison with conventional crime in news broadcasts and in crime series of films and so on.

　　与传统犯罪相比，公司犯罪在新闻广播片和犯罪电影、电视中都往往被忽视。

【记】understand *v.* 懂，理解

understake *v.* 承担，从事；答应；承诺

underwear *n.* 衬衣，内衣

in comparison with 与……比较，同……比较起来

【例】Corporate crime tends to be underreported **in comparison with** conventional crime in news broadcasts and in crime series of films and so on.

　　与传统犯罪**相比**，公司犯罪在新闻广播片和犯罪电影、电视中都往往被忽视。

【记】comparison *n.* 比较，对照；[语] 比喻；比较级

compass *n.* 罗盘；指南针；圆规；界限

compact *v.* 压紧，（使）坚实；把……弄紧密，把……弄结实；使（文体）简洁

conventional [kənˈvenʃnl] *a.* 符合习俗的，传统的；常见的；惯例的

【例】Corporate crime tends to be underreported in comparison with **conventional** crime in news broadcasts and in crime series of films and so on.

　　与**传统**犯罪相比，公司犯罪在新闻广播片和犯罪电影、电视中都往往被忽视。

【搭】conventional accounting 会计惯例，常规会计

conventional form 惯例形式

【记】convention *n.* 会议；全体与会者；国际公约；习俗，规矩

conversation *n.* 交谈，会话；交往，交际；会谈；（人与计算机的）人机对话

series ['siəriːz] *n.* 系列，连续；[电] 串联；级数；丛书

【变】series

【例】Corporate crime tends to be underreported in comparison with conventional crime in news broadcasts and in crime **series** of films and so on.

与传统犯罪相比，公司犯罪在新闻广播片和犯罪电影、电视中都往往被忽视。

【搭】a series of attack 一连串攻击　a series of movies 一系列电影

【记】serious *a.* 严肃的；认真的；重要的；危险的

sermon *n.* 布道；讲道；讲道文章；一大通教训

词汇听写

1. _____ 2. _____ 3. _____

句子听写

2. They think their misfortune is an accident, or that is the fault of no one in particular. They're unaware that they've been victims of a crime.

他们认为他们的不幸是一个意外，或者说是一个错误，只是犯错的不是某个特定的人。他们不知道，他们已经成为犯罪的受害者。

fault [fɔːlt] *n.* 故障；错误；缺点；毛病　*v.* 弄错；产生断层

【变】faulted　faulted　faulting　faults

【例】They think their misfortune is an accident, or that is the **fault** of no one in particular. They're unaware that they've been victims of a crime.

他们认为他们的不幸是一个意外，或者说是一个**错误**，只是犯错的不是某个特定的人。他们不知道，他们已经成为犯罪的受害者。

【搭】fault assessment 故障（后果）评定　fault group 断层组

【记】faultless *a.* 完美的；无缺点的；无疵

faulty *a.* 错误的；有错误的，有过失的，有缺点的；不完美的

favour *n.* 帮助；恩惠；赞同；善行

in particular 尤其，特别

【例】They think their misfortune is an accident, or that is the fault of no one **in particular**. They're unaware that they've been victims of a crime.

他们认为他们的不幸是一个意外，或者说是一个错误，只是犯错的不是某个**特定的**人。他们不知道，他们已经成为犯罪的受害者。

【记】particularly *ad.* 特别；尤其；异乎寻常地

partition *n.* 划分，分开；分割；隔离物；隔墙

partly *ad.* 在一定程度上；部分地；不完全地；半

unaware [ˌʌnəˈweə] *a.* 不知道的，无意的；未察觉到的　*ad.* 意外地；不知不觉地

【例】They think their misfortune is an accident, or that is the fault of no one in particular. They're **unaware** that they've been victims of a crime.

他们认为他们的不幸是一个意外，或者说是一个错误，只是犯错的不是某个特定的人。他们**不知道**，他们已经成为犯罪的受害者。

【记】aware *a.* 意识到的；知道的；觉察到的

award *v.* 授予，奖给，判给；判归，判定

unwilling *a.* 不愿意的，不情愿的；勉强的；厌恶的；不甘的

victim [ˈviktim] *n.* 受害人；牺牲品；牺牲者

【变】victims

【例】They think their misfortune is an accident, or that is the fault of no one in particular. They're unaware that they've been **victims** of a crime.

他们认为他们的不幸是一个意外，或者说是一个错误，只是犯错的不是某个特定的人。他们不知道，他们已经成为犯罪的**受害者**。

【记】victorious *a.* 胜利的；得胜的

video *n.* 磁带录像；录像磁带；录像机，电视；（指方法）录像

view *n.* 看；[建筑学] 视图；风景；意图

词汇听写

1. _____ 2. _____ 3. _____

句子听写

3. We have been offering a wide variety of walking holidays to <u>suit</u> all <u>tastes</u> for just three years, but already we have won two <u>awards</u> for <u>excellence</u> in this field.

短短三年里，我们一直在提供各种各样的徒步旅行假期，以适应各种旅客的要求，尽管才三年，但在这一领域，我们以优质的服务已经赢得了两个奖项。

suit [suːt] *v.* 适合；使适应 *n.* 诉讼；组；套装；恳求

【变】suited　suited　suiting　suits

【例】We have been offering a wide variety of walking holidays to **suit** all tastes for just three years，but already we have won two awards for excellence in this field.

短短三年里，我们一直在提供各种各样的徒步旅行假期，以**适应**各种旅客的要求，尽管才三年，但在这一领域，我们以优质的服务已经赢得了两个奖项。

【搭】suit all tastes 人人中意　suit oneself 随自己的意愿行事；自便

【记】suitcase *n.* 手提箱；衣箱

suitable *a.* 合适的，适当的，适宜的，恰当的

sullen *a.* 愠怒的，不高兴的；（天气）阴沉的；悲哀的

taste [teist] *n.* 味道；品味；审美 *v.* 尝；体验

【例】We have been offering a wide variety of walking holidays to suit all **tastes** for just three years，but already we have won two awards for excellence in this field.

短短三年里，我们一直在提供各种各样的徒步旅行假期，以适应各种旅客的**要求**，尽管才三年，但在这一领域，我们以优质的服务已经赢得了两个奖项。

【搭】taste blood 尝到甜头，初识真味　taste bud 味蕾

【记】task *n.* 工作，任务；作业；苦差事

　　tax *v.* 使负重担；消耗精力；向······征税；责备，谴责

award 英 [ə'wɔːd] *v.* 授予；判定　*n.* 奖品；判决

【变】awarded　awarded　awarding　awards

【例】We have been offering a wide variety of walking holidays to suit all tastes for just three years, but already we have won two **awards** for excellence in this field.

　　　短短三年里，我们一直在提供各种各样的徒步旅行假期，以适应各种旅客的要求，尽管才三年，但在这一领域，我们以优质的服务已经赢得了两个**奖项**。

【搭】award meeting 决算会议　　award the contract to a factory 把合同给了一家工厂

【记】aware *a.* 意识到的；知道的；觉察到的

　　away *ad.* 离开，远离；在远处；消失

　　await *v.* 等候；等待；期待

excellence ['ekslns] *n.* 优秀；美德；长处

【变】excellences

【例】We have been offering a wide variety of walking holidays to suit all tastes for just three years, but already we have won two awards for **excellence** in this field.

　　　短短三年里，我们一直在提供各种各样的徒步旅行假期，以适应各种旅客的要求，尽管才三年，但在这一领域，我们以优质的服务已经赢得了两个奖项。

【记】excellent *a.* 卓越的；杰出的；优秀的

　　except *v.* 把······除外；不计

　　exceed *v.* 超过；超越；（在数量和质量等方面）胜过；越过······的界限

词汇听写

1. _____　2. _____　3. _____

句子听写

Monday ··· ‹‹‹

1. After our dinner at communal tables designed to make all our guests feel part of a family atmosphere, entertainment is laid on nearly every night with tour leaders on hand to organize lectures , quizzes and respond to any special requests from guests.

我们在公共餐桌上吃晚餐，这是为了让我们的客人感受到家庭的氛围，晚餐后，几乎每天晚上都有娱乐活动，领队现场组织演讲、问答等游戏，并且应对客人的任何特殊要求。

communal [ˈkɔmjunl] a. 公共的；公社的

【例】After our dinner at **communal** tables designed to make all our guests feel part of a family atmosphere, entertainment is laid on nearly every night with tour leaders on hand to organize lectures , quizzes and respond to any special requests from guests.

我们在**公共**餐桌上吃晚餐，这是为了让我们的客人感受到家庭的氛围，晚餐后，几乎每天晚上都有娱乐活动，领队现场组织演讲、问答等游戏，并且应对客人的任何特殊要求。

【搭】communal aerial 公用天线　communal habitat 群落居住地

【记】communicate v. 传达，表达；表明；传染扩散

communication n. 通信；交流；书信；传达

communism n. 共产主义；共产主义制度

atmosphere [ˈætməˌsfiə] n. 气氛；大气；空气

【变】atmospheres

【例】After our dinner at communal tables designed to make all our guests feel part of a family **atmosphere**, entertainment is laid on nearly every night with tour leaders on hand to organize lectures，quizzes and respond to any special requests from guests.

我们在公共餐桌上吃晚餐，这是为了让我们的客人感受到家庭的**氛围**，晚餐后，几乎每天晚上都有娱乐活动，领队现场组织演讲、问答等游戏，并且应对客人的任何特殊要求。

【搭】atmosphere analyzer 大气分析器　atmosphere dust 大气尘埃

【记】atmospheric a. 大气的；大气引起的；有……气氛的

atom n. 原子；原子能；微粒，微量

sphere n. 球（体）；（兴趣或活动的）范围；势力范围；天体，如行星或恒星

entertainment [entə'teinmnt] n. 娱乐；消遣；款待

【变】entertainments

【例】After our dinner at communal tables designed to make all our guests feel part of a family atmosphere，**entertainment** is laid on nearly every night with tour leaders on hand to organize lectures，quizzes and respond to any special requests from guests.

我们在公共餐桌上吃晚餐，这是为了让我们的客人感受到家庭的氛围，晚餐后，几乎每天晚上都有**娱乐**活动，领队现场组织演讲、问答等游戏，并且应对客人的任何特殊要求。

【搭】entertainment car 娱乐车　entertainment center 娱乐中心

【记】entertain v. 热情款待；使有兴趣；抱着，怀有；考虑

enthusiasm n. 热情，热忱；热衷的事物；宗教的狂热

entire a. 全部的；整个的；全体的

quiz [kwiz] n. 考查；恶作剧；课堂测验　v. 挖苦；张望；对……进行测验

【变】quizzes

【例】After our dinner at communal tables designed to make all our guests feel part of a family atmosphere，entertainment is laid on nearly every night with tour leaders on hand to organize lectures，**quizzes** and respond to any special requests from guests.

我们在公共餐桌上吃晚餐，这是为了让我们的客人感受到家庭的氛

围，晚餐后，几乎每天晚上都有娱乐活动，领队现场组织演讲、**问答**等游戏，并且应对客人的任何特殊要求。

【搭】quiz game 答问比赛；猜谜游戏　a general knowledge quiz 常识问答竞赛

【记】quotation *n.* 引用，引证；行市；估价单；引用语

qualification *n.* 资格，授权；条件，限制；合格证书

qualitative *a.* 定性的，定质的；性质上的；质量的

词汇听写

1. _____　2. _____　3. _____

句子听写

2. Sharks have a <u>tough</u> elastic skeleton of <u>cartilage</u>, unlike bone, this firm, <u>pliable</u> material is rather like your nose, and allows the sharks to bend easily as it swims.

鲨鱼有一种坚韧且有弹性的软骨骨架，和骨头不同，这种坚硬、柔韧的材料就像你的鼻子，能够让鲨鱼在游泳时容易弯曲。

tough [tʌf] *a.* 艰苦的，困难的；坚强的，不屈不挠的；坚韧的，牢固的；强壮的，结实的　*n.* 恶棍　*v.* 坚持；忍受，忍耐　*ad.* 强硬地，顽强地

【变】toughed　toughed　toughing　toughs

【例】Sharks have a **tough** elastic skeleton of cartilage, unlike bone, this firm, pliable material is rather like your nose, and allows the sharks to bend easily as it swims.

鲨鱼有一种**坚韧**且有弹性的软骨骨架，和骨头不同，这种坚硬、柔韧的材料就像你的鼻子，能够让鲨鱼在游泳时容易弯曲。

【记】tour *n.* 旅行，观光；巡回演出；任职期；轮班

tourist *n.* 旅行者，观光客；

tow *v.* 拖，拉；牵引

elastic [iˈlæstik] *a.* 有弹性的；灵活的；易伸缩的　*n.* 松紧带；橡皮圈

【变】elastics

【例】Sharks have a tough **elastic** skeleton of cartilage, unlike bone, this firm, pliable material is rather like your nose, and allows the sharks to bend easily as it swims.

鲨鱼有一种坚韧且**有弹性的**软骨骨架，和骨头不同，这种坚硬、柔韧的材料就像你的鼻子，能够让鲨鱼在游泳时容易弯曲。

【记】elaborate *v.* 详尽说明；变得复杂

elapse *v.* 消逝；时间过去

elbow *n.* 肘部；弯头，扶手；肘形管，弯管

cartilage [ˈkɑːt(i)lidʒ] *n.* 软骨

【变】cartilages

【例】Sharks have a tough elastic skeleton of **cartilage**, unlike bone, this firm, pliable material is rather like your nose, and allows the sharks to bend easily as it swims.

鲨鱼有一种坚韧且有弹性的**软骨**骨架，和骨头不同，这种坚硬、柔韧的材料就像你的鼻子，能够让鲨鱼在游泳时容易弯曲。

【记】cartoon *n.* 漫画；讽刺画；动画片；草图

cartridge *n.* 子弹，弹药筒；笔芯

cart *n.* 运货马车，手推车

pliable [ˈplaiəbl] *a.* 柔韧的；柔软的；圆滑的；易曲折的

【例】Sharks have a tough elastic skeleton of cartilage, unlike bone, this firm, **pliable** material is rather like your nose, and allows the sharks to bend easily as it swims.

鲨鱼有一种坚韧且有弹性的软骨骨架，和骨头不同，这种坚硬、**柔韧的**材料就像你的鼻子，能够让鲨鱼在游泳时容易弯曲。

【记】plot *n.* 地基；（戏剧、小说等的）情节

split *v.* & *n.* 裂开，切开　*a.* 分裂的

plague *n.* 瘟疫；灾害，折磨

词汇听写

1. _____ 2. _____ 3. _____

句子听写

3. The shark's skin isn't <u>covered</u> with <u>scales</u>, like other fish, instead the skin's covered with <u>barbs</u>, giving it a rough <u>texture</u> like sandpaper.

鲨鱼的皮肤不像其他的鱼那样覆盖着鳞片，而是覆盖着倒钩，使皮肤像砂纸一样质感粗糙。

cover [ˈkʌvə] *v.* 包括；采访，报导；涉及；覆盖；代替　*n.* 封面，封皮；盖子；掩蔽物

【变】covered　covered　covering　covers

【例】The shark's skin isn't **covered** with scales, like other fish, instead the skin's covered with barbs, giving it a rough texture like sandpaper.

鲨鱼的皮肤不像其他的鱼那样**覆盖**着鳞片，而是覆盖着倒钩，使皮肤像砂纸一样质感粗糙。

【搭】fish adhesive 鱼胶　fish and chips 炸鱼，加炸土豆片

【记】cow *n.* 奶牛

coach *n.* 教练；（铁路）旅客车厢；长途客运汽车；四轮大马车

coal *n.* 煤；煤块；煤堆；木炭

scale [skeil] *n.* 规模；比例；鳞；刻度；天平；数值范围　*v.* 衡量；攀登；剥落；刮鳞

【变】scaled　scaled　scaling　scales

【例】The shark's skin isn't covered with **scales**, like other fish, instead the skin's covered with barbs, giving it a rough texture like sandpaper.

鲨鱼的皮肤不像其他的鱼那样覆盖着**鳞**片，而是覆盖着倒钩，使皮肤像砂纸一样质感粗糙。

【搭】scale arc 标度弧　scale beam 秤杆

【记】scan *v.*（计）扫描；细看；细查；（雷达）对……进行扫描

scandal *n.* 丑闻，丑名，丑事，丢脸的事件

scar *n.* 伤痕；精神上的创伤；露岩，断崖

barb ［bɑːb］ *v.* 装倒钩于　*n.* 箭头鱼钩等的倒钩；伤人的话

【变】barbs

【例】The shark's skin isn't covered with scales, like other fish, instead the skin's covered with **barbs**, giving it a rough texture like sandpaper.

　　鲨鱼的皮肤不像其他的鱼那样覆盖着鳞片，而是覆盖着**倒钩**，使皮肤像砂纸一样质感粗糙。

【搭】cover her face 盖住她的脸　cover against 为⋯⋯投保

【记】barber *n.* 理发师；理发店（＝ barber's shop）

　　bare *a.* 光秃秃的；（房间、柜子等）空的；赤裸的；刚好够的

　　bar *n.* 条，棒；（门、窗等的）闩；障碍；酒吧间

texture ［'tekstʃə］ *n.* 质地；纹理；结构；本质，实质

【变】textures

【例】The shark's skin isn't covered with scales, like other fish, instead the skin's covered with barbs, giving it a rough **texture** like sandpaper.

　　鲨鱼的皮肤不像其他的鱼那样覆盖着鳞片，而是覆盖着倒钩，使皮肤像砂纸一样**质感**粗糙。

【搭】texture characteristic 纹理特征，组织特性　texture class 质地（分）级

【记】text *n.* 文本，原文；课文，教科书；主题；版本

　　textbook *n.* 教科书，课本

　　textile *n.* 纺织品，织物；纺织业

词汇听写

1. ＿＿＿＿＿＿　2. ＿＿＿＿＿＿　3. ＿＿＿＿＿＿

句子听写

Tuesday ································· «

1. Sharks rarely swim at the <u>surface</u>. Mostly, they swim at the bottom of ocean, <u>scavenging</u>. While most other animals hunt their <u>prey</u> by means of their eyesight, shark hunt by their <u>acute</u> sense of smell.

   鲨鱼很少在水面游泳。大多数情况下，他们在海洋的底部畅游、寻找。大多数其他动物通过他们的视力捕捉猎物，而鲨鱼则是依靠他们敏锐的嗅觉追捕猎物。

surface ['səːfis] *n.* 表面；表层；外观　*a.* 表面的，肤浅的　*v.* 浮出水面
v. 使浮出水面；使成平面

   【变】surfaced　surfaced　surfacing　surfaces

   【例】Sharks rarely swim at the **surface**. Mostly, they swim at the bottom of ocean, scavenging. While most other animals hunt their prey by means of their eyesight, shark hunt by their acute sense of smell.

   　　鲨鱼很少在**水面**游泳。大多数情况下，他们在海洋的底部畅游、寻找。大多数其他动物通过他们的视力捕捉猎物，而鲨鱼则是依靠他们敏锐的嗅觉追捕猎物。

   【搭】road surface 路面　surface abrasion 表面磨蚀

   【记】surgeon *n.* 外科医生；［军］军医

   　　sure *a.* 确信的，确实的；有把握的；无疑的；一定的

   　　face *n.* 面容；表面；脸；方面

scavenge ['skævin(d)ʒ] *v.* 打扫；排除废气；以……为食　*v.* 清除污物；
打扫

   【变】scavenged　scavenged　scavenging　scavenges

   【例】Sharks rarely swim at the surface. Mostly, they swim at the bottom of ocean, **scavenging**. While most other animals hunt their prey by means of their eyesight, shark hunt by their acute sense of smell.

   　　鲨鱼很少在水面游泳。大多数情况下，他们在海洋的底部畅游、寻找。大多数其他动物通过他们的视力捕捉猎物，而鲨鱼则是依靠他们敏锐的嗅觉追捕猎物。

   【搭】scavenge delivery 油泵输出管　scavenge gears 油泵回油器（装置）

【记】scene *n.* 场面，现场；（戏剧的）一场；景色，风景；事件

scenery *n.* 风景，景色；舞台布景；风景画；舞台面

scent *n.* 香味，气味；嗅觉；（动物的）臭迹；痕迹，踪迹

prey ［prei］ *v.* 捕食；掠夺；折磨 *n.* 捕食；牺牲者；被捕食的动物

【变】preyed preyed preying preys

【例】Sharks rarely swim at the surface. Mostly, they swim at the bottom of ocean, scavenging. While most other animals hunt their **prey** by means of their eyesight, shark hunt by their acute sense of smell.

鲨鱼很少在水面游泳。大多数情况下，他们在海洋的底部畅游、寻找。大多数其他动物通过他们的视力捕捉**猎物**，而鲨鱼则是依靠他们敏锐的嗅觉追捕猎物。

【搭】attack its prey 攻击它的猎物 prey upon 捕食，掠夺，折磨

【记】price *n.* 价格，价钱；代价；价值；赏金

prick *v.* 刺，扎，戳；刺伤，刺痛

pride *n.* 自尊；骄傲；自满；（狮）群

acute ［əˈkjuːt］ *a.* 严重的，[医] 急性的；敏锐的；激烈的；尖声的

【例】Sharks rarely swim at the surface. Mostly, they swim at the bottom of ocean, scavenging. While most other animals hunt their prey by means of their eyesight, shark hunt by their **acute** sense of smell.

鲨鱼很少在水面游泳。大多数情况下，他们在海洋的底部畅游、寻找。大多数其他动物通过他们的视力捕捉猎物，而鲨鱼则是依靠他们**敏锐的**嗅觉追捕猎物。

【搭】acute shortage 严重的短缺 acute accent 重音符

【记】academic *a.* 学院的，大学的，学会的，（学术、文艺）协会的

academy *n.* 专科学校；学会，学院

accelerate *v.* （使）加快，（使）增速；促进

词汇听写

1. _____ 2. _____ 3. _____

句子听写

2. If you don't want to do the whale watch <u>cruise</u>, your guide will take anyone who is interested either on a <u>bushwalk</u> through the national park near the hotel, and there's no extra <u>charge</u> for that, or on a fishing trip. And there's also a <u>reptile</u> park in town.

如果你不想坐观鲸游船，而是对旅馆附近的国家公园徒步行感兴趣或者是对钓鱼之旅感兴趣，无论哪一种选择，导游都会带着你去，不收额外的费用，附近，还有一个爬行动物公园。

cruise [kruːz] *v.* 巡航，巡游；漫游 *n.* 巡航，巡游；乘船游览

【变】cruised cruised cruising cruises

【例】If you don't want to do the whale watch **cruise**, your guide will take anyone who is interested either on a bushwalk through the national park near the hotel, and there's no extra charge for that, or on a fishing trip. And there's also a reptile park in town.

如果你不想坐观鲸游**船**，而是对旅馆附近的国家公园徒步行感兴趣或者是对钓鱼之旅感兴趣，无论哪一种选择，导游都会带着你去，不收额外的费用，附近，还有一个爬行动物公园。

【搭】cruise attitude 巡航姿态（巡航状态的俯仰角）   cruise car 巡逻警车

【记】crush *v.* 压破，压碎；镇压；弄皱

crust *n.* 面包皮；硬外皮；地壳

clockwise *a.* & *ad.* 顺时针方向转的（地）

bushwalk ['buʃwɔːk] *n.* 丛林徒步旅行

【例】If you don't want to do the whale watch cruise, your guide will take anyone who is interested either on a **bushwalk** through the national park near the hotel, and there's no extra charge for that, or on a fishing trip. And there's also a reptile park in town.

如果你不想坐观鲸游船，而是对旅馆附近的国家公园**徒步行**感兴趣或者是对钓鱼之旅感兴趣，无论哪一种选择，导游都会带着你去，不收额外的费用，附近，还有一个爬行动物公园。

【记】bush *n.* 灌木（<u>丛</u>）

bubble *n.* 泡，水泡；冒泡，起泡

charge [tʃɑːdʒ] *n.* 费用；电荷；掌管；控告；命令；负载　*v.* 使充电；使承担；指责；装载；对……索费；向……冲去

【变】charged　charged　charging　charges

【例】If you don't want to do the whale watch cruise, your guide will take anyone who is interested either on a bushwalk through the national park near the hotel, and there's no extra **charge** for that, or on a fishing trip. And there's also a reptile park in town.

　　如果你不想坐观鲸游船，而是对旅馆附近的国家公园徒步行感兴趣或者是对钓鱼之旅感兴趣，无论哪一种选择，导游都会带着你去，不收额外的**费用**，附近，还有一个爬行动物公园。

【搭】charge account 赊账　charge against 控告

【记】charity *n.* 慈善（行为）；施舍，捐助；仁爱

　　charm *n.* 魔力；魅力

　　character *n.* 性格，特征；字母；人物

reptile ['reptail] *a.* 爬虫类的；卑鄙的　*n.* 爬行动物；卑鄙的人

【变】reptiles

【例】If you don't want to do the whale watch cruise, your guide will take anyone who is interested either on a bushwalk through the national park near the hotel, and there's no extra charge for that, or on a fishing trip. And there's also a **reptile** park in town.

　　如果你不想坐观鲸游船，而是对旅馆附近的国家公园徒步行感兴趣或者是对钓鱼之旅感兴趣，无论哪一种选择，导游都会带着你去，不收额外的费用，附近，还有一个**爬行动物**公园。

【搭】keep a reptile as a pet 养一只爬行动物为宠物

【记】repair *v.* 修理；纠正；恢复；弥补

　　repay *v.* 偿还；付还；报答；酬报

　　reach *v.* 到达，走到，完成

　　fertile *a.* （创造力）丰富的

　　hostile *a.* 敌对的；不友好的

　　tile *n.* 瓦片，瓷砖；贴砖

词汇听写

1. _____ 2. _____ 3. _____

句子听写

3. I have to tell you that if you cancel within seven day departure you will have to pay 50% of your total booking. Now you need to pay a 20% deposit at the time of booking. So I'll make a provisional booking. Let me issue you with a customer reference number.

　　我必须告知的是如果在离开之前七日内取消预订，你将支付你的总预订金额的 50%。现在你要预订就需要支付 20% 的定金。我将给您作临时预订，并发给你一个顾客参考号码。

departure [di'pɑːtʃə] *n.* 离开；出发；违背

【变】departures

【例】I have to tell you that if you cancel within seven day departure you will have to pay 50% of your total booking. Now you need to pay a 20% deposit at the time of booking. So I'll make a provisional booking. Let me issue you with a customer reference number.

　　我必须告知的是如果在离开之前七日内取消预订，你将支付你的总预订金额的 50%。现在你要预订就需要支付 20% 的定金。我将给您作临时预订，并发给你一个顾客参考号码。

【搭】departure from 违反，违背　departure indication lamp 离去（发车）表示灯

【记】depart *v.* 离开，出发；去世

　　department *n.* 部门；系，学部；车间

　　depend *v.* 依靠；信赖；决定于

deposit [di'pɒzit] *n.* 存款；保证金；沉淀物　*v.* 使沉积；存放

【变】deposited　deposited　depositing　deposits

【例】I have to tell you that if you cancel within seven day departure you will have to pay 50% of your total booking. Now you need to pay a 20%

deposit at the time of booking. So I'll make a provisional booking. Let me issue you with a customer reference number.

我必须告知的是如果在离开之前七日内取消预订，你将支付你的总预订金额的 50％。现在你要预订就需要支付 20％ 的定金。我将给您作临时预订，并发给你一个顾客参考号码。

【搭】deposit account 有息存款，储蓄存款　deposit allowance 存款利息

【记】deposition n. 沉积（物）；证词；免职，革职

depress v. 压下，压低；使沮丧；使萧条；使跌价

deprive v. 剥夺，夺去，使丧失

---

provisional [prəˈviʒnl] a. 临时的，暂时的；暂定的　n. 临时邮票

【变】provisionals

【例】I have to tell you that if you cancel within seven day departure you will have to pay 50％ of your total booking. Now you need to pay a 20％ deposit at the time of booking. So I'll make a provisional booking. Let me issue you with a customer reference number.

我必须告知的是如果在离开之前七日内取消预订，你将支付你的总预订金额的 50％。现在你要预订就需要支付 20％ 的定金。我将给您作临时预订，并发给你一个顾客参考号码。

【搭】provisional acceptance 临时接受　provisional account 临时账户

【记】provision n. 规定，条项，准备，设备；供应，（一批）供应品

provoke v. 激起，招致；触怒，使愤怒

prove v. 证明，证实；检定；显示

---

issue [ˈiʃuː] n. 问题；流出；期号；发行物　v. 发行，发布；发给；放出，排出；造成……结果；传下

【变】issued　issued　issuing　issues

【例】I have to tell you that if you cancel within seven day departure you will have to pay 50％ of your total booking. Now you need to pay a 20％ deposit at the time of booking. So I'll make a provisional booking. Let me issue you with a customer reference number.

我必须告知的是如果在离开之前七日内取消预订，你将支付你的总

预订金额的 50%。现在你要预订就需要支付 20%的定金。我将给您作临时预订，并发给你一个顾客参考号码。

【搭】issue at the market price 按市价发行　issue cost 发行成本

【记】Islam *n.* 伊斯兰教；伊斯兰教义；伊斯兰教国家

　　isolate *v.* 使隔离，使孤立；［电］使绝缘；island *n.* 岛，岛屿

词汇听写

1. ＿＿＿＿＿＿＿＿　2. ＿＿＿＿＿＿＿＿　3. ＿＿＿＿＿＿＿＿

句子听写

Wednesday ·································· ◄◄◄

1. We tested three different <u>cots</u> all in the <u>budget</u> price range and, as usual, we will <u>feature</u> the good points, the problems and our <u>verdict</u>.

我们测试了在预算价格范围内的三种不同的婴儿床，和往常一样，我们将特别描述床的好处、存在的问题和我们的判决。

cot [kɔt] *n.* 简易床；小屋；轻便小床；婴儿

【变】cots

【例】We tested three different **cots** all in the budget price range and, as usual, we will feature the good points, the problems and our verdict.

我们测试了在预算价格范围内的三种不同的**婴儿床**，和往常一样，我们将特别描述床的好处、存在的问题和我们的判决。

【搭】cot bar 槛杆　cot death 婴儿猝死综合症

【记】cottage *n.* 小屋，村舍；（农舍式的）小别墅；（大院内的）单幢住宅

cost *n.* 价钱，代价；花费，费用；牺牲

cosmic *a.* 宇宙的；极广阔的

budget [ˈbʌdʒit] *n.* 预算，预算费　*v.* 安排，预定；把……编入预算
a. 廉价的

【变】budgeted　budgeted　budgeting　budgets

【例】We tested three different cots all in the **budget** price range and, as usual, we will feature the good points, the problems and our verdict.

我们测试了在**预算**价格范围内的三种不同的婴儿床，和往常一样，我们将特别描述床的好处、存在的问题和我们的判决。

【搭】budget account 预算账户　budget amendment 追加预算

【记】bud *n.* 芽，萌芽；蓓蕾

bubble *n.* 泡，水泡；冒泡，

bucket *n.* 水桶；一桶（的量）；大量

feature [ˈfiːtʃə] *n.* 特色，特征；容貌；特写或专题节目　*v.* 特写；以……
为特色；由……主演

【变】featured　featured　featuring　features

【例】We tested three different cots all in the budget price range and，as usual，we will **feature** the good points，the problems and our verdict.

我们测试了在预算价格范围内的三种不同的婴儿床，和往常一样，我们将**特别描述**床的好处、存在的问题和我们的判决。

【搭】feature bundle 特征束　feature changing rule 特征变化规则

【记】feather *n*. 羽毛，翎毛

February *n*. 二月

verdict [ˈvəːdikt] *n*. 结论；裁定

【变】verdicts

【例】We tested three different cots all in the budget price range and，as usual，we will feature the good points，the problems and our **verdict**.

我们测试了在预算价格范围内的三种不同的婴儿床，和往常一样，我们将特别描述床的好处、存在的问题和我们的**判决**。

【搭】verdict of not guilty 无罪的判决

【记】verge *n*. 边，边缘；界限

verb *n*. 动词；动词结构

verify *v*. 核实；证明；判定

词汇听写

1. _____ 2. _____ 3. _____

句子听写

2. The real problem cot was the space between the bars; our testers found they were too wide and a baby could easily trap his head. We felt this was a real safety hazard and so we have labelled this one dangerous.

真正的问题是婴儿床围栏条之间的间隙，我们的测试者发现间隙太宽，一个婴儿可以很容易地把他的头伸进去并卡在那里。我们觉得这是一个真正的安全隐患，因此我们认为这婴儿床危险。

bar [baː] *n.* 条，棒；酒吧；障碍　*v.* 禁止；阻拦　*prep.* 除……外

【变】barred　barred　barring　bars

【例】The real problem cot was the space between the **bars**; our testers found they were too wide and a baby could easily trap his head. We felt this was a real safety hazard and so we have labelled this one dangerous.

真正的问题是婴儿床围**栏条**之间的间隙，我们的测试者发现间隙太宽，一个婴儿可以很容易地把他的头伸进去并卡在那里。我们觉得这是一个真正的安全隐患，因此我们认为这婴儿床危险。

【搭】bar and shape mill 型材轧机　bar and grill 烤肉酒吧

【记】barber *n.* 理发师；理发店（＝ barber's shop）

bare *a.* 光秃秃的；（房间、柜子等）空的；赤裸的；刚好够的

bargain *n.* 契约，协定；交易；特价商品；便宜货

trap [træp] *v.* 诱捕；使……受限制；使……陷入困境　*n.* 陷阱；圈套

【变】trapped　trapped　trapping　traps

【例】The real problem cot was the space between the bars; our testers found they were too wide and a baby could easily **trap** his head. We felt this was a real safety hazard and so we have labelled this one dangerous.

真正的问题是婴儿床围栏条之间的间隙，我们的测试者发现间隙太宽，一个婴儿可以很容易地把他的头伸进去并**卡**在那里。我们觉得这是一个真正的安全隐患，因此我们认为这婴儿床危险。

【搭】trap address 陷阱地址　trap amplifier（监测）隔离放大器

【记】travel *n.* 旅行；进行；移动；漫游

traverse *n.* 穿过；横贯，横切；横木；[建] 横梁

tray *n.* 盘子；托盘；浅盘；满盘

hazard ['hæzəd] *v.* 赌运气；冒……的危险，使遭受危险　*n.* 危险，冒险；冒险的事

【变】hazarded　hazarded　hazarding　hazards

【例】The real problem cot was the space between the bars; our testers found they were too wide and a baby could easily trap his head. We felt this was a real safety **hazard** and so we have labelled this one dangerous.

真正的问题是婴儿床围栏条之间的间隙，我们的测试者发现间隙太宽，一个婴儿可以很容易地把他的头伸进去并卡在那里。我们觉得这是一个真正的安全**隐患**，因此我们认为这婴儿床危险。

【搭】at the hazard of his life 他冒着生命危险　hazard beacon 危险警告信标，濒危标志　full of hazard 充满了冒险

【记】habit *n.* 习惯，习性；气质

habitual *a.* 习惯的；惯常的；习以为常的

hail *n.* 冰雹；一阵

label ['leibl] *v.* 标注；贴标签于　*n.* 标签；商标；签条

【变】labelled　labelled　labelling　labels

【例】The real problem cot was the space between the bars; our testers found they were too wide and a baby could easily trap his head. We felt this was a real safety hazard and so we have **labelled** this one dangerous.

真正的问题是婴儿床围栏条之间的间隙，我们的测试者发现间隙太宽，一个婴儿可以很容易地把他的头伸进去并卡在那里。我们觉得这是一个真正的安全隐患，因此我们认为这婴儿床危险。

【搭】label address table 标号地址表　label block 标号信息组

【记】label *n.* 标签；称标记，符号

laboratory *n.* 实验室；实验课；研究室；药厂

lace *n.* 蕾丝；透孔织品；鞋带；系带

词汇听写

1. _____ 2. _____ 3. _____

句子听写

3. There is diploma course prospectus. To do the course by full-time or part-time depends on your financial circumstances.

这里有文凭课程的内容大纲。是参加全日制还是非全日制取决于你的财务情况。

diploma [di'pləumə] n. 毕业证书，学位证书；公文，文书；奖状　v. 发给……毕业文凭

【变】diplomas

【例】There is **diploma** course prospectus. To do the course by full-time or part-time depends on your financial circumstances.

这里有**文凭**课程的内容大纲。是参加全日制还是非全日制取决于你的财务情况。

【搭】diploma mill（美口）文凭工厂，野鸡大学　high school diploma 高中毕业文凭　music diploma 音乐学位证书

【记】diplomatic a. 外交上的；外交人员的；策略的

direct a. 直接的；直的

direction n. 方向，指南；指挥，导演，（乐队）指挥

prospectus [prə'spektəs] n. 内容说明书；样张；创办计划书

【变】prospectuses

【例】There is diploma course **prospectus**. To do the course by full-time or part-time depends on your financial circumstances.

这里有文凭课程的内容**大纲**。是参加全日制还是非全日制取决于你的财务情况。

【记】prosperity n. 繁荣；兴旺，昌盛；成功

prosperous a. 繁荣的，兴旺的；富裕的；幸福的，运气好的；良好的

prospect n. 前景；期望；眺望处；景象

depend on 取决于；依赖；依靠

【变】depended　depended　depending　depends

【例】There is diploma course prospectus. To do the course by full-time or part-time **depends on** your financial circumstances.

这里有文凭课程的内容大纲。是参加全日制还是非全日制**取决于你**的财务情况。

【搭】depend upon 依赖，依靠　depend crucially on 主要取决于　it depends 视情况而定

【记】depend v. 依靠；依赖；信赖；决定于

　　dependent a. 依靠的；依赖的；取决于……的；有瘾的

circumstance [ˈsəːkəmstns] n. 环境，情况；事件；境遇

【变】circumstances

【例】There is diploma course prospectus. To do the course by full-time or part-time depends on your financial **circumstances**.

　　这里有文凭课程的内容大纲。是参加全日制还是非全日制取决于你的财务**情况**。

【记】circumference n. 周围，圆周；胸围

　　circus n. 马戏，马戏团；马戏表演，圆形广场

词汇听写

1. _____　2. _____　3. _____

句子听写

Thursday ·· 《

1. Winning the Enterprise Award helped raise our profile, and the money enabled us to pay all our shipping costs, which represent our greatest expense.

　　赢得企业奖有助于提高我们的形象，奖金让我们能够支付船只运费，这项费用是我们最大的支出。

enterprise [ˈentəpraiz] *n.* 企业；事业；进取心；事业心

【变】enterprises

【例】Winning the **Enterprise** Award helped raise our profile, and the money enabled us to pay all our shipping costs, which represent our greatest expense.

　　赢得**企业**奖有助于提高我们的形象，奖金让我们能够支付船只运费，这项费用是我们最大的支出。

【搭】enterprise accounting 企业会计　enterprise cost 企业成本

【记】enter *v.* 进入；开始；参加；登记

　　entertain *v.* 热情款待；使有兴趣；抱着，怀有；考虑

　　enthusiasm *n.* 热情，热忱；热衷的事物；宗教的狂热

raise [reiz] *v.* 提高；筹集；养育；升起　*n.* 高地；上升；加薪

【变】raised　raised　raising　raises

【例】Winning the Enterprise Award helped **raise** our profile, and the money enabled us to pay all our shipping costs, which represent our greatest expense.

　　赢得企业奖有助于**提高**我们的形象，奖金让我们能够支付船只运费，这项费用是我们最大的支出。

【搭】raise a big fanfare 大吹大擂　raise a blockade 解除封锁

【记】raisin *n.* 葡萄干

　　rake *n.* 耙子；放荡的男人

　　ramble *v.* 漫游；漫步；漫谈；蔓延

profile [ˈprəufail] *n.* 侧面；轮廓；外形；剖面；简况　*v.* 描……的轮廓；扼要描述

【变】profiled　profiled　profiling　profiles

【例】Winning the Enterprise Award helped raise our **profile**, and the money enabled us to pay all our shipping costs, which represent our greatest expense.

　　赢得企业奖有助于提高我们的**形象**，奖金让我们能够支付船只运费，这项费用是我们最大的支出。

【搭】profile analysis〈美〉个人能力测验图分析　profile angle 齿形角，齿廓角

【记】profit *n*. 收益，得益；利润

proficiency *n*. 熟练，精通，娴熟

proficient *a*. 精通的，熟练的

enable [in'eibl] *v*. **使能够，使成为可能；授予权利或方法**

【例】Winning the Enterprise Award helped raise our profile, and the money **enabled** us to pay all our shipping costs, which represent our greatest expense.

　　赢得企业奖有助于提高我们的形象，奖金让我们**能够**支付船只运费，这项费用是我们最大的支出。

【搭】enable input 启动输入，允许输入　enable interruption 允许中断

【记】enchant *v*. 使心醉，使迷惑；用魔法迷惑

able *a*. 能够的；有能力的；有才干的；干练的

ensure *v*. 确保；担保获得；使（某人）获得；使安全

词汇听写

1. _____　　2. _____　　3. _____

句子听写

2. I'm going to talk to you about that remarkable continent Antarctica — remote, hostile and at present uninhabited on a permanent basis.

　　我要和你谈谈引人注目的南极洲大陆——一个遥远的、不利于人类居住的，以及目前为止无人曾居住过的地方。

continent [ˈkɔntinənt] *n.* **大陆，洲，陆地** *a.* **自制的，克制的**

【变】continents

【例】I'm going to talk to you about that remarkable **continent** Antarctica — remote, hostile and at present uninhabited on a permanent basis.

　　我要和你谈谈引人注目的南极洲**大陆**——一个遥远的、不利于人类居住的，以及目前为止无人曾居住过的地方。

【搭】continent making movement 造陆运动　　continent sea 内陆海

【记】continental *a.* 大陆的，大陆性的，欧洲大陆的；〈美〉（独立战争时）美洲殖民地的

　　continual *a.* 不间断的；不停的；多次重复的；频繁的

remote [riˈməut] *a.* **遥远的；偏僻的；疏远的** *n.* **远程**

【变】remoter　remotest

【例】I'm going to talk to you about that remarkable continent Antarctica — **remote**, hostile and at present uninhabited on a permanent basis.

　　我要和你谈谈引人注目的南极洲大陆——一个**遥远的**、不利于人类居住的，以及目前为止无人曾居住过的地方。

【搭】remote access 远程存取（访问）　　remote adjustment 遥控，远程调整

【记】removal *n.* 免职；除去；移走；搬迁

　　remove *v.* 开除；去除；脱掉，拿下；迁移

　　render *v.* 提出，开出；放弃，让与；报答；归还

hostile [ˈhɔstail] *a.* **敌对的，敌方的；怀敌意的；不利的** *n.* **敌对**

【例】I'm going to talk to you about that remarkable continent Antarctica — remote, **hostile** and at present uninhabited on a permanent basis.

　　我要和你谈谈引人注目的南极洲大陆——一个遥远的、**不利于人类居住的**，以及目前为止无人曾居住过的地方。

【搭】hostile air 敌空军（部队），敌占区上空 hostile witness 恶意证人

【记】host *n.* ［计算机］主机；主人，东道主；节目主持人；酒店业主

　　hospital *n.* 医院；收容所；养老院

　　hostage *n.* 人质；抵押品

uninhabited [ˌʌninˈhæbitid] *a.* 无人居住的，杳无人迹的

【例】I'm going to talk to you about that remarkable continent Antarctica — remote, hostile and at present **uninhabited** on a permanent basis.

我要和你谈谈引人注目的南极洲大陆——一个遥远的、不利于人类居住的，以及目前为止**无人曾居住过**的地方。

【记】union *n.* 同盟，联盟；协会，工会；联合，团结

uniform *n.* 制服；军服

inhabited *a.* 有人居住的

词汇听写

1. _____ 2. _____ 3. _____

句子听写

3. Here science and technical support have been <u>integrated</u> in a very cost-effective way. The station <u>generates</u> its own electricity and communicates with the outside world using a satellite <u>link</u>.

在这里，科学和技术支持已经以一种具有成本效益的方式融合在一起。这个地方生成自己的电力，并通过卫星通信与外界联系。

integrate [ˈintiɡreit] *v.* 使……完整；使……成整体；求……的积分；表示……的总和 *a.* 整合的；完全的 *n.* 一体化；集成体

【变】integrated integrated integrating integrates

【例】Here science and technical support have been **integrated** in a very cost-effective way. The station generates its own electricity and communicates with the outside world using a satellite link.

在这里，科学和技术支持已经以一种具有成本效益的方式融合在一起。这个地方生成自己的电力，并通过卫星通信与外界联系。

【搭】integrate with（使）与……结合在一起 integrate with us 和我们联合；

integrate theory with practice 把理论与实际结合起来

【记】integral *a.* 完整的；积分的；必须的

integrity *n.* 正直，诚实；完整；[计算机] 保存；健全

intellect *n.* 智力，理解力；有才智的人；知识分子

cost-effective [ˈkɔːstəˈfektiv] *a.* 划算的；成本效益好的（等于 cost-efficient）

【例】IIere science and technical support have been integrated in a very **cost-effective** way. The station generates its own electricity and communicates with the outside world using a satellite link.

在这里，科学和技术支持已经以一种具有**成本效益**的方式融合在一起。这个地方生成自己的电力，并通过卫星通信与外界联系。

【记】cost *n.* 价钱，代价；花费

effective *a.* 有效的；起作用的

cottage *n.* 小屋，村舍；（农舍式的）小别墅

generate [ˈdʒenəreit] *v.* 使形成；发生；生殖

【变】generated generated generating generates

【例】Here science and technical support have been integrated in a very cost-effective way. The station **generates** its own electricity and communicates with the outside world using a satellite link.

在这里，科学和技术支持已经以一种具有成本效益的方式融合在一起。这个地方**生成**自己的电力，并通过卫星通信与外界联系。

【搭】generate electricity 发电 generate form 生成形式

【记】generation *n.* 一代人；代（约 30 年），时代；生殖；产生

generosity *n.* 慷慨，大方；宽容或慷慨的行为；丰富

genius *n.* 天才；天赋；天才人物；（特别的）才能

link [liŋk] *n.* [计] 链环，环节；联系，关系 *v.* 连接，连结；联合，结合 *v.* 连接起来；联系在一起；将人或物连接或联系起来

【变】links linked linked linking links

【例】Here science and technical support have been integrated in a very cost-effective way. The station generates its own electricity and communicates with the outside world using a satellite **link.**

　　在这里，科学和技术支持已经以一种具有成本效益的方式融合在一起。这个地方生成自己的电力，并通过卫星通信与外界**联系**。

【搭】link address 连接地址　　link field 链接域　　click this link 点击此链接

【记】wink *v.* 眨眼；使眼色

linear *a.* 直线的，线形的；长度的

linen *n.* 亚麻布，亚麻线；家庭日用织品

词汇听写

1. _____ 2. _____ 3. _____

句子听写

Friday ··· ◀◀◀

1. A second important area is monitoring the size of the hole in the <u>ozone</u> <u>layer</u> above Antarctica, since this is an <u>indicator</u> of global <u>ultra-violet</u> radiation levels.

第二个重要的研究领域是监测南极洲上空臭氧层洞的大小，因为这是全球紫外线辐射水平的指标。

ozone [ˈəuzəun] *n.* ［化］臭氧；新鲜的空气

【例】A second important area is monitoring the size of the hole in the **ozone** layer above Antarctica, since this is an indicator of global ultra-violet radiation levels.

第二个重要的研究领域是监测南极洲上空**臭氧**层洞的大小，因为这是全球紫外线辐射水平的指标。

【搭】ozone cloud 臭氧云　ozone value 臭氧值，臭氧价

【记】zone *n.* 地带；区域，范围

oar *n.* 桨，橹；划手

oath *n.* 誓言，誓约

layer [ˈleiə] *n.* 层，阶层；地层　*v.* 用压条法培植；把……堆积成层

【变】layered　layered　layering　layers

【例】A second important area is monitoring the size of the hole in the ozone **layer** above Antarctica, since this is an indicator of global ultra-violet radiation levels.

第二个重要的研究领域是监测南极洲上空臭氧**层**洞的大小，因为这是全球紫外线辐射水平的指标。

【搭】layer board 衬垫用纸板　layer of no motion 无流层

【记】layout *n.* 布局，安排，设计

lazy *a.* 懒惰的；没精打采的；慢吞吞的

clay *n.* 黏土，泥土，陶土

indicator [ˈindikeitə] *n.* 指示器；（试剂）指示剂；［计］指示符；压力计

【变】indicators

【例】A second important area is monitoring the size of the hole in the ozone layer above Antarctica，since this is an **indicator** of global ultra-violet radiation levels.

第二个重要的研究领域是监测南极洲上空臭氧层洞的大小，因为这是全球紫外线辐射水平的**指标**。

【搭】indicator apparatus 指示装置　indicator function 指标函数

【记】indicate *v.* 表明；象征，暗示，预示

indication *n.* 指示；象征，标示

indifferent *a.* 漠不关心的；无关紧要的

ultra-violet [ˌʌltrəˈvaiələt] *n.* 紫外线

【例】A second important area is monitoring the size of the hole in the ozone layer above Antarctica，since this is an indicator of global **ultra-violet** radiation levels.

第二个重要的研究领域是监测南极洲上空臭氧层洞的大小，因为这是全球**紫外线**辐射水平的指标。

【记】ultrasonic *a.* ［声］超声的；超音波的，超音速的

ultra *a.* 过激的，极端的

violet *n.* 紫罗兰；蓝紫色；羞怯的人

词汇听写

1. _____ 2. _____ 3. _____

句子听写

2. Salesman：What kind of gear change do you want? I presume you'd want a manual.

Customer：I'll go for the automatic one.

售货员：你想要什么样的车？我相信你想要手动挡。

顾客：我喜欢这个自动挡。

gear [giə] *n.* 齿轮；装置，工具；传动装置　*v.* 适合；搭上齿轮；开始工作

【变】geared　geared　gearing　gears

【例】Salesman：What kind of **gear** change do you want? I presume you'd want a manual.

　　Customer：I'll go for the automatic one.

　　售货员：你想要什么样的**车**？我相信你想要手动挡。

　　顾客：我喜欢这个自动挡。

【搭】gear assembly 齿轮传动装置，减速器

　　gear change shift fork 变速杆拨叉，齿轮拨叉

【记】general *a.* 大致的；综合的；全体的；普遍的

　　generalization *n.* 一般化；普通化；概论

　　generalize *v.* 概括，归纳；普及；使一般化

presume [pri'zjuːm] *v.* 假定；推测；擅自；意味着

【变】presumed　presumed　presuming　presumes

【例】Salesman：What kind of gear change do you want? I **presume** you'd want a manual.

　　Customer：I'll go for the automatic one.

　　售货员：你想要什么样的车？我**相信**你想要手动挡。

　　顾客：我喜欢这个自动挡。

【搭】I presume 我想

【记】presumably *ad.* 据推测；大概；可能；想来

　　pretend *v.* 假装，伪装；假称；装扮

　　pretty *a.* 漂亮的；机灵的，聪明的

manual ['mænjul] *a.* 手工的；体力的　　*n.* 手册，指南

【变】manuals

【例】Salesman：What kind of gear change do you want? I presume you'd want a **manual**.

　　Customer：I'll go for the automatic one.

　　售货员：你想要什么样的车？我相信你想要**手动**挡。

　　顾客：我喜欢这个自动挡。

【搭】manual adjustment 手调　manual degaussing 人工消磁

【记】manufacture *v.* 制造，生产；捏造，虚构；加工；从事制造

　　　manufacturer *n.* 制造商，制造厂；厂主；[经] 厂商

　　　manuscript *n.* 手稿；原稿；底稿；手写本

go for 去找；被认为；主张；拥护；努力获取；喜欢

【变】went　went　going　goes

【例】Salesman：What kind of gear change do you want? I presume you'd want a manual.

　　　Customer：I'll **go for** the automatic one.

　　　售货员：你想要什么样的车？我相信你想要手动挡。

　　　顾客：我**喜欢**这个自动挡。

【搭】go for a picnic 去野餐；go for a drink 去喝一杯；go for restaurants 适用于餐馆

【记】waggon *n.* 敞蓬车厢

　　　gorgeous *a.* 绚丽的；极好的

　　　gossip *n.* 闲谈；碎嘴子

词汇听写

1. _____　2. _____　3. _____

句子听写

3. By 2008, we must reduce our carbon dioxide emissions by 12.5%, compared with 1990. And recycling can help to achieve that goal, in two main ways.

　　到 2008 年，与 1990 年相比，我们必须减少 12.5% 的二氧化碳排放量。而回收利用可以帮助实现这一目标，主要通过两种方式。

carbon ['kɑːbn] *n.* [化] 碳；碳棒；复写纸　*a.* 碳的；碳处理的

【变】carbons

【例】By 2008，we must reduce our **carbon** dioxide emissions by 12.5％, compared with 1990. And recycling can help to achieve that goal，in two main ways.

　　到 2008 年，与 1990 年相比，我们必须减少 12.5％的二氧化**碳**排放量。而回收利用可以帮助实现这一目标，主要通过两种方式。

【搭】carbon amplifier 碳质放大器　　carbon block lining 碳砖炉衬

【记】card *n.* 卡片；纸牌；信用卡

　　care *v.* 关心；担心；在乎；介意

　　career *n.* 生涯；职业；事业

dioxide [daiˈɔksaid] *n.* 二氧化物

【变】dioxides

【例】By 2008，we must reduce our carbon **dioxide** emissions by 12.5％, compared with 1990. And recycling can help to achieve that goal，in two main ways.

　　到 2008 年，与 1990 年相比，我们必须减少 12.5％的**二氧化**碳排放量。而回收利用可以帮助实现这一目标，主要通过两种方式。

【记】diagnose *v.* 诊断；判断

　　diagram *n.* 图表；图解；示意图；[数] 线图

　　dial *n.* 日晷；钟（表）面，标度盘；拨号盘；表盘

emission [iˈmiʃn] *n.* （光、热等的）发射，散发；喷射；发行

【变】emissions

【例】By 2008，we must reduce our carbon dioxide **emissions** by 12.5％, compared with 1990. And recycling can help to achieve that goal，in two main ways.

　　到 2008 年，与 1990 年相比，我们必须减少 12.5％的二氧化碳**排放**量。而回收利用可以帮助实现这一目标，主要通过两种方式。

【搭】emission angle 发射角　　emission measurement 排放计量

【记】emigrate *v.* 移居国外

　　emit *v.* 发出；发射；颁布；发表

　　emotion *n.* 情感，感情；情绪；感动，激动

recycle [ri:'saikl] *n.* (资源、垃圾的）回收利用 *v.* 回收；再循环利用

【变】recycled recycled recycling recycles

【例】By 2008，we must reduce our carbon dioxide emissions by 12.5%, compared with 1990. And **recycling** can help to achieve that goal, in two main ways.

到 2008 年，与 1990 年相比，我们必须减少 12.5% 的二氧化碳排放量。而**回收利用**可以帮助实现这一目标，主要通过两种方式。

【搭】recycle back 反向循环 recycle valve 再循环阀

【记】recall *v.* 叫回，召回；使想起，取消

receipt *n.* 收据，发票；收入

receive *v.* 收到；接纳；接待

词汇听写

1. _____ 2. _____ 3. _____

句子听写

Saturday ·· ≪

1. The production of recycled glass and paper uses much less energy than producing them from virgin materials, and also recycling reduces greenhouse gas emissions from landfill sites and incineration plants.

　　和从原材料生产玻璃与纸张相比，回收再利用玻璃和纸张的生产使用的能源要少得多，而且，回收利用使垃圾填埋场和焚烧厂排放的温室气体减少。

virgin ['vəːdʒin] *a.* 处女的；纯洁的；未经利用的，处于原始状态的　*n.* 处女

【变】virgins

【例】The production of recycled glass and paper uses much less energy than producing them from **virgin** materials, and also recycling reduces greenhouse gas emissions from landfill sites and incineration plants.

　　和从原材料生产玻璃与纸张相比，回收再利用玻璃和纸张的生产使用的能源要少得多，而且，回收利用使垃圾填埋场和焚烧厂排放的温室气体减少。

【搭】virgin oil 直馏油（石油），初榨橄榄油

【记】virtual *a.* 事实上的；（计算机）虚拟的；虚像的

　　virtually *ad.* 实际上，实质上

　　virtue *n.* 美德；德行；价值；长处

greenhouse ['griːnhaus] *n.* 温室

【变】greenhouses

【例】The production of recycled glass and paper uses much less energy than producing them from virgin materials, and also recycling reduces **greenhouse** gas emissions from landfill sites and incineration plants.

　　和从原材料生产玻璃与纸张相比，回收再利用玻璃和纸张的生产使用的能源要少得多，而且，回收利用使垃圾填埋场和焚烧厂排放的**温室**气体减少。

【搭】greenhouse effect 温室效应　greenhouse gas（二氧化碳、甲烷等）导致温室效应的气体

【记】green *a.* 绿色的；青春的；未成熟的；主张保护环境的

greedy *a.* 贪吃的；贪心的

house *n.* 住宅；家庭

landfill ['lænfil] *n.* 垃圾填埋地；垃圾堆

【变】landfills

【例】The production of recycled glass and paper uses much less energy than producing them from virgin materials, and also recycling reduces greenhouse gas emissions from **landfill** sites and incineration plants.

和从原材料生产玻璃与纸张相比，回收再利用玻璃和纸张的生产使用的能源要少得多，而且，回收利用使**垃圾填埋场**和焚烧厂排放的温室气体减少。

【记】inland *a.* 国内的；内地的

landing *n.* 登陆，着陆；终点；楼梯的

landlord *n.* 房东，地主；店主

landscape *n.* 风景，景色

incineration [in,sinə'reiʃn] *n.* 焚化；烧成灰

【例】The production of recycled glass and paper uses much less energy than producing them from virgin materials, and also recycling reduces greenhouse gas emissions from landfill sites and **incineration** plants.

和从原材料生产玻璃与纸张相比，回收再利用玻璃和纸张的生产使用的能源要少得多，而且，回收利用使垃圾填埋场和**焚烧**厂排放的温室气体减少。

【搭】incineration by pyrolysis 高温分解焚烧　incineration dish 煅烧盘

【记】inclination *n.* 倾向；爱好；斜坡

incline *v.* （使）倾斜，弄斜；（使）偏向，倾向于

cineration *n.* 灰化，煅灰

词汇听写

1. _____ 2. _____ 3. _____

句子听写

2. Government officials knew that Fuller had <u>developed</u> a <u>prototype</u> of family <u>dwelling</u> which could be produced rapidly, using the same equipment which had <u>previously</u> built war-time airplanes.

政府官员都知道，富勒开发了一种家庭住宅的原型，它可以迅速建立，所使用的设备此前曾用于制造战时飞机。

---

develop [di'veləp] *v.* 开发；进步；使成长；使显影；发育；生长；进化；显露

【变】developed　developed　developing　develops

【例】Government officials knew that Fuller had **developed** a prototype of family dwelling which could be produced rapidly, using the same equipment which had previously built war-time airplanes.

政府官员都知道，富勒**开发**了一种家庭住宅的原型，它可以迅速建立，所使用的设备此前曾用于制造战时飞机。

【记】development *n.* 发展，进化；被发展的状态；新生事物，新产品；开发区

deviate *v.* 脱离，使脱离常轨

device *n.* 装置，设备；策略

---

prototype ['prəutaip] *v.* 开发；进步；（使）成长；（使）显影

【变】prototypes

【例】Government officials knew that Fuller had developed a **prototype** of family dwelling which could be produced rapidly, using the same equipment which had previously built war-time airplanes.

政府官员都知道，富勒开发了一种家庭住宅的**原型**，它可以迅速建立，所使用的设备此前曾用于制造战时飞机。

【搭】prototype aeroplane 样机　prototype casting 试生产铸件

【记】proud *a.* 自豪的，得意的；光荣的，高尚的；傲慢的；有自尊心的

practicable *a.* 切实可行的，行得通的；实际的；实用的；可以通行的

practical *a.* 实践的，实际的；可实现的，实用的；注重实际的；可用的

---

dwell ['dwel] *n.* 住处；寓所　*v.* 居住

【变】dwellings

【例】Government officials knew that Fuller had developed a prototype of family **dwelling** which could be produced rapidly，using the same equipment which had previously built war-time airplanes.

　　政府官员都知道，富勒开发了一种家庭**住宅**的原型，它可以迅速建立，所使用的设备此前曾用于制造战时飞机。

【搭】dwelling district 居住区

【记】dwell *v.* 居住；存在于；细想某事

　　dwarf *n.* 侏儒，矮子；矮小的动物（植物）；［天］矮星

　　dye *n.* 染料，染色；颜色

previously ［ˈpriviəsli］ *ad.* 以前；预先；仓促地

【变】more previously　most previously

【例】Government officials knew that Fuller had developed a prototype of family dwelling which could be produced rapidly，using the same equipment which had **previously** built war-time airplanes.

　　政府官员都知道，富勒开发了一种家庭住宅的原型，它可以迅速建立，所使用的设备**此前**曾用于制造战时飞机。

【记】previous *a.* 先前的；以前的；过早的

　　prey *n.* 被捕食的动物；捕食（习性）；受害者；受骗者

　　preach *v.* 布道，讲道；说教

词汇听写

1. ＿＿＿＿＿＿　　2. ＿＿＿＿＿＿　　3. ＿＿＿＿＿＿

句子听写

3. This principle directed his studies toward creating a new architectural design, the geodesic dome, based also upon his idea of "doing more with less". Fuller discovered that if a spherical structure was created from triangles, it would have unparalleled strength.

　　这一原则指导他的研究，推动他创造了一种新的建筑设计方向发

展——穹顶，这一设计也是基于他"以少做多"的观点。富勒发现，如果球状结构是以三角形为基础，那么这种结构将会很结实。

geodesic [ˌdʒiːəˈdesik] *a.* 测地线的；测量的（等于 geodetic）   *n.* ［测］测地线

【例】This principle directed his studies toward creating a new architectural design, the **geodesic** dome, based also upon his idea of "doing more with less". Fuller discovered that if a spherical structure was created from triangles, it would have unparalleled strength.

这一原则指导他的研究，推动他创造了一种新的建筑设计方向发展——穹顶，这一设计也是基于他"以少做多"的观点。富勒发现，如果球状结构是以三角形为基础，那么这种结构将会很结实。

【搭】geodesic circle 测地圆   geodesic conic 测地二次曲线

【记】geographical *a.* 地理学的，地理的

　　geography *n.* 地理（学）；地形，地势；布局

　　geology *n.* 地质学；（某地区的）地质情况；地质学的著作

spherical [ˈsferikəl] *a.* 球形的，球面的；天体的

【例】This principle directed his studies toward creating a new architectural design, the geodesic dome, based also upon his idea of "doing more with less". Fuller discovered that if a **spherical** structure was created from triangles, it would have unparalleled strength.

这一原则指导他的研究，推动他创造了一种新的建筑设计方向发展——穹顶，这一设计也是基于他"以少做多"的观点。富勒发现，如果球状结构是以三角形为基础，那么这种结构将会很结实。

【搭】spherical angle 球面角

【记】sphere *n.* 球（体）；（兴趣或活动的）范围；势力范围；天体，如行星或恒星

　　spice *n.* 香料，调味品；香味；情趣；少许

　　spider *n.* 蜘蛛；三脚架

triangle [ˈtraiæŋgl] *n.* 三角（形）；三角关系；三角形之物；三人一组

【变】triangles

【例】This principle directed his studies toward creating a new architectural design, the geodesic dome, based also upon his idea of "doing more with less". Fuller discovered that if a spherical structure was created from **triangles**, it would have unparalleled strength.

这一原则指导他的研究，推动他创造了一种新的建筑设计方向发展——穹顶，这一设计也是基于他"以少做多"的观点。富勒发现，如果球状结构是以**三角形**为基础，那么这种结构将会很结实。

【搭】triangle generator 三角波发生器　triangle knife 三角刮刀

【记】triangular *a.* 三角（形）的；三方面的

tribute *n.* 礼物；颂辞；证据；贡品

trick *n.* 戏法，把戏；骗局；恶作剧

unparallel [ʌn'pærəlel] *a.* 不平行的；无法匹敌的

【例】This principle directed his studies toward creating a new architectural design, the geodesic dome, based also upon his idea of "doing more with less". Fuller discovered that if a spherical structure was created from triangles, it would have **unparalleled** strength.

这一原则指导他的研究，推动他创造了一种新的建筑设计方向发展——穹顶，这一设计也是基于他"以少做多"的观点。富勒发现，如果球状结构是以三角形为基础，那么这种结构将会很结实。

【记】paralleled 平行的

parallel *a.* 平行的；相同的，类似的；[电] 并联的；[计] 并行的

paralyse *v.* 使瘫痪 [麻痹]；使不能正常活动；[电] 关闭

词汇听写

1. _____　2. _____　3. _____

句子听写

Sunday ·· ≪

1. The <u>concave</u> interior creates a natural airflow that allows the hot or cool air to flow <u>evenly</u> throughout the <u>dome</u> with the help of return air <u>ducts</u>.

凹部的内部创建了一个自然的空气流，空气流允许热的或冷的空气在回风管道的帮助下均匀流动于整个圆顶。

---

concave [ˈkɔnkeiv] · *a.* **凹的，凹面的** *n.* **凹面** *v.* **使成凹形**

【变】concaved concaved concaving concaves

【例】The **concave** interior creates a natural airflow that allows the hot or cool air to flow evenly throughout the dome with the help of return air ducts.

凹部的内部创建了一个自然的空气流，空气流允许热的或冷的空气在回风管道的帮助下均匀流动于整个圆顶。

【搭】concave adjusting bolt 凹板调节螺栓

concave adjusting lever 凹板（间隙）调节杆

【记】conceal *v.* 隐藏，隐瞒，遮住

conceit *n.* 自负；幻想；观点；巧妙构思

conceive *v.* 怀孕；构思；想象

---

evenly [ˈiːvənli] *ad.* **均匀地；平衡地；平坦地；平等地**

【例】The concave interior creates a natural airflow that allows the hot or cool air to flow **evenly** throughout the dome with the help of return air ducts.

凹部的内部创建了一个自然的空气流，空气流允许热的或冷的空气在回风管道的帮助下均匀流动于整个圆顶。

【搭】evenly divided scale 等分刻度 cover the surface evenly 均匀地涂在表面上

【记】even *ad.* 甚至；更加；即使；恰巧在……时候

revenue *n.* 收入

event *n.* 事件，大事

revenge *n.* & *v.* 报复，复仇 eventually 终于

---

dome [dəum] *n.* **圆屋顶** *v.* **成圆顶状**

【变】domed domed doming domes

【例】The concave interior creates a natural airflow that allows the hot or cool air to flow evenly throughout the **dome** with the help of return air ducts.

凹部的内部创建了一个自然的空气流，空气流允许热的或冷的空气在回风管道的帮助下均匀流动于整个圆顶。

【搭】dome cap 气包盖

【记】domestic *a.* 家庭的，家的；国内的

dominant *a.* 占优势的；统治的，支配的

donkey *n.* 驴，毛驴；傻瓜；（美国）民主党的象征

duct [dʌkt] *n.* 输送管，导管　*v.* 用导管输送；以导管封住

【变】ducts

【例】The concave interior creates a natural airflow that allows the hot or cool air to flow evenly throughout the dome with the help of return air **ducts**.

凹部的内部创建了一个自然的空气流，空气流允许热的或冷的空气在回风**管道**的帮助下均匀流动于整个圆顶。

【搭】duct cleaner 电缆管道清洁器　duct cleaning tool 清洁管道的工具

【记】due *a.* 预定；适当的；应有的；由于

duke *n.* 公爵；君主

induce *v.* 劝诱；引起

conduct *n.* 行为，品行

deduce *v.* 演绎，推断

词汇听写

1. _____ 2. _____ 3. _____

句子听写

2. The fastness of the color, or its permanency, depends upon the dye and the process used. True dyeing is a permanent color change, and the dye is absorbed by, or chemically combined with, the fiber.

着色的速度或着色的永久性取决于染料和使用的程序。真正的染色是一次永久性的颜色变化，染料被纤维吸收，或和纤维结合在一起。

permanency [ˈpəːmənənsi] *n.* 永久；耐久性；永久的事物

【变】permanencies

【例】The fastness of the color, or its **permanency**, depends upon the dye and the process used. True dyeing is a permanent color change, and the dye is absorbed by, or chemically combined with, the fiber.

着色的速度或着色的**永久性**取决于染料和使用的程序。真正的染色是一次永久性的颜色变化，染料被纤维吸收，或和纤维结合在一起。

【记】permanent *a.* 永久（性）的，永恒的，不变的，稳定的

permanently *ad.* 永久地，长期不变地

permission *n.* 允许；批准

pregnant *a.* 怀孕的

dye [dai] *n.* 染料；染色　*v.* 染；把……染上颜色　*v.* 被染色

【变】dyed　dyed　dyeing　dyes

【例】The fastness of the color, or its permanency, depends upon the **dye** and the process used. True dyeing is a permanent color change, and the dye is absorbed by, or chemically combined with, the fiber.

着色的速度或着色的永久性取决于**染料**和使用的程序。真正的染色是一次永久性的颜色变化，染料被纤维吸收，或和纤维结合在一起。

【搭】dye absorption 染料渗透

【记】dying *a.* 〈口〉渴望的，切盼的；临终的；会死的

dynamic *a.* 动态的；动力的；充满活力的；不断变化的

absorb [əbˈzɔːb] *v.* 吸收；吸引；承受；理解；使……全神贯注

【变】absorbed　absorbed　absorbing　absorbs

【例】The fastness of the color, or its permanency, depends upon the dye and the process used. True dyeing is a permanent color change, and the dye is **absorbed** by, or chemically combined with, the fiber.

着色的速度或着色的永久性取决于染料和使用的程序。真正的染色是一次永久性的颜色变化，染料被纤维**吸收**，或和纤维结合在一起。

【搭】absorber 吸收者减震器；吸收器

【记】absorption *n.* 吸收；专注；合并

absurd *a.* 荒谬的；荒唐的

abundance *n.* 丰富，充裕

abstract *a.* 抽象的；深奥的 *n.* 摘要

forbid *v.* 禁止

absolute *a.* 绝对的；完全的

combine [kəm'bain] *v.* **联合，结合；化合** *n.* **联合收割机；联合企业**

【变】combined combined combining combines

【例】The fastness of the color, or its permanency, depends upon the dye and the process used. True dyeing is a permanent color change, and the dye is absorbed by, or chemically **combined** with, the fiber.

　　着色的速度或着色的永久性取决于染料和使用的程序。真正的染色是一次永久性的颜色变化，染料被纤维吸收，或和纤维**结合**在一起。

【搭】combine to form water 合成水　combined effects 复合疗效（效果）

【记】combination *n.* 合作；密码组合；联合体；排列

　　combustion *n.* 燃烧，烧毁；氧化；骚动

词汇听写

1. ＿＿＿＿＿＿　　2. ＿＿＿＿＿＿　　3. ＿＿＿＿＿＿

句子听写

3. The dyestuffs were extracts from plants, mollusks, insects, woods, or naturally occurring minerals. There are many plants which produce dye, and many were heavily cultivated.

　　这些染料是植物、软体动物、昆虫、树林、或天然矿物的提取物。有许多植物生产染料，人们对其中一些植物进行大量种植。

stuff [stʌf] *n.* **东西；材料；填充物；素材资料** *v.* **塞满；填塞；让吃饱**

【例】The dye**stuffs** were extracts from plants, mollusks, insects, woods, or naturally occurring minerals. There are many plants which produce dye, and many were heavily cultivated.

　　这些染料是植物、软体动物、昆虫、树林、或天然矿物的提取物。有许多植物生产染料，人们对其中一些植物进行大量种植。

【搭】sticky stuff 黏乎乎的东西　antique stuff 古玩物件　stuff it full 把它塞满

【记】stuffy *a.* 不透气的，闷热的

　　studio *n.* （电影）制片厂；（电台）播音室

　　stubborn *a.* 顽固的；顽强的

　　sturdy *a.* 坚定的；牢固的

extract [ikˈstrækt] *v.* 提取；取出；摘录；榨取　*n.* 汁；摘录；榨出物；选粹

【变】extracted　extracted　extracting　extracts

【例】The dyestuffs were **extracts** from plants, mollusks, insects, woods, or naturally occurring minerals. There are many plants which produce dye, and many were heavily cultivated.

　　这些染料是植物、软体动物、昆虫、树林、或天然矿物的**提取物**。有许多植物生产染料，人们对其中一些植物进行大量种植。

【搭】extract atmospheric flash tower 常压蒸发塔　extract content 浸出物量，提出物的含量

【记】extraction *n.* 取出，抽出；[化] 提取（法），萃取（法），提出物

　　extraordinarily *ad.* 很，十分，特别，极其

　　extraordinary *a.* 非凡的，特别的；意外的，离奇的

mollusk [ˈmɒləsk] *n.* （美）（无脊椎）软体动物

【变】mollusks

【例】The dyestuffs were extracts from plants, **mollusks**, insects, woods, or naturally occurring minerals. There are many plants which produce dye, and many were heavily cultivated.

　　这些染料是植物、**软体动物**、昆虫、树林、或天然矿物的提取物。有许多植物生产染料，人们对其中一些植物进行大量种植。

【记】moment *n.* 瞬间；时刻；紧要；[物] 力矩

　　momentary *a.* 短暂的；瞬间的；随时会发生的

　　monarch *n.* 君主，帝王；最高统治者

cultivate ['kʌltiveit] v. 培养；陶冶；耕作

【变】cultivated　cultivated　cultivating　cultivates

【例】The dyestuffs were extracts from plants, mollusks, insects, woods, or naturally occurring minerals. There are many plants which produce dye, and many were heavily **cultivated.**

这些染料是植物、软体动物、昆虫、树林、或天然矿物的提取物。有许多植物生产染料，人们对其中一些植物进行大量**种植**。

【搭】cultivate land 种地

【记】culture n. 文化；　［生物学］　（微生物等的）培养；修养；养殖
　　 cultivation n. 教养；栽培；耕作；（关系的）培植

词汇听写

1. ＿＿＿＿＿＿　　2. ＿＿＿＿＿＿　　3. ＿＿＿＿＿＿

句子听写

第 4 周

1. In contrast to dyes, pigments are highly <u>insoluble</u> coloring materials, which are incorporated into an applications medium by <u>dispersion</u>, and they remain as <u>discrete</u> solid particles.

和染料相比，颜料是高度不溶性的着色剂，通过分散，融入到一种应用介质。并且它们保持成离散的固体颗粒。

in contrast to 与……形成对照

【例】**In contrast to** dyes, pigments are highly insoluble coloring materials, which are incorporated into an applications medium by dispersion, and they remain as discrete solid particles.

和染料**相比**，颜料是高度不溶性的着色剂，通过分散，融入到一种应用介质。并且它们保持成离散的固体颗粒。

【搭】contrast agent 造影剂，对比剂

【记】in contrast with 相比之下

contrast with 与……截然不同，形成鲜明的对照；把（一方）与（另一方）对比；相映

contrast *n.* 对比，对照；差异；对照物，对立面

insoluble [in'sɔljubl] *a.* 不能解决的；［化］不能溶解的；难以解释的

【例】In contrast to dyes, pigments are highly **insoluble** coloring materials, which are incorporated into an applications medium by dispersion, and they remain as discrete solid particles.

和染料相比，颜料是高度**不溶性**的着色剂，通过分散，融入到一种应用介质。并且它们保持成离散的固体颗粒。

【搭】insoluble in water 不溶于水

【记】inspect *v.* 检查，检验；视察

insect *n.* 昆虫；卑鄙的人；微贱的人，小人

soluble *a.* [化] 可溶的；可以解决的；[数] 可解的

dispersion [dis'pəːʃən] *n.* 散布；[数] 离差；驱散

【例】In contrast to dyes, pigments are highly insoluble coloring materials, which are incorporated into an applications medium by **dispersion**, and they remain as discrete solid particles.

和染料相比，颜料是高度不溶性的着色剂，通过**分散**，融入到一种应用介质。并且它们保持成离散的固体颗粒。

【搭】dispersion angle 色散角　atmospheric dispersion phenomena 大气扩散现象

【记】disperse *v.* （使）分散，（使）散开；散播，使（光）色散

displace *v.* 移动，替换；排水；撤职

discrete [die'skriːt] *a.* 离散的，不连续的　*n.* 分立元件；独立部件

【例】In contrast to dyes, pigments are highly insoluble coloring materials, which are incorporated into an applications medium by dispersion, and they remain as **discrete** solid particles.

和染料相比，颜料是高度不溶性的着色剂，通过分散，融入到一种应用介质。并且它们保持成**离散**的固体颗粒。

【搭】discrete air ports 射流空气口　discrete amount 个别量

【记】discrimination *n.* 歧视；区别；识别力；不公平的待遇

discuss *v.* 讨论，详述；商量

disable *v.* 使无能力；使伤残；使无资格

discipline *n.* 纪律；学科

词汇听写

1. _____　2. _____　3. _____

句子听写

2. The origins of the synthetic inorganic pigment industry may be traced to the introduction of Prussian blue in the early 18th century.

合成无机颜料行业的起源可追溯到 18 世纪初，那时普鲁士蓝被引入该行业。

origin [ˈɔridʒin] *n.* 起源；原点；出身；开端

【变】origins

【例】The **origins** of the synthetic inorganic pigment industry may be traced to the introduction of Prussian blue in the early 18th century.

　　合成无机颜料行业的**起源**可追溯到 18 世纪初，那时普鲁士蓝被引入该行业。

【搭】origin of life 生命的起源　　origin distortion 原始失真

【记】original *a.* 原始的；独创的；最初的；新颖的

　　originate *v.* 引起；创始，创作；开始

　　ornament *n.* 装饰；装饰物

synthetic [sinˈθetik] *a.* 综合的；合成的，人造的 *n.* 合成物

【变】synthetics

【例】The origins of the **synthetic** inorganic pigment industry may be traced to the introduction of Prussian blue in the early 18th century.

　　合成无机颜料行业的起源可追溯到 18 世纪初，那时普鲁士蓝被引入该行业。

【搭】synthetic address 合成地址　　synthetic adhesive 合成胶，人造胶

【记】system *n.* 体系，系统；制度；身体；方法

　　systematic *a.* 有系统的，有规则的；有条不紊的，一贯的，惯常的

　　systematically *ad.* 有系统地；有组织地；有条不紊地

　　pathetic *a.* 哀婉动人的；可怜的

pigment [ˈpigmnt] *n.* [物] 色素；颜料　*v.* 给……着色；呈现颜色

【变】pigments

【例】The origins of the synthetic inorganic **pigment** industry may be traced to the introduction of Prussian blue in the early 18th century.

合成无机**颜料**行业的起源可追溯到 18 世纪初，那时普鲁士蓝被引入该行业。

【搭】pigment body 色素体　pigment brown 颜料棕

【记】pile *n.* 桩；一堆；绒头；摞

　　pilgrim *n.* 香客，朝圣者；旅行者；追寻者

　　pill *n.* 药丸；弹丸

trace [treis] *v.* 追踪，查探；描绘；回溯　*n.* 痕迹，踪迹

【变】traced　traced　tracing　traces

【例】The origins of the synthetic inorganic pigment industry may be **traced** to the introduction of Prussian blue in the early 18th century.

　　合成无机颜料行业的起源可**追溯**到 18 世纪初，那时普鲁士蓝被引入该行业。

【搭】trace amount 痕量　trace analysis 痕量分析

【记】track *n.* 小路；踪迹；轨道，音轨；方针，路线

　　tractor *n.* 拖拉机；牵引器

词汇听写

1. _____ 2. _____ 3. _____

句子听写

3. Dragline silk forms the <u>radial</u> <u>spokes</u> of the web; bridge line silk is the first <u>strand</u>, by which the web hangs from its support; yet another silk forms the great <u>spiral</u>.

　　牵引丝形成网络的径向辐条；桥丝是第一链，给整个蜘蛛网提供支持力；而牵引丝形成了一个大的螺旋形网。

radial ['reidiəl] *a.* 半径的；放射状的；光线的；光线状的　*n.* 射线，光线

【变】radials

【例】Dragline silk forms the **radial** spokes of the web; bridge line silk is the

127

first strand, by which the web hangs from its support; yet another silk forms the great spiral.

牵引丝形成网络的**径向**辐条；桥丝是第一链，给整个蜘蛛网提供支持力；而牵引丝形成了一个大的螺旋形网。

【记】radar *n.* 雷达；雷达装置；无线电探测器

radiant *a.* 照耀的；辐射的；容光焕发的

spoke ［spəuk］ *v.* 说话（speak 的过去分词）；为……装轮辐　　*n.* 轮辐；刹车；扶梯棍

【变】spokes

【例】Dragline silk forms the radial **spokes** of the web; bridge ine silk is the first strand, by which the web hangs from its support; yet another silk forms the great spiral.

牵引丝形成网络的径向**辐条**；桥丝是第一链，给整个蜘蛛网提供支持力；而牵引丝形成了一个大的螺旋形网。

【记】spokesman *n.* 发言人，代言人

sponge *n.* 海绵；海绵状物

sponsor *n.* 发起者，主办者；担保者；倡议者，提案人；后援组织

strand ［strænd］ *n.* 线；串；海滨　　*v.* 使搁浅；使陷于困境；弄断；使落后

【变】stranded　stranded　stranding　strands

【例】Dragline silk forms the radial spokes of the web; bridge line silk is the first **strand**, by which the web hangs from its support; yet another silk forms the great spiral.

牵引丝形成网络的径向辐条；桥丝是第一链，给整个蜘蛛网提供支持力；而牵引丝形成了一个大的螺旋形网。

【搭】a strand of wool 一股羊毛

【记】strange *a.* 陌生的，生疏的；古怪的

stranger *n.* 陌生人；外地人

strap *v.* 用带捆扎；用皮带抽打；拼命工作

random *n.* 随机 *a.* 随机的

wander *v.* 漫步；迷路

spiral ['spairl] *n.* **螺旋；旋涡；螺旋形之物**　*a.* **螺旋形的；盘旋的**　*v.* **盘旋；成螺旋形；螺旋形上升**

【变】spiraled　spiraled　spiraling　spirals

【例】Dragline silk forms the radial spokes of the web; bridgeline silk is the first strand, by which the web hangs from its support; yet another silk forms the great **spiral**.

　　牵引丝形成网络的径向辐条；桥丝是第一链，给整个蜘蛛网提供支持力；而牵引丝形成了一个大的**螺旋形网**。

【搭】spiral agitator 螺旋搅拌器　spiral auger 螺旋钻

【记】spirit *n.* 精神，心灵；潮流，风气

spiritual *a.* 精神的；心灵的；高尚的，崇高的；宗教的

spite *n.* 恶意；怨恨；恶事

词汇听写

1. _____　2. _____　3. _____

句子听写

Tuesday ·· 《

1. Embedded in the amorphous portions of both proteins are two kinds of crystalline regions that toughen the silk.

　　嵌入在这两种蛋白的不规则部分的是两种结晶区，这种结晶区使丝绸更加坚韧。

embed [im'bed] *v.* 栽种；使嵌入，使插入；使深留脑中

【变】embedded　embedded　embedding　embeds

【例】**Embedded** in the amorphous portions of both proteins are two kinds of crystalline regions that toughen the silk.

　　　嵌入在这两种蛋白的不规则部分的是两种结晶区，这种结晶区使丝绸更加坚韧。

【搭】embedded in hard sandstone 嵌在坚硬的砂岩中；be deeply embedded in our society 在我们的社会中根深蒂固；be embedded in a state treaty 被纳入国家条约中

【记】embody *v.* 表现，象征；包含，收录

　　　embrace *v.* 拥抱

　　　embroidery *n.* 刺绣；刺绣品；粉饰，修饰

amorphous [ə'mɔːfəs] *a.* 无定形的；无组织的；[物] 非晶形的

【例】Embedded in the **amorphous** portions of both proteins are two kinds of crystalline regions that toughen the silk.

　　　嵌入在这两种蛋白的**不规则**部分的是两种结晶区，这种结晶区使丝绸更加坚韧。

【搭】amorphous binder 黏合剂　amorphous body 非晶形体

【记】amount *n.* 量，数量；总额；本利之和；全部效果，全部含义

　　　ampere *n.* [电] 安培

　　　ample *a.* 足够的；充足的，丰富的；宽敞的，广大的；富裕的

protein ['prəutiːn] *n.* 蛋白质；朊　*a.* 蛋白质的

【变】proteins

【例】Embedded in the amorphous portions of both **proteins** are two kinds of crystalline regions that toughen the silk.

嵌入在这两种**蛋白**的不规则部分的是两种结晶区，这种结晶区使丝绸更加坚韧。

【搭】protein and fat 蛋白质和脂肪   rich in protein 蛋白质丰富

【记】protest *n.* 抗议；反对；申明

proton *n.* ［物］质子

prototype *n.* 原型，雏形，蓝本

crystalline ['kristlain] *a.* 透明的；水晶般的；水晶制的

【例】Embedded in the amorphous portions of both proteins are two kinds of **crystalline** regions that toughen the silk.

嵌入在这两种蛋白的不规则部分的是两种**结晶区**，这种**结晶区**使丝绸更加坚韧。

【搭】crystalline structure 结晶结构   crystalline rocks 结晶岩

【记】crystal *n.* 结晶（体）；晶体；水晶；水晶饰品

cube *n.* 立方形，立方体；立方，小房间

cubic *a.* 立方体的

词汇听写

1. _____   2. _____   3. _____

句子听写

2. Any good marketer will confidently remark that the key to success is to have good campaign and to never give up. And to make it in the job market today one has to be aware of that and to do just that.

任何一位优秀的营销员都会理直气壮地说，成功的关键是要有良好的竞争并且永不放弃。要在今天的人才市场上获得成功，求职者得意识到这一点，并做到这一点。

marketer [ˈmɑːkitə] *n.* （贸易）市场商人；市场营销人员

【例】Any good **marketer** will confidently remark that the key to success is to have good campaign and to never give up. And to make it in the job market today one has to be aware of that and to do just that.

　　任何一位优秀的**营销员**都会理直气壮地说，成功的关键是要有良好的竞争并且永不放弃。要在今天的人才市场上获得成功，求职者得意识到这一点，并做到这一点。

【记】market *n.* 交易；市集；需求；交易情况，行情

marriage *n.* 结婚；婚姻生活；密切结合；合并

marry *v.* （使）结婚；娶；嫁；结合

remark [riˈmɑːk] *n.* 注意；言辞　*v.* 评论；觉察；谈论

【变】remarked　remarked　remarking　remarks

【例】Any good marketer will confidently **remark** that the key to success is to have good campaign and to never give up. And to make it in the job market today one has to be aware of that and to do just that.

　　任何一位优秀的营销员都会理直气壮地**说**，成功的关键是要有良好的竞争并且永不放弃。要在今天的人才市场上获得成功，求职者得意识到这一点，并做到这一点。

【搭】remark measures 补救措施；remark on 就……发表意见 ；a casual remark 随便说说

【记】remarkable *a.* 异常的，引人注目的，卓越的；非凡的，非常（好）的

remedy *n.* 治疗法；纠正办法

remind *v.* 使想起，使记起；提醒

campaign [kæmˈpein] *v.* 作战；参加竞选；参加活动　*n.* 运动；活动；战役

【变】campaigns

【例】Any good marketer will confidently remark that the key to success is to have good **campaign** and to never give up. And to make it in the job market today one has to be aware of that and to do just that.

　　任何一位优秀的营销员都会理直气壮地说，成功的关键是要有良好的**竞争**并且永不放弃。要在今天的人才市场上获得成功，求职者得意识

到这一点，并做到这一点。

【搭】campaign badge 随军记者　campaign chest 竞选用专款，一种有抽屉的柜子

【记】campus *n.* （大学）校园；学校范围内；大学生活

cabin *n.* 〈美〉小木屋；客舱；（轮船上工作或生活的）隔间

camp *n.* 野营；营地 *v.* 设营

be aware of 知道

【例】Any good marketer will confidently remark that the key to success is to have good campaign and to never give up. And to make it in the job market today one has to **be aware of** that and to do just that.

任何一位优秀的营销员都会理直气壮地说，成功的关键是要有良好的竞争并且永不放弃。要在今天的人才市场上获得成功，求职者得**意识到这一点**，并做到这一点。

【记】aware *a.* 意识到的；知道的；觉察到的

away *ad.* 离开，远离；在远处；消失

awake *a.* 醒着的；警惕的

beware *v.* 谨防，当心

software *n.* （计算机的）软件

ware *n.* 商品，货物

warehouse *n.* 仓库，货栈

词汇听写

1. ＿＿＿＿＿＿＿＿　2. ＿＿＿＿＿＿＿＿　3. ＿＿＿＿＿＿＿＿

句子听写

3. Happiness is the ultimate principle whoever one is, a prince or a pauper. And undeniably smile and friendly approach will make one look upbeat and interesting.

无论是王子还是穷光蛋，幸福都是最终的原则。毋庸置疑的是，微笑

和友好的态度让一个人看起来让人愉快且令人感兴趣。

ultimate [ˈʌltimət] a. 最终的；极限的；根本的 n. 终极；根本；基本原则

【变】ultimates

【例】Happiness is the **ultimate** principle whoever one is, a prince or a pauper. And undeniably smile and friendly approach will make one look upbeat and interesting.

无论是王子还是穷光蛋，幸福都是**最终的**原则。毋庸置疑的是，微笑和友好的态度让一个人看起来让人愉快且令人感兴趣。

【搭】ultimate analysis 最后分析   ultimate bearing strength 弯曲极限强度

【记】ultimately ad. 最后，最终；基本上；根本

ultrasonic a. [声] 超声的；超音波的，超音速的

umbrella n. 雨伞；〈比喻〉保护物；[军] 空中掩护幕

pauper [ˈpɔːpə] n. 乞丐；穷人；靠救济度日者   a. 贫民的

【变】paupers

【例】Happiness is the ultimate principle whoever one is, a prince or a **pauper**. And undeniably smile and friendly approach will make one look upbeat and interesting.

无论是王子还是**穷光蛋**，幸福都是最终的原则。毋庸置疑的是，微笑和友好的态度让一个人看起来让人愉快且令人感兴趣。

【记】pause n. 暂时的停顿；犹豫；（诗中）节奏的停顿

pave v. 铺设；为……铺平道路；安排

paw n. 爪子；手；〈俚〉笔迹

undeniably [ˌʌndiˈnaiəbli] ad. 不可否认地；确凿无疑地

【例】Happiness is the ultimate principle whoever one is, a prince or a pauper. And **undeniably** smile and friendly approach will make one look upbeat and interesting.

无论是王子还是穷光蛋，幸福都是最终的原则。**毋庸置疑**的是，微笑和友好的态度让一个人看起来让人愉快且令人感兴趣。

【记】under prep. 在……下面，在表面之下；小于；在……情况下

underestimate v. 低估；看轻

undergo v. 经历，经验；遭受，承受

upbeat [ˈʌpbiːt] *n.* 兴旺；上升；弱拍 *a.* 乐观的；上升的

【变】upbeats

【例】Happiness is the ultimate principle whoever one is，a prince or a pauper. And undeniably smile and friendly approach will make one look **upbeat** and interesting.

无论是王子还是穷光蛋，幸福都是最终的原则。毋庸置疑的是，微笑和友好的态度让一个人看起来让人**愉快**且令人感兴趣。

【记】beat v.（心脏等）跳动；搜索；（风、雨等）吹打；（鼓）咚咚地响

uphold v. 支持；维持；赞成；支撑

upon *prep.* 在……上面；当……时候

词汇听写

1. _____ 2. _____ 3. _____

句子听写

Wednesday ·· 《《《

1. Get a friend to pretend as the interviewer and then rehearse how to tackle him. Even if the job applied for does not require professional attire, one should still wear a business suit, unless told otherwise.

邀请一个朋友扮演面试官，然后排练如何面对他。即使申请的职位没有要求穿职业装，应聘者还是应该穿西装，除非面试官有另行通知。

---

rehearse [ri'hə:s] *v.* **排练；预演；演习**

【变】rehearsed　rehearsed　rehearsing　rehearses

【例】Get a friend to pretend as the interviewer and then **rehearse** how to tackle him. Even if the job applied for does not require professional attire, one should still wear a business suit, unless told otherwise.

邀请一个朋友扮演面试官，然后**排练**如何面对他。即使申请的职位没有要求穿职业装，应聘者还是应该穿西装，除非面试官有另行通知。

【记】rehearsal *n.* 排练，排演；彩排，演习；复述，详述

reign *v.* 当政，统治；占主导地位

rein *n.* 驾驭（法）；统治手段；缰绳

---

tackle ['tækl] *n.* **滑车；装备；用具；扭倒**　　*v.* **处理；抓住；固定；**
与……交涉

【变】tackled　tackled　tackling　tackles

【例】Get a friend to pretend as the interviewer and then rehearse how to **tackle** him. Even if the job applied for does not require professional attire, one should still wear a business suit, unless told otherwise.

邀请一个朋友扮演面试官，然后排练如何**面对**他。即使申请的职位没有要求穿职业装，应聘者还是应该穿西装，除非面试官有另行通知。

【搭】tackle below the belt 暗中伤人，不择手段　　tackle down（足球、橄榄球中）把对方弄倒

【记】tact *n.* 机智，机敏；老练

tack *n.* [航] 食物；方针，方法；航向

tactics *n.* 战术；策略，手段；用兵学

attire [əˈtaiə] *n.* 服装；盛装　*v.* 打扮；使穿衣

【变】attired　attired　attiring　attires

【例】Get a friend to pretend as the interviewer and then rehearse how to tackle him. Even if the job applied for does not require professional **attire**, one should still wear a business suit, unless told otherwise.

邀请一个朋友扮演面试官，然后排练如何面对他。即使申请的职位没有要求穿职业装，应聘者还是应该穿西装，除非面试官有另行通知。

【搭】attire in 穿上

【记】attitude *n.* 态度，看法；[戏剧]（表演时的）姿势

attorney *n.* 代理人；律师

attraction *n.* 吸引；[物] 引力；魅力；引人注意的东西，有趣的东西

otherwise [ˈʌðəwaiz] *ad.* 否则；另外；在其他方面　*a.* 另外的；其他方面的

【例】Get a friend to pretend as the interviewer and then rehearse how to tackle him. Even if the job applied for does not require professional attire, one should still wear a business suit, unless told **otherwise**.

邀请一个朋友扮演面试官，然后排练如何面对他。即使申请的职位没有要求穿职业装，应聘者还是应该穿西装，除非面试官有**另行通知**。

【搭】otherwise from 不同于

【记】other *a.* 别的；其他的；（两个中的）另一个；其余的

ought *aux.* 应该（指道义上有责任）；应当（显示所采取行动正确或明智）；可能会；预料会做（某事）

ounce *n.* 盎司；〈口〉少量，一点儿；雪豹

词汇听写

1. ＿＿＿＿＿＿＿＿　2. ＿＿＿＿＿＿＿＿　3. ＿＿＿＿＿＿＿＿

句子听写

2. If one wants to land a specific role within a company, find out exactly what experience, qualifications, and requirements are needed to secure the position. Then target sufficient energies into obtaining these things.

　　如果一个人想要在公司内获得一个特定的职位，找出这个职位所需要的经验、资历和要求能够让他更有把握获得这个职位。然后以此为目标，用足够的能力去争取这些东西。

specific [spə'sifik] *a.* 特殊的，特定的；明确的；详细的；[药] 具有特效的　*n.* 特性；细节；特效药

【变】more specific　most specific

【例】If one wants to land a **specific** role within a company, find out exactly what experience, qualifications, and requirements are needed to secure the position. Then target sufficient energies into obtaining these things.

　　如果一个人想要在公司内获得一个**特定的**职位，找出这个职位所需要的经验、资历和要求能够让他更有把握获得这个职位。然后以此为目标，用足够的能力去争取这些东西。

【搭】specific absorption 吸收率　specific accelerating force 单位加速力

【记】specification *n.* 规格；详述；说明书

　　specify *v.* 指定；详述；提出……的条件；使具有特性

　　specimen *n.* 样品；范例；（化验的）抽样；某种类型的人

secure [si'kjuə] *a.* 安全的；无虑的；有把握的；稳当的　*v.* 保护；弄到；招致；缚住

【变】secured　secured　securing　secures

【例】If one wants to land a specific role within a company, find out exactly what experience, qualifications, and requirements are needed to **secure** the position. Then target sufficient energies into obtaining these things.

　　如果一个人想要在公司内获得一个特定的职位，找出这个职位所需要的经验、资历和要求能够让他更**有把握**获得这个职位。然后以此为目标，用足够的能力去争取这些东西。

【搭】secure foothold 稳固的脚踏处　secure currency 稳定的通货

【记】security *n.* 安全；保证；保护；有价证券

　　seam *n.* 接缝，接合处；煤层；线缝；裂缝

obscure *a.* 阴暗的；蒙昧的

target [ˈtɑːgit] *n.* **目标；靶子** *v.* **把……作为目标；规定……的指标；瞄准某物**

【变】targets targeted targeted targeting targets

【例】If one wants to land a specific role within a company, find out exactly what experience, qualifications, and requirements are needed to secure the position. Then **target** sufficient energies into obtaining these things.

如果一个人想要在公司内获得一个特定的职位，找出这个职位所需要的经验、资历和要求能够让他更有把握获得这个职位。然后**以此为目标**，用足够的能力去争取这些东西。

【搭】target acceleration 目标加速度 target acquisition radar 目标搜索雷达

【记】task *n.* 工作，任务；作业；苦差事

taste *n.* 体验；滋味；味觉；风味

tax *v.* 使负重担；消耗精力；向……征税；责备，谴责

sufficient [səˈfiʃnt] *a.* **足够的；充分的**

【例】If one wants to land a specific role within a company, find out exactly what experience, qualifications, and requirements are needed to secure the position. Then target **sufficient** energies into obtaining these things.

如果一个人想要在公司内获得一个特定的职位，找出这个职位所需要的经验、资历和要求能够让他更有把握获得这个职位。然后以此为目标，用**足够的**能力去争取这些东西。

【搭】sufficient cause 充分理由 sufficient condition 充分条件

【记】sufficiently *ad.* 足够地，充分地；十分，相当

sugar *n.* 糖；一块（茶匙等）糖；（植物、水果等所含的）糖；（爱称）宝贝儿，亲爱的

suicide *n.* 自杀；自杀者；自杀行为

词汇听写

1. _____ 2. _____ 3. _____

句子听写

3. A competent translator should be very acquainted with the following point：A detailed knowledge of the subject matter is equally as important as academic knowledge of the language pairs, in certain cases it plays a greater role.

一位优秀的翻译者应该非常熟悉以下原则：需要翻译的科目的详细知识和翻译目标语的语言知识同等重要，在某些情况下，它发挥更大的作用。

competent [ˈkɔmpitnt] *a.* 胜任的；有能力的；能干的；足够的

【例】A **competent** translator should be very acquainted with the following point：A detailed knowledge of the subject matter is equally as important as academic knowledge of the language pairs, in certain cases it plays a greater role.

一位**优秀的**翻译者应该非常熟悉以下原则：需要翻译的科目的详细知识和翻译目标语的语言知识同等重要，在某些情况下，它发挥更大的作用。

【搭】competent authority 主管当局　a competent secretary 一名能干的秘书

【记】competition *n.* 竞争；比赛

competitive *a.* 竞争的，比赛的；（价格等）有竞争力的

competitor *n.* 竞争者；对手

acquaint [əˈkweint] *v.* 使熟悉；使认识

【变】acquainted　acquainted　acquainting　acquaints

【例】A competent translator should be very **acquainted** with the following point：A detailed knowledge of the subject matter is equally as important as academic knowledge of the language pairs, in certain cases it plays a greater role.

一位优秀的翻译者应该非常**熟悉**以下原则：需要翻译的科目的详细知识和翻译目标语的语言知识同等重要，在某些情况下，它发挥更大的作用。

【搭】acquaint oneself of 开始知道　acquaint oneself with 开始知道

【记】acquaintance *n.* 相识的人，熟人；相识；对……有了解；知识，心得

acquire *v.* 获得，取得；学到

pair [peə] *n.* 一对，一双，一副　*v.* 把……组成一对

【变】paired　paired　pairing　pairs

【例】A competent translator should be very acquainted with the following point：A detailed knowledge of the subject matter is equally as important as academic knowledge of the language **pairs**，in certain cases it plays a greater role.

一位优秀的翻译者应该非常熟悉以下原则：需要翻译的科目的详细知识和翻译**目标语**的语言知识同等重要，在某些情况下，它发挥更大的作用。

【搭】pair assembly 双机组　pair cable 双股电缆

【记】pal *n.* 朋友；老兄，兄弟；小子；（对男子的不友好称呼）家伙

pacific *a.* 和平的，爱好和平的；平静的；平时的

pack *n.* 一群；包裹；（纸牌的）一副；一组

case [keis] *n.* 情况；实例；箱　*v.* 包围；把……装于容器中

【变】cases　cased　cased　casing　cases

【例】A competent translator should be very acquainted with the following point：A detailed knowledge of the subject matter is equally as important as academic knowledge of the language pairs，in certain **cases** it plays a greater role.

一位优秀的翻译者应该非常熟悉以下原则：需要翻译的科目的详细知识和翻译目标语的语言知识同等重要，在某些**情况**下，它发挥更大的作用。

【搭】case back flaw 表壳后盖裂缝　case band 箱箍

【记】cash *n.* 现金；支付金额

cassette *n.* 盒式录音带；珠宝箱

casual *a.* 偶然的；临时的；随便的

词汇听写

1. _____　2. _____　3. _____

句子听写

Thursday ··· ◁◁◁

1. Interpretation is generally categorized into consecutive interpretation and simultaneous interpretation.

口译一般分为交替传译和同声传译。

---

interpretation [intə:pri'teiʃn] *n.* **解释；翻译；演出**

【变】interpretations

【例】**Interpretation** is generally categorized into consecutive interpretation and simultaneous interpretation.

口译一般分为交替传译和同声传译。

【搭】interpretation of air photograph 航空照片判读　interpretation of data 数据判读

【记】interpreter *n.* 解释者；口译译员；［军事］判读员；翻译器

interrupt *v.* 打断（别人的话等）；阻止；截断

interruption *n.* 中断；打断；障碍物；打岔的事

---

categorize ['kætəgə'raiz] *v.* **分类**

【变】categorized　categorized　categorizing　categorizes

【例】Interpretation is generally **categorized** into consecutive interpretation and simultaneous interpretation.

口译一般**分为**交替传译和同声传译。

【记】category *n.* 类型，部门，种类，类别，类目；［逻、哲］范畴；体重等级

cater *v.* 提供饮食及服务

cathedral *n.* 总教堂，大教堂

---

consecutive [kən'sekjutiv] *a.* **连贯的；连续不断的**

【例】Interpretation is generally categorized into **consecutive** interpretation and simultaneous interpretation.

口译一般分为**交替**传译和同声传译。

【搭】consecutive action 连续动作　consecutive clause（表结果的）连续从句

【记】consent *n.* 准许，赞同；同意；（意见等的）一致

consequence *n.* 结果，成果；[逻] 结论；重要性；推论

consequently *ad.* 所以，因此；因此，因而；终于，这样；合乎逻辑的推论是

simultaneous [ˌsɪmlˈteɪnɪəs] *a.* **同时的；联立的；同时发生的** *n.* **同时译员**

【变】simultaneouses

【例】Interpretation is generally categorized into consecutive interpretation and **simultaneous** interpretation.

口译一般分为交替传译和**同声传译**。

【搭】simultaneous adaptation 同时适应 simultaneous approximation 联立逼近，同时逼近

【记】similar *a.* 类似的；同类的；同样的

simple *a.* 单纯的；易受骗的；天真的

sin *n.* 违背宗教的恶行；罪恶；可耻的事

词汇听写

1. _____ 2. _____ 3. _____

句子听写

2. Consecutive interpretation is used primarily to interpret witness testimony, a situation in which foreign affairs are concerned and everyone in the courtroom needs to hear the interpretation.

交替传译主要是用于法庭上翻译证人的证词，在涉外案件的法庭上，每个人都需要听到证人的证词。

primarily [ˈpraɪmrɪlɪ] *ad.* **首先；主要地，根本上**

【例】Consecutive interpretation is used **primarily** to interpret witness testimony, a situation in which foreign affairs are concerned and everyone in the courtroom needs to hear the interpretation.

交替传译**主要**是用于法庭上翻译证人的证词，在涉外案件的法庭

上，每个人都需要听到证人的证词。

【记】prick *v.* 刺，戳；刺伤

pride *n.* 自尊；骄傲；自满

witness ['witnis] *n.* 证人；目击者；证据　*v.* 目击；证明；为……作证

【变】witnessed　witnessed　witnessing　witnesses

【例】Consecutive interpretation is used primarily to interpret **witness** testimony, a situation in which foreign affairs are concerned and everyone in the courtroom needs to hear the interpretation.

交替传译主要是用于法庭上翻译**证人**的证词，在涉外案件的法庭上，每个人都需要听到证人的证词。

【搭】no witness 没有证人　bear witness to... 见证……

【记】witty *a.* 诙谐的；会说俏皮话的；聪明的

woe *n.* 悲哀；悲伤；灾难，灾殃；苦恼

wade *v.*（从水、泥等）蹚，走过；跋涉

testimony ['testiməni] *n.* [法] 证词，证言；证据

【变】testimonies

【例】Consecutive interpretation is used primarily to interpret witness **testimony**, a situation in which foreign affairs are concerned and everyone in the courtroom needs to hear the interpretation.

交替传译主要是用于法庭上翻译证人的**证词**，在涉外案件的法庭上，每个人都需要听到证人的证词。

【搭】testimony of a witness [法] 人证

【记】testify *v.* 作证；声明；证明；证实　textile *n.* 纺织品，织物；纺织业

court [kɔːt] *n.* 法院；球场；朝廷；奉承　*v.* 招致（失败、危险等）；向……献殷勤；设法获得

【变】courtrooms

【例】Consecutive interpretation is used primarily to interpret witness testimony, a situation in which foreign affairs are concerned and everyone in the **court**room needs to hear the interpretation.

交替传译主要是用于法庭上翻译证人的证词，在涉外案件的**法庭**上，每个人都需要听到证人的证词。

【搭】appear in court 出庭　civil/criminal courts 民事/刑事法庭　facing court action 面临法庭诉讼

【记】cousin *n.* 堂（表）兄弟姊妹；远亲，同辈

counter *a.* & *ad.* 相反的（地）

courageous *a.* 勇敢的，无畏的

courteous *a.* 有礼貌的，谦恭的

词汇听写

1. _____　2. _____　3. _____

句子听写

3. Non-designated languages are languages for which there are no state certifying examinations. Registered interpreters must pass an English proficiency exam that tests their knowledge of English, court procedure, and professional ethics.

　　非指定的语言是指没有国家认证考试的语言。注册的口译员必须通过英语水平考试，测试他们的英语知识、法院程序和职业道德。

designate [ˈdezigneit] *v.* 指定；指派；标出；把……定名为　*a.* 指定的；选定的

【变】designated　designated　designating　designates

【例】Non-**designated** languages are languages for which there are no state certifying examinations. Registered interpreters must pass an English proficiency exam that tests their knowledge of English, court procedure, and professional ethics.

　　非**指定**的语言是指没有国家认证考试的语言。注册的口译员必须通过英语水平考试，测试他们的英语知识、法院程序和职业道德。

【搭】designated bank 指定的银行　designated instructor 指定的教员

【记】design *v.* 设计；绘制

desirable *a.* 令人满意的；值得拥有的；性感的

certify ['səːtifai] v. 证明；保证

【变】certified　certified　certifying　certifies

【例】Non-designated languages are languages for which there are no state **certifying** examinations. Registered interpreters must pass an English proficiency exam that tests their knowledge of English, court procedure, and professional ethics.

　　非指定的语言是指没有国家**认证**考试的语言。注册的口译员必须通过英语水平考试，测试他们的英语知识、法院程序和职业道德。

【搭】certify to 证明

【记】certificate n. 证明书；文凭，结业证书

　　chain n. 链子，链条；连锁，连续；拘束；连锁店或旅馆系列的事物

proficiency [prə'fiʃnsi] n. 精通，熟练

【例】Non-designated languages are languages for which there are no state certifying examinations. Registered interpreters must pass an English **proficiency** exam that tests their knowledge of English, court procedure, and professional ethics.

　　非指定的语言是指没有国家认证考试的语言。注册的口译员必须通过英语水平考试，测试他们的英语知识、法院程序和职业道德。

【记】proficient a. 精通的，熟练的

　　profit n. 收益，得益；利润

　　profitable a. 有利可图的，有益的；可赚钱的，合算的

ethic ['eθik] n. 伦理；道德规范　a. 伦理的；道德的（等于 ethical）

【例】Non-designated languages are languages for which there are no state certifying examinations. Registered interpreters must pass an English proficiency exam that tests their knowledge of English, court procedure, and professional **ethics**.

　　非指定的语言是指没有国家认证考试的语言。注册的口译员必须通过英语水平考试，测试他们的英语知识、法院程序和职业**道德**。

【记】eternal a. 永恒的，永久的；似乎不停的；不朽的

　　Europe n. 欧洲；欧盟；（除英国以外的）全欧洲

evaluate *v.* 评价；对······评价

词汇听写

1. _____ 2. _____ 3. _____

句子听写

Friday ·································· ◁◁

1. A butterfly farm is a piece of land <u>dedicated</u> to raising a <u>spectacular</u> and unusual cash crop：various <u>species</u> of those beautiful，<u>delicate</u> insects.

　　蝴蝶农场致力于养殖一种壮观的、不寻常的经济作物——各种各样的美丽的、精致的昆虫。

dedicate ['dedikeit] v. 致力；献身；题献

【变】dedicated　dedicated　dedicating　dedicates

【例】A butterfly farm is a piece of land **dedicated** to raising a spectacular and unusual cash crop：various species of those beautiful，delicate insects.

　　蝴蝶农场**致力**于养殖一种壮观的、不寻常的经济作物——各种各样的美丽的、精致的昆虫。

【搭】dedicate oneself to 专心致力于；全力以赴　dedicate to 宣告……是供奉（上帝）的；献（身）于

【记】deduce v. 推论，推断；演绎；追溯根源

　　deed n. 行为；行动；证书

spectacular [spek'tækjulə] a. 壮观的，惊人的；公开展示的

【变】spectaculars

【例】A butterfly farm is a piece of land dedicated to raising a **spectacular** and unusual cash crop：various species of those beautiful，delicate insects.

　　蝴蝶农场致力于养殖一种**壮观的**、不寻常的经济作物——各种各样的美丽的、精致的昆虫。

【记】spectator n. 观众，旁观者

　　spectrum n. [物理学] 谱，光谱辐射源，能谱；光谱相片；系列，幅度

　　speculate v. 思索，猜测，推测

species ['s pi:ʃi:z] n. [生物] 物种；种类　a. 物种上的

【变】species

【例】A butterfly farm is a piece of land dedicated to raising a spectacular and unusual cash crop：various **species** of those beautiful，delicate insects.

　　蝴蝶农场致力于养殖一种壮观的、不寻常的经济作物——各种各样

的美丽的、精致的昆虫。

【搭】species certificate 品种证明书　species complex 物种综合

【记】special *a.* 特殊的；专门的；专用的；重要的

　　specialist *n.* 专家；行家；专科医生

　　specialize *v.* 专门从事；专攻；详细说明；特化

delicate [ˈdelikət] *a.* 微妙的；精美的，雅致的；柔和的；易碎的；纤弱的；清淡可口的

【例】A butterfly farm is a piece of land dedicated to raising a spectacular and unusual cash crop: various species of those beautiful, **delicate** insects.

　　蝴蝶农场致力于养殖一种壮观的、不寻常的经济作物——各种各样的美丽的、**精致的**昆虫。

【搭】delicate adjusting 精调　delicate adjustment 精调，微调

【记】delicious *a.* 美味的，可口的；有趣的；香的

　　delight *n.* 快乐，高兴；使人高兴的东西或人

　　deliver *v.* 发表；递送；交付；使分娩

词汇听写

1. _____　2. _____　3. _____

句子听写

2. On the farm the insects go through their entire life cycle in captivity. These farms provide protective control over the stock.

　　昆虫在这个农场上被圈养着，经历着它们整个生命周期。这些农场对家畜提供保护性的控制。

cycle [ˈsaikl] *n.* 循环；周期；自行车；整套；一段时间　*v.* 循环；骑自行车；轮转

【变】cycled　cycled　cycling　cycles

【例】On the farm the insects go through their entire life **cycle** in captivity.

These farms provide protective control over the stock.

　　昆虫在这个农场上被圈养着，经历着它们整个生命**周期**。这些农场对家畜提供保护性的控制。

【搭】cycle amplitude 循环振幅

【记】cabbage *n.* 甘蓝（洋白菜、卷心菜）

　　cabin *n.* 〈美〉小木屋；客舱；（轮船上工作或生活的）隔间

captivity [kæp'tiviti] *n.* 囚禁；被关

【例】On the farm the insects go through their entire life cycle in **captivity**. These farms provide protective control over the stock.

　　昆虫在这个农场上被**圈养**着，经历着它们整个生命周期。这些农场对家畜提供保护性的控制。

【记】capture *v.* 俘获；引起（注意、想象、兴趣）

　　captain *n.* 船长；领袖；上尉

　　caption *n.* 标题，说明文字，字幕

protective [prəu'tektiv] *a.* 防护的；关切保护的；保护贸易的

【例】On the farm the insects go through their entire life cycle in captivity. These farms provide **protective** control over the stock.

　　昆虫在这个农场上被圈养着，经历着它们整个生命周期。这些农场对家畜提供**保护性**的控制。

【搭】protective agent 防护剂，保护剂，防老（化）剂　protective antibody 保护性抗体

【记】protection *n.* 保护；护照；［经］保护贸易制，保护政策

　　protein *n.* 蛋白（质）

　　protest *n.* 抗议；反对；申明

stock [stɔk] *n.* 股份，股票；库存；血统；树干；家畜　*a.* 存货的，常备的；平凡的　*v.* 进货；备有；装把手于

【变】stocked　stocked　stocking　stocks

【例】On the farm the insects go through their entire life cycle in captivity. These farms provide protective control over the **stock**.

　　昆虫在这个农场上被圈养着，经历着它们整个生命周期。这些农场

对**家畜**提供保护性的控制。

【搭】stock account 存货账　breeding stock 种畜

【记】stocking *n.* 长袜；似长袜之物

　　　stomach *n.* 腹部；食欲；欲望

　　　flock *v.* 群集，聚集

　　　dock *n.* 码头

词汇听写

1. _____ 2. _____ 3. _____

句子听写

3. People have always been <u>fascinated</u> by butterflies. So great was the butterfly <u>craze</u> during the Victorian Age that public <u>auctions</u> of <u>exotic</u> specimens were frequently held in London.

　　人们对蝴蝶一直很着迷。在维多利亚时代，人们对蝴蝶是如此疯狂，以致于在伦敦经常举行公开拍卖奇特蝴蝶标本的拍卖会。

fascinate [ˈfæsineit] *v.* （使）着迷，（使）神魂颠倒

【变】fascinated　fascinated　fascinating　fascinates

【例】People have always been **fascinated** by butterflies. So great was the butterfly craze during the Victorian Age that public auctions of exotic specimens were frequently held in London.

　　人们对蝴蝶一直很**着迷**。在维多利亚时代，人们对蝴蝶是如此疯狂，以致于在伦敦经常举行公开拍卖奇特蝴蝶标本的拍卖会。

【记】fashion *n.* 时尚，时装；方式，方法

　　　fashionable *a.* 流行的；时髦的，符合时尚的

　　　coordinate *a.* 同等的，并列的；坐标的 *n.* 坐标 *v.* 整理

　　　illuminate *v.* 照明，照亮；阐明

craze [kreiz] n. 狂热 v. 发狂；产生纹裂

【变】crazes

【例】People have always been fascinated by butterflies. So great was the butterfly **craze** during the Victorian Age that public auctions of exotic specimens were frequently held in London.

人们对蝴蝶一直很着迷。在维多利亚时代，人们对蝴蝶是如此**疯狂**，以致于在伦敦经常举行公开拍卖奇特蝴蝶标本的拍卖会。

【搭】craze crack 龟裂；latest craze 最新时尚

【记】crazy *a.* 疯狂的；不理智的；离奇的；生气的

cream *n.* 乳霜；奶油色

blaze *v.* 燃烧

gaze *v.* & *n.* 凝视，注视

auction ['ɔːkʃn] v. 拍卖；竞卖 n. 拍卖

【变】auctioned auctioned auctioning auctions

【例】People have always been fascinated by butterflies. So great was the butterfly craze during the Victorian Age that public **auctions** of exotic specimens were frequently held in London.

人们对蝴蝶一直很着迷。在维多利亚时代，人们对蝴蝶是如此疯狂，以致于在伦敦经常举行公开**拍卖**奇特蝴蝶标本的拍卖会。

【记】audience *n.* 观众，听众，读者；接见；拥护者

sauce *n.* 调味汁，酱汁

saucer *n.* 茶托，碟子

sausage *n.* 香肠

exotic [ig'zɔtik] a. 异国的；外来的；异国情调的

【例】People have always been fascinated by butterflies. So great was the butterfly craze during the Victorian Age that public auctions of **exotic** specimens were frequently held in London.

人们对蝴蝶一直很着迷。在维多利亚时代，人们对蝴蝶是如此疯狂，以致于在伦敦经常举行公开拍卖**奇特**蝴蝶标本的拍卖会。

【搭】exotic composition 特殊高能燃料 exotic currency 外来货币

【记】expand *v.* 使……变大；扩张；详述

    expansion *n.* 扩大；扩张；膨胀物

    expedition *n.* 探险；探险队

词汇听写

1. _____ 2. _____ 3. _____

句子听写

1. In this regard, he made his contribution to the betterment of Costa Rica economy. In the past few years, Costa Rica was suffering its most devastating economic crunch.

在这方面，他对哥斯达黎加经济的改善作出了他的贡献。在过去的几年中，哥斯达黎加一直遭受其最具破坏性的经济紧缩。

in this regard 就这一点而言

【例】**In this regard**, he made his contribution to the betterment of Costa Rica economy. In the past few years, Costa Rica was suffering its most devastating economic crunch.

在这方面，他对哥斯达黎加经济的改善作出了他的贡献。在过去的几年中，哥斯达黎加一直遭受其最具破坏性的经济紧缩。

【搭】regard as 把……认作；当做；看成；看做　regard with great detestation 非常讨厌；视如蛇蝎

【记】regard *v.* 关系；注意；（尤指以某种方式）注视；尊敬

in this way *ad.* 这样

betterment [ˈbetəmnt] *n.* 改善，改进；改良；涨价

【变】betterments

【例】In this regard, he made his contribution to the **betterment** of Costa Rica economy. In the past few years, Costa Rica was suffering its most devastating economic crunch.

在这方面，他对哥斯达黎加经济的**改善**作出了他的贡献。在过去的几年中，哥斯达黎加一直遭受其最具破坏性的经济紧缩。

【搭】betterment costs 改良费用

【记】bet *v. & n.* 赌，打赌；相信

betray *v.* 背叛，出卖

beyond *prep.* 在（或向）……的那边，远于

beware *v.* 当心；提防

devastate [ˈdevəsteit] *a.* 毁灭性的；全然的　*v.* 摧毁

【变】devastated　devastated　devastating　devastates

【例】In this regard, he made his contribution to the betterment of Costa Rica economy. In the past few years, Costa Rica was suffering its most **devastating** economic crunch.

　　在这方面，他对哥斯达黎加经济的改善作出了他的贡献。在过去的几年中，哥斯达黎加一直受其**最具破坏性的**经济紧缩。

【记】develop *v.* 发展；生长；形成；发达

develolment *n.* 发展，新生事物，新产品；开发区

deviate *v.* 脱离，越轨，误入歧途

crunch [krʌn(t)ʃ] *n.* 咬碎，咬碎声；扎扎地踏　*v.* 压碎；嘎扎嘎扎的咬嚼；扎扎地踏过

【变】crunched　crunched　crunching　crunches

【例】In this regard, he made his contribution to the betterment of Costa Rica economy. In the past few years, Costa Rica was suffering its most devastating economic **crunch**.

　　在这方面，他对哥斯达黎加经济的改善作出了他的贡献。在过去的几年中，哥斯达黎加一直遭受其最具破坏性的经济**紧缩**。

【搭】crunch seal 陶瓷（金属）封接　when it comes to the crunch 到了关键时刻　a loud crunch 嘎吱一声巨响

【记】crust *n.* 面包皮；外壳；硬外皮；地壳

cruel *a.* 残酷的，残忍的；使人痛苦的，让人受难的；无情的，严酷的

cruise *v.* 巡游；漫游；巡航

词汇听写

1. _____　2. _____　3. _____

句子听写

2. In many jurisdictions, there is one generic category of "lawyer", although some may specialise in advocacy and specialist legal advice whereas others do deals and rarely go to Court.

在许多司法管辖区，"律师"只分一类，虽然有些人可能专门出庭替人辩护和提供专业的法律意见，而另外一些人则专门处理案件，很少出庭。

jurisdiction [ˌdʒuərisˈdikʃn] *n.* 司法权，审判权，管辖权；权限，权力

【变】jurisdictions

【例】In many **jurisdictions**, there is one generic category of "lawyer", although some may specialise in advocacy and specialist legal advice whereas others do deals and rarely go to Court.

在许多**司法管辖区**，"律师"只分一类，虽然有些人可能专门出庭替人辩护和提供专业的法律意见，而另外一些人则专门处理案件，很少出庭。

【搭】no jurisdiction 无裁判权　under the jurisdiction of... 隶属······

【记】jury *n.* 陪审团；（展览会、竞赛等的）全体评审员

justify *v.* 证明······有理；为······辩护；对······作出解释

adjustable *a.* 可调整的，可校准的

justice *n.* 公正，公平

generic [dʒiˈnerik] *a.* 类的；一般的；属的；非商标的

【变】generics

【例】In many jurisdictions, there is one **generic** category of "lawyer", although some may specialise in advocacy and specialist legal advice whereas others do deals and rarely go to Court.

在许多司法管辖区，"律师"只分一**类**，虽然有些人可能专门出庭替人辩护和提供专业的法律意见，而另外一些人则专门处理案件，很少出庭。

【搭】generic coefficient 种属系数　generic description 货物分类名称（运价表）

【记】generosity *n.* 慷慨，大方；宽容或慷慨的行为；丰富

generous *a.* 慷慨的，大方的；丰盛的；肥沃的；浓厚的

genius *n.* 天才；天赋；天才人物；（特别的）才能

specialise [ˈspeʃəlaiz] *v.* **专门研究**（等于 specialize）　*v.* **使专门化；限定……的范围；深入**（等于 specialize）

【变】specialized　specialized　specializing　specializes

【例】In many jurisdictions, there is one generic category of "lawyer", although some may **specialize** in advocacy and specialist legal advice whereas others do deals and rarely go to Court.

在许多司法管辖区，"律师"只分一类，虽然有些人可能**专门**出庭替人辩护和提供专业的法意见，而另外一些人则专门处理案件，很少出庭。

【记】specialist *n.* 专家；行家；专科医生

speciality *n.* 专业，专长；特性

specify *v.* 指定；详述；提出……的条件；使具有特性

advocacy [ˈædvəkəsi] *n.* **主张；拥护；辩护**

【变】advocacies

【例】In many jurisdictions, there is one generic category of "lawyer", although some may specialise in **advocacy** and specialist legal advice whereas others do deals and rarely go to Court.

在许多司法管辖区，"律师"只分一类，虽然有些人可能专门出庭替人**辩护**和提供专业的法律意见，而另外一些人则专门处理案件，很少出庭。

【记】advocate *v.* 提倡；拥护；鼓吹；为……辩护

aerial *a.* 空气的；航空的，空中的；空想的

aeroplane *n.* 飞机

词汇听写

1. ＿＿＿＿＿＿＿　2. ＿＿＿＿＿＿＿　3. ＿＿＿＿＿＿＿

句子听写

3. Most solicitors are employed by a private practice, which is a firm of solicitors run by the "partners" of the firm who regulate the flow of work to the solicitors.

　　大多数律师受雇于私人事务所，这是由律师组成的公司，由"合作伙伴"共同运营，并且对工作进行分配。

solicitor [sə'lisitə] *n.* 律师；法务官；募捐者

【变】solicitors

【例】Most **solicitors** are employed by a private practice, which is a firm of solicitors run by the "partners" of the firm who regulate the flow of work to the solicitors.

　　大多数**律师**受雇于私人事务所，这是由律师组成的公司，由"合作伙伴"共同运营，并且对工作进行分配。

【记】solid *a.* 固体的；实心的；结实的，可靠的；可信赖的

solidarity *n.* 团结

solidify *v.* 使凝固，固化；使结晶；使团结

practice ['præktis] *n.* 实践；练习；惯例；（律师或医师的）业务　*v.* 练习；实习；实行

【变】practiced　practiced　practicing　practices

【例】Most solicitors are employed by a private **practice**, which is a firm of solicitors run by the "partners" of the firm who regulate the flow of work to the solicitors.

　　大多数律师受雇于私人**事务**所，这是由律师组成的公司，由"合作伙伴"共同运营，并且对工作进行分配。

【搭】practice board 练习板　practice factor 实施系数

【记】practical *a.* 实践的，实际的；可实现的

pray *v.* 请求；祈祷

preach *v.* 宣讲（教义），宣传

partner ['pɑ:tnə] *n.* 伙伴；合伙人；配偶　*v.* 合伙；合股；成为搭档

【变】partnered　partnered　partnering　partners

【例】Most solicitors are employed by a private practice，which is a firm of solicitors run by the **"partners"** of the firm who regulate the flow of work to the solicitors.

　　大多数律师受雇于私人事务所，这是由律师组成的公司，由"**合作伙伴**"共同运营，并且对工作进行分配。

【记】party *n.* 社交聚会；党，党派；当事人；同类，伙伴

　　partial *a.* 部分的；偏爱的；偏袒的；钟爱的

　　participant *n.* 参加者，参与者；与会代表；参与国；关系者

flow [fləu] *v.* 流动，涌流；川流不息；飘扬　*n.* 流动；流量；涨潮，泛滥

【变】flowed　flowed　flowing　flows

【例】Most solicitors are employed by a private practice，which is a firm of solicitors run by the "partners" of the firm who regulate the **flow** of work to the solicitors.

　　大多数律师受雇于私人事务所，这是由律师组成的公司，由"合作伙伴"共同运营，并且对工作进行**分配**。

【搭】flow away 流逝；流失

【记】float *v.* （使）浮动；（使）漂浮；自由浮动

　　flock *n.* 兽群，鸟群；群众；棉束；大堆，大量

　　flour *n.* 面粉；粉状物

　　flourish *v.* 繁荣，兴旺

词汇听写

1. ＿＿＿＿＿＿　2. ＿＿＿＿＿＿　3. ＿＿＿＿＿＿

句子听写

Sunday ⋯⋯⋯⋯⋯⋯⋯⋯⋯⋯⋯⋯⋯⋯⋯⋯⋯⋯ «

1. The work will involve matters such as conveyancing, personal injury claims, representing clients in court in divorce cases or making wills, as well as offering services to businesses such as advice on contracts and partnerships.

工作涉及的事项有转让、人身伤害索赔、离婚案件中代表客户出庭或立遗嘱；也包括向商业事务提供服务，如对合同和合作伙伴关系的建议等。

conveyance [kən'veiəns] *n.* 运输；运输工具；财产让与

【变】conveyances

【例】The work will involve matters such as **conveyancing**，personal injury claims, representing clients in court in divorce cases or making wills, as well as offering services to businesses such as advice on contracts and partnerships.

工作涉及的事项有**转让**、人身伤害索赔、离婚案件中代表客户出庭或立遗嘱；也包括向商业事务提供服务，如对合同和合作伙伴关系的建议等。

【记】conviction *n.* 定罪；说服；信念

convince *v.* 使相信，说服，使承认；使明白

convention *n.* 公约

convert *v.* 转变

controversy *n.* 争论，辩论

claim [kleim] *v.* 提出要求　*v.* 要求；声称；需要；认领　*n.* 要求；声称；索赔；断言；值得

【变】claimed　claimed　claiming　claims

【例】The work will involve matters such as conveyancing, personal injury **claims**，representing clients in court in divorce cases or making wills, as well as offering services to businesses such as advice on contracts and partnerships.

工作涉及的事项有转让、人身伤害**索赔**、离婚案件中代表客户出庭或立遗嘱；也包括向商业事务提供服务，如对合同和合作伙伴关系的建议等。

【搭】claim a foul 声明对方犯规，要求宣布对方的胜利无效   claim against a company for compensation 要求公司赔偿

【记】clamp v. 夹紧，夹住；堆存；脚步很重地走

clap v. 拍手，鼓掌；振翼，拍翅膀

clarify v. 使清楚，澄清

client [ˈklaiənt] n. [经] 客户；顾客；委托人

【变】clients

【例】The work will involve matters such as conveyancing, personal injury claims, representing **clients** in court in divorce cases or making wills, as well as offering services to businesses such as advice on contracts and partnerships.

工作涉及的事项有转让、人身伤害索赔、离婚案件中代表**客户**出庭或立遗嘱；也包括向商业事务提供服务，如对合同和合作伙伴关系的建议等。

【搭】client applications 客户应用程序   client's interests 客户的利益

【记】cliff n. 悬崖，峭壁

climate n. 气候；水土，风土

climax n. 顶点，极点；高潮

contract [ˈkɔntrækt] v. 收缩；感染；订约；使缩短   n. 合同；婚约

【变】contracts   contracted   contracted   contracting   contracts

【例】The work will involve matters such as conveyancing, personal injury claims, representing clients in court in divorce cases or making wills, as well as offering services to businesses such as advice on **contracts** and partnerships.

工作涉及的事项有转让、人身伤害索赔、离婚案件中代表客户出庭或立遗嘱；也包括向商业事务提供服务，如对**合同**和合作伙伴关系的建议等。

【搭】contract authority 订约授权   contract award date 合同签订日期

【记】contradict *v.* 驳斥；否认；与……抵触

contradiction *n.* 矛盾；否认，反驳

contrast *n.* 对比，对照；差异；对照物，对立面；［摄］反差

词汇听写

1. _____ 2. _____ 3. _____

句子听写

2. Anthropologists have discovered that fear, happiness, sadness, and surprise are universally reflected in facial expressions.

人类学家们已经发现，恐惧、快乐、悲伤和惊奇都会行之于色，这在全人类是共通的。

anthropologist [ˌænθrəˈpɒlədʒist] *n.* 人类学家

【变】Anthropologists

【例】**Anthropologists** have discovered that fear, happiness, sadness, and surprise are universally reflected in facial expressions.

人类学家们已经发现，恐惧、快乐、悲伤和惊奇都会行之于色，这在全人类是共通的。

【记】anthropological *a.* 人类学的

anthropology *n.* 人类学

apologist *n.* 辩解者

universally [ˌjuːniˈvɜːsəli] *ad.* 普遍地；一般地；人人；处处

【例】Anthropologists have discovered that fear, happiness, sadness, and surprise are **universally** reflected in facial expressions.

人类学家们已经发现，恐惧、快乐、悲伤和惊奇都会行之于色，这在全人类是**共通**的。

【搭】universally valid formula 普遍有效公式

【记】universal *a.* 普遍的

university *n.* 综合性大学；大学人员

universe *n.* 宇宙，全人类；［天］银河系，恒星与星辰系

reflect [ri'flekt] *v.* 反射（光、热、声或影像）；考虑；表达；折转

【变】reflected　reflected　reflecting　reflects

【例】Anthropologists have discovered that fear, happiness, sadness, and surprise are universally **reflected** in facial expressions.

　　人类学家们已经发现，恐惧、快乐、悲伤和惊奇都会行之于色，这在全人类是共通的。

【搭】reflect credit on 使……增光　reflect on 仔细想；回忆，影响……的荣誉

【记】reflection *n.* 倒影，影响

　　reflective *a.* 沉思的

　　reflexion *n.* 反射，反射光；反射作用（等于 reflection）

facial ['feiʃl] *a.* 面部的；面部用的；表面的　*n.* 美容；面部按摩

【变】facials

【例】Anthropologists have discovered that fear, happiness, sadness, and surprise are universally reflected in **facial** expressions.

　　人类学家们已经发现，恐惧、快乐、悲伤和惊奇都会行之于色，这在全人类是共通的。

【搭】facial expression 脸色，脸部表情　facial area 正面区

【记】fabricate *v.* 制作，组合；捏造

　　facility *n.* 设备；灵巧

　　facilitate *v.* 促进，助长；使容易；帮助

　　fade *v.* 褪色；衰减

　　faint *a.* 微弱的，不明显的

词汇听写

1. _____ 　2. _____ 　3. _____

句子听写

3. In group to remain in existence, a profit-making organization must, in the long run, produce something consumers consider useful or desirable.

任何营利组织若要生存，最终都必须生产出消费者可用或需要的产品。

---

remain [riˈmein] *n.* 剩余物，残骸；遗迹；遗体　*v.* 留下；保持；留待；依然；终属，归于

【变】remained　remained　remaining　remains

【例】In group to **remain** in existence, a profit-making organization must, in the long run, produce something consumers consider useful or desirable.

任何**营利**组织若要生存，最终都必须生产出消费者可用或需要的产品。

【搭】remain with 属于，归于　remain up 继续处于一个适当位置

【记】remaining *a.* 剩余的，剩下的

remainder *n.* 剩余物；其他人员　*a.* 剩余的；留存下的

remind *v.* 使想起，使记起；提醒

---

existence [igˈzistəns] *n.* 存在，实在；实体，存在物，生物

【变】existences

【例】In group to remain in **existence**, a profit-making organization must, in the long run, produce something consumers consider useful or desirable.

任何营利组织若要**生存**，最终都必须生产出消费者可用或需要的产品。

【搭】existence condition 存在条件，现状　existence domain 存在域

【记】existential *a.* 有关存在的

exit *n.* 出口，通道 *v.* 离开；退出；去世

exist *v.* 存在；生活；继续存在

---

in the long run 从长远来看，终究

【例】In group to remain in existence, a profit-making organization must, **in the long run**, produce something consumers consider useful or desirable.

任何营利组织若要生存，**最终**都必须生产出消费者可用或需要的

产品。

【记】in the end 最终

in the short run 在不久的将来

on the run 忙碌，奔波；奔跑，逃跑

in the soup 在困境中

desirable [diˈzaiərəbl] *a.* 令人满意的；值得拥有的；可取的；性感的

n. 称心如意的人/东西

【变】desirables

【例】In group to remain in existence, a profit-making organization must, in the long run, produce something consumers consider useful or **desirable**.

任何营利组织若要生存，最终都必须生产出消费者可用或**需要**的产品。

【搭】desirable animal nuance 令人愉快的动物香料（指天然动物香料）

desirable criterion 必要标准/判据

【记】desirability *n.* 愿望，希求

desirably *ad.* 愿望地

desire *v.* & *n.* 希望；渴望；要求；请求

词汇听写

1. _____ 2. _____ 3. _____

句子听写

第 5 周

1. The greater the population there is in a locality; the greater the need there is for water, transportation, and disposal of refuse.

　　一个地方的人口越多，其对水、交通和垃圾处理的要求就会越大。

---

population [ˌpɒpjuˈleiʃn] *n.* 人口；全体居民；特定（生物）种群

【变】populations

【例】The greater the **population** there is in a locality; the greater the need there is for water, transportation, and disposal of refuse.

　　　一个地方的**人口**越多，其对水、交通和垃圾处理的要求就会越大。

【搭】population biology 群体生物学　population ecology 种群生态学

【记】populate *v.* 居住于；生活于；落户于

　　popular *a.* 流行的，大众化的；普通的

　　popularity *n.* 流行；名气；大众性

---

locality [ləuˈkæləti] *n.* 位置；地区；产地

【变】localities

【例】The greater the population there is in a **locality**; the greater the need there is for water, transportation, and disposal of refuse.

　　　一个**地方**的人口越多，其对水、交通和垃圾处理的要求就会越大。

【搭】locality disinfection 区域消毒　locality protection 区域保护

【记】local *a.* 地方的；当地的；局部的 *n.* 本地居民（律师、教士、医生）；本地新闻

　　locate *v.* 位于；说出来源；确定……的位置

　　lock *n.* 锁；水闸 *v.* 锁上；锁好，关好；使固定

disposal [di'spəuzl] *n.* （事情的）处置；（自由）处置权；清理；排列
a. 处理（或置放）废品的

【变】disposals

【例】The greater the population there is in a locality；the greater the need there is for water，transportation，and **disposal** of refuse.

一个地方的人口越多，其对水、交通和垃圾**处理**的要求就会越大。

【搭】disposal area 处置区　disposal value 清算价值，清理价值

【记】dispose *v.* 处理，处置；安排

dispute *v.* 辩论，争论；怀疑；争夺

refuse [ri'fjuːz] *n.* 废物，垃圾　*v.* 拒绝，回绝，推却；拒绝给（所需之物）；不愿，不肯

【变】refused　refused　refusing　refuses

【例】The greater the population there is in a locality；the greater the need there is for water，transportation，and disposal of refuse.

一个地方的人口越多，其对水、交通和垃圾处理的要求就会越大。

【搭】refuse an offer 拒绝一个提议　refuse channel 垃圾（输送）道

【记】refuser *n.* 拒绝（抗拒、推辞者）

refute *v.* 驳斥，驳倒；否认真实性

refugee *n.* 避难者，难民

词汇听写

1. _____ 2. _____ 3. _____

句子听写

2. It is more difficult to write simply, directly, and effectively than to employ flowery but vague expressions that only obscure one's meaning.

简明、直接、有力的写作比花哨、含混而意义模糊的表达难度高。

effectively [i'fektivli] *ad.* 有效地；实际上，事实上

【例】It is more difficult to write simply, directly, and **effectively** than to employ

167

flowery but vague expressions that only obscure one's meaning.

　　简明、直接、**有力**的写作比花哨、含混而意义模糊的表达难度高。

【搭】effectively computable function 能行可计算函数

【记】effective *a.* 有效的；起作用的；给人深刻印象的

efficiency *n.* 效率，效能；能力；功效

efficient *a.* 有效率的；能干的

flowery ［ˈflauəri］ *a.* 用花装饰的；（贬）（说话或作品）辞藻华丽的

【例】It is more difficult to write simply, directly, and effectively than to employ **flowery** but vague expressions that only obscure one's meaning.

　　简明、直接、有力的写作比**花哨**、含混而意义模糊的表达难度高。

【搭】flowery odour 花香（味）　　flowery language 漂亮的辞藻　　flowery carpets 花卉地毯

【记】flow *v.* 流；垂；（谈话、文体等）流畅 *n.* 流动；连贯

overflow *v.* 从……中溢出

vague ［veig］ *a.* 模糊的；（思想上）不清楚的；（表达或感知）含糊的；暧昧的　*n.* 模糊不定状态

【变】vaguer　vaguest

【例】It is more difficult to write simply, directly, and effectively than to employ flowery but **vague** expressions that only obscure one's meaning.

　　简明、直接、有力的写作比花哨、**含混**而意义模糊的表达难度高。

【搭】vague mathematics 模糊数学　　vague response 不明确的回复

【记】vaguely *ad.* 含糊地；茫然地；暧昧地

vacant *a.* 空闲的；空虚的；茫然的

vacation *n.* 假期，休假 *v.* 度假

obscure ［əbˈskjuə］ *a.* 昏暗的；晦涩的；不著名的　*v.* 使……模糊不清，隐藏；使难理解　*n.* 某种模糊的或不清楚的东西

【变】obscured　obscured　obscuring　obscures

【例】It is more difficult to write simply, directly, and effectively than to employ flowery but vague expressions that only **obscure** one's meaning.

　　简明、直接、有力的写作比花哨、含混而意义**模糊**的表达难度高。

【搭】obscure the fact/issue 搞混，使难以理解　　obscure poets 不知名的诗人

obscure charges 模糊的指控

【记】obscuration *n.* 昏暗，暗淡，朦胧

observe *v.* 观察；研究；遵守；庆祝

obstacle *n.* 障碍（物）；障碍物

词汇听写

1. _____ 2. _____ 3. _____

句子听写

3. Acids are chemical <u>compounds</u> that, in water <u>solution</u>, have a sharp taste, a <u>corrosive</u> action on metals, and the ability to turn certain blue vegetable dyes red.

　　酸是一种化合物，它在溶于水时具有强烈的气味和对金属的腐蚀性，并且能够使某些蓝色植物染料变红。

---

acid ['æsid] *a.* 酸味的；尖刻的；酸性的　*n.* [化] 酸；酸味物质

【变】acids

【例】**Acids** are chemical compounds that, in water solution, have a sharp taste, a corrosive action on metals, and the ability to turn certain blue vegetable dyes red.

　　　酸是一种化合物，它在溶于水时具有强烈的气味和对金属的腐蚀性，并且能够使某些蓝色植物染料变红。

【搭】acid accelerator 酸性促进剂　acid soil 酸性土壤　acid humour 尖酸的幽默

【记】acidy *a.* 有些酸味的

acre *n.* 英亩；耕地

achieve *v.* 完成，达到

acquaint *v.* (sb. with) 使认识，使了解

---

compound ['kɔmpaund] *n.* 场地；复合物；（筑有围墙的）院子

　　　　　　[kəm'paund] *v.* 调和；使混合；调停　*a.* [语法学]（句子）复合的；合成的；多功能的

【变】compounded　compounded　compounding　compounds

【例】Acids are chemical **compounds** that，in water solution，have a sharp taste, a corrosive action on metals，and the ability to turn certain blue vegetable dyes red.

　　酸是一种化合物，它在溶于水时具有强烈的气味和对金属的腐蚀性，并且能够使某些蓝色植物染料变红。

【搭】compound sentences 复合句　problems get compounded 问题进一步复杂
　　embassy compound 使馆大院

【记】compoundable *a.* 能混合的，能缓解的，能化合的
　　comprehend *v.* 理解，领会；包含
　　compress *v.* 压紧；压缩；精简 *n.* 止血敷布；打包机

solution [sə'lu:ʃn] *n.* 解决；溶解；溶液；答案

【变】solutions

【例】Acids are chemical compounds that，in water **solution**，have a sharp taste, a corrosive action on metals，and the ability to turn certain blue vegetable dyes red.

　　酸是一种化合物，它在**溶**于水时具有强烈的气味和对金属的腐蚀性，并且能够使某些蓝色植物染料变红。

【搭】solution assay 溶液分析　simple, effective solutions 简单有效的解决方法
　　solution to crossword 纵横字谜的答案

【记】solute *n.* 溶解物，溶质
　　solve *v.* 解决；解答；解释；清偿（债务）

corrosive [kə'rəusiv] *a.* 腐蚀性的；侵蚀性的；（对社会、个人情感等）有害的　*n.* 腐蚀性物品

【例】Acids are chemical compounds that，in water solution，have a sharp taste, a **corrosive** action on metals，and the ability to turn certain blue vegetable dyes red.

　　酸是一种化合物，它在溶于水时具有强烈的气味和对金属的**腐蚀**性，并且能够使某些蓝色植物染料变红。

【搭】corrosive agent 腐蚀剂　corrosive atmosphere 腐蚀性空气

【记】corrosively *ad.* 腐蚀地，侵蚀地
　　corrupt *a.* 堕落的，道德败坏的；腐烂的 *v.* 使腐败

correctly *ad.* 正确地，得体地

dye [dai] *n.* 染料，染色；颜色　*v.* 染色；给……染色

【变】dyes　dyed　dyed　dyeing

【例】Acids are chemical compounds that, in water solution, have a sharp taste, a corrosive action on metals, and the ability to turn certain blue vegetable **dyes** red.

酸是一种化合物，它在溶于水时具有强烈的气味和对金属的腐蚀性，并且能够使某些蓝色植物**染料**变红。

【搭】dye absorption 染料渗透试验法（测定陶瓷气孔率）

【记】dyeable *a.* 可染色的

dynamic *a.* 动态的；动力的；充满活力的，精力充沛的；不断变化的 *n.* 动态；动力学；活力

dynamo *n.* 精力充沛的人；[物] 发电机

词汇听写

1. _____　2. _____　3. _____

句子听写

Tuesday ··· ≪≪

1. Essentially, a theory is an <u>abstract</u>, <u>symbolic</u> <u>representation</u> of what is <u>conceived</u> to be reality.

理论在本质上是对认识了的现实的一种抽象和符号化的表达。

---

abstract ['æbstrækt] *a.* 抽象的，理论上的；难解的　*n.* 抽象概念；抽象派艺术作品；摘要；［化］萃取物　*v.* 提取，分离；转移（注意等）；摘录

【变】abstracted　abstracted　abstracting　abstracts

【例】Essentially, a theory is an **abstract**, symbolic representation of what is conceived to be reality.

理论在本质上是对认识了的现实的一种**抽象**和符号化的表达。

【搭】abstract account 摘要账户　　in the abstract 泛泛地；总体地；抽象地
abstract concept 抽象概念　　abstract words 抽象名词　　abstract painting
抽象画

【记】abstractly *ad.* 抽象地，理论上地

absurd *a.* 荒谬的；荒唐的；荒诞的　*n.* 无价值，无意义

abundance *n.* 丰富，充裕；极多；盈余

---

symbolic [sim'bɔlik] *a.* 象征的，象征性的

【例】Essentially, a theory is an abstract, **symbolic** representation of what is conceived to be reality.

理论在本质上是对认识了的现实的一种抽象和**符号化的**表达。

【搭】symbolic address 符号地址　　symbolic colour 象征色（如白色象征光明、纯洁、信念，黑色象征悲哀、邪恶、死亡）

【记】symbolical *a.* 表示象征的，符号的

symmetrical *a.* 对称的，匀称的

symmetry *n.* 对称；对称美；整齐，匀称

---

representation [ˌreprizen'teiʃn] *n.* 表现；陈述；表现……的事物；有代理人

【变】representations

【例】Essentially, a theory is an abstract, symbolic **representation** of what is conceived to be reality.

　　理论在本质上是对认识了的现实的一种抽象和符号化的**表达**。

【搭】representation formula 表示公式　　negative representation letter 负面描述

【记】represent *n.* 受陈述者

　　representative *n.* 代表；继任者 *a.* 典型的；有代表性的

　　reproduce *v.* 复制，再版；生殖

conceive [kənˈsiːv] *v.* 怀孕；构思；想象，设想；持有

【变】conceived　conceived　conceiving　conceives

【例】Essentially, a theory is an abstract, symbolic representation of what is **conceived** to be reality.

　　理论在本质上是对**认识了的**现实的一种抽象和符号化的表达。

【搭】conceive of 想象，设想

【记】conceiving *v.* 想出（conceive 的现在分词）；构想；设想；怀孕

　　concentrate *v.* 专心于；注意；聚集

　　concept *n.* 观念，概念；观点

词汇听写

1. ＿＿＿＿＿＿＿＿　2. ＿＿＿＿＿＿＿＿　3. ＿＿＿＿＿＿＿＿

句子听写

2. Thanks to modern irrigation, crops now grow abundantly in areas where once nothing but cacti and sagebrush could live.

　　受当代灌溉技术之赐，农作物在原来只有仙人掌和荞属科植物才能生存的地方旺盛地生长。

thanks to 幸亏，多亏，由于

【例】**Thanks to** modern irrigation, crops now grow abundantly in areas where once nothing but cacti and sagebrush could live.

　　受当代灌溉技术之赐，农作物在原来只有仙人掌和荞属科植物才能

生存的地方旺盛地生长。

【搭】give thanks to 对……感恩　no thanks to you 并非由于你的帮助　thanks to your help 亏得你们帮忙

【记】due to 因为；由于

owing to 因为；由于（可与 due to 互换）

irrigation [ˌiriˈgeiʃn] *n.* 灌溉；水利；[医] 冲洗

【变】irrigations

【例】Thanks to modern **irrigation**, crops now grow abundantly in areas where once nothing but cacti and sagebrush could live.

受当代**灌溉**技术之赐，农作物在原来只有仙人掌和荞属科植物才能生存的地方旺盛地生长。

【搭】irrigation area 灌溉面积　irrigation ditcher 灌渠挖掘机

【记】irrigate *v.* 灌溉；冲洗（伤口）

irritate *v.* 刺激，使兴奋；使发怒；引起不愉快

irregular *a.* 不规则的，不对称的；不合规范的

abundantly [əˈbʌndəntli] *ad.* 丰富地；大量地；十分清楚；非常明白

【例】Thanks to modern irrigation, crops now grow **abundantly** in areas where once nothing but cacti and sagebrush could live.

受当代灌溉技术之赐，农作物在原来只有仙人掌和荞属科植物才能生存的地方**旺盛**地生长。

【搭】in abundance 丰富　an abundance of 充裕，丰富

【记】abundant *a.* 丰富的，充裕的

abuse *n.* & *v.* 滥用；恶习；侮辱；恶言

nothing but 只有，只不过；无非（相当于 only）

【例】Thanks to modern irrigation, crops now grow abundantly in areas where once **nothing but** cacti and sagebrush could live.

受当代灌溉技术之赐，农作物在原来**只有**仙人掌和荞属科植物才能生存的地方旺盛地生长。

【搭】nothing but misery 只有痛苦　nothing but gas and hot air 只是吹牛和空话　nothing but an impostor 不过是个骗子

【记】all but（＝almost，nearly）表示"几乎，差一点"

anything but（＝not at all，by no means，never）表示"决不，根本不"

none but（＝no one except）表示"只有；除……外谁也不"

词汇听写

1. _____ 2. _____ 3. _____

句子听写

3. The development of <u>mechanical</u> timepieces <u>spurred</u> the search for more <u>accurate</u> sundials with which to <u>regulate</u> them.

　　机械计时器的发展促使人们寻求更精确的日晷，以便校准机械计时器。

mechanical [məˈkænɪkl] *a.* 机械的；呆板的；体力的；手工操作的

【例】The development of **mechanical** timepieces spurred the search for more accurate sundials with which to regulate them.

机械计时器的发展促使人们寻求更精确的日晷，以便校准机械计时器。

【搭】mechanical abrasion 机械性擦伤　mechanical action 机械作用

【记】mechanically *ad.* 机械方面地；机械地；物理上地

mechanic *n.* 技工，机修工

spur [spəː] *n.* 马刺；激励因素；支柱　*v.* 策（马）前进；（尤指用马刺）策（马）加速；鞭策

【变】spurred　spurred　spurring　spurs

【例】The development of mechanical timepieces **spurred** the search for more accurate sundials with which to regulate them.

　　机械计时器的发展**促使**人们寻求更精确的日晷，以便校准机械计时器。

【搭】spur a willing horse *v.* 给予不必要的刺激　spur him into taking part 促使他投身参与

【记】spurred *a.* 装有马刺的 *v.* 策（马）前进（spur 的过去式和过去分词）策马飞奔

spy *n.* 间谍；密探 *v.* 看见；秘密监视

accurate [ˈækjərət] *a.* 精确的，准确的；正确无误的

【变】more accurate　most accurate

【例】The development of mechanical timepieces spurred the search for more **accurate** sundials with which to regulate them.

　　机械计时器的发展促使人们寻求更**精确的**日晷，以便校准机械计时器。

【搭】accurate adjustment 精调　accurate arrival time 准确抵达时间

【记】accurately *ad.* 正确无误地，准确地；精确地

accuse *v.* 指责，谴责；指控

accustomed *a.* 习惯的；通常的

regulate [ˈregjuleit] *v.* 调节，调整；校准；控制，管理

【变】regulated　regulated　regulating　regulates

【例】The development of mechanical timepieces spurred the search for more accurate sundials with which to **regulate** them.

　　机械计时器的发展促使人们寻求更精确的日晷，以便**校准**机械计时器。

【搭】regulate a clock 根据……对钟　regulate capital 约束资本

【记】regulative *a.* 调整的，调节的

regulation *n.* 管理；规章；规则

reign *v.* 当政，统治；占主导地位 *n.* 君主的统治；任期

词汇听写

1. _____　2. _____　3. _____

句子听写

Wednesday ··· ≪≪

1. Anthropology is a <u>science</u> in that anthropologists use a <u>rigorous</u> set of methods and techniques to <u>document</u> <u>observations</u> that can be checked by others.

人类学是一门科学，因为人类学家采用一整套强有力的方法和技术来记录观测结果，这样的观测结果可供他人核查。

---

science [ˈsaiəns] *n.* **科学；技术，知识；学科；理科**

【变】sciences

【例】Anthropology is a **science** in that anthropologists use a rigorous set of methods and techniques to document observations that can be checked by others.

人类学是一门**科学**，因为人类学家采用一整套强有力的方法和技术来记录观测结果，这样的观测结果可供他人核查。

【搭】science abstract 科技文摘，科学文摘　science education 自然科学教育

【记】scientific *a.* 科学的；有系统的

scientist *n.* 科学家；科学工作者

scissors *n.* 剪刀 *v.* 剪开（scissor 的第三人称单数）

---

rigorous [ˈrigərəs] *a.* **严密的；缜密的；严格的；枯燥的**

【例】Anthropology is a science in that anthropologists use a **rigorous** set of methods and techniques to document observations that can be checked by others.

人类学是一门科学，因为人类学家采用一整套**强有力的**方法和技术来记录观测结果，这样的观测结果可供他人核查。

【搭】rigorous error limits 严格误差限　rigorous scholarship 严谨的治学态度

【记】rigorously *ad.* 严厉地，残酷地；严密地

rigorousness *n.* 严厉，残酷

rigid *a.* 严格的；僵硬的；（规则、方法等）死板的

---

document [ˈdɔkjumənt] *n.* [计算机] 文档，证件；公文　*v.* 证明；记录；为……提供证明

【变】documented　documented　documenting　documents

【例】Anthropology is a science in that anthropologists use a rigorous set of methods and techniques to **document** observations that can be checked by others.

人类学是一门科学，因为人类学家采用一整套强有力的方法和技术来**记录**观测结果，这样的观测结果可供他人核查。

【搭】document alignment 文件对齐（定位）　document copying 文件复制

【记】documental *a.* 公文的，文件的

documentary *n.* 纪录片 *a.* 记录的；文书的；纪实的

commentary *n.* 解说词；评注；个人生平传记

observation [ˌɔbzəˈveiʃn] *n.* 观察；观察力；注意；观察报告

【变】observations

【例】Anthropology is a science in that anthropologists use a rigorous set of methods and techniques to document **observations** that can be checked by others.

人类学是一门科学，因为人类学家采用一整套强有力的方法和技术来记录**观测**结果，这样的观测结果可供他人核查。

【搭】observation aeroplane 观测机　observation balloon 观测气球

【记】observational *a.* 观察的，观测的

observationally *ad.* 根据观察地

observe *v.* 观察；研究；遵守；观察；庆祝；评述；当观察员

词汇听写

1. ＿＿＿＿＿＿＿　2. ＿＿＿＿＿＿＿　3. ＿＿＿＿＿＿＿

句子听写

2. Fungi are important in the process of decay, which returns ingredients to the soil, enhances soil fertility, and decomposes animal debris.

真菌在腐化过程中十分重要，而腐化过程将化学物质回馈于土壤，提高其肥力，并分解动物粪便。

decay [diˈkei] *v.* (使）腐烂，腐朽；衰败，衰退，衰落　*n.* 腐败、衰退的状态

【变】decayed　decyed　decaying　decays

【例】Fungi are important in the process of **decay**, which returns ingredients to the soil, enhances soil fertility, and decomposes animal debris.

真菌在**腐化**过程中十分重要，而腐化过程将化学物质回馈于土壤，提高其肥力，并分解动物粪便。

【搭】decay chain 衰变链，放射系　decay chamber 衰变室

【记】deceit *n.* 欺骗，欺诈

deceive *v.* 欺诈；误导

decadal *a.* 十的

decade *n.* 十年，十年间；十个一组；十年期

decadent *a.* 堕落的；颓废派的；衰微的　*n.* 堕落者

ingredient [inˈɡriːdiənt] *n.* （混合物的）组成部分；（烹调的）原料；（构成）要素；因素

【变】ingredients

【例】Fungi are important in the process of decay, which returns **ingredients** to the soil, enhances soil fertility, and decomposes animal debris.

真菌在腐化过程中十分重要，而腐化过程将化学**物质**回馈于土壤，提高其肥力，并分解动物粪便。

【记】inhabit *v.* 居住；在……出现；填满 *v.* 居住

adient *a.* 趋近的

enhance [inˈhɑːns] *v.* 提高，增加；加强

【变】enhanced　enhanced　enhancing　enhances

【例】Fungi are important in the process of decay, which returns ingredients to the soil, **enhances** soil fertility, and decomposes animal debris.

真菌在腐化过程中十分重要，而腐化过程将化学物质回馈于土壤，提**高**其肥力，并分解动物粪便。

【记】enhancement *n.* 增强；增加；提高；改善

enhancer *n.* 增加者；加强者；提高者；增强子

enable *v.* 使能够；使可能；授予权利或方法

decomposes [di:kəm'pəuziz] *v.* 腐烂（decompose 的第三人称单数）；（使）分解；（化）分解（某物质、光线等）

【变】decomposed decomposed decomposing decomposes

【例】Fungi are important in the process of decay，which returns ingredients to the soil，enhances soil fertility，and **decomposes** animal debris.

真菌在腐化过程中十分重要，而腐化过程将化学物质回馈于土壤，提高其肥力，并**分解**动物粪便。

【记】decomposable *a.* 可分解的

decomposition *n.* 分解；腐烂

decorate *v.* 装饰；点缀；粉刷；布置

词汇听写

1. _____ 2. _____ 3. _____

句子听写

3. Eliminating problems by transferring the blame to others is often called scape-goating.

用怪罪别人的办法来解决问题通常被称为寻找替罪羊。

eliminate [i'limineit] *v.* 排除，消除；淘汰；除掉

【变】eliminated eliminated eliminating eliminates

【例】**Eliminating** problems by transferring the blame to others is often called scape-goating.

用怪罪别人的办法来**解决**问题通常被称为寻找替罪羊。

【搭】eliminate illiteracy 扫盲 eliminate the negative〈美俚〉消除自卑感

【记】eliminable *a.* 可消除的，可消去的，可排除的

elimination *n.* 排除；除去；根除；淘汰

elliptical *a.* 椭圆的；像椭圆形的；省略的

transfer [trænsˈfəː] *v.* （使）转移；使调动；转让（权利等）；让与　*n.* 转移；调动；换乘；（运动员）转会

【变】transferred　transferred　transferring　transfers

【例】Eliminating problems by **transferring** the blame to others is often called scape-goating.

　　用怪罪别人的办法来解决问题通常被称为寻找替罪羊。

【搭】transfer address 转移地址　transfer account 转账账户

【记】transferee *n.* （财产、权利等）受让人，被调任者

　　transform *v.* 改变；改观；变换 *n.* ［数］变换式

　　transistor *n.* 晶体管；晶体管收音机，半导体收音机

blame [bleim] *v.* 指责，责怪；归咎于　*n.* 责备；责任；过失

【变】blamed　blamed　blaming　blames

【例】Eliminating problems by transferring the **blame** to others is often called scape-goating.

　　用怪罪别人的办法来解决问题通常被称为寻找替罪羊。

【搭】be blame of 该受责备的

【记】blameable *a.* 可责备的，有过失的

　　blameful *a.* 该受责备的，有过错的

　　blank *a.* 空白的；无信息的；茫然的 *n.* 填空处，空白表格

scape-goat [ˈskeip-gəutiŋ] *v.* 使成为替罪羊

【变】scapegoats　scapegoated　scapegoated　scape-goating　scapegoats

【例】Eliminating problems by transferring the blame to others is often called **scape-goating.**

　　用怪罪别人的办法来解决问题通常被称为**寻找替罪羊。**

【搭】avoid favouritism and scapegoating 杜绝偏袒和乱扣帽子　be made a scapegoat 成了替罪羊

【记】whipping boy *n.* 代人受罪者，代罪羔羊

词汇听写

1. _____　2. _____　3. _____

句子听写

Thursday ·· ◄◄

1. Most substances contract when they freeze so that the density of a substance's solid is higher than the density of its liquid.

　　大多数物质遇冷收缩，所以它们的密度在固态时高于液态。

---

substance [ˈsʌbstəns] *n.* **物质，材料；实质，内容；（织品的）质地**

【变】substances

【例】Most **substances** contract when they freeze so that the density of a substance's solid is higher than the density of its liquid.

　　　　大多数**物质**遇冷收缩，所以它们的密度在固态时高于液态。

【搭】substance of value 价值实体

【记】substantial *a.* 大量的；结实的；重大的 *n.* 本质；重要材料

　　　substitute *v.* 代替，替换，代用 *n.* 代替者；替补（运动员）；替代物

　　　subtle *a.* 微妙的；敏感的；狡猾的；巧妙的

---

contract [ˈkɒntrækt] *v.* **染上（恶习、疾病等）；缩小，紧缩；订契约，承包**
　　　　　　[ˈkɒntrækt] *n.* **契约；婚约；[法] 契约法；行贿**

【变】contracted　contracted　contracting　contracts

【例】Most substances **contract** when they freeze so that the density of a substance's solid is higher than the density of its liquid.

　　　　大多数物质遇冷**收缩**，所以它们的密度在固态时高于液态。

【搭】contract authority 订约授权　　a contracting market 萎缩的市场

【记】contractive *a.* 收缩的，有收缩性的

　　　contradict *v.* 反驳；否认；与……抵触

　　　contrary *a.* 相反的；违反的 *n.* 对立或相反的事物；对立方

---

freeze [friːz] *v.* **（使）结冰，使冻僵；冷藏；吓呆；冻结（存款等）** *n.* **冻结；严寒时期**

【变】froze　frozen　freezing　freezes

【例】Most substances contract when they **freeze** so that the density of a substance's solid is higher than the density of its liquid.

大多数物质**遇冷**收缩，所以它们的密度在固态时高于液态。

【搭】water freezes 水冻结成冰　freeze drier 冷冻干燥机

【记】frozen *a.* 冻结的，（资产等被）冻结的；冷漠的

freight *n.* 货运，货物；运费 *v.* 运输；装货于

frequency *n.* 频繁性

density ['densəti] *n.* 密度；稠密，浓厚；［物］浓度，比重；愚钝

【变】densities

【例】Most substances contract when they freeze so that the **density** of a substance's solid is higher than the density of its liquid.

大多数物质遇冷收缩，所以它们的**密度**在固态时高于液态。

【搭】density airspeed 密度空速　density class 密度级

【记】dense *a.* 密集的，稠密的；浓厚的；愚钝的

dentist *n.* 牙科医生

deny *v.* 拒绝；拒绝承认

词汇听写

1. _____　2. _____　3. _____

句子听写

2. Although apparently rigid, bones exhibit a degree of elasticity that enables the skeleton to withstand considerable impact.

骨头看起来是脆硬的，但它也有一定的弹性，使得骨骼能够承受相当大的打击。

rigid ['ridʒid] *a.* 严格的；僵硬的；（规则、方法等）死板的；刚硬的，顽固的

【变】more rigid　most rigid

【例】Although apparently **rigid**, bones exhibit a degree of elasticity that enables the skeleton to withstand considerable impact.

骨头看起来是**脆硬的**，但它也有一定的弹性，使得骨骼能够承受相当大的打击。

【搭】rigid airship 硬式飞艇   rigid body 刚体，刚性体

【记】rigidify v. 使……僵化；使……固定

rigorous a. 严密的；缜密的；严格的；枯燥的

rim n.（圆形器皿的）边，缘，框 v. 环绕（圆形或环形物的）边缘；镶边

---

exhibit [ig'zibit] v. 陈列，展览；呈现；证明；［法］提交证据 n. 展览，陈列；展览品；公开展示；［法］证据

【变】exhibited   exhibited   exhibiting   exhibits

【例】Although apparently rigid, bones **exhibit** a degree of elasticity that enables the skeleton to withstand considerable impact.

骨头看起来是脆硬的，但它也有一定的弹性，使得骨骼能够承受相当大的打击。

【搭】on exhibit 展出中

【记】exhibition n. 展览会

exhibitor n. 参展者

exile v. & n. 放逐，流放；背井离乡

---

elasticity [ˌiːlæ'stisəti] n. 弹性；弹力；灵活性；伸缩性

【变】elasticities

【例】Although apparently rigid, bones exhibit a degree of **elasticity** that enables the skeleton to withstand considerable impact.

骨头看起来是脆硬的，但它也有一定的**弹性**，使得骨骼能够承受相当大的打击。

【搭】elasticity approach 弹性分析法   elasticity correction 空气密度修正量

【记】elastic a. 有弹力的；可伸缩的；灵活的 n. 松紧带，橡皮圈

bounce v. 弹跳；使弹起；（使）上下晃动 n. 弹跳；弹性；活力

---

withstand [wið'stænd] v. 经受，承受，禁得起；反抗

【变】withstood   withstood   withstanding   withstands

【例】Although apparently rigid, bones exhibit a degree of elasticity that enables

---

dynamic [dai'næmik] *a.* 动态的；充满活力的；不断变化的 *n.* 动态；动力学；活力

【变】dynamics

【例】Research into the **dynamics** of storms is directed toward improving the ability to predict these events and thus to minimize damage and avoid loss of life.

对风暴**动力学**的研究是为了提高风暴预测，从而减少损失，避免人员伤亡。

【搭】dynamic accent 力重音，动力重音　dynamic address translation 动态地址变换

【记】dynamical *a.* 动力（学）的，有力量的

dynamo *n.* 精力充沛的人；[物] 发电机

dye *n.* 染料，染色；颜色 *v.* 染色；给……染色

---

predict [pri'dikt] *v.* 预言，预测；预示，预告

【变】predicted　predicted　predicting　predicts

【例】Research into the dynamics of storms is directed toward improving the ability to **predict** these events and thus to minimize damage and avoid loss of life.

对风暴动力学的研究是为了提高风暴**预测**，从而减少损失，避免人员伤亡。

【记】predictor *n.* 预言者，预报器

prediction *n.* 预报；预言；预言的事物

predominant *a.* 主要的，占主导地位的；卓越的；有影响的

---

minimize ['minimaiz] *v.* 把……减至最低数量（程度）；对（某事物）作最低估计，极力贬低（某事物）的价值（重要性）；极度轻视

【变】minimized　minimized　minimizing　minimizes

【例】Research into the dynamics of storms is directed toward improving the ability to predict these events and thus to **minimize** damage and avoid loss of life.

对风暴动力学的研究是为了提高风暴预测，从而**减少**损失，避免人员伤亡。

【搭】minimize button 最小化按钮　minimize the risk of infection 最大限度减小感染的危险

【记】minimization *n.* 最小限度，轻视；极小化

minimizer *n.* 把事情估计得最低的人

minimum *n.* 最低消费；［数］极小值 *a.* 最低的；最小的；最少的

avoid [əˈvɔid] *v.* 避开，避免，预防；［法］使无效，撤销，废止

【变】avoided　avoided　avoiding　avoids

【例】Research into the dynamics of storms is directed toward improving the ability to predict these events and thus to minimize damage and **avoid** loss of life.

　　对风暴动力学的研究是为了提高风暴预测，从而减少损失，**避免**人员伤亡。

【搭】avoid ambiguity 避免歧义　avoid a strike 避免罢工

【记】avoidable *a.* 能避免的，可回避的；可作为无效的

avoidance *n.* 逃避；职位空缺；废止；无效

award *v.* 授予，奖给，判给；判归，判定 *n.* 奖品

词汇听写

1. ＿＿＿＿＿＿＿＿　2. ＿＿＿＿＿＿＿＿　3. ＿＿＿＿＿＿＿＿

句子听写

【例】Before staring on a sea voyage, **prudent** navigators learn the sea charts, study the sailing directions, and memorize lighthouse locations to prepare themselves for any conditions they might encounter.

　　谨慎的航海员在出航前，会研究航向，记录灯塔的位置，以便对各种可能出现的情况做到有备无患。

【搭】prudent investment 明智投资，审慎投资

【记】prudence *n.* 谨慎；节俭；精明

prudently *ad.* 智虑地；谨慎地；精明地

imprudent *a.* 不明智的，不谨慎的

chart [tʃɑːt] *n.* 图表；航海图；排行榜　*v.* 绘制地图；记录；记述；跟踪（进展或发展）

【变】charted　charted　charting　charts

【例】Before staring on a sea voyage, prudent navigators learn the sea **charts**, study the sailing directions, and memorize lighthouse locations to prepare themselves for any conditions they might encounter.

　　谨慎的航海员在出航前，会研究**航向**，记录灯塔的位置，以便对各种可能出现的情况做到有备无患。

【搭】chart board 图板　chart desk 海图桌；图板

【记】charting *v.* 制图，图表研究，图示行为法；填图

character *n.* 性格，特征；品行；字母，符号；人物 *v.* 刻，印；使具有特征

charge *v.* 装载；控诉；使充电；索（价）*n.* 费用；指示；掌管；指责

memorize [ˈmeməraiz] *v.* 记住，熟记；[计算机科学] 存储，记忆

【变】memorized　memorized　memorizing　memorizes

【例】Before staring on a sea voyage, prudent navigators learn the sea charts, study the sailing directions, and **memorize** lighthouse locations to prepare themselves for any conditions they might encounter.

　　谨慎的航海员在出航前，会研究航向，**记录**灯塔的位置，以便对各种可能出现的情况做到有备无患。

【记】memorable *a.* 值得纪念的；显著的；重大的，著名的

memorization *n.* 记住，默记；识记

menace *n.* & *v.* 威胁；恐吓

encounter [in'kauntə] *v.* 不期而遇；遭遇；对抗　　*n.* 相遇，碰见；遭遇战；对决，冲突

【变】encountered　encountered　encountering　encounters

【例】Before staring on a sea voyage, prudent navigators learn the sea charts, study the sailing directions, and memorize lighthouse locations to prepare themselves for any conditions they might **encounter**.

　　谨慎的航海员在出航前，会研究航向，记录灯塔的位置，以便对各种可能**出现**的情况做到有备无患。

【搭】encountering *v.* 遇到（encounter 的现在分词）；遭遇；偶然碰到；与（人、部队）冲突

【记】encourage *v.* 鼓励，鼓舞；支持；促进；鼓动

　　enchant *v.* 使心醉，使迷惑；用魔法迷惑

词汇听写

1. _____　2. _____　3. _____

句子听写

3. The human skeleton consists of more than two hundred bones bound together by tough and relatively inelastic connective tissues called ligaments.

　　人类骨骼由两百多块骨头组成，这些骨头是由坚韧而相对缺乏弹性的，被称为韧带的结缔组织连在一起。

skeleton ['skelitn] *n.* （建筑物等的）骨架；梗概　　*a.* 骨骼的；骨瘦如柴的；概略的；基本的

【变】skeletons

【例】The human **skeleton** consists of more than two hundred bones bound together by tough and relatively inelastic connective tissues called ligaments.

　　人类**骨骼**由两百多块骨头组成，这些骨头是由坚韧而相对缺乏弹性

Saturday ·· ≪

1. Scientists do not know why <u>dinosaurs</u> became <u>extinct</u>, but some theories <u>postulate</u> that changes in geography, climate, and sea levels were <u>responsible</u>.

科学家不知道恐龙为何绝种了，但是一些理论推断是地理、气候和海平面的变化造成的。

dinosaur [ˈdainəsɔ:] *n.* [生] 恐龙；守旧落伍的人，过时落后的东西

【变】dinosaurs

【例】Scientists do not know why **dinosaurs** became extinct，but some theories postulate that changes in geography, climate, and sea levels were responsible.

科学家不知道**恐龙**为何绝种了，但是一些理论推断是地理、气候和海平面的变化造成的。

【记】dinosaurian *a.* 恐龙的，似恐龙的 *n.* 恐龙

diploma *n.* 毕业文凭；学位证书；公文；奖状 *v.* 发毕业文凭

diplomatic *a.* 外交上的；外交人员的；策略的

extinct [ikˈstiŋkt] *a.* 灭绝的；绝种的；消逝的；破灭的

【例】Scientists do not know why dinosaurs became **extinct**，but some theories postulate that changes in geography, climate, and sea levels were responsible.

科学家不知道恐龙为何**绝种**了，但是一些理论推断是地理、气候和海平面的变化造成的。

【搭】extinct books 绝版书　extinct language 死语，消亡语

【记】extincting *v.* 灭绝

extinguish *v.* 熄灭（火）；使（希望、爱情等）不复存在；偿清

extraction *n.* 取出，抽出；血统，家世，出身；[化] 提取（法），萃取（法），提出物，精炼

postulate [ˈpɔstjuleit] *v.* 假定；提出要求；视……为理所当然　*n.* 假定；先决条件；基本原理

【变】postulated　postulated　postulating　postulates

【例】Scientists do not know why dinosaurs became extinct，but some theories

postulate that changes in geography, climate, and sea levels were responsible.

科学家不知道恐龙为何绝种了，但是一些理论**推断**是地理、气候和海平面的变化造成的。

【搭】challeage the postulate 质疑这种假设　postulate of induction 归纳法公设

【记】postulation *n.* 假定；公设

potential *a.* 潜在的，有可能的；有能力的 *n.* 潜力，潜能

responsible [ri'spɒnsəbl] *a.* **尽责的；承担责任；负有责任的；懂道理的**

【变】more responsible　most responsible

【例】Scientists do not know why dinosaurs became extinct, but some theories postulate that changes in geography, climate, and sea levels were **responsible**.

科学家不知道恐龙为何绝种了，但是一些理论推断是地理、气候和海平面的变化**造成的**。

【搭】responsible administration 责任局（部门）　responsible editor 责任编辑者

【记】responsibleness *n.* 负责

responsibility *n.* 责任；职责；责任感，责任心；负责任

response *n.* 反应；回答，答复

词汇听写

1. _____　2. _____　3. _____

句子听写

2. When Henry Ford first <u>sought</u> financial <u>backing</u> for making cars, the very <u>notion</u> of farmers and clerks owning automobiles was considered <u>ridiculous</u>.

当亨利・福特最初制造汽车为寻求资金支持时，农民和一般职员也能拥有汽车的想法被认为是可笑的。

seek [siːk] *v.* **寻找，探寻；追求，谋求；往或朝……而去**

【变】sought　sought　seeking　seeks

been going on so long in the United States as to constitute a tradition.

根据**默默无闻**的小说制作优秀影片在美国由来已久，已经成为传统。

【记】obscuration *n.* 昏暗，暗淡，朦胧

observation *n.* 观察；观察力；注意；观察报告

observe *v.* 观察；研究

constitute [ˈkɒnstitjuːt] *v.* 构成，组成；制定，设立；等同于；指派

【变】constituted   constituted   constituting   constitutes

【例】The practice of making excellent films based on rather obscure novels has been going on so long in the United States as to **constitute** a tradition.

根据默默无闻的小说制作优秀影片在美国由来已久，已经**成为**传统。

【记】constitution *n.* 建立，组成；构成方式；宪法

constraint *n.* 强制；限制；约束

construct *v.* 修建，建造；构成；创立；[数]作图 *n.* 结构（物）；构想；概念

tradition [trəˈdiʃn] *n.* 传统；惯例

【变】traditions

【例】The practice of making excellent films based on rather obscure novels has been going on so long in the United States as to constitute a **tradition.**

根据默默无闻的小说制作优秀影片在美国由来已久，已经成为**传统**。

【搭】by tradition 根据传统习俗   break tradition 打破传统

【记】traditionary *a.* 世袭的，传统的，惯例的

traditionalism *n.* 传统主义（尤指宗教、道德、习俗等方面）

traditional *a.* 传统的；口传的；惯例的；因袭的

词汇听写

1. _____   2. _____   3. _____

句子听写

Sunday ·· ⋘

1. His students in <u>advanced</u> composition found him terrifyingly <u>frigid</u> in the classroom but <u>sympathetic</u> and understanding in their personal conferences.

　　他的高级作文课上的学生觉得他在课上古板得可怕，但私下交流却富有同情心和善解人意。

> **advance** [əd'vɑːns] *v.* （使）前进；将……提前；预付；提出；（数量等）增加；向前推（至下一步）；上涨　*n.* 增长；借款；（价格、价值的）上涨；预付款　*a.* 预先的；先行的

【变】advanced　advanced　advancing　advances

【例】His students in **advanced** composition found him terrifyingly frigid in the classroom but sympathetic and understanding in their personal conferences.

　　他的**高级**作文课上的学生觉得他在课上古板得可怕，但私下交流却富有同情心和善解人意。

【搭】advance account 预支款　advance allocation 预付拨款

【记】advancer *n.* 前进者；进相机

　　advantage *n.* 有利条件；益处；优越（性）；处于支配地位 *v.* 有利于；有益于；促进；使处于有利地位

> **frigid** ['fridʒid] *a.* 寒冷的；极冷的；冷漠的　*ad.* 寒冷地，冷漠地　*n.* 寒冷，冷漠

【例】His students in advanced composition found him terrifyingly **frigid** in the classroom but sympathetic and understanding in their personal conferences.

　　他的高级作文课上的学生觉得他在课上**古板**得可怕，但私下交流却富有同情心和善解人意。

【搭】frigid manners 冷淡的态度　frigid zone 寒带

【记】frigidity *n.* 寒冷；冷淡；索然无味

　　frigidly *ad.* 寒冷地；冷漠地；冷淡地；呆板地

　　fringe *n.* 穗；边缘；刘海 *v.* 作为……的边缘，围绕着

各样的材料制成，比如蜡和玻璃；其制作如此精巧，**几乎**可以以假乱真。

【搭】scarcely any 几乎没有　scarcely ever 几乎从不

【记】scarce *a.* 缺乏的，罕见的 *ad.* 勉强；仅仅；几乎不；简直不

scarcity *n.* 不足，缺乏；稀少；萧条

scare *v.* 使惊恐，惊吓；使害怕，使恐惧；把……吓跑 *n.* 惊恐，惊吓；恐惧；恐慌

---

distinguish [diˈstiŋgwiʃ] *v.* 区分，辨别，分清；辨别出，识别；引人注目，有别于；使杰出，使著名

【变】distinguished　distinguished　distinguishing　distinguishes

【例】Artificial flowers are used for scientific as well as for decorative purposes. They are made from a variety of materials, such as wax and glass, so skillfully that they can scarcely be **distinguished** from natural flowers.

　　人造花卉既可用于科学目的，也可用于装饰目的，它们可以用各种各样的材料制成，比如蜡和玻璃；其制作如此精巧，几乎可以以假乱真。

【搭】distinguish between 辨别，识别（两者）之间的不同；辨明　distinguish from 辨别；显示出特性；将……与……区别开

【记】distinguishable *a.* 可区别的，可辨别的；可分辨

distinction *n.* 区别；荣誉；特质；卓越

distinct *a.* 清楚的；卓越的，不寻常的；有区别的；确切的

词汇听写

1. _____　2. _____　3. _____

句子听写

3. The United States Constitution requires that President be a natural-born citizen, thirty-five years of age or older, who has lived in the United States for a minimum of fourteen years.

　　美国宪法要求总统是生于美国本土的公民，三十五岁以上，并且在美国居住了至少十四年。

constitution [ˌkɔnstiˈtjuːʃən] n. 建立，组成；体格；构成方式；宪法

【变】constitutions

【例】The United States **Constitution** requires that President be a natural-born citizen，thirty-five years of age or older，who has lived in the United States for a minimum of fourteen years.

美国**宪法**要求总统是生于美国本土的公民，三十五岁以上，并且在美国居住了至少十四年。

【搭】constitution day 行宪纪念日　according to the constitutiong 根据宪法

【记】constitute v. 构成，组成；制定，设立；等同于；指派

constant a. 持续的；始终如一的；忠实的 n. ［数］常数，常量；不变的事物；永恒值

president [ˈprezidənt] n. 校长；总统；总裁；董事长

【变】presidents

【例】The United States Constitution requires that **President** be a natural-born citizen，thirty-five years of age or older，who has lived in the United States for a minimum of fourteen years.

美国宪法要求**总统**是生于美国本土的公民，三十五岁以上，并且在美国居住了至少十四年。

【搭】president of a society 会长　president of raiway 铁路总经理

【记】presidential a. 总统（总裁、议长、董事长、校长等）（职务）的；统辖的，指挥的；总统制的

presidentship（英）总统（议长、会长、社长、总裁、校长等）职位（任期）

preside v. 主持，指挥；担任会议主席

natural-born [ˈnætʃərəl bɔːn] a. 生就的，生来的

【例】The United States Constitution requires that President be a **natural-born** citizen，thirty-five years of age or older，who has lived in the United States for a minimum of fourteen years.

美国宪法要求总统是生于美国**本土**的公民，三十五岁以上，并且在美国居住了至少十四年。

对多数年轻人来说，校园刚开始的日子并不是什么愉快的经历。

【搭】mention of 提及

【记】mentionable *a.* 可以提起的，值得一提的

mental *a.* 内心的，精神的，思想的，心理的；智慧的，智力的 *n.* 精神病患者

pleasant [ˈpleznt] *a.* 可爱的；令人愉快的；有趣的；晴朗的

【变】more pleasant　most pleasant

【例】Nowadays, many students always go into raptures at the mere mention of the coming life of high school or college they will begin. Unfortunately, for most young people, it is not **pleasant** experience on their first day on campus.

当前，一提到即将开始的学校生活，许多学生都会兴高采烈。然而，对多数年轻人来说，校园刚开始的日子并不是什么**愉快的**经历。

【搭】pleasant memory 愉快的记忆

【记】pleasantly *ad.* 愉快地；快活地；和气地；和蔼地

pleasantness *n.* 愉快

pleasure *n.* 愉快；娱乐；希望；令人高兴的事 *v.* 使高兴；使满意

on campus 在校内

【例】Nowadays, many students always go into raptures at the mere mention of the coming life of high school or college they will begin. Unfortunately, for most young people, it is not pleasant experience on their first day **on campus.**

当前，一提到即将开始的学校生活，许多学生都会兴高采烈。然而，对多数年轻人来说，**校园**刚开始的日子并不是什么愉快的经历。

词汇听写

1. _____　2. _____　3. _____

句子听写

2. According to a recent survey, four-million people die each year from diseases linked to smoking. In view of the seriousness of this problem, effective measures should be taken before things get worse.

　　根据最近的一项调查，每年有 4,000,000 人死于与吸烟相关的疾病。考虑到问题的严重性，在事态进一步恶化之前，必须采取有效的措施。

survey [ˈsəːvei] *v.* 调查；勘测；俯瞰　*n.* 调查（表），调查所，测量

【变】surveyed　surveyed　surveying　surveys

【例】According to a recent **survey**, four-million people die each year from diseases linked to smoking. In view of the seriousness of this problem, effective measures should be taken before things get worse.

　　根据最近的一项**调查**，每年有 4,000,000 人死于与吸烟相关的疾病。考虑到问题的严重性，在事态进一步恶化之前，必须采取有效的措施。

【搭】survey agent 检验代理人　survey clause 检验条款

【记】survival *n.* 幸存，生存；幸存者；遗物；遗风

　　survive *v.* 幸存，活下来 *v.* 比……活得长，经历……之后还存在；幸存；艰难度过

link [liŋk] *n.* 环，节；[计算机] 链接；关联，关系　*v.* 连接；挽住，勾住；用环连接；联系在一起

【变】linked　linked　linking　links

【例】According to a recent survey, four-million people die each year from diseases **linked** to smoking. In view of the seriousness of this problem, effective measures should be taken before things get worse.

　　根据最近的一项调查，每年有 4,000,000 人死于与吸烟**相关**的疾病。考虑到问题的严重性，在事态进一步恶化之前，必须采取有效的措施。

【搭】link address 链接地址　only link 唯一的纽带

【记】linkage *n.* 关联原则　line *n.* 排；线路；线条；方法 *v.* 排队；用线标出

in view of 由于，鉴于；基于

【例】According to a recent survey, four-million people die each year from diseases linked to smoking. **In view of** the seriousness of this problem, effective measures should be taken before things get worse.

resident [ˈrezidənt] *a.* 定居的，常驻的；[计] 常驻的，常存于内存中的；[动] 不迁徙的（鸟兽等）；固有的，内在的　*n.* 居民；（旅馆的）住宿者；住院医师

【变】residents

【例】An increasing number of experts believe that migrants will exert positive effects on construction of city. However, this opinion is now being questioned by more and more city **residents.**

越来越多的专家相信移民对城市的建设起到积极作用。然而，越来越多的城市**居民**却怀疑这种说法。

【搭】resident auditor 常驻审计员　local resident 当地居民

【记】residentship *n.* 居住

residual *a.* 残余的；残留的 *n.* 剩余；残渣

reside *v.* 住，居住，（官吏）留驻；（性质）存在，具备

词汇听写

1. ＿＿＿＿＿＿＿　2. ＿＿＿＿＿＿＿　3. ＿＿＿＿＿＿＿

句子听写

Tuesday ·· ≪

1. There is no <u>denying</u> the fact that air pollution is an extremely serious problem: the city <u>authorities</u> should take strong measures to <u>deal with</u> it. Any government which <u>is blind to</u> this point may pay a heavy price.

　　无可否认，空气污染是一个极其严重的问题，城市当局应该采取有力措施来解决它。任何政府忽视这一点都将付出巨大的代价。

---

deny [di'nai] *v.* 拒绝；拒绝承认；拒绝……占有；否认知情

【变】denied　denied　denying　denies

【例】There is no **denying** the fact that air pollution is an extremely serious problem: the city authorities should take strong measures to deal with it. Any government which is blind to this point may pay a heavy price.

　　　无可**否认**，空气污染是一个极其严重的问题，城市当局应该采取有力措施来解决它。任何政府忽视这一点都将付出巨大的代价。

【搭】deny oneself to 不会见；谢绝　deny other's impeachment 拒绝他人的责难（非议）

【记】denial *n.* 否认，否定；克制；拒绝，拒绝接受　denote *v.* 表示，指示

---

authority [ɔː'θɔrəti] *n.* 权威；权力；学术权威；[复数] 当权者

【变】authorities

【例】There is no denying the fact that air pollution is an extremely serious problem: the city **authorities** should take strong measures to deal with it. Any government which is blind to this point may pay a heavy price.

　　　无可否认，空气污染是一个极其严重的问题，城市**当局**应该采取有力措施来解决它。任何政府忽视这一点都将付出巨大的代价。

【搭】authority figure 权威人物　authority for payment 付款权

【记】author *n.* 著作家；作者；创造者；发起人 *v.* 创作出版

---

deal with 惠顾；与……交易；应付；对待

【例】There is no denying the fact that air pollution is an extremely serious problem: the city authorities should take strong measures to **deal with** it.

211

3. Once your return is received and inspected, we will send you an email to notify you that we have received your returned item. We will also notify you of the approval or rejection of your refund.

一旦收到你的回复并对其检查后，我们将向您发送一封电子邮件，通知您，我们已经收到你返回的物品。我们也将通知你关于你方退款的同意或拒绝意见。

inspect [in'spekt] *v.* 检查，检验；视察；进行检查；进行视察

【变】inspected inspected inspecting inspects

【例】Once your return is received and **inspected**，we will send you an email to notify you that we have received your returned item. We will also notify you of the approval or rejection of your refund.

一旦收到你的回复并对其**检查**后，我们将向您发送一封电子邮件，通知您，我们已经收到你返回的物品。我们也将通知你关于你方退款的同意或拒绝意见。

【搭】inspect sth. for cracks/faults 检查某物有无裂缝/缺陷

【记】inspection *n.* 检查，inspector *n.* 检察员，督察员

notify ['nəutifai] *v.* 通知；布告

【变】notified notified notifying notifies

【例】Once your return is received and inspected，we will send you an email to **notify** you that we have received your returned item. We will also notify you of the approval or rejection of your refund.

一旦收到你的回复并对其检查后，我们将向您发送一封电子邮件，**通知**您，我们已经收到你返回的物品。我们也将通知你关于你方退款的同意或拒绝意见。

【搭】notify sb. of 通知某人

【记】notification *n.* 通知，告知   notice *n. & v.* 注意，通知

rejection [ri'dʒekʃn] *n.* 拒绝；摒弃；剔除物；（医）排斥

【变】rejections

【例】Once your return is received and inspected，we will send you an email to notify you that we have received your returned item. We will also notify you of the approval or **rejection** of your refund.

一旦收到你的回复并对其检查后，我们将向您发送一封电子邮件，通知您，我们已经收到你返回的物品。我们也将通知你关于你方退款的同意或**拒绝**意见。

【记】reject *v.* 提议，建议，不雇佣，摒弃，（因质量不好而）废弃

refund [ˈriːfʌnd] *n.* 资金偿还；偿还数额　*v.* 退还；归还或偿还

【变】refunded　refunded　refunding　refunds

【例】Once your return is received and inspected，we will send you an email to notify you that we have received your returned item. We will also notify you of the approval or rejection of your **refund.**

一旦收到你的回复并对其检查后，我们将向您发送一封电子邮件，通知您，我们已经收到你返回的物品。我们也将通知你关于你方**退款**的同意或拒绝意见。

【搭】refund of fare 退还票款　refund order 退款单

【记】refundable *a.* 可归还的，可退还的

词汇听写

1. _____　2. _____　3. _____

句子听写

【例】By living on campus or participating in intramural sports, a trivia bowl, dances, and other social activitie, you can make friends from all over the globe. You can also attend college **prep** workshops.

通过校园生活或参与校内体育活动，玩小板球，跳舞或其他社交活动，你都可以与来自世界各地的人交朋友。你也可以参加大学里的**预科**研习班。

【记】prepare *v.* 准备

preposition *n.* 介词

workshop ['wəːkʃɒp] *n.* **车间；专题讨论会，研究会；创作室；实习班，实验班**

【变】workshops

【例】By living on campus or participating in intramural sports, a trivia bowl, dances, and other social activitie, you can make friends from all over the globe. You can also attend college prep **workshops.**

通过校园生活或参与校内体育活动，玩小板球，跳舞或其他社交活动，你都可以与来自世界各地的人交朋友。你也可以参加大学里的预科**研习班**。

【记】workshop appliance 车间设备

词汇听写

1. _____ 2. _____ 3. _____

句子听写

2. On-campus residential buildings have various configurations. All buildings are coed. Most buildings have suites, typically featuring a common room, two to four bedrooms, and a shared bathroom.

校园宿舍有各种配置。所有的宿舍楼都是男女共用。大多数建筑物有套房，通常具有一个公共休息室，两到四个卧室，一个公共浴室。

residential [ˌrezi'denʃl] *a.* **住宅的，适于作住宅的；与居住有关的；适宜作住宅的**

【例】On-campus **residential** buildings have various configurations. All buildings

217

are coed. Most buildings have suites, typically featuring a common room, two to four bedrooms, and a shared bathroom.

　　校园**宿舍**有各种配置。所有的宿舍楼都是男女共用。大多数建筑物有套房，通常具有一个公共休息室，两到四个卧室，一个公共浴室。

【搭】residential account 居民账户（住在本国居民的账户）　　residential area 居民区，住宅区　　residential college（美）住宿学院

【记】resident *n.* 居民，住客

residence *n.* 住宅，宅第

configuration [kənˌfigəˈreiʃn] *n.* 组合，布置；结构，构造；［化］（分子中原子的）组态，排列；［物］位形，组态

【变】configurations

【例】On-campus residential buildings have various **configurations**. All buildings are coed. Most buildings have suites, typically featuring a common room, two to four bedrooms, and a shared bathroom.

　　校园宿舍有各种**配置**。所有的宿舍楼都是男女共用。大多数建筑物有套房，通常具有一个公共休息室，两到四个卧室，一个公共浴室。

【搭】configuration control register 配置控制寄存器　　configuration counting series 构形计数级数　　configuration section 结构节

【记】configure *v.* ［术语］装配，配置（尤指计算机设备等）

coed [ˌkəuˈed] *a.* （非正）（教育、学校等）男女同校的　　*n.* （过时，美，非正）（男女同校大学中的）女大学生

【例】On-campus residential buildings have various configurations. All buildings are **coed**. Most buildings have suites, typically featuring a common room, two to four bedrooms, and a shared bathroom.

　　校园宿舍有各种配置。所有的宿舍楼都是**男女共用**。大多数建筑物有套房，通常具有一个公共休息室，两到四个卧室，一个公共浴室。

【搭】coeducation 男女同校制　　coefficient 系数

suite [swiːt] *n.* ［计］（软件的）套件；（房间，器具等）一套，一副；［乐］组曲；随从

【变】suites

【例】On-campus residential buildings have various configurations. All buildings are coed. Most buildings have **suites**，typically featuring a common room，two to four bedrooms，and a shared bathroom.

　　校园宿舍有各种配置。所有的宿舍楼都是男女共用。大多数建筑物有**套房**，通常具有一个公共休息室，两到四个卧室，一个公共浴室。

【搭】suite of rooms（旅馆的）套房　three-piece suite 三件套家具

【记】suiting *n.* 西服

　　suit *n.* 西服；诉讼 *v.* 适合；相称

词汇听写

1. _____ 2. _____ 3. _____

句子听写

3. Housing will be assigned to eligible students who submit full payment of tuition，housing，and all other fees by the housing request deadline of May 20.

　　住宿申请的最后期限是 5 月 20 日，只有在这期限前全额支付学费、住宿费和其他费用，符合这些条件的学生才会分配到住宿。

assign [əˈsain] *v.* 分派，选派，分配；归于，归属；[法] 把（财产、权利、利息）从一人转让给另一人；把……编制　*n.*（常用复数）[法] 受让人，接受财产等转让的人，受托者

【变】assigned　assigned　assigning　assigns

【例】Housing will be **assigned** to eligible students who submit full payment of tuition，housing，and all other fees by the housing request deadline of May 20.

　　住宿申请的最后期限是 5 月 20 日，只有在这期限前全额支付学费、住宿费和其他费用，符合这些条件的学生才会**分配**到住宿。

【搭】assign mark 评分

【记】assignable *a.* 可分配的，可归属的，可指定的；不可忽视

　　assigner *n.* 分配人，指定人

eligible [ˈelidʒəbl] *a.* 合适的；在（法律上或道德上）合格的；有资格当选的；称心如意的 *n.* 合格者；合适者；称心如意的人；合乎条件的人（或东西）

【变】eligibles

【例】Housing will be assigned to **eligible** students who submit full payment of tuition, housing, and all other fees by the housing request deadline of May 20.

住宿申请的最后期限是 5 月 20 日，只有在这期限前全额支付学费、住宿费和其他费用，**符合这些条件的学生才会分配到住宿**。

【搭】eligible bankers acceptance 合格的银行承兑汇票 eligible value date 有效交割日

【记】eligibility *n.* 适任，合格；被选举资格

eligibly *ad.* 适当地

tuition [tjuˈiʃn] *n.* 学费；教学，讲授

【例】Housing will be assigned to eligible students who submit full payment of **tuition**, housing, and all other fees by the housing request deadline of May20.

住宿申请的最后期限是 5 月 20 日，只有在这期限前全额支付**学费**、住宿费和其他费用，符合这些条件的学生才会分配到住宿。

【搭】tuition fee *n.* 学费，（某一学科的）教学 tuition scholarship 学费助学金

【记】tuitional *a.* 讲授的，学费的

deadline [ˈdedlain] *n.* 最后期限；截止期限；原稿截止时间

【变】deadlines

【例】Housing will be assigned to eligible students who submit full payment of tuition, housing, and all other fees by the housing request **deadline** of May 20.

住宿申请的**最后期限**是 5 月 20 日，只有在这期限前全额支付学费、住宿费和其他费用，符合这些条件的学生才会分配到住宿。

【搭】meet deadline 到达截期限 beat deadline 赶工期完成 to miss deadline 没赶上最后期限

词汇听写

1. _____ 2. _____ 3. _____

句子听写

Thursday ·· ≪

1. Every Summer School student has an <u>assistant</u> dean to whom he or she can go for advice and <u>counsel</u> in all matters. Assistant deans manage the <u>proctors</u> and oversee the safety and welfare of students.

　　每个暑期学校的学生有一个助理院长，学生可以去向助理院长建议和商讨全部事情。助理院长管理学监和监督学生的安全和福利。

assistant [ə'sistənt] *n.* 助手，助理；[化学]（染色的）助剂；辅助物；店
员，伙计　*a.* 助理的；辅助的；有帮助的；副的

【变】assistants

【例】Every Summer School student has an **assistant** dean to whom he or she can go for advice and counsel in all matters. Assistant deans manage the proctors and oversee the safety and welfare of students.

　　每个暑期学校的学生有一个**助理**院长，学生可以去向助理院长建议和商讨全部事情。助理院长管理学监和监督学生的安全和福利。

【搭】assistant accountant 助理会计　assistant accounts clerk 会计助理员
assistant teacher 一般教学人员

【记】assist *v.* 帮助

counsel ['kaunsl] *n.* 协商，讨论；建议；策略；法律顾问，辩护人
v. 劝告，建议；提供专业咨询

【变】counseled counseled counseling counsels

【例】Every Summer School student has an assistant dean to whom he or she can go for advice and **counsel** in all matters. Assistant deans manage the proctors and oversee the safety and welfare of students.

　　每个暑期学校的学生有一个助理院长，学生可以去向助理院长建议和**商讨**全部事情。助理院长管理学监和监督学生的安全和福利。

【搭】counsel for the defence 辩护律师，被告律师　counsel of perfection 理想
但不切实际的劝告　take counsel 商量问题；商讨问题

proctor [ˈprɔktə] *n.* （大学的）学监，监考人；代理人　*v.* 监督

【变】proctored　proctored　proctoring　proctors

【例】Every Summer School student has an assistant dean to whom he or she can go for advice and counsel in all matters. Assistant deans manage the **proctors** and oversee the safety and welfare of students.

　　每个暑期学校的学生有一个助理院长，学生可以去向助理院长建议和商讨全部事情。助理院长管理**学监**和监督学生的安全和福利。

【记】proctorship *n.* 代理人之职

　　proctorial *a.* 代诉人的，训导长的

词汇听写

1. _____　2. _____　3. _____

句子听写

2. These tour pamphlets can be purchased from our office for a minimal charge. You may also download audio files.

　　你可以以最少的费用从我们办公室购买这些旅行小册子，也可以下载音频文件。

pamphlet [ˈpæmflət] *n.* 小册子；活页文选

【变】pamphlets

【例】These tour **pamphlets** can be purchased from our office for a minimal charge. You may also download audio files.

　　你可以以最少的费用从我们办公室购买这些旅行**小册子**，也可以下载音频文件。

【记】palm *n.* 手掌；棕榈树

purchase [ˈpəːtʃəs] *v.* 购买；采购；换得；依靠机械力移动　*n.* 购买；购买行为；购置物；紧握

【变】purchased　purchased　purchasing　purchases

【例】These tour pamphlets can be **purchased** from our office for a minimal charge. You may also download audio files.

你可以以最少的费用从我们办公室**购买**这些旅行小册子，也可以下载音频文件。

【搭】purchase account 进货账　purchase agreement 采购合同，购买契约

【记】purchaser *n.* 买家

charge [tʃɑːdʒ] *v.* 装载；控诉；使充电；索（价）；记在账上；充电　*n.* 费用；指示；掌管；指责

【例】These tour pamphlets can be purchased from our office for a minimal **charge**. You may also download audio files.

你可以以最少的**费用**从我们办公室购买这些旅行小册子，也可以下载音频文件。

【搭】free of charge 免费　lay something to someone's charge 指责某人做过某事　press（或 prefer）charges 正式控告（某人的）罪行　in charge 主管，领导，负责处于领导或管理的职位

【记】charity *n.* 慈善（行为）；施舍；仁爱

charm *n.* 魔力；魅力

character *n.* 性格，特征，字母，人物

audio [ˈɔːdiəu] *a.* 听觉的，声音的；音频的　*n.* 声音回路；音响；可听到的声音；声音信号

【例】These tour pamphlets can be purchased from our office for a minimal charge. You may also download **audio** files.

你可以以最少的费用从我们办公室购买这些旅行小册子，也可以下载**音频**文件。

【搭】audio acuity 听力检查

audio aids 听觉教具，听音设备

audio cassette 盒式录音磁带

词汇听写

1. _____　2. _____　3. _____

句子听写

3. You may find yourself <u>navigating</u> new cultural <u>encounters</u> and experiencing new foods, different customs, and unfamiliar <u>domestic</u> patterns. To apply this program, students must be at least 18, have completed one year of college or be a first-year student, and be in good <u>academic standing</u>.

你会发现自己在经历和应对新的文化境遇和尝试新的食物，适应不同的风俗和陌生的家庭模式。申请这个活动的学生必须年满 18 岁，已经完成大学一年的课程或是大一学生，而且要有良好的学习成绩。

navigate [ˈnævigeit] *v.* 驾驶；航行于；使通过；航行

【变】navigated navigated navigating navigates

【例】You may find yourself **navigating** new cultural encounters and experiencing new foods, different customs, and unfamiliar domestic patterns. To apply this program, students must be at least 18, have completed one year of college or be a first-year student, and be in good academic standing.

你会发现自己在**经历**和应对新的文化境遇和尝试新的食物，适应不同的风俗和陌生的家庭模式。申请这个活动的学生必须年满 18 岁，已经完成大学一年的课程或是大一学生，而且要有良好的学习成绩。

【搭】navigate by the stars/sun 靠星辰确定方向

【记】navigable *a.* 可通航的，可航行的

navigation *n.* 航行学

navigator *n.* 领航员

encounter [inˈkauntə] *v.* 不期而遇；遭遇；对抗；碰见，尤指不期而遇

n. 相遇，碰见；遭遇战；对决，冲突

【变】encounters encountered encountered encountering encounters

【例】You may find yourself navigating new cultural **encounters** and experiencing new foods, different customs, and unfamiliar domestic patterns. To apply this program, students must be at least 18, have completed one year of college or be a first-year student, and be in good academic standing.

你会发现自己在经历和应对新的文化**境遇**和尝试新的食物，适应不同的风俗和陌生的家庭模式。申请这个活动的学生必须年满 18 岁，已经完成大学一年的课程或是大一学生，而且要有良好的学习成绩。

【搭】encounter group 交友小组　　chance encounter 巧遇

【记】encourage *v.* 鼓励，支持；促进

enchant *v.* 使迷惑

domestic [dəˈmestik] *a.* 家庭的，家的；国内的；驯养的；热心家务的
          n. 佣人；国货

【变】domestics

【例】You may find yourself navigating new cultural encounters and experiencing new foods, different customs, and unfamiliar **domestic** patterns. To apply this program, students must be at least 18, have completed one year of college or be a first-year student, and be in good academic standing.

    你会发现自己在经历和应对新的文化境遇和尝试新的食物，适应不同的风俗和陌生的**家庭**模式。申请这个活动的学生必须年满 18 岁，已经完成大学一年的课程或是大一学生，而且要有良好的学习成绩。

【搭】domestic appliance/equipment 家用　domestic violence/ problem/trouble 家庭暴力/问题/麻烦

【记】domesticate *v.* 驯养

    dome *n.* 圆屋顶 *v.* 呈圆顶状

standing [ˈstændiŋ] *n.* 起立，站立；身份，地位；持续时间　*a.* 长期有效的；直立的；固定的　*v.* 站立；坚持不变

【例】You may find yourself navigating new cultural encounters and experiencing new foods, different customs, and unfamiliar domestic patterns. To apply this program, students must be at least 18, have completed one year of college or be a first-year student, and be in good academic **standing.**

    你会发现自己在经历和应对新的文化境遇和尝试新的食物，适应不同的风俗和陌生的家庭模式。申请这个活动的学生必须年满 18 岁，已经完成大学一年的课程或是大一学生，而且要有良好的学习**成绩**。

【搭】standing and responsibility（公司的）信誉与偿付能力　standing army 常备军，现役部队　standing joke 笑料

词汇听写

1. _____ 2. _____ 3. _____

句子听写

Friday ·· ⟪⟪⟪

1. Donald Pfiste has been appointed <u>interim</u> dean of Harvard College. Pfiste's career at Harvard <u>spans</u> nearly 40 years, where he has been an award-winning teacher, an influential scholar and a <u>committed</u> student <u>advocate</u>.

Donald Pfiste 一直被任命为哈佛大学的临时院长，他已经在哈佛大学工作大约40年了，他是一位获奖的、有影响力的学者，同时还是一个忠实的学生支持者。

interim [ˈintərim] *a.* 暂时的，临时的；期中的　*n.* 间歇，过渡期间；临时协定

【例】Donald Pfiste has been appointed **interim** dean of Harvard College. Pfiste's career at Harvard spans nearly 40 years, where he has been an award-winning teacher, an influential scholar and a committed student advocate.

Donald Pfiste 一直被任命为哈佛大学的**临时**院长，他已经在哈佛大学工作大约40年了，他是一位获奖的、有影响力的学者，同时还是一个忠实的学生支持者。

【搭】interim award 临时裁决　interim credit 临时贷款

span [spæn] *n.* 共轭（马、骡）；跨度，墩距；一段时间；［航］跨绳　　*v.* 缚住或扎牢；跨越时间或空间；以掌测量；以手围绕测量类似测量

【变】spanned　spanned　spanning　spans

【例】Donald Pfiste has been appointed interim dean of Harvard College. Pfiste's career at Harvard **spans** nearly 40 years, where he has been an award-winning teacher, an influential scholar and a committed student advocate.

Donald Pfiste 一直被任命为哈佛大学的临时院长，他已经在哈佛大学工作大约40年了，他是一位获奖的、有影响力的学者，同时还是一个忠实的学生支持者。

【搭】span length 杆间距离，跨度距离　　a span of 6 years 六年的时间

committed [kəˈmitid] *a.* 忠诚的，坚定的　*v.* 保证（做某事、遵守协议或遵从安排等）（commit 的过去式和过去分词）；把……托付给；把……记（或写）下来；承诺

【例】Donald Pfiste has been appointed interim dean of Harvard College. Pfiste's career at Harvard spans nearly 40 years, where he has been an award-winning teacher, an influential scholar and a **committed** student advocate.

Donald Pfiste 一直被任命为哈佛大学的临时院长，他已经在哈佛大学工作大约 40 年了，他是一位获奖的、有影响力的学者，同时还是一个**忠实的**学生支持者

【搭】committed socialists 坚定的社会主义者　committed member of the team 忠于职守的队员

advocate [ˈædvəkeit] *v.* 提倡；拥护；鼓吹；为……辩护　*n.*（辩护）律师；提倡者；支持者

【变】advocates　advocated　advocated　advocating　advocates

【例】Donald Pfiste has been appointed interim dean of Harvard College. Pfiste's career at Harvard spans nearly 40 years, where he has been an award-winning teacher, an influential scholar and a committed student **advocate.**

Donald Pfiste 一直被任命为哈佛大学的临时院长，他已经在哈佛大学工作大约 40 年了，他是一位获奖的、有影响力的学者，同时还是一个忠实的学生**支持者**。

【搭】advocate of netclear power 核能的坚定拥护者　be an advocate of 提倡者，鼓吹者

【记】advocacy *n.* 支持，拥护
　　adverse *a.* 不利的，有害的

词汇听写

1. ＿＿＿＿＿＿　2. ＿＿＿＿＿＿　3. ＿＿＿＿＿＿

句子听写

2. Refreshing gazpacho, pizza peppered with crisp basil, and fruit smoothies for dessert — something about summertime brings out the gourmand in us all.

  提神的西班牙凉菜汤、洒满脆罗勒的披萨和香滑的甜点水果沙冰——一些关于夏令时节的食品把美食主义在我们面前展露无遗。

refreshing [riˈfreʃiŋ] *a.* 使人精神焕发的；提神的；使人耳目一新的
v. 使恢复，使振作（refresh 的现在分词）

【变】more refreshing   most refreshing

【例】**Refreshing** gazpacho, pizza peppered with crisp basil, and fruit smoothies for dessert — something about summertime brings out the gourmand in us all.

  提神的西班牙凉菜汤、洒满脆罗勒的披萨和香滑的甜点水果沙冰——一些关于夏令时节的食品把美食主义在我们面前展露无遗。

【记】refreshingly *ad.* 清爽地，有精神地   refreshment *n.* 茶点，点心

pepper [ˈpepə] *n.* 胡椒；辣椒；胡椒粉   *v.* 在……上撒胡椒粉；使布满

【变】peppered   peppered   peppering   peppers

【例】Refreshing gazpacho, pizza **peppered** with crisp basil, and fruit smoothies for dessert — something about summertime brings out the gourmand in us all.

  提神的西班牙凉菜汤、**洒满**脆罗勒的披萨和香滑的甜点水果沙冰——一些关于夏令时节的食品把美食主义在我们面前展露无遗。

smoothy [ˈsmuːði] *n.* 善于讨好女人的男子，举止优雅的人，*a.* 口感柔滑的

【例】Refreshing gazpacho, pizza peppered with crisp basil, and fruit **smoothies** for dessert — something about summertime brings out the gourmand in us all.

  提神的西班牙凉菜汤、洒满脆罗勒的披萨和**香滑的**甜点水果沙冰——一些关于夏令时节的食品把美食主义在我们面前展露无遗。

【记】smoothly *ad.* 平稳地，顺畅地

smooth *v.* 顺利摆脱困境，使平滑，*a.* 柔软的，平坦的

booth *n.* 摊位；公用电话亭；隔开的小间

gourmand [ɡuəˈmɑːnd] *n.* **喜欢吃喝的人，贪吃的人；美食主义**

【变】gourmands

【例】Refreshing gazpacho, pizza peppered with crisp basil, and fruit smoothies for dessert — something about summertime brings out the **gourmand** in us all.

提神的西班牙凉菜汤、洒满脆罗勒的披萨和香滑的甜点水果沙冰——一些关于夏令时节的食品引诱着我们对**美食**的渴望。

【记】gourmandism *n.* 美食主义

gourmet *n.* 美食家，讲究吃喝的人

demand *v.* & *n.* 要求，请求

词汇听写

1. _____ 2. _____ 3. _____

句子听写

3. Nora is stuck inside the life she never wanted after caring for an ailing parent for four years, and watching those crucial years sail by like balloons that slipped out of her hands.

照顾了她生病的父（母）亲四年，看着这关键的四年就像气球一样从她的指尖悄悄流逝，诺拉觉得她被这种从来就不是她想要的生活给**困住了**。

stuck [stʌk] *v.* 刺（stick 的过去式及过去分词） *a.* **动不了的；被卡住的；被……缠住的；被……难住的，不知所措的**

【变】stuck stuck sticking sticks

【例】Nora is **stuck** inside the life she never wanted after caring for an ailing parent for four years, and watching those crucial years sail by like balloons that slipped out of her hands.

229

照顾了她生病的父（母）亲四年，看着这关键的四年就像气球一样从她的指尖悄悄流逝，诺拉觉得她被这种从来就不是她想要的生活给困住了。

【搭】stick and carrot 软硬兼施　stick and stone 全部，一切　stick by 忠实于

【记】stickpin *n.* 装饰别针　pluck *v.* 来，拔掉；拉 *n.* 勇气

caring [ˈkeəriŋ] *a.* 关心的；有同情心的　*v.* 关心（care 的现在分词）

【例】Nora is stuck inside the life she never wanted after **caring** for an ailing parent for four years, and watching those crucial years sail by like balloons that slipped out of her hands.

照顾了她生病的父（母）亲四年，看着这关键的四年就像气球一样从她的指尖悄悄流逝，诺拉觉得她被这种从来就不是她想要的生活给困住了。

【搭】be past caring（因劳累、沮丧或担心别的事而）无暇顾及，无心考虑，caring profession 关心照顾人的职业

ailing [ˈeiliŋ] *a.* 生病的；不舒服的　*v.* 使受病痛；使痛苦（ail 的 ing 形式）

【例】Nora is stuck inside the life she never wanted after caring for an **ailing** parent for four years, and watching those crucial years sail by like balloons that slipped out of her hands.

照顾了她生病的父（母）亲四年，看着这关键的四年就像气球一样从她的指尖悄悄流逝，诺拉觉得她被这种从来就不是她想要的生活给困住了。

【搭】ailing aircraft 有故障的飞机　ailing economy 病态经济

【记】ailment *n.* 小病，微恙

slip out 无意中说出（或泄露）；悄悄溜走

【例】Nora is stuck inside the life she never wanted after caring for an ailing parent for four years, and watching those crucial years sail by like balloons that **slipped out** of her hands.

照顾了她生病的父（母）亲四年，看着这关键的四年就像气球一样从她的指尖悄悄流逝，诺拉觉得她被这种从来就不是她想要的生活给困住了。

230

【记】slippery *a.* 狡猾的；不可靠的

　　slide *v.* 下跌，滑落

　　slipper *n.* 拖鞋

词汇听写

1. _____ 2. _____ 3. _____

句子听写

Saturday ⋯⋯⋯⋯⋯⋯⋯⋯⋯⋯⋯⋯⋯⋯⋯⋯⋯⋯⋯⋯⋯⋯⋯⋯ ◅◅

1. While she appears placid, she is fuming on the inside until the captivating Shahid family moves to town and reawakens something inside her.

虽然她显得波澜不惊，但是她内心却烦恼不已，直到吸引她注意力的沙希德一家搬到这个城镇，她们焕发了她内心的渴望。

---

placid [ˈplæsid] *a.* 平和的，宁静的；温和的；满意的，满足的；平缓

【例】While she appears **placid**, she is fuming on the inside until the captivating Shahid family moves to town and reawakens something inside her.

虽然她显得**波澜不惊**，但是她内心却烦恼不已，直到吸引她注意力的沙希德一家搬到这个城镇，她们焕发了她内心的渴望。

【记】plaguesome *a.* 讨厌的，麻烦的，瘟疫的

planet *n.* [天] 行星；[占星]（左右人命运的）星相

place *n.* 位；地方；职位；座位

---

fume on 烦恼不已

【例】While she appears placid, she is **fuming on** the inside until the captivating Shahid family moves to town and reawakens something inside her.

虽然她显得波澜不惊，但是她内心却**烦恼不已**，直到吸引她注意力的沙希德一家搬到这个城镇，她们焕发了她内心的渴望。

【记】fumy *a.* 冒烟的，多蒸汽的

fun *n.* 乐趣；娱乐活动；嬉戏，嬉闹；有趣的事 *a.* 使人愉快的；开心的 *v.* 嬉闹；开玩笑

full *a.* 满的，装满的；完全的，完整的；丰富的；详尽的

---

captivate [ˈkæptiveit] *a.* 迷人的，有魅力的，有吸引力的 *v.* 迷住（某人），迷惑

【变】captivated captivated captivating captivates

【例】While she appears placid, she is fuming on the inside until the **captivating** Shahid family moves to town and reawakens something inside her.

虽然她显得波澜不惊，但是她内心却烦恼不已，直到**吸引**她注意力

的沙希德一家搬到这个城镇，她们焕发了她内心的渴望。

【记】capture *v.* 俘获；夺取；夺得；引起（注意、想象、兴趣）

carpenter *n.* 木工，木匠

reawaken [ˌriːəˈweɪkən] *v.* 再度觉醒

【变】reawakened　reawakened　reawakening　reawakens

【例】While she appears placid, she is fuming on the inside until the captivating Shahid family moves to town and **reawakens** something inside her.

　　虽然她显得波澜不惊，但是她内心却烦恼不已，直到吸引她注意力的沙希德一家搬到这个城镇，她们**焕发**了她内心的渴望。

【记】refresh *v.* 使恢复，使振作；使焕然一新，翻新；给（电池）充电

reward *n.* 报酬；报答；赏金；酬金

reaction *n.* 反应；反作用力；反动；保守

词汇听写

1. _____　2. _____　3. _____

句子听写

2. Often it seems that apathy reigns supreme among millennials, the 20-somethings who in poll after poll show their distrust of elected leaders, political institutions, and the courts.

　　冷漠的"千禧一代"——20 多岁的年轻人，往往会在投票后的民意调查中表现出他们对所选出的领导人、政治机构和法院不信任。

apathy [ˈæpəθi] *n.* 冷漠，无兴趣，漠不关心；无感情

【例】Often it seems that **apathy** reigns supreme among millennials, the 20-somethings who in poll after poll show their distrust of elected leaders, political institutions, and the courts.

　　冷漠的"千禧一代"——20 多岁的年轻人，往往会在投票后的民意调查中表现出他们对所选出的领导人、政治机构和法院不信任。

【记】apologize *v.* 道歉，认错；辩解，辩护

apparent *a.* 易看见的，可看见的；显然的；表面的

apparatus *n.* 仪器，器械；机器；机构；器官

reign [rein] *v.* 统治；支配；盛行；君临　*n.* 统治；统治时期；支配

【变】reigned　reigned　reigning　reigns

【例】Often it seems that apathy **reigns** supreme among millennials, the 20-somethings who in poll after poll show their distrust of elected leaders, political institutions, and the courts.

冷漠的"千禧一代"——20多岁的年轻人，往往会在投票后的民意调查中表现出他们对所选出的领导人、政治机构和法院不信任。

【搭】reign of terror 恐怖统治

【记】rein *n.* 驾驭（法）；统治手段；控制（权）；缰绳

regard *v.* 关系；注意；（尤指以某种方式）注视；尊敬

region *n.* 地区，地域，地带；行政区，管辖区；（大气、海水等的）层，界，境；（学问等的）范围，领域

supreme [su:'pri:m] *n.* 至高；霸权　*a.* 最高的；至高的；最重要的

【例】Often it seems that apathy reigns **supreme** among millennials, the 20-somethings who in poll after poll show their distrust of elected leaders, political institutions, and the courts.

冷漠的"千禧一代"——20多岁的年轻人，往往会在投票后的民意调查中表现出他们对所选出的领导人、政治机构和法院不信任。

【搭】supreme being 上帝；神王　supreme count（英国）最高法院

【记】supremely *ad.* 极其，极为

surpass *v.* 超过；优于；胜过；非……所能办到

surprise *v.* 使惊奇，使诧异；意外发现，出其不意获得；突袭

poll [pəul] *n.* 投票；民意测验；投票数；投票所　*v.* 修剪；投票；对……进行调查

【变】polled　polled　polling　polls

【例】Often it seems that apathy reigns supreme among millennials, the 20-somethings who in poll after **poll** show their distrust of elected leaders, political institutions, and the courts.

冷漠的"千禧一代"——20 多岁的年轻人，往往会在投票后的**民意调查**中表现出他们对所选出的领导人、政治机构和法院不信任。

【搭】weekly poll 每周一次的调查　the latest poll 最近的民意调查

【记】pollute v. 污染；玷污，亵渎；破坏（品性），使堕落

　　　pull v. 拉；扯；拉过来；划（船）v. 赢得；吸引异性

词汇听写

1. ＿＿＿＿＿＿＿＿　2. ＿＿＿＿＿＿＿＿　3. ＿＿＿＿＿＿＿＿

句子听写

3. In this area, impoverished residents were burning broken electronic parts, discarded and dumped by wealthier nations, to extract the metal components.

　　在这个地方，一些富有国家把破损的电子零件丢弃并倾倒在这里，贫困居民熔化破损电子零件，以提炼出金属部件。

impoverish [imˈpɒvriʃ] v. 使贫穷；使枯竭

【变】impoverished　impoverished　impoverishing　impoverishes

【例】In this area, **impoverished** residents were burning broken electronic parts, discarded and dumped by wealthier nations, to extract the metal components.

　　在这个地方，一些富有国家把破损的电子零件丢弃并倾倒在这里，**贫困**居民熔化破损电子零件，以提炼出金属部件。

【搭】impoverished areas 贫穷的地区

【记】impoverishment n. 贫穷，穷困；贫化

　　　imprison v. 关押，监禁；束缚，禁锢；使……不自由

　　　improper a. 不合适的，非正常的；不正确的；不正派的，不合礼仪的；不道德的

discard [diˈskɑːd] n. 抛弃；被丢弃的东西或人　v. 抛弃；放弃；丢弃

【变】discarded　discarded　discarding　discards

【例】In this area, impoverished residents were burning broken electronic parts, **discarded** and dumped by wealthier nations, to extract the metal components.

在这个地方，一些富有国家把破损的电子零件**丢弃**并倾倒在这里，贫困居民熔化破损电子零件，以提炼出金属部件。

【搭】discard solution 废液　　discard tobacco 废烟丝

【记】discardable *a.* 可废弃的　　discern *v.* 看出；理解，了解；识别，辨别
discharge *v.* 下（客）；卸船；免除（自己的义务、负担等）；执行

dump [dʌmp] *n.* 垃圾场　*v.* 倾倒；倾卸

【变】dumped　dumped　dumping　dumps

【例】In this area, impoverished residents were burning broken electronic parts, discarded and **dumped** by wealthier nations, to extract the metal components.

在这个地方，一些富有国家把破损的电子零件丢弃并**倾倒**在这里，贫困居民熔化破损电子零件，以提炼出金属部件。

【搭】dump bin 废料箱　　dump box 倾卸式车厢

【记】dumb *a.* 哑的；无声的；无言的

jump *v.* 跳；跳过；（因吃惊、害怕或激动而）猛地一动

duty *n.* 职责，责任；义务；职责或工作；税收

extract [iks'trækt] *v.* 提取；（费力地）拔出；选取；获得　*n.* 汁；摘录；提炼物；浓缩物

【变】extracted　extracted　extracting　extracts

【例】In this area, impoverished residents were burning broken electronic parts, discarded and dumped by wealthier nations, to **extract** the metal components.

在这个地方，一些富有国家把破损的电子零件丢弃并倾倒在这里，贫困居民熔化破损电子零件，以**提炼**出金属部件。

【搭】extract content 抽提率

【记】extractability *n.* 可萃性，萃取率

extractable *a.* 可引出的，可拔出的

extraction *n.* 取出；血统，[化] 提取（法），萃取（法），回收物

词汇听写

1. _____　　2. _____　　3. _____

句子听写

Sunday ·· «

1. Crouched around bonfires, they <u>inhaled</u> <u>toxic</u> smoke and unwittingly leached heavy metals into a nearby river, just to <u>eke</u> out a living.

　　蹲伏在篝火周围，他们吸入有毒的烟雾，并在不知不觉中把滤出的重金属排入附近的河流中，而他们这么做只是为了糊口。

crouch ［krautʃ］ *n.* 蹲伏　*v.* 低头；屈膝；蹲伏，蜷伏；卑躬屈膝

【变】crouched　crouched　crouching　crouches

【例】**Crouched** around bonfires, they inhaled toxic smoke and unwittingly leached heavy metals into a nearby river, just to eke out a living.

　　　蹲伏在篝火周围，他们吸入有毒的烟雾，并在不知不觉中把滤出的重金属排入附近的河流中，而他们这么做只是为了糊口。

【搭】crouch start 蹲伏式起跑

【记】creche *n.* 托儿所，孤儿院

　　crush *v.* 压破，压碎；镇压；弄皱；挤榨，榨出

　　crude *a.* 粗糙的，粗杂的；粗鲁的；天然的，未加工的；简陋的

inhale ［in'heil］ *v.* 吸入；猛吃猛喝；吸气

【变】inhaled　inhaled　inhaling　inhales

【例】Crouched around bonfires, they **inhaled** toxic smoke and unwittingly leached heavy metals into a nearby river, just to eke out a living.

　　　蹲伏在篝火周围，他们**吸入**有毒的烟雾，并在不知不觉中把滤出的重金属排入附近的河流中，而他们这么做只是为了糊口。

【记】inherent *a.* 固有的，内在的；天生的

　　inherit *v.* 经遗传获得（品质、身体特征等），继任

　　inhabit *v.* 居住；在······出现；填满

toxic ［'tɔksik］ *a.* 有毒的；中毒的

【变】toxics

【例】Crouched around bonfires, they inhaled **toxic** smoke and unwittingly leached heavy metals into a nearby river, just to eke out a living.

蹲伏在篝火周围，他们吸入**有毒的**烟雾，并在不知不觉中把滤出的
重金属排入附近的河流中，而他们这么做只是为了糊口。

【搭】toxic amine 毒胺　toxic animal 有毒动物

【记】toxically *ad.* 有毒地

　　toxicity *n.* 毒性，毒力

　　toilet *n.* 厕所，洗手间；马桶

eke [iːk] *v.* 补充；增加；放长

【变】eked　eked　eking　ekes

【例】Crouched around bonfires, they inhaled toxic smoke and unwittingly leached heavy metals into a nearby river, just to **eke** out a living.

　　　　蹲伏在篝火周围，他们吸入有毒的烟雾，并在不知不觉中把滤出的
重金属排入附近的河流中，而他们这么做只是为了糊口。

【搭】eke out a living 勉强维持生活

【记】elect *v.* 选举；挑出，挑选；决定

　　electric *a.* 电的，带电的；发电的，导电的；令人激动的；电动的

词汇听写

1. ＿＿＿＿＿＿　2. ＿＿＿＿＿＿　3. ＿＿＿＿＿＿

句子听写

2. The new coating could be used to create durable, scratch-resistant lenses for eyeglasses, self-cleaning windows, improved solar panels, and new medical diagnostic devices.

　　　　新的涂层可用于创建耐用眼镜的防刮镜片，用于制造自动清洗的窗
户，改进的太阳能电池板，改善新的医疗诊断设备。

durable [ˈdjuərəbl] *n.* 耐用品　*a.* 耐用的，持久的

【变】more durable　most durable

【例】The new coating could be used to create **durable**, scratch-resistant lenses for eyeglasses, self-cleaning windows, improved solar panels, and new medical diagnostic devices.

　　新的涂层可用于创建**耐用**眼镜的防刮镜片，用于制造自动清洗的窗户，改进的太阳能电池板，改善新的医疗诊断设备。

【搭】durable aroma 持久香气　durable facility 耐用设备

【记】durability *n.* 耐久性；持久性

durableness *n.* 耐用性

durably *ad.* 经久地，坚牢地

scratch [skrætʃ] *n.* 擦伤；抓痕；刮擦声；乱写　*v.* 抓；刮；挖出；乱涂　*a.* 打草稿用的；凑合的；碰巧的

【变】scratched　scratched　scratching　scratches

【例】The new coating could be used to create durable, **scratch**-resistant lenses for eyeglasses, self-cleaning windows, improved solar panels, and new medical diagnostic devices.

　　新的涂层可用于创建耐用眼镜的防**刮**镜片，用于制造自动清洗的窗户，改进的太阳能电池板，改善新的医疗诊断设备。

【搭】scratch about 扒，刨　scratch along 勉强糊口，艰难地谋生

【记】scratcher *n.* 抓扒者，抓扒工具

scream *v.* 尖声喊叫，拼命叫喊；喊叫着说出；尖叫得使变

scramble *v.* 攀登，爬；争夺，抢夺；（植物）蔓延；［航］紧急起飞

solar [ˈsəʊlə] *n.* 日光浴室　*a.* 太阳的；日光的；利用太阳光的；与太阳相关的

【例】The new coating could be used to create durable, scratch-resistant lenses for eyeglasses, self-cleaning windows, improved **solar** panels, and new medical diagnostic devices.

　　新的涂层可用于创建耐用眼镜的防刮镜片，用于制造自动清洗的窗户，改进的**太阳能**电池板，改善新的医疗诊断设备。

【搭】solar array 太阳能电池阵

【记】soldier *n.* 士兵，军人；军事家

solid *a.* 固体的；实心的；结实的，可信赖的

solo *n.* 独唱（曲），独奏（曲）；单飞；单人表演

diagnostic [daiəɡ'nɔstik] *n.* 诊断法；诊断结论 *a.* 诊断的；特征的

【例】The new coating could be used to create durable, scratch-resistant lenses for eyeglasses, self-cleaning windows, improved solar panels, and new medical **diagnostic** devices.

新的涂层可用于创建耐用眼镜的防刮镜片，用于制造自动清洗的窗户，改进的太阳能电池板，改善新的医疗**诊断**设备。

【搭】diagnostic agent 诊断剂　diagnostic character 鉴别性状

【记】diametral *a.* 直径的

diamond *n.* 钻石，金刚石；菱形；方块

diary *n.* 日记，日志；日记簿

词汇听写

1. _____ 2. _____ 3. _____

句子听写

3. The plant lures insects onto the ultra slippery surface of its leaves, where they slide to their doom.

植物吸引昆虫到额外滑溜的叶面上，在那里昆虫将走向厄运。

lure [l(j)uə] *n.* 诱惑；饵；诱惑物 *v.* 诱惑；引诱

【变】lured　lured　luring　lures

【例】The plant **lures** insects onto the ultra slippery surface of its leaves, where they slide to their doom.

植物**吸引**昆虫到额外滑溜的叶面上，在那里昆虫将走向厄运。

【记】luxury *n.* 奢侈，豪华；奢侈品，美食，美衣；乐趣，享受

luck *n.* 运气；好运；机遇；命运

lecture *n.* 演讲；训斥，教训

ultra ['ʌltrə] *a.* 过激的，极端的 *n.* 过激论者

【例】The plant **lures** insects onto the **ultra** slippery surface of its leaves, where they slide to their doom.

　　植物吸引昆虫到**额外**滑溜的叶面上，在那里昆虫将走向厄运。

【搭】ultra centrifuge 超（速）离心机　ultra conservative 老古董

【记】ultrasonic *a.* ［声］超声的；超音波的，超音速的

　　ultraviolet *a.* 紫外的；紫外线的；产生紫外线的

　　umbrella *n.* 雨伞；〈比喻〉保护物；［军］空中掩护幕；总括

slide ［slaid］*n.* 滑动；幻灯片；滑梯；雪崩　　*v.* 滑动；使滑动；悄悄地迅速放置

【变】slid　slid　sliding　slides

【例】The plant lures insects onto the ultra slippery surface of its leaves, where they **slide** to their doom.

　　植物吸引昆虫到额外滑溜的叶面上，在那里昆虫将**走向**厄运。

【搭】slide advertising 幻灯广告

【记】slidable *a.* 滑动的

　　laudably *ad.* 值得赞赏地，可称赞地

　　slight *a.* 微小的；细小的；不结实的；无须重视的

doom ［du:m］*n.* 厄运；死亡；判决；世界末日　　*v.* 注定；判决；使失败

【变】doomed doomed dooming dooms

【例】The plant lures insects onto the ultra slippery surface of its leaves, where they **slide** to their **doom**.

　　植物吸引昆虫到额外滑溜的叶面上，在那里昆虫将走向**厄运**。

【搭】doom and gloom 悲观失望　　be doomed from the start 一开始就注定失败

【记】door *n.* 门，户；出入口；一家；通道

　　dorm *n.* 宿舍

　　room *n.* 房间；空间；余地；房间里所有的人

　　deem *v.* 视为，认为；断定

词汇听写

1. ＿＿＿＿＿＿　　2. ＿＿＿＿＿＿　　3. ＿＿＿＿＿＿

句子听写

241

1. By adjusting the width of the honeycomb cells to make their diameter much smaller than the wavelength of visible light, the researchers kept the coating from reflecting light.

　. 研究人员调整蜂窝孔格的宽度，使它们的直径远小于可见光的波长，通过这种方式，研究人员保护涂层避免反射光。

honeycomb cells 蜂窝孔格

【例】By adjusting the width of the **honeycomb cells** to make their diameter much smaller than the wavelength of visible light, the researchers kept the coating from reflecting light.

　　研究人员调整**蜂窝孔格**的宽度，使它们的直径远小于可见光的波长，通过这种方式，研究人员保护涂层避免反射光。

【记】honeymoon *n.* 蜜月；蜜月期；蜜月旅行；短暂的和谐时期

honourable *a.* 诚实的，正直的；光荣的，荣耀的；尊敬的；高尚的

honesty *n.* 诚实，真诚；正直

diameter [dai'æmitə] *n.* 直径

【变】diameters

【例】By adjusting the width of the honeycomb cells to make their **diameter** much smaller than the wavelength of visible light, the researchers kept the coating from reflecting light.

　　研究人员调整蜂窝孔格的宽度，使它们的**直径**远小于可见光的波长，通过这种方式，研究人员保护涂层避免反射光。

【搭】diameter of the ring 戒指的直径　　the diameter of a tree trunk 树干的直径

【记】cell-like *a.* 细胞样的

cellar *n.* 地下室，地窖；酒窖；（英）（都市住宅的）地下煤窖

wavelength [ˈweivleŋθ] *n.* [物] 波长

【变】wavelengths

【例】By adjusting the width of the honeycomb cells to make their diameter much smaller than the **wavelength** of visible light, the researchers kept the coating from reflecting light.

研究人员调整蜂窝孔格的宽度，使它们的直径远小于可见光的**波长**，通过这种方式，研究人员保护涂层避免反射光。

【搭】wavelength adjustment 波长调节　　wavelength loss 波长损失

【记】wealthy *a.* 富有的；充分的

wave *n.* 波浪，波动；挥手；涌现的人（或事物）；汹涌的行动（或思想）态势

visible [ˈvizibl] *n.* 可见物；进出口贸易中的有形项目　*a.* 明显的；看得见的；现有的；可得到的

【例】By adjusting the width of the honeycomb cells to make their diameter much smaller than the wavelength of **visible** light, the researchers kept the coating from reflecting light.

研究人员调整蜂窝孔格的宽度，使它们的直径远小于**可见光的**波长，通过这种方式，研究人员保护涂层避免反射光。

【搭】visible arc 明弧　　visible brightness 可见亮度

【记】visibility *n.* 能见度；可见性；可见距离；清晰度

vision *n.* 视力，视觉；美景，绝妙的东西；幻影；想象力

词汇听写

1. ＿＿＿＿＿＿　　2. ＿＿＿＿＿＿　　3. ＿＿＿＿＿＿

句子听写

2. While women slightly <u>outnumber</u> men, <u>instructors</u> have <u>devised</u> a creative solution. Female dancers stand in an inner circle facing out, and are surrounded by an outer circle of male dancers, who <u>rotate</u> to a new partner every few minutes.

　　由于女性略多于男性，教师设计了一个创造性的解决方案。女舞者站在内圈，脸朝外，外圈的男舞者围着内圈，每隔几分钟，男舞者就旋转到一个新的舞伴面前。

---

outnumber [aut'nʌmbə] v. 数目超过；比……多

【变】outnumbered　outnumbered　outnumbering　outnumbers

【例】While women slightly **outnumber** men, instructors have devised a creative solution. Female dancers stand in an inner circle facing out, and are surrounded by an outer circle of male dancers, who rotate to a new partner every few minutes.

　　由于女性略**多于**男性，教师设计了一个创造性的解决方案。女舞者站在内圈，脸朝外，外圈的男舞者围着内圈，每隔几分钟，男舞者就旋转到一个新的舞伴面前。

【记】output n. 产量；输出；作品；[计] 输出信号

outward a. 向外的；外面的；公开的

outermost a. 最外面的，离中心最远的

---

instructor [in'strʌktə] n. 指导书；教员；指导者

【变】instructors

【例】While women slightly outnumber men, **instructors** have devised a creative solution. Female dancers stand in an inner circle facing out, and are surrounded by an outer circle of male dancers, who rotate to a new partner every few minutes.

　　由于女性略多于男性，**教师**设计了一个创造性的解决方案。女舞者站在内圈，脸朝外，外圈的男舞者围着内圈，每隔几分钟，男舞者就旋转到一个新的舞伴面前。

【搭】instructor of gymnastics 体操指导员

【记】instructorship n. 〈美〉（大学）讲师职位（或职务）

instrument n. 仪器；手段，工具；乐器；法律文件 v. 用仪器装备；为演奏谱曲

instruction n. 授课；教诲；传授的或获得的知识，课程；[计算机科学] 指令

devise [di'vaiz] *n.* 遗赠　*v.* 设计；想出；发明；图谋；遗赠给

【变】devises　devised　devised　devising　devises

【例】While women slightly outnumber men, instructors have **devised** a creative solution. Female dancers stand in an inner circle facing out, and are surrounded by an outer circle of male dancers, who rotate to a new partner every few minutes.

由于女性略多于男性，教师**设计**了一个创造性的解决方案。女舞者站在内圈，脸朝外，外圈的男舞者围着内圈，每隔几分钟，男舞者就旋转到一个新的舞伴面前。

【搭】devise a scheme 想出一个计策　devise new methods 想出新方法

【记】devisable *a.* 可发明的，可设计的

devourer *n.* 贪食的人

devouringly *ad.* 贪婪地，贪食地

devote *v.* 把……奉献（给），把……专用（于）；奉献

rotate [rə(u)'teit] *v.* 使旋转；使转动；使轮流　*a.* [植] 辐状的
v. 旋转；循环

【变】rotated　rotated　rotating　rotates

【例】While women slightly outnumber men, instructors have devised a creative solution. Female dancers stand in an inner circle facing out, and are surrounded by an outer circle of male dancers, who **rotate** to a new partner every few minutes.

由于女性略多于男性，教师设计了一个创造性的解决方案。女舞者站在内圈，脸朝外，外圈的男舞者围着内圈，每隔几分钟，男舞者就**旋转**到一个新的舞伴面前。

【搭】rotate mode flag 转动式标志　rotate the aircraft into the climb 使飞机旋转爬高

【记】rotatable *a.* 可旋转的，可转动的

rotative *a.* 回转的，循环的；旋转性的

rotatory *a.* 回转的；使回转的；轮流的；引起旋转的

词汇听写

1. _____ 2. _____ 3. _____

句子听写

3. In the era of the iPhone, Facebook, and Twitter, we've become <u>enamored</u> of ideas that spread as effortlessly as <u>ether</u>. We want <u>frictionless</u>, "turnkey" solutions to the major difficulties of the world-hunger, disease, poverty.

在 iPhone、Facebook 和 Twitter 的时代，我们迷恋于无穷无尽的创意，面对世界饥饿、疾病和贫穷等巨大的困难，我们想要的是能顺利解决问题和能"马上见效的"方法。

enamor [iˈnæmə] v. 使迷恋，使倾心

【变】enamored   enamored   enamoring   enamors

【例】In the era of the iPhone, Facebook, and Twitter, we've become **enamored** of ideas that spread as effortlessly as ether. We want frictionless, "turnkey" solutions to the major difficulties of the world-hunger, disease, poverty.

　　在 iPhone、Facebook 和 Twitter 的时代，我们**迷恋**于无穷无尽的创意，面对世界饥饿、疾病和贫穷等巨大的困难，我们想要的是能顺利解决问题和能"马上见效的"方法。

【记】enchant v. 使心醉，使迷惑；用魔法迷惑

　　enclose v. （用墙、篱笆等）把……围起来；把……装入信封；附入

　　enumerable a. 可点数的，可列举的

ether [ˈiːθə] n. 乙醚；[有化] 以太；苍天

【例】In the era of the iPhone, Facebook, and Twitter, we've become enamored of ideas that spread as effortlessly as **ether**. We want frictionless, "turnkey" solutions to the major difficulties of the world-hunger, disease, poverty.

　　在 iPhone、Facebook 和 Twitter 的时代，我们迷恋于无穷无尽的创意，面对世界饥饿、疾病和贫穷等巨大的困难，我们想要的是能顺利解决问题和能"马上见效的"方法。

【搭】ether alcohol 醚醇　the ether 苍天；太空　disappear into the ether 消失

在九霄云外

【记】etheric *a.* 醚的

either *pron.* （两者之中）任何一个

event *n.* 事件，大事；活动，经历；结果；运动项目

frictionless ['frikʃnlis] *a.* 无摩擦的；光滑的

【例】In the era of the iPhone, Facebook, and Twitter, we've become enamored of ideas that spread as effortlessly as ether. We want **frictionless**, "turnkey" solutions to the major difficulties of the world-hunger, disease, poverty.

在 iPhone、Facebook 和 Twitter 的时代，我们迷恋于无穷无尽的创意，面对世界饥饿、疾病和贫穷等巨大的困难，我们想要的是能顺利解决问题和能"马上见效的"方法。

【记】friction *n.* 摩擦；冲突，不和；摩擦力

frictional *a.* 摩擦的，摩擦力的

fridge *n.* 电冰箱；冷冻机

turnkey ['təːnkiː] *n.* 狱吏；监狱的看守；总控钥匙

【变】turnkeys

【例】In the era of the iPhone, Facebook, and Twitter, we've become enamored of ideas that spread as effortlessly as ether. We want frictionless, "**turnkey**" solutions to the major difficulties of the world-hunger, disease, poverty.

在 iPhone、Facebook 和 Twitter 的时代，我们迷恋于无穷无尽的创意，面对世界饥饿、疾病和贫穷等巨大的困难，我们想要的是能顺利解决问题和能"马上见效的"方法。

【搭】turnkey contract 交钥匙合同　　turnkey system 承包系统

【记】turtle *n.* ［动］龟；［动］海龟

turning *n.* 旋转；转向；转弯处；车工工艺

turnip *n.* 芜青，萝卜；芜菁作物

词汇听写

1. _____　　2. _____　　3. _____

句子听写

Tuesday ·· ◀◀

1. Chemicals generated by <u>bacteria</u> in the <u>colon</u> help important <u>immune</u> cells in the colon grow and function well.

结肠中细菌产生的化学物质帮助重要的免疫细胞在结肠中繁殖并发挥作用。

bacteria [bæk'tiəriə] *n.* [微] 细菌

【例】Chemicals generated by **bacteria** in the colon help important immune cells in the colon grow and function well.

结肠中**细菌**产生的化学物质帮助重要的免疫细胞在结肠中繁殖并发挥作用。

【搭】bacteria carrier 带菌者

【记】bacterium *n.* 细菌（复数为 bacteria）

baffle *v.* 使受挫折；使困惑，使迷惑；用隔音板隔音；挡住（水流等）

background *n.* （画等的）背景；底色；背景资料；配乐

colon ['kəulən] *n.* [解剖] 结肠；冒号（用于引语、说明、例证等之前）；科郎（哥斯达黎加货币单位）

【变】colons

【例】Chemicals generated by bacteria in the **colon** help important immune cells in the colon grow and function well.

结肠中细菌产生的化学物质帮助重要的免疫细胞在结肠中繁殖并发挥作用。

【搭】colon bacillus 大肠杆菌

【记】colonel *n.* 上校

colonial *a.* 殖民地的；殖民地化的；[生] 群体的，集群的；英领殖民地时期的

colony *n.* 侨民；侨居地；聚居地；聚居人群

immune [i'mju:n] *n.* 免疫者；免除者　*a.* 免疫的；免于……的，免除的

【例】Chemicals generated by bacteria in the colon help important **immune** cells in the colon grow and function well.

　　结肠中细菌产生的化学物质帮助重要的**免疫**细胞在结肠中繁殖并发挥作用。

【搭】immune adherence 抗原抗体粘着　　immune system 免疫系统

【记】immediate *a.* 立即的；直接的，最接近的；目前的，当前的；直觉的

　　immense *a.* 极大的，巨大的；浩瀚的，无边际的

　　immigrant *n.* 移民，侨民；从异地移入的动物〈植物〉

cell [sel] *n.* 细胞；电池；蜂房的巢室；单人小室　*v.* 住在牢房或小室中

【变】cells

【例】Chemicals generated by bacteria in the colon help important immune **cells** in the colon grow and function well.

　　结肠中细菌产生的化学物质帮助重要的免疫**细胞**在结肠中繁殖并发挥作用。

【搭】cell area 单元面积；面积元；存储单元区　　blood cells 血细胞

　　the nucleus of a cell 细胞核

【记】cell-like 细胞样的

　　cellar *n.* 地下室，地窖；酒窖；〈英〉（都市住宅的）地下煤窖

词汇听写

1. ＿＿＿＿＿＿　　2. ＿＿＿＿＿＿　　3. ＿＿＿＿＿＿

句子听写

2. Researchers have long suspected a link between gut microbes and immune-related diseases, such as obesity, allergies, and colon cancer.

　　研究人员早就怀疑肠道微生物与免疫相关的疾病，如肥胖、过敏和结肠癌之间有联系。

suspect [səˈspekt] *n.* 嫌疑犯　*a.* 可疑的；不可信的　*v.* 怀疑；猜想

【变】suspected　suspected　suspecting　suspects

【例】Researchers have long **suspected** a link between gut microbes and immune-related diseases，such as obesity，allergies，and colon cancer.

　　研究人员早就**怀疑**肠道微生物与免疫相关的疾病，如肥胖、过敏和结肠癌之间有联系。

【搭】suspect of 怀疑　　suspect patient 疑似症患者，可疑病人

【记】suspicion n. 怀疑；嫌疑；疑心

　　spend v. 用钱，花钱

gut [gʌt] n. 内脏；肠子；剧情；胆量；海峡　v. 取出内脏；摧毁内部装置
　　　　　　a. 简单的；本质的，根本的

【变】gutted　gutted　gutting　guts

【例】Researchers have long suspected a link between **gut** microbes and immune-related diseases，such as obesity，allergies，and colon cancer.

　　研究人员早就怀疑**肠道**微生物与免疫相关的疾病，如肥胖、过敏和结肠癌之间有联系。

【搭】gut cleaning 刮肠　　gut hasher 内脏切碎机

【记】gutless a. 无胆量的；没勇气的；没有生气的

　　get v. 使得；获得；受到；变成

　　gust n. 狂风；（感情）迸发 v. 猛刮

obesity [ə(u)'biːsiti] n. 肥大，肥胖

【例】Researchers have long suspected a link between gut microbes and immune-related diseases，such as **obesity**，allergies，and colon cancer.

　　研究人员早就怀疑肠道微生物与免疫相关的疾病，如**肥胖**、过敏和结肠癌之间有联系。

【记】obese a. 肥胖的，过胖的

　　obey v. 服从，听从；按照……行动

allergy ['ælədʒi] n. 过敏症；反感；厌恶

【例】Researchers have long suspected a link between gut microbes and immune-related diseases，such as obesity，**allergies**，and colon cancer.

　　研究人员早就怀疑肠道微生物与免疫相关的疾病，如肥胖、**过敏**和结肠癌之间有联系。

【记】allergist *n.* 过敏症专科医师

allergenic *a.* 引起过敏症的

allergenicity *n.* 变应原性

词汇听写

1. _____ 2. _____ 3. _____

句子听写

3. The subscription based-channel will now offer broadcasts streamed in HD, with improved graphics and in-game statistical information.

以电视频道为主的订阅活动将提供节目，在高清电视中播放，显示改良的图表和游戏中的统计信息。

subscription [səb'skripʃn] *n.* 捐献；订阅；订金；签署

【变】subscriptions

【例】The **subscription** based-channel will now offer broadcasts streamed in HD, with improved graphics and in-game statistical information.

以电视频道为主的**订阅**活动将提供节目，在高清电视中播放，显示改良的图表和游戏中的统计信息。

【搭】subscription agent 期刊预订代理商

【记】subscriber *n.* 订户；签署者；捐献者

subscribe *v.* 订阅；捐款；认购；赞成；签署

stream [striːm] *n.* 溪流；流动；潮流；光线 *v.* 流出；涌出；（使）飘动

【变】streamed streamed streaming streams

【例】The subscription based-channel will now offer broadcasts **streamed** in HD, with improved graphics and in-game statistical information.

以电视频道为主的订阅活动将提供节目，在高清电视中播放，**显示**改良的图表和游戏中的统计信息。

【搭】stream down 流下 stream of visitors 游客流量

【记】streaming *n*. 流；〈英〉按能力分组

streamlet *n*. 小河；细流

graphic ['græfik] *a.* 形象的；图表的；绘画似的

【例】The subscription based-channel will now offer broadcasts streamed in HD, with improved **graphics** and in-game statistical information.

以电视频道为主的订阅活动将提供节目，在高清电视中播放，显示改良的**图表**和游戏中的统计信息。

【搭】graph data 图形数据，图表资料　graph grammar 图文法

【记】graphical *a.* 图解的；绘画的；生动的

graphically *ad.* 生动地；活灵活现地；用图表表示地；轮廓分明地

graph *n.* 图表；曲线图

in-game ['in-geim] *a.* 游戏中的

【例】The subscription based-channel will now offer broadcasts streamed in HD, with improved graphics and **in-game** statistical information.

以电视频道为主的订阅活动将提供节目，在高清电视中播放，显示改良的图表和**游戏中**的统计信息。

【搭】in-game advertisement（电脑、电子）游戏中出现的广告

词汇听写

1. _____　2. _____　3. _____

句子听写

1. He oversees two long-term studies generating numerous insights on healthy living. He and his colleagues have found that red meat is associated with increased risk of diabetes while coffee is linked to reduced risk.

　　他跟踪了两项长期的研究，通过研究，他对健康生活有了许多看法。他和他的同事们发现，红色肉类会增加患糖尿病的风险，而咖啡则可以降低该风险。

oversee [ˌəuvə'siː] *v.* 监督；审查；俯瞰；偷看到，无意中看到

【变】oversaw　oversaw　overseeing　oversees

【例】He **oversees** two long-term studies generating numerous insights on healthy living. He and his colleagues have found that red meat is associated with increased risk of diabetes while coffee is linked to reduced risk.

　　他**跟踪**了两项长期的研究，通过研究，他对健康生活有了许多看法。他和他的同事们发现，红色肉类会增加患糖尿病的风险，而咖啡则可以降低该风险。

【记】overseer *n.* 监督；工头

　　oversea *a.* 外国的；在海外的

　　overseam *n.* 包边帽，包缝

insight ['insait] *n.* 洞察力；洞悉

【变】insights

【例】He oversees two long-term studies generating numerous **insights** on healthy living. He and his colleagues have found that red meat is associated with increased risk of diabetes while coffee is linked to reduced risk.

　　他跟踪了两项长期的研究，通过研究，他对健康生活有了许多**看法**。他和他的同事们发现，红色肉类会增加患糖尿病的风险，而咖啡则可以降低该风险。

【搭】insight into social affairs 对社会时事的观察

【记】insightful *a.* 有深刻见解的，富有洞察力的

insigne *n.* 勋章；徽章

insignificance *n.* 无意义；不重要；无价值

colleague ['kɔliːg] *n.* 同事，同僚

【变】colleagues

【例】He oversees two long-term studies generating numerous insights on healthy living. He and his **colleagues** have found that red meat is associated with increased risk of diabetes while coffee is linked to reduced risk.

他跟踪了两项长期的研究，通过研究，他对健康生活有了许多看法。他和他的**同事们**发现，红色肉类会增加患糖尿病的风险，而咖啡则可以降低该风险。

【记】college *n.* 大学；学院；学会

collected *a.* 镇定的；收集成的

collet *n.* 夹头；宝石座；筒夹

diabetes [ˌdaiə'biːtiːz] *n.* 糖尿病；多尿症

【例】He oversees two long-term studies generating numerous insights on healthy living. He and his colleagues have found that red meat is associated with increased risk of **diabetes** while coffee is linked to reduced risk.

他跟踪了两项长期的研究，通过研究，他对健康生活有了许多看法。他和他的同事们发现，红色肉类会增加患**糖尿病**的风险，而咖啡则可以降低该风险。

【搭】in case of diabetes mellitus 对于糖尿病患者

【记】diabetic *a.* 糖尿病的，患糖尿病的

diabolic *a.* 残忍的；魔鬼似的；恶魔的

词汇听写

1. _____   2. _____   3. _____

句子听写

2. Underlying all these exciting efforts is the awareness that <u>experimentation</u> is key and that we do not yet know how to best <u>harness</u> the enormous positive potential of the online <u>revolution</u> for on-campus learning.

所有这些激动人心的努力让大家意识到，实验是关键，而且，我们还不知道该如何最好地利用学校网络教育革命所拥有的巨大潜力。

underlie [ˌʌndəˈlai] *v.* 成为……的基础；位于……之下

【变】underlay　underlain　underlying　underlies

【例】**Underlying** all these exciting efforts is the awareness that experimentation is key and that we do not yet know how to best harness the enormous positive potential of the online revolution for on-campus learning.

　　所有这些激动人心的努力让大家意识到，实验是关键，而且，我们还不知道该如何最好地利用学校网络教育革命所拥有的巨大潜力。

【记】underachiever *n.* 后进生；学校学习成绩低于智商的学生

　　underbid *n.* 叫牌偏低；出价较低

　　underestimate *v.* 低估

experimentation [ikˌsperimenˈteiʃən] *n.* 实验；试验；实验法；实验过程

【变】experimentations

【例】Underlying all these exciting efforts is the awareness that **experimentation** is key and that we do not yet know how to best harness the enormous positive potential of the online revolution for on-campus learning.

　　所有这些激动人心的努力让大家意识到，**实验**是关键，而且，我们还不知道该如何最好地利用学校网络教育革命所拥有的巨大潜力。

【搭】experimentation cost 试验费用

【记】experimental *a.* 实验的；根据实验的；试验性的

　　experimentally *ad.* 实验上地；用实验方法地

　　experimentalism *n.* 经验主义

　　experiment *v.* 尝试；进行实验

harness [ˈhɑːnis] *n.*　马具；甲胄；挽具状带子；降落伞背带
　　　　　　　　　　v. 治理；套；驾驭；利用

【变】harnessed　harnessed　harnessing　harnesses

【例】Underlying all these exciting efforts is the awareness that experimentation is key and that we do not yet know how to best **harness** the enormous positive potential of the online revolution for on-campus learning.

所有这些激动人心的努力让大家意识到，实验是关键，而且，我们还不知道该如何最好地利用学校网络教育革命所拥有的巨大潜力。

【搭】harness a horse 给马上挽具　how to harness the power of the sun 如何使用太阳能

【记】harass *v.* 使困扰；使烦恼；反复袭击

harmful *a.* 有害的；能造成损害的

revolution [ˌrevəˈluːʃn] *n.* 革命；旋转；运行；循环

【变】revolutions

【例】Underlying all these exciting efforts is the awareness that experimentation is key and that we do not yet know how to best harness the enormous positive potential of the online **revolution** for on-campus learning.

所有这些激动人心的努力让大家意识到，实验是关键，而且，我们还不知道该如何最好地利用学校网络教育**革命**所拥有的巨大潜力。

【搭】days of revolution 革命期间　French Revolution 法国大革命

【记】revolutionary *a.* 革命的；旋转的；大变革的

revolve *n.* 旋转；循环；旋转舞台

revolutionist *n.* 革命家

词汇听写

1. _____　2. _____　3. _____

句子听写

3. Adults may already be getting bone-building <u>calcium</u> from other <u>sources</u> such as <u>fortified</u> orange juice. Whether children should be drinking whole or <u>skim</u> milk is up for debate.

成人可能已经从其他来源得到骨头生长需要的钙，如强化橙汁。孩子们是否应该喝全脂或脱脂牛奶尚存异议。

calcium [ˈkælsiəm] *n.* [化] 钙

【例】Adults may already be getting bone-building **calcium** from other sources such as fortified orange juice. Whether children should be drinking whole or skim milk is up for debate.

成人可能已经从其他来源得到骨头生长需要的**钙**，如强化橙汁。孩子们是否应该喝全脂或脱脂牛奶尚存异议。

【搭】calcium acetate 乙酸钙　calcium alginate 藻酸钙

【记】calculable *a.* 可计算的；能预测的；可靠的

calculous *a.* 结石的，结石症的；石一般的 *n.* 微积分

callout *n.* 插图编号

source [sɔːs] *n.* 来源；水源；原始资料

【变】sources　sourced　sourced　sourcing　sources

【例】Adults may already be getting bone-building calcium from other **sources** such as fortified orange juice. Whether children should be drinking whole or skim milk is up for debate.

成人可能已经从其他**来源**得到骨头生长需要的钙，如强化橙汁。孩子们是否应该喝全脂或脱脂牛奶尚存异议。

【搭】source address 源地址　source alphabet 信源字母集

【记】sour *a.* 酸的；发酵的；刺耳的；酸臭的；讨厌的

south *n.* 南方；南部；美国南方各州；（南半球的）发展中国家

fortify [ˈfɔːtifai] *v.* 加强，增强；增加营养物；使体力增加；鼓励，使（意志等）坚定；构筑防御工事

【变】fortified　fortified　fortifying　fortifies

【例】Adults may already be getting bone-building calcium from other sources such as **fortified** orange juice. Whether children should be drinking whole or skim milk is up for debate.

成人可能已经从其他来源得到骨头生长需要的钙，如**强化**橙汁。孩子们是否应该喝全脂或脱脂牛奶尚存异议。

【搭】fortifiable *a.* 可以弄巩固的，宜于设防的

【记】fortify *v.* 加强，增强；增加营养物；使体力增加；鼓励，使（意志等）坚定

fortifiable *a.* 可以弄巩固的，宜于设防的

fortifier *n.* 使坚固的东西，筑城者，增强论点力量（或体力等的）人

skim [skim] *n.* 撇；撇去的东西；表层物；瞒报所得的收入　*a.* 脱脂的；撇去浮沫的；表层的　*v.* 略读；撇去……的浮物；从……表面飞掠而过；去除；（为逃税而）隐瞒（部分收入）

【变】skimmed　skimmed　skimming　skims

【例】Adults may already be getting bone-building calcium from other sources such as fortified orange juice. Whether children should be drinking whole or **skim** milk is up for debate.

成人可能已经从其他来源得到骨头生长需要的钙，如强化橙汁。孩子们是否应该喝全脂或*脱脂*牛奶尚存异议。

【搭】skim the instruction 浏览使用说明

【记】skimmed *a.* 脱脂的

skimming *n.* 撇取浮沫；浮渣

skimmer *n.* 大略阅读的人；撇去浮沫的器具

词汇听写

1. _____　　2. _____　　3. _____

句子听写

Thursday ·· ≪

1. The U. S. suffers higher rates of gun-related <u>homicides</u>, gun-related <u>suicides</u> because so many more people here own and use <u>firearms</u> and because of permissive gun laws.

因为美国允许使用枪支的法律，很多美国人拥有和使用枪支，这让美国承受着较高的和枪支有关的凶杀、自杀的死亡率。

homicide [ˈhɔmisaid] *n.* 杀人；杀人犯

【变】homicides

【例】The U. S. suffers higher rates of gun-related **homicides**, gun-related suicides because so many more people here own and use firearms and because of permissive gun laws.

因为美国允许使用枪支的法律，很多美国人拥有和使用枪支，这让美国承受着较高的和枪支有关的**凶杀**、自杀的死亡率。

【记】suicide *v.* 自杀

decide *v.* 决定，决心

suicide [ˈs(j)uːisaid] *n.* 自杀；自杀行为；自杀者 *a.* 自杀的 *v.* 自杀 *v.* 自杀

【变】suicides

【例】The U. S. suffers higher rates of gun-related homicides, gun-related **suicides** because so many more people here own and use firearms and because of permissive gun laws.

因为美国允许使用枪支的法律，很多美国人拥有和使用枪支，这让美国承受着较高的和枪支有关的凶杀、**自杀**的死亡率。

【搭】suicide bomber 自杀炸弹

【记】suitcase *n.* （旅行用的）手提箱

suicidal *a.* 自杀的，自杀性的；自我毁灭的；自取灭亡的

suicidally *ad.* 毁灭性地；自杀性地

firearm [ˈfaiərɑːm] *n.* 火器；枪炮

【变】firearms

【例】The U. S. suffers higher rates of gun-related homicides，gun-related suicides because so many more people here own and use **firearms** and because of permissive gun laws.

　　因为美国允许使用枪支的法律，很多美国人拥有和使用**枪支**，这让美国承受着较高的和枪支有关的凶杀、自杀的死亡率。

【记】fireman n. 消防队员；［矿］救火员，爆破工；司炉工

firework n.（常 pl.）烟火，烟花；（热情、怒气等的）迸发

fireplace n. 壁炉

permissive [pə'misiv] a. 许可的；自由的；宽容的；放任的

【例】The U. S. suffers higher rates of gun-related homicides，gun-related suicides because so many more people here own and use firearms and because of **permissive** gun laws.

　　因为美国**允许**使用枪支的法律，很多美国人拥有和使用枪支，这让美国承受着较高的和枪支有关的凶杀、自杀的死亡率。

【搭】permissive tolerance 姑息纵容　permissive temperature 许可的温度

【记】permissible a. 可允许的；获得准许的

permissibly ad. 获准地；得到许可地

permission n. 允许，许可

词汇听写

1. _____　　2. _____　　3. _____

句子听写

2. He is a true visionary, and he consistently shows how boundaries can be pushed and expanded to further the cause of education and knowledge.

　　他是一位真正的梦想家，他一再展示如何推动与扩展教育事业和知识的边界。

visionary ['viʒnri] n. 空想家；梦想者；有眼力的人　a. 梦想的；幻影的

【变】visionaries

【例】He is a true **visionary**，and he consistently shows how boundaries can be pushed and expanded to further the cause of education and knowledge.

　　他是一位真正的**梦想家**，他一再展示如何推动与扩展教育事业和知识的边界。

【记】vision *n.* 视力；美景；眼力；幻象；想象力 *v.* 想象；显现；梦见

　　visionaries *n.* 空想主义者；愿景者；远见者（visionary 的复数）

consistently [kən'sistəntli] *ad.* 一贯地；一致地；坚实地

【例】He is a true visionary，and he **consistently** shows how boundaries can be pushed and expanded to further the cause of education and knowledge.

　　他是一位真正的梦想家，他**一再**展示如何推动与扩展教育事业和知识的边界。

【搭】consistently approve 一致同意

【记】consistent *a.* 始终如一的，一致的；坚持的

　　consistency *n.* ［计］一致性；稠度；相容性

　　consist *v.* 组成；在于；符合

boundary ['baundri] *n.* 边界；范围；分界线

【变】boundaries

【例】He is a true visionary，and he consistently shows how **boundaries** can be pushed and expanded to further the cause of education and knowledge.

　　他是一位真正的梦想家，他一再展示如何推动与扩展教育事业和知识的**边界**。

【搭】boundary angle 边界角　boundary diffusion 界面扩散

【记】bound *a.* 被束缚的，装订的

　　bound *v.* 跳跃

further ['fə:ðə] *a.* 更远的；深一层的　*v.* 促进，助长；增进　*ad.* 进一步地；而且；更远地

【变】furthered　furthered　furthering　furthers

【例】He is a true visionary，and he consistently shows how boundaries can be pushed and expanded to **further** the cause of education and knowledge.

　　他是一位真正的梦想家，他一再展示如何推动与扩展教育事业和知

识的边界。

【搭】further charge 追补价款 furthermore 而且，此外

【记】furthermost *a.* 最远方的

furtherance *n.* 促进；助成；助长

词汇听写

1. _____ 2. _____ 3. _____

句子听写

3. This fellowship <u>formalizes</u> the <u>intersection</u> of the theater and the Institute by providing an opportunity for young aspiring theater producers to be <u>nurtured</u> by a professional theater company.

　　这家剧院通过为年轻有抱负的戏剧制作人提供机会，正式与学院建立了合作关系。

formalize [ˈfɔːmlaiz] *v.* 使形式化；使正式；拘泥礼仪

【变】formalized formalized formalizing formalizes

【例】This fellowship **formalizes** the intersection of the theater and the Institute by providing an opportunity for young aspiring theater producers to be nurtured by a professional theater company.

　　这家剧院通过为年轻有抱负的戏剧制作人提供机会，**正式**与学院建立了合作关系。

【记】formalization *n.* 形式化；礼仪化

formalism *n.* 形式主义；形式体系

formalin *n.* [药] 福尔马林

intersection [intəˈsekʃn] *n.* 交叉；十字路口；交集；交叉点

【变】intersections

【例】This fellowship formalizes the **intersection** of the theater and the Institute by providing an opportunity for young aspiring theater producers to be nurtured by a professional theater company.

这家剧院通过为年轻有抱负的戏剧制作人提供机会，正式与学院建立了合作**关系**。

【搭】intersection chart 网络图，交织图　intersection cover 相交覆盖

【记】intersectant *a.* 交叉的，相交的

intersect *v.* 相交，交叉

nurture [ˈnəːtʃə] *n.* **养育；教养；营养物** *v.* **养育；鼓励；培植**

【变】nurtured　nurtured　nurturing　nurtures

【例】This fellowship formalizes the intersection of the theater and the Institute by providing an opportunity for young aspiring theater producers to be **nurtured** by a professional theater company.

这家剧院通过为年轻有抱负的戏剧制作人**提供机会**，正式与学院建立了合作关系。

【记】nurturant *a.* 抚育的；抚养的

nursing *n.* 护理；看护；养育

nurturance *n.* 养成；教育；培养（形容词 nurturant）；养育

nature *n.* 大自然；本质

词汇听写

1. ＿＿＿＿＿＿＿＿　2. ＿＿＿＿＿＿＿＿　3. ＿＿＿＿＿＿＿＿

句子听写

Friday ·· «

1. Its <u>mission</u> is to protect genetic diversity in <u>livestock</u> and <u>poultry</u> species through the conservation and promotion of <u>endangered</u> breeds.

　　它的使命是通过保存和促进濒危品种的发展来保护畜禽品种遗传的多样性。

mission [ˈmiʃn] *n.* **使命，任务；代表团；布道** *v.* **派遣；向……传教**

【变】missioned　missioned　missioning　missions

【例】Its **mission** is to protect genetic diversity in livestock and poultry species through the conservation and promotion of endangered breeds.

　　　它的**使命**是通过保存和促进濒危品种的发展来保护畜禽品种遗传的多样性。

【搭】mission allowance 出差津贴　　mission description 游戏描述，任务说明

【记】missionary *a.* 传教的；传教士的

　　　missionary *n.* 传教士

　　　missioner *n.* 传教士，教区传教士

livestock [ˈlaivstɔk] *n.* **牲畜；家畜**

【例】Its mission is to protect genetic diversity in **livestock** and poultry species through the conservation and promotion of endangered breeds.

　　　它的使命是通过保存和促进濒危品种的发展来保护**畜禽**品种遗传的多样性。

【记】live-science *n.* 生活科学

　　　lives *n.* 生命；生物，活物；一生；生活方式

　　　lively *a.* 充满活力的；活泼的；充满趣味的

poultry [ˈpəultri] *n.* **家禽**

【例】Its mission is to protect genetic diversity in livestock and **poultry** species through the conservation and promotion of endangered breeds.

　　　它的使命是通过保存和促进濒危品种的发展来保护**畜禽**品种遗传的多样性。

【搭】poultry breeding 饲养家禽

【记】poulterer *n.* 鸟贩；家禽贩

poult *n.* 幼禽

pool *n.* 联营；撞球；水塘；共同资金

endanger [inˈdein(d)ʒə] *v.* 危及；使遭到危险

【变】endangered　endangered　endangering　endangers

【例】Its mission is to protect genetic diversity in livestock and poultry species through the conservation and promotion of **endangered** breeds.

　　它的使命是通过保存和促进**濒危**品种的发展来保护畜禽品种遗传的多样性。

【搭】endangerment *n.* 危害；受到危害　endangered species *n.* 濒于灭绝的物种

【记】endangered *a.* 濒临灭绝的；有生命危险的

endangerment *n.* 危害，受到危害

endorsing *n.* ［商］背书

词汇听写

1. ＿＿＿＿＿＿＿＿　2. ＿＿＿＿＿＿＿＿　3. ＿＿＿＿＿＿＿＿

句子听写

2. There have been significant improvements in patient safety, citing the elimination of bloodstream infections from central lines, hand hygiene, and surgical time-outs.

　　病人的安全已经有显著改善，比如，由血液感染、手部卫生和手术暂停引起的问题已经有所减少。

elimination [iˌlimiˈneiʃən] *n.* 消除；淘汰；除去

【变】eliminations

【例】There have been significant improvements in patient safety, citing the

elimination of bloodstream infections from central lines, hand hygiene, and surgical time-outs.

病人的安全已经有显著**改善**，比如，由血液感染、手部卫生和手术暂停引起的问题已经有所减少。

【搭】elimination of jobs 减少就业机会　elimination of mistakes 消除错误

【记】eliminator *n.* 消除器；消除者

eliminate *v.* 消除；排除

limit *n.* 限制；限度；界线

infection [inˈfekʃn] *n.* 感染；传染；影响；传染病

【变】infections

【例】There have been significant improvements in patient safety, citing the elimination of bloodstream **infections** from central lines, hand hygiene, and surgical time-outs.

病人的安全已经有显著改善，比如，由血液**感染**、手部卫生和手术暂停引起的问题已经有所减少。

【搭】infection atrium 传染入口

【记】infectious *a.* 传染的；传染性的；易传染的

infective *a.* 有传染性的，感染别人的

infect *v.* 感染，传染

hygiene [ˈhaidʒiːn] *n.* 卫生；卫生学；保健法

【例】There have been significant improvements in patient safety, citing the elimination of bloodstream infections from central lines, hand **hygiene**, and surgical time-outs.

病人的安全已经有显著改善，比如，由血液感染、手部**卫生**和手术暂停引起的问题已经有所减少。

【记】hygienic *a.* 卫生的，保健的；卫生学的

hygienically *ad.* 卫生地

hygienics *n.* 卫生学

surgical [ˈsəːdʒikl] *n.* 外科手术；外科病房　*a.* 外科的；手术上的

【例】There have been significant improvements in patient safety, citing the elimination of bloodstream infections from central lines, hand hygiene, and **surgical** time-outs.

病人的安全已经有显著改善，比如，由血液感染、手部卫生和**手术**暂停引起的问题已经有所减少。

【搭】surgical operations 外科手术

【记】surgically *ad.* 如外科手术般地

surgery *n.* 外科；外科手术；手术室；诊疗室

surgeon *n.* 外科医生

词汇听写

1. _____ 2. _____ 3. _____

句子听写

3. I find that librarians especially tend to be very service-oriented. We often feel guilty about taking time for ourselves like doing exercises. This yoga class is great because anyone can carve out 30 minutes once a week.

我发现图书馆管理员的服务意识特别强烈，我们会因为在自己身上花费时间如做运动而感到内疚。这个瑜伽课程设置得很棒，因为每个人都能每周腾出 30 分钟。

librarian [laiˈbreəriən] *n.* 图书馆员；图书管理员

【变】librarians

【例】I find that **librarians** especially tend to be very service-oriented. We often feel guilty about taking time for ourselves like doing exercises. This yoga class is great because anyone can carve out 30 minutes once a week.

我发现**图书馆管理员**的服务意识特别强烈，我们会因为在自己身上花费时间如做运动而感到内疚。这个瑜伽课程设置得很棒，因为每个人都能每周腾出 30 分钟。

【记】library *n.* 图书馆，藏书室；文库

librarianship *n.* 图书馆事业；图书馆管理员职位；图书馆管理业务

orient [ˈɔːriənt] *n.* 东方；东方诸国　*a.* 东方的　*v.* 使适应；确定方向；使朝东；以……为中心

【变】oriented　oriented　orienting　orients

【例】I find that librarians especially tend to be very service-**oriented**. We often feel guilty about taking time for ourselves like doing exercises. This yoga class is great because anyone can carve out 30 minutes once a week.

我发现图书馆管理员的**服务意识**特别强烈，我们会因为在自己身上花费时间如做运动而感到内疚。这个瑜伽课程设置得很棒，因为每个人都能每周腾出 30 分钟。

【搭】orient core 方位中心　orient pink 珍珠粉红色　quality-oriented education 素质教育

【记】oriented *a.* 导向的；定向的；以……为方向的

oriental *a.* 东方的；东方人的

orientation *n.* 方向；定向；适应；情况介绍；向东方

guilty [ˈgilti] *a.* 有罪的；内疚的

【变】guiltier　guiltiest

【例】I find that librarians especially tend to be very service-oriented. We often feel **guilty** about taking time for ourselves like doing exercises. This yoga class is great because anyone can carve out 30 minutes once a week.

我发现图书馆管理员的服务意识特别强烈，我们会因为在自己身上花费时间如做运动而感到**内疚**。这个瑜伽课程设置得很棒，因为每个人都能每周腾出 30 分钟。

【搭】guilty party 有罪一方，当事人

【记】guiltless *a.* 无罪的，无辜的；没有……的，不知……的

guiltily *ad.* 内疚地；有罪地

guilt *n.* 犯罪，过失；内疚

carve [kɑːv] *v.* 雕刻；切开；开创；做雕刻工作

【变】carved　carved　carving　carves

【例】I find that librarians especially tend to be very service-oriented. We often feel guilty about taking time for ourselves like doing exercises. This yoga class is great because anyone can **carve** out 30 minutes once a week.

　　我发现图书馆管理员的服务意识特别强烈，我们会因为在自己身上花费时间如做运动而感到内疚。这个瑜伽课程设置得很棒，因为每个人都能每周**腾出** 30 分钟。

【搭】carve out 雕刻出……；用辛勤的劳动创造出……　　carve for oneself 自由行动

【记】carved *a.* 有雕刻的

　　carven *a.* 雕刻的

　　carving *n.* 雕刻；雕刻品；雕刻术

词汇听写

1. ＿＿＿＿＿＿＿　　2. ＿＿＿＿＿＿＿　　3. ＿＿＿＿＿＿＿

句子听写

Saturday ·· ≪

1. Chair yoga serves to reset posture—which has a tendency to sag after a few hours in front of a screen. Gentle neck stretches, seated spine twists and hand and wrist stretches are especially helpful for people who type a lot.

在椅子上做瑜伽是为了重塑身形——在屏幕前坐上几个小时后，身形下垂。轻柔的颈部伸展，坐着扭动脊柱，手腕和腰部伸展对打字多的人特别有帮助。

posture [ˈpɒstʃə] *n.* 姿势；态度；情形 *v.* 做……的姿势，摆姿势

【变】postured postured posturing postures

【例】Chair yoga serves to reset **posture**—which has a tendency to sag after a few hours in front of a screen. Gentle neck stretches, seated spine twists and hand and wrist stretches are especially helpful for people who type a lot.

在椅子上做瑜伽是为了重塑**身形**——在屏幕前坐上几个小时后，身形下垂。轻柔的颈部伸展，坐着扭动脊柱，手腕和腰部伸展对打字多的人特别有帮助。

【搭】posture map 态势图 posture switch 姿势开关

【记】postural *a.* 姿势的，位置的；心态的

posturing *n.* 故作姿态；摆姿势；并非由衷的言行

posturer 杂技演员；装腔作势的人；做出某种姿态的人

sag [sæg] *n.* 松弛；下跌；漂流；萧条 *v.* 下垂；下降；萎靡

【变】sagged sagged sagging sags

【例】Chair yoga serves to reset posture—which has a tendency to **sag** after a few hours in front of a screen. Gentle neck stretches, seated spine twists and hand and wrist stretches are especially helpful for people who type a lot.

在椅子上做瑜伽是为了重塑身形——在屏幕前坐上几个小时后，身形**下垂**。轻柔的颈部伸展，坐着扭动脊柱，手腕和腰部伸展对打字多的人特别有帮助。

【搭】sag adjustment 垂度调节

【记】sagging *n.* 下垂

signal *n.* 信号；暗号；导火线 *v.* 标志；用信号通知

stretch [stretʃ] *n.* 伸展，延伸　*v.* 伸展，张开　*a.* 可伸缩的

【变】stretched　stretched　stretching　stretches

【例】Chair yoga serves to reset posture—which has a tendency to sag after a few hours in front of a screen. Gentle neck **stretches**, seated spine twists and hand and wrist stretches are especially helpful for people who type a lot.

在椅子上做瑜伽是为了重塑身形——在屏幕前坐上几个小时后，身形下垂。轻柔的颈部**伸展**，坐着扭动脊柱，手腕和腰部伸展对打字多的人特别有帮助。

【搭】stretch legs 伸伸腿　stretch elongation 伸长

【记】stretchy *a.* 有弹性的；能伸展的

stretchable *a.* 能伸展的；可伸缩的

stretcher *n.* 担架；延伸器

stretchability *n.* （力）拉伸性；延性

spine [spain] *n.* 脊柱，脊椎；刺；书脊

【变】spines

【例】Chair yoga serves to reset posture—which has a tendency to sag after a few hours in front of a screen. Gentle neck stretches, seated **spine** twists and hand and wrist stretches are especially helpful for people who type a lot.

在椅子上做瑜伽是为了重塑身形——在屏幕前坐上几个小时后，身形下垂。轻柔的颈部伸展，坐着扭动**脊柱**，手腕和腰部伸展对打字多的人特别有帮助。

【记】spinal *a.* 脊髓的；脊柱的；针的；脊骨的；尖刺的

spineless *a.* 没有骨气的；无脊椎的；懦弱的

spinally *ad.* 在脊骨方面地；沿着脊骨地

词汇听写

1. _____　2. _____　3. _____

句子听写

2. Science suggests if we want to have a breakthrough <u>impact</u> on children, we have to transform the lives of adults who take care of them. Adults have to be prepared to <u>buffer</u> children from stress in their lives——to help children learn to be <u>resilient</u> and overcome <u>adversity</u>.

科学表明，如果我们希望对儿童的影响有一个突破，我们必须转变照顾他们的成年人的生活。成人必须做好准备，减轻孩子的压力——帮助孩子学会抗压和克服逆境。

impact [ˈimpækt] *n.* 影响；效果；碰撞；冲击力　　*v.* 影响；撞击；冲突；压紧；产生影响

【变】impacted　impacted　impacting　impacts

【例】Science suggests if we want to have a breakthrough **impact** on children，we have to transform the lives of adults who take care of them. Adults have to be prepared to buffer children from stress in their lives—to help children learn to be resilient and overcome adversity.

科学表明，如果我们希望对儿童的**影响**有一个突破，我们必须转变照顾他们的成年人的生活。成人必须做好准备，减轻孩子的压力——帮助孩子学会抗压和克服逆境。

【搭】impact acceleration 撞击加速度，撞击过载

【记】impacted *a.* 压紧的；结实的；嵌入的；（人口）稠密的

impactive *a.* 冲击的；有不良影响的

impaction *n.* 压紧；装紧；嵌入

buffer [ˈbʌfə] *n.* ［计］缓冲区；缓冲器，（车辆）减震器　　*v.* 缓冲

【变】buffers　buffered　buffered　buffering　buffers

【例】Science suggests if we want to have a breakthrough impact on children，we have to transform the lives of adults who take care of them. Adults have to be prepared to **buffer** children from stress in their lives—to help children learn to be resilient and overcome adversity.

科学表明，如果我们希望对儿童的影响有一个突破，我们必须转变照顾他们的成年人的生活。成人必须做好准备，**减轻**孩子的压力——帮助孩子学会抗压和克服逆境。

【搭】buffer action 缓冲作用

【记】buff *n.* 浅黄色；软皮 *v.* 缓冲；擦亮

resilient [ri'ziliənt] *a.* 弹回的，有弹力的

【例】Science suggests if we want to have a breakthrough impact on children, we have to transform the lives of adults who take care of them. Adults have to be prepared to buffer children from stress in their lives—to help children learn to be **resilient** and overcome adversity.

科学表明，如果我们希望对儿童的影响有一个突破，我们必须转变照顾他们的成年人的生活。成人必须做好准备，减轻孩子的压力——帮助孩子学会**抗压**和克服逆境。

【搭】resilient rope 有弹力的绳子

【记】resilience *n.* 恢复力；弹力；顺应力

resile *v.* 弹回；恢复原状；被撤销

adversity [əd'vəːsiti] *n.* 厄运，不幸；逆境，悲惨的境遇；（尤指经济方面的）窘境

【变】adversities

【例】Science suggests if we want to have a breakthrough impact on children, we have to transform the lives of adults who take care of them. Adults have to be prepared to buffer children from stress in their lives—to help children learn to be resilient and overcome **adversity**.

科学表明，如果我们希望对儿童的影响有一个突破，我们必须转变照顾他们的成年人的生活。成人必须做好准备，减轻孩子的压力——帮助孩子学会抗压和克服**逆境**。

【搭】in time of adversity 在患难中　triumph over adversity 战胜逆境

【记】advertisement *n.* 广告，宣传

adventage *n.* 有利

词汇听写

1. _____ 2. _____ 3. _____

句子听写

3. Although institution welcomes any proposals that catalyze innovation around teaching and learning at Harvard, grant proposals are particularly encouraged.

尽管机构欢迎任何有关促进哈佛教学和学习创新的建议，但是学校还是特别鼓励各种拨款和补助。

proposal [prəˈpəuzl] *n.* 提议，建议；求婚

【变】proposals

【例】Although institution welcomes any **proposals** that catalyze innovation around teaching and learning at Harvard, grant proposals are particularly encouraged.

尽管机构欢迎任何有关促进哈佛教学和学习创新的**建议**，但是学校还是特别鼓励各种拨款和补助。

【搭】proposal accepted 接受了的提议

【记】proposed *a.* 被提议的；所推荐的

proposition *n.* ［数］命题；提议；主题；议题

catalyze [ˈkætəlaiz] *v.* 催化；刺激，促进

【变】catalyzed catalyzed catalyzing catalyzes

【例】Although institution welcomes any proposals that **catalyze** innovation around teaching and learning at Harvard, grant proposals are particularly encouraged.

尽管机构欢迎任何有关促进哈佛教学和学习创新的建议，但是学校还是特别鼓励各种拨款和补助。

【记】catalytic *a.* 接触反应的；起催化作用的

catalytically *ad.* 催化地

274

innovation [ɪnəˈveɪʃn] *n.* 创新，革新；新方法

【变】innovations

【例】Although institution welcomes any proposals that catalyze **innovation** around teaching and learning at Harvard, grant proposals are particularly encouraged.

　　尽管机构欢迎任何有关促进哈佛教学和学习**创新**的建议，但是学校还是特别鼓励各种拨款和补助。

【搭】innovation function 革新职能　　encourage innovation 鼓励创新

【记】innovative *a.* 革新的，创新的

　　innovator *n.* 改革者，创新者

　　innovate *v.* 创新；改革；革新

grant [grɑːnt] *n.* 拨款；[法] 授予物　　*v.* 授予；允许；承认；同意

【变】granted　granted　granting　grants

【例】Although institution welcomes any proposals that catalyze innovation around teaching and learning at Harvard, **grant** proposals are particularly encouraged.

　　尽管机构欢迎任何有关促进哈佛教学和学习创新的建议，但是学校还是特别鼓励各种**拨款**和补助。

【搭】I grant you 我同意你的观点　　grant a loan 同意贷款

【记】grantee *n.* 受让人；被授与者

　　grantor *n.* 授予者；[法] 让与人

　　grain *n.* 谷物粮食

词汇听写

1. _____　2. _____　3. _____

句子听写

Sunday ·· 《

1. These findings suggest that strategies focused on enhanced outpatient management of chronic disease may not be focused on the problems plaguing Medicare's high-cost patients.

　　这些发现表明，要加强管理罹患慢性疾病的门诊病人，不能只着眼于受医疗保险费用高昂所困扰的患者。

outpatient [ˈaʊtpeɪʃnt] *n.* 门诊病人

【变】outpatients

【例】These findings suggest that strategies focused on enhanced **outpatient** management of chronic disease may not be focused on the problems plaguing Medicare's high-cost patients.

　　这些发现表明，要加强管理罹患慢性疾病的**门诊病人**，不能只着眼于受医疗保险费用高昂所困扰的患者。

【记】patient *a.* 有耐性的，能容忍的 *n.* 病人；患者

patiently *ad.* 耐心地；有毅力地

patience *n.* 耐性，耐心；忍耐，容忍

chronic [ˈkrɒnik] *a.* 慢性的；长期的；习惯性的

【例】These findings suggest that strategies focused on enhanced outpatient management of **chronic** disease may not be focused on the problems plaguing Medicare's high-cost patients.

　　这些发现表明，要加强管理罹患**慢性**疾病的门诊病人，不能只着眼于受医疗保险费用高昂所困扰的患者。

【记】chronically *ad.* 长期地；慢性地；习惯性地

chronicles *n.* 历代记（旧约）

plague [pleig] *n.* 瘟疫；灾祸；麻烦；讨厌的人
　　　　　 v. 折磨；使苦恼；使得灾祸

【变】plagues

【例】These findings suggest that strategies focused on enhanced outpatient management of chronic disease may not be focused on the problems **plaguing** Medicare's high-cost patients.

这些发现表明，要加强管理罹患慢性疾病的门诊病人，不能只着眼于受医疗保险费用高昂所**困扰**的患者。

【搭】outbreak of plague 鼠疫的爆发　recurrent plague 周期性的烦扰

【记】plaguily *ad.* 讨厌地；烦恼地；极其

　lagging *n.* 绝缘层材料 *a.* 落后的

词汇听写

1. _____　2. _____　3. _____

句子听写

2. In an analysis of data from 92 <u>randomized</u> trials by a researcher in <u>epidemiology</u> and <u>nutrition</u> researchers found that a daily iron supplement lowered a woman's risk of <u>anemia</u> by 12%.

研究员对流行病学和营养学进行了研究，他们从 92 个随机试验数据的分析发现，每天补充铁能让女性患贫血的危险降低 12%。

randomize [ˈrændəmaiz] *v.* 使随机化；（使）作任意排列或不规则分布

【变】randomized　randomized　randomized　randomizes

【例】In an analysis of data from 92 **randomized** trials by a researcher in epidemiology and nutrition researchers found that a daily iron supplement lowered a woman's risk of anemia by 12%.

研究员对流行病学和营养学进行了研究，他们从 92 个**随机**试验数据的分析发现，每天补充铁能让女性患贫血的危险降低 12%。

【搭】randomize routine 随机化程序　randomize the order 打乱顺序

【记】random *a.* ［数］随机的；任意的；胡乱的 *n.* 随意

epidemiology [ˌepidiːmiˈɒlədʒi] *n.* 流行病学；传染病学

【例】In an analysis of data from 92 randomized trials by a researcher in

277

epidemiology and nutrition researchers found that a daily iron supplement lowered a woman's risk of anemia by 12%.

研究员对**流行病学**和营养学进行了研究，他们从 92 个随机试验数据的分析发现，每天补充铁能让女性患贫血的危险降低 12%。

【搭】Journal of Epidemiology《流行病学杂志》

【记】epidemic *a.* 流行的；传染性的

epidemiological *a.* 流行病学的

epidemiologic *a.* 流行病学的；传染病学的

nutrition [nju'triʃn] *n.* 营养，营养学；营养品

【例】In an analysis of data from 92 randomized trials by a researcher in epidemiology and **nutrition** researchers found that a daily iron supplement lowered a woman's risk of anemia by 12%.

研究员对流行病学和**营养学**进行了研究，他们从 92 个随机试验数据的分析发现，每天补充铁能让女性患贫血的危险降低 12%。

【搭】nutrition fat 消化吸收性脂肪　nutrition foundation 营养基础

【记】nutrient *a.* 营养的；滋养的

nutritious *a.* 有营养的，滋养的

nutritional *a.* 营养的；滋养的

anemia [ə'ni:miə] *n.* 贫血；贫血症

【例】In an analysis of data from 92 randomized trials by a researcher in epidemiology and nutrition researchers found that a daily iron supplement lowered a woman's risk of **anemia** by 12%.

研究员对流行病学和营养学进行了研究，他们从 92 个随机试验数据的分析发现，每天补充铁能让女性患**贫血**的危险降低 12%。

【记】anemic *a.* 患贫血症的，贫血的

anesthetization *n.* 麻醉；麻痹

academia *n.* 学术界；学术生涯

词汇听写

1. _____　　2. _____　　3. _____

句子听写

3. It has been a privilege to help steer this inaugural Harvard Library strategy to unanimous approval by the Harvard Library Board.

　　能够帮助引导哈佛图书馆董事会一致批准这个首届哈佛图书馆战略是一种殊荣。

privilege ['privilidʒ] *n.* 特权；优待；基本权利　*v.* 给与……特权；特免

【变】privileged　privileged　privileging　privileges

【例】It has been a **privilege** to help steer this inaugural Harvard Library strategy to unanimous approval by the Harvard Library Board.

　　能够帮助引导哈佛图书馆董事会一致批准这个首届哈佛图书馆战略是一种**殊荣**。

【搭】privilege cab〈英〉特许在车站候客的马车

【记】privileged *a.* 享有特权的；有特别恩典的

　　privacy *n.* 隐私；秘密；隐居；隐居处

steer [stiə] *v.* 控制，引导；驾驶　*n.* 阉牛

【变】steered　steered　steering　steers

【例】It has been a privilege to help **steer** this inaugural Harvard Library strategy to unanimous approval by the Harvard Library Board.

　　能够帮助**引导**哈佛图书馆董事会一致批准这个首届哈佛图书馆战略是一种殊荣。

【搭】steer a middle course 取中庸之道，避免极端

【记】steerable *a.* 易驾驶的；可操纵的；易改变位置的

　　steering *n.* 操纵；指导；掌舵

inaugural [in'ɔːgjərəl] *a.* 就职的，就任的；创始的，最早的　*n.* 就职典礼；就职演说

【变】inaugurals

【例】It has been a privilege to help steer this **inaugural** Harvard Library strategy to unanimous approval by the Harvard Library Board.

能够帮助引导哈佛图书馆董事会一致批准这个**首届**哈佛图书馆战略是一种殊荣。

【记】inauguration *n.* 就职典礼；开始，开创；开幕式

　　inaugurate *v.* 创新；开辟；开创；举行开幕典礼；举行就职典礼

unanimous [juːˈnænɪməs] *a.* **全体一致的；意见一致的；无异议的**

【例】It has been a privilege to help steer this inaugural Harvard Library strategy to **unanimous** approval by the Harvard Library Board.

　　　　能够帮助引导哈佛图书馆董事会**一致**批准这个首届哈佛图书馆战略是一种殊荣。

【搭】unanimous vote 投票一致同意　　no unanimous conclusion 没有一致的结论

【记】unanimously *ad.* 全体一致地

　　unanimity *n.* 同意，全体一致

　　unanimousness *n.* 一致同意

词汇听写

1. _____　2. _____　3. _____

句子听写

第 8 周

Monday ·· ≪

1. An <u>adjacent</u> <u>lounge</u> below a large <u>opening</u> along 20th street provides a <u>spatial</u> connection between the conference center and the open office.

第 20 大街的一大片空地下有一间较近的休息室，在会议中心和开放式办公室之间提供了宽敞的空间。

---

adjacent [ə'dʒeisnt] *a.* 邻近的，毗连的

【例】An **adjacent** lounge below a large opening along 20th street provides a spatial connection between the conference center and the open office.

第 20 大街的一大片空地下有一间**较近的**休息室，在会议中心和开放式办公室之间提供了宽敞的空间。

【搭】adjacent angles 邻角　　adjacent village 相邻的村落

【记】adjacence *n.* 毗邻；接近

adhesive *n.* 黏合剂；胶黏剂

adhesion *n.* 粘附；支持；固守

---

lounge [laun(d)ʒ] *n.* 休息室；闲逛；躺椅；〈英〉酒吧间
v. 闲逛；懒洋洋地躺卧；闲混

【变】lounged　lounged　lounging　lounges

【例】An adjacent **lounge** below a large opening along 20th street provides a spatial connection between the conference center and the open office.

第 20 大街的一大片空地下有一间较近的**休息室**，在会议中心和开放式办公室之间提供了宽敞的空间。

【搭】lounge away 虚度　　lounge car 火车上的上等车厢

【记】lounger *n.* 闲荡的人；懒人

loungewear *n.* 家常便服

opening [ˈəupniŋ] *n.* 开始；机会；通路；空缺的职位

【变】openings

【例】An adjacent lounge below a large **opening** along 20th street provides a spatial connection between the conference center and the open office.

第20大街的一大片**空地**下有一间较近的休息室，在会议中心和开放式办公室之间提供了宽敞的空间。

【记】open *a.* 公开的；敞开的；空旷的；坦率的；营业着的

openness *n.* 公开；宽阔；率真

opener *n.* 开启工具；开启的人

spatial [ˈspeiʃl] *a.* 空间的；存在于空间的；受空间条件限制的

【例】An adjacent lounge below a large opening along 20th street provides a **spatial** connection between the conference center and the open office.

第20大街的一大片空地下有一间较近的休息室，在会议中心和开放式办公室之间提供了**宽敞的**空间。

【搭】spatial distribution 空间分布　　spatial relationship 空间关系

【记】spatiotemporal *a.* 时空的；存在于时间与空间上的

spatially *ad.* 空间地；存在于空间地

special *n.* 特使，特派人员；特刊；特色菜；专车；特价商品 *a.* 特别的；专门的，专用的

词汇听写

1. _____　　2. _____　　3. _____

句子听写

2. There were very few windows on the perimeter, and a very deep interior space. Before the redesign, the space was a very typical office with poorly positioned offices lacking good ventilation and natural light.

侧边的窗口数极少，内部空间非常深。在重新设计之前，这个地方就

是一个典型的办公室，位置不佳，缺乏良好的通风和自然光。

perimeter [pəˈrimitə] *n.* 周长；周界；[眼科] 视野计

【变】perimeters

【例】There were very few windows on the **perimeter**, and a very deep interior space. Before the redesign, the space was a very typical office with poorly positioned offices lacking good ventilation and natural light.

　　　侧边的窗口数极少，内部空间非常深。在重新设计之前，这个地方就是一个典型的办公室，位置不佳，缺乏良好的通风和自然光。

【搭】perimeter arc 视野计弧　perimeter path 环行道路

【记】perinatal *a.* 围产期的，出生前后的

　　　peristalsis *n.* 蠕动

　　　peri *n.* 妖精；美人；仙女

interior [inˈtiəriə] *n.* 内部；本质　*a.* 内部的；国内的；本质的

【变】interiors

【例】There were very few windows on the perimeter, and a very deep **interior** space. Before the redesign, the space was a very typical office with poorly positioned offices lacking good ventilation and natural light.

　　　侧边的窗口数极少，**内部**空间非常深。在重新设计之前，这个地方就是一个典型的办公室，位置不佳，缺乏良好的通风和自然光。

【搭】interior angle 内角　interior core 内部型芯

【记】interiorize *v.* 使看法深入内心；使成内景

　　　interim *a.* 临时的，暂时的；中间的；间歇的

　　　intercept *v.* 拦截；截断；窃听 *n.* 拦截；[数] 截距；截获的情报

typical [ˈtipikl] *a.* 典型的；特有的；象征性的

【变】more typical　most typical

【例】There were very few windows on the perimeter, and a very deep interior space. Before the redesign, the space was a very **typical** office with poorly positioned offices lacking good ventilation and natural light.

　　　侧边的窗口数极少，内部空间非常深。在重新设计之前，这个地方就是一个**典型的**办公室，位置不佳，缺乏良好的通风和自然光。

【搭】be typical of the period 那个时期的典型

【记】typic a. 典型的；正规的；象征性的

typically ad. 代表性地；作为特色地

typicality n. 典型性

ventilation [ˌventiˈleiʃn] n. 通风设备；空气流通

【例】There were very few windows on the perimeter, and a very deep interior space. Before the redesign, the space was a very typical office with poorly positioned offices lacking good **ventilation** and natural light.

　　侧边的窗口数极少，内部空间非常深。在重新设计之前，这个地方就是一个典型的办公室，位置不佳，缺乏良好的**通风**和自然光。

【搭】ventilation breather 通气器，呼吸孔　　ventilation system 通风系统

【记】ventilated a. 通风的

ventilatory a. 通气的，通风的

vent n. （感情的）发泄；出口；通风

词汇听写

1. _____　　　2. _____　　　3. _____

句子听写

3. The <u>acclaimed</u> architect released new <u>renderings</u> of the One Thousand Museum Tower located in downtown Miami. The project consists of a 215 meters high tower which will contains 60 luxury <u>condominiums</u> and it will have a <u>concrete exoskeleton</u>.

　　著名的建筑师发布了新的"一千博物馆塔楼"的透视图，该塔楼位于迈阿密市中心。该项目包括215米高的塔，塔里有60套豪华公寓，这个项目将会有具体的结构骨架。

acclaim [əˈkleim] n. 欢呼，喝彩；称赞　v. 称赞；为……喝彩，向……欢呼

【变】acclaimed　acclaimed　acclaiming　acclaims

【例】The **acclaimed** architect released new renderings of the One Thousand Museum Tower located in downtown Miami. The project consists of a 215 meters high tower which will contains 60 luxury condominiums and it will have a concrete exoskeleton.

著名的建筑师发布了新的"一千博物馆塔楼"的透视图，该塔楼位于迈阿密市中心。该项目包括 215 米高的塔，塔里有 60 套豪华公寓，这个项目将会有具体的结构骨架。

【记】acclamation *n.* 欢呼，喝彩；鼓掌欢呼表示通过

acclimation *n.* 适应环境（气候、水土等）

accelerate *v.* 加速；促进；增加

render ［ˈrendə］ *n.* 打底；缴纳；粉刷　　*v.* 致使；提出；实施；着色；以……回报；给予补偿

【变】rendered　rendered　rendering　renders

【例】The acclaimed architect released new **renderings** of the One Thousand Museum Tower located in downtown Miami. The project consists of a 215 meters high tower which will contains 60 luxury condominiums and it will have a concrete exoskeleton.

著名的建筑师发布了新的"一千博物馆塔楼"的**透视图**，该塔楼位于迈阿密市中心。该项目包括 215 米高的塔，塔里有 60 套豪华公寓，这个项目将会有具体的结构骨架。

【搭】render a service to 效劳；贡献

【记】rendering *n.* 翻译；表现；表演；描写；打底；（建筑物等）透视图

condominium ［ˌkɔndəˈminiəm］ *n.* 共同统治；财产共有权

【变】condominiums

【例】The acclaimed architect released new renderings of the One Thousand Museum Tower located in downtown Miami. The project consists of a 215 meters high tower which will contains 60 luxury **condominiums** and it will have a concrete exoskeleton.

著名的建筑师发布了新的"一千博物馆塔楼"的透视图，该塔楼位于迈阿密市中心。该项目包括 215 米高的塔，塔里有 60 套豪华**公寓**，这

285

个项目将会有具体的结构骨架。

【记】contained *a.* 泰然自若的，从容的；被控制的

container *n.* 集装箱；容器

containment 包含；牵制；容量；密闭度

containable *a.* 可控制的；可容纳的

concrete [ˈkɔŋkriːt] *n.* 具体物；凝结物　*a.* 混凝土的；实在的，具体的；
　　　　　　　　　　　有形的　*v.* （使）凝固；用混凝土修筑

【变】concretes

【例】The acclaimed architect released new renderings of the One Thousand Museum Tower located in downtown Miami. The project consists of a 215 meters high tower which will contains 60 luxury condominiums and it will have a **concrete** exoskeleton.

　　著名的建筑师发布了新的"一千博物馆塔楼"的透视图，该塔楼位于迈阿密市中心。该项目包括 215 米高的塔，塔里有 60 套豪华公寓，这个项目将会有**具体**的结构骨架。

【搭】concrete anchor bolt 混凝土锚固螺栓　concrete accelerator 混凝土速凝剂

【记】concretely *ad.* 具体地

concreteness *n.* 具体；具体性；确实

concretise *v.* 〈英〉使……具体化（等于 concretize）

词汇听写

1. ＿＿＿＿＿＿＿　2. ＿＿＿＿＿＿＿　3. ＿＿＿＿＿＿＿

句子听写

Tuesday .... ◁◁

1. There will also be a <u>helipad</u>, a <u>deck</u> with pools, <u>rooftop</u> event areas, <u>billiards</u> rooms, a fitness center to ensure that the tower is a small city in itself.

 这里将有一个直升机停机坪，配备游泳池的板层，屋顶的活动区，台球室，一个健身中心，以确保这个塔本身是一个小城市。

---

helipad ['helipæd] *n.* 直升机起飞及降落场

【变】helipads

【例】There will also be a **helipad**, a deck with pools, rooftop event areas, billiards rooms, a fitness center to ensure that the tower is a small city in itself.

 这里将有一个**直升机停机坪**，配备游泳池的板层，屋顶的活动区，台球室，一个健身中心，以确保这个塔本身是一个小城市。

【记】heliport *n.* ［航］直升飞机场，直升机停机坪

 heliport *n.* 螺旋电位计；螺旋线圈分压器

 helicopt *n.* 直升机 *v.* 乘直升机

---

deck [dek] *n.* 甲板；行李仓；露天平台　　*v.* 装饰；装甲板；打扮

【变】decked　decked　decking　decks

【例】There will also be a helipad, a **deck** with pools, rooftop event areas, billiards rooms, a fitness center to ensure that the tower is a small city in itself.

 这里将有一个直升机停机坪，配备游泳池的**板层**，屋顶的活动区，台球室，一个健身中心，以确保这个塔本身是一个小城市。

【搭】deck bolt 平圆柱头螺栓，甲板螺栓　　deck beam 甲板梁

【记】decker *n.* 装饰者；甲板水手

 dust *n.* 灰尘；尘埃；尘土

---

rooftop ['ruf'tɔp] *n.* 屋顶　　*a.* 屋顶上的

【变】rooftops

【例】There will also be a helipad, a deck with pools, **rooftop** event areas, billiards rooms, a fitness center to ensure that the tower is a small city in itself.

 这里将有一个直升机停机坪，配备游泳池的板层，**屋顶的**活动区，

287

台球室，一个健身中心，以确保这个塔本身是一个小城市。

【记】roofing *a.* 屋顶用的

roofed *a.* 有屋顶的

billiard [ˈbiljəd] *n.* 连撞两球所得的分数　*a.* 台球的；撞球用的

【例】There will also be a helipad, a deck with pools, rooftop event areas, **billiards** rooms, a fitness center to ensure that the tower is a small city in itself.

这里将有一个直升机停机坪，配备游泳池的板层，屋顶的活动区，**台球室**，一个健身中心，以确保这个塔本身是一个小城市。

【记】billiards *n.* 台球，桌球；弹子戏

billi *n.* ［计量］千兆分之一（忽，毫微）

billy *n.* 棍棒，警棍；伙伴

liar *n.* 说谎者

词汇听写

1. _____   2. _____   3. _____

句子听写

2. The theater will be the largest and resembles the shape of a shell with three elevated platforms that pass through a large atrium towards the performance hall that can host 1,800 persons, making it the biggest theater in the city.

该剧院将是最大的、形状酷似贝壳的建筑物，三个高架平台可以穿过巨大的天井，移到表演厅，该演出大厅可容纳 1800 人，使其成为全市最大的剧院。

resemble [riˈzembl] *v.* 类似，像

【变】resembled　resembled　resembling　resembles

【例】The theater will be the largest and **resembles** the shape of a shell with three elevated platforms that pass through a large atrium towards the performance hall that can host 1800 persons, making it the biggest theater in the city.

该剧院将是最大的、形状**酷似**贝壳的建筑物，三个高架平台可以穿过巨大的天井，移到表演厅，该演出大厅可容纳 1800 人，使其成为全市最大的剧院。

【搭】resemble her mother 像她母亲　resemble each other 彼此相像

【记】resemblance *n.* 相似；相似之处；相似物；肖像

resume *v.* 重新开始；恢复

shell [ʃel] *n.* 壳，贝壳；炮弹；外形　*v.* 剥皮；炮轰；设定命令行解释器的位置

【变】shelled　shelled　shelling　shells

【例】The theater will be the largest and resembles the shape of a **shell** with three elevated platforms that pass through a large atrium towards the performance hall that can host 1800 persons, making it the biggest theater in the city.

该剧院将是最大的、形状酷似**贝壳**的建筑物，三个高架平台可以穿过巨大的天井，移到表演厅，该演出大厅可容纳 1800 人，使其成为全市最大的剧院。

【搭】shell fragments 弹片　egg shell 蛋壳

【记】shelled *a.* 带壳的；去壳的

shelling *n.* 去皮；去壳

sheller *n.* 脱壳机；剥壳者

elevate ['eliveit] *v.* 提升；举起；振奋情绪等；提升……的职位

【变】elevated　elevated　elevating　elevates

【例】The theater will be the largest and resembles the shape of a shell with three **elevated** platforms that pass through a large atrium towards the performance hall that can host 1800 persons, making it the biggest theater in the city.

该剧院将是最大的、形状酷似贝壳的建筑物，三个**高架**平台可以穿过巨大的天井，移到表演厅，该演出大厅可容纳 1800 人，使其成为全市最大的剧院。

【搭】elevated approach 高架引道　elevated car 高架电车

atrium ['eitriəm] n. 中庭，天井前厅；[解剖] 心房

【变】atriums

【例】The theater will be the largest and resembles the shape of a shell with three elevated platforms that pass through a large **atrium** towards the performance hall that can host 1800 persons, making it the biggest theater in the city.

该剧院将是最大的、形状酷似贝壳的建筑物，三个高架平台可以穿过巨大的**天井**，移到表演厅，该演出大厅可容纳 1800 人，使其成为全市最大的剧院。

【搭】left atrium 左心房　atrium of ventricle 心室前房

【记】atrial a. 心房的；门廊的

atrip ad. 起锚地

trim v. 修剪；整理；装点；削减

词汇听写

1. _____　2. _____　3. _____

句子听写

3. Site selection supports environmental sustainability, incorporating the needs of both client and community, to revitalize municipalities and campuses and to energize commercial areas.

选择地址时，要注意环境的可持续性，要结合客户和社会的需求，以振兴市区和校园的发展，并给该商业区注入活力。

sustainability [sə'steinəbiləti] n. 持续性；永续性；能维持性

【例】Site selection supports environmental **sustainability**, incorporating the needs of both client and community, to revitalize municipalities and campuses and to energize commercial areas.

选择地址时，要注意环境的**可持续性**，要结合客户和社会的需求，以振兴市区和校园的发展，并给该商业区注入活力。

【记】sustainable *a.* 可以忍受的；足可支撑的；养得起的

sustained *a.* 持续的；持久的；持久不变的

sustainer *n.* 支持者，维持者；主发动机；支撑的人物

community [kəˈmjuːniti] *n.* 社区；[生态] 群落；共同体；团体

【变】communities

【例】Site selection supports environmental sustainability, incorporating the needs of both client and **community**, to revitalize municipalities and campuses and to energize commercial areas.

选择地址时，要注意环境的可持续性，要结合客户和**社会**的需求，以振兴市区和校园的发展，并给该商业区注入活力。

【搭】community antenna television 共天线电视，电缆电视　community center 社区活动中心（供社区居民开会、娱乐、休闲等的建筑物）

【记】communal *a.* 公共的；公社的

communally *ad.* 社区地；公有地

commune *n.* 公社

revitalize [ˌriːˈvaitəlaiz] *v.* 使……复活；使……复兴；使……恢复生气

【变】revitalized　revitalized　revitalizing　revitalizes

【例】Site selection supports environmental sustainability, incorporating the needs of both client and community, to **revitalize** municipalities and campuses and to energize commercial areas.

选择地址时，要注意环境的可持续性，要结合客户和社会的需求，以**振兴**市区和校园的发展，并给该商业区注入活力。

【搭】revitalize the inner cities 让市中心更加繁荣

【记】revitalization *n.* 复兴；复苏；新生

revitalizer *n.* 复苏剂；活肤霜

reviser *n.* 校订者；修订者

municipality [mjuːˌnisiˈpæliti] *n.* 市民；市政当局；自治市或区

【变】municipalities

291

【例】Site selection supports environmental sustainability, incorporating the needs of both client and community, to revitalize **municipalities** and campuses and to energize commercial areas.

选择地址时，要注意环境的可持续性，要结合客户和社会的需求，以振兴**市区**和校园的发展，并给该商业区注入活力。

【记】municipal *a.* 市政的，市的；地方自治的

municipally *ad.* 市制上；市政上；依市的规定

muniment *n.* 契据；不动产所有权状；防卫手段

词汇听写

1. _____ 2. _____ 3. _____

句子听写

Wednesday ··· ⫷

1. Rumors swirled this week that the country was considering suspending a ban on the export of lethal weapons to the neighboring new government.

有关这个国家正在考虑暂停禁止致命武器出口到邻近新政府的流言在这周开始大面积传开。

---

rumor [ˈruːmə] *n.* 谣言；传闻　*v.* 谣传；传说

【变】rumored　rumored　rumoring　rumors

【例】**Rumors** swirled this week that the country was considering suspending a ban on the export of lethal weapons to the neighboring new government.

有关这个国家正在考虑暂停禁止致命武器出口到邻近新政府的**流言**在这周开始大面积传开。

【记】rumormonger *n.* 造谣者；散布谣言者

rumple *v.* 弄皱；弄得乱七八糟

---

swirl [swəːl] *n.* 漩涡；打旋；涡状形　*v.* 盘绕；打旋；眩晕；大口喝酒

【变】swirled　swirled　swirling　swirls

【例】Rumors **swirled** this week that the country was considering suspending a ban on the export of lethal weapons to the neighboring new government.

有关这个国家正在考虑暂停禁止致命武器出口到邻近新政府的流言在这周开始**大面积传开**。

【搭】swirl atomizer 旋涡式喷油嘴　swirl crotch figure（木材）涡卷纹，羽状纹；涡卷花纹

【记】swirler *n.* 旋流器，回旋式喷嘴

twirl *v.* 快速扭动；卷曲 *n.* 旋转，转动

---

suspend [səˈspend] *v.* 延缓，推迟；（使）暂停；（使）悬浮

【变】suspended　suspended　suspending　suspends

【例】Rumors swirled this week that the country was considering **suspending** a ban on the export of lethal weapons to the neighboring new government.

有关这个国家正在考虑**暂停**禁止致命武器出口到邻近新政府的流言

在这周开始大面积传开。

【搭】suspend breathing 闭气　suspend pay 无力支付，宣布破产

【记】suspender *n.* 吊裤带；悬挂物；吊杆；袜吊

suspense *n.* 悬而未决，含糊不定；焦虑，挂念；悬念；中止，暂停

suspension *n.* 悬浮；暂停；悬架；悬浮液

lethal [ˈliːθl] *n.* 致死因子　*a.* 致命的，致死的

【例】Rumors swirled this week that the country was considering suspending a ban on the export of **lethal** weapons to the neighboring new government.

　　有关这个国家正在考虑暂停禁止**致命**武器出口到邻近新政府的流言在这周开始大面积传开。

【搭】lethal agent 致死剂　lethal chamber（执行死刑的）毒气行刑室

【记】lethargic *a.* 昏睡的；没精打采的，懒洋洋的

lethargy *n.* 昏睡；没精打采；懒洋洋；嗜眠症

词汇听写

1. _____　2. _____　3. _____

句子听写

2. Over the past decade, the US legislation has dropped tariffs on 1,800 African imports, including agricultural products, apparel and some textiles.

　　在过去的十年中，美国的法律已经降低了 1800 种非洲进口货物的关税，包括农产品、服装和部分纺织品。

legislation [ledʒisˈleiʃn] *n.* 立法；法律

【变】legislations

【例】Over the past decade, the US **legislation** has dropped tariffs on 1,800 African imports, including agricultural products, apparel and some textiles.

　　在过去的十年中，美国的**法律**已经降低了 1800 种非洲进口货物的关税，包括农产品、服装和部分纺织品。

【记】legislative *a.* （关于）立法的；立法决定的；有权立法的，用以立法的；立法机构的 *n.* 立法权；立法机关

legislator *n.* 立法委员；立法者

legislature *n.* 立法机关；立法机构；立法部；（特指）州议会

tariff ['tærif] *n.* 关税表；收费表　*v.* 定税率；征收关税

【变】tariffs

【例】Over the past decade, the US legislation has dropped **tariffs** on 1,800 African imports, including agricultural products, apparel and some textiles.

在过去的十年中，美国的法律已经降低了 1800 种非洲进口货物的**关税**，包括农产品、服装和部分纺织品。

【记】tarn *n.* （地）冰斗湖，山中小湖

sheriff *n.* 州长，执行吏

apparel [ə'pærl] *n.* 服装；衣服　*v.* 给……穿衣

【变】appareled　appareled　appareling　apparels

【例】Over the past decade, the US legislation has dropped tariffs on 1,800 African imports, including agricultural products, **apparel** and some textiles.

在过去的十年中，美国的法律已经降低了 1800 种非洲进口货物的关税，包括农产品、**服装**和部分纺织品。

【记】apparently *ad.* 显然地；表面上；似乎；显而易见

apparatus *n.* 仪器；机构；机关

textile ['tekstail] *n.* 纺织品，织物　*a.* 纺织的

【变】textiles

【例】Over the past decade, the US legislation has dropped tariffs on 1,800 African imports, including agricultural products, apparel and some **textiles**.

在过去的十年中，美国的法律已经降低了 1800 种非洲进口货物的关税，包括农产品、服装和部分**纺织品**。

【搭】textile auxiliary 纺织助剂　textile design 织物图案

【记】text *n.* 文本，原文；课文，教科书；主题；版本

textual *a.* 正文的，版本的，原文的

texture *n.* 质地；结构；本质

词汇听写

1. _____ 2. _____ 3. _____

句子听写

3. The vine is used to treat arthritis, gout and inflammation as well as a weight loss remedy.

这种藤被用于治疗关节炎、痛风和炎症以及减肥治疗。

---

vine [vain] *n.* 藤；葡萄树；藤本植物；攀缘植物 *v.* 长成藤蔓；爬藤

【变】vined vined vining vines

【例】The **vine** is used to treat arthritis, gout and inflammation as well as a weight loss remedy.

这种**藤**被用于治疗关节炎、痛风和炎症以及减肥治疗。

【记】vinegar *n.* 醋；尖酸刻薄

vinegary *a.* 有酸味的

vineyard *n.* 葡萄园；工作场所；苦心经营的地方

---

arthritis [ɑ:ˈθraitis] *n.* [外科] 关节炎

【例】The vine is used to treat **arthritis**, gout and inflammation as well as a weight loss remedy.

这种藤被用于治疗**关节炎**、痛风和炎症以及减肥治疗。

【记】article *n.* （报章杂志中的）文章，论文；条款；物品；[语] 冠词

articulacy *n.* 口齿清楚的说话能力

articulate *a.* 发音清晰的；善于表达的；有关节的

---

gout [gaut] *n.* [遗][外科] 痛风；一滴；一团

【例】The vine is used to treat arthritis, **gout** and inflammation as well as a weight loss remedy.

这种藤被用于治疗关节炎、**痛风**和炎症以及减肥治疗。

【搭】my gout troubles me these days 这些天我的痛风闹得厉害。

【记】govern *v.* 统治；管理；治理；支配（词或短语的形式或用法）

  gouge *v.* 挖凿；欺诈，诈取

  gourd *n.* 葫芦

inflammation [inflə'meiʃn] *n.* ［病理］炎症；［医］发炎；燃烧；发火

【变】inflammations

【例】The vine is used to treat arthritis, gout and **inflammation** as well as a weight loss remedy.

  这种藤被用于治疗关节炎、痛风和**炎症**以及减肥治疗。

【搭】inflammation of a joint 关节炎

【记】inflame *v.*（使）发怒，过热；使发炎

  inflammable *a.* 易燃的；〈口〉易激动的，易激怒的 *n.* 易燃物

  inflammatory *a.* 令人激动的；有煽动性的；炎性的，发炎的

词汇听写

1. _____ 2. _____ 3. _____

句子听写

Thursday

1. The 2011 research on the H5N1 influenza strain ignited a fierce ethical debate.

2011 年有关 H5N1 流感病菌类型的研究引发了激烈的伦理道德的争论。

influenza ［influ'enzə］ *n.* ［内科］流行性感冒（简写 flu）；**家畜流行性感冒**

【例】The 2011 research on the H5N1 **influenza** strain ignited a fierce ethical debate.

2011 年有关 H5N1 **流感**病菌类型的研究引发了激烈的伦理道德的争论。

【搭】influenza virus 流感病毒

【记】influx *n.* 流入，注入；汇集，充斥；注入口，河口

influential *a.* 有影响的；有权势的 *n.* 有影响力的人物

strain ［strein］ *n.* 张力；拉紧；负担；扭伤；血缘；家族 *v.* 拉紧；滥用；滤去；竭力

【变】strained strained straining strains

【例】The 2011 research on the H5N1 influenza **strain** ignited a fierce ethical debate.

2011 年有关 H5N1 流感病菌类型的研究引发了激烈的伦理道德的争论。

【搭】strain after 竭力做某事 strain amplifier 应变放大器

【记】strainer *n.* 滤器，滤盆，滤网

strait *n.* 海峡；（常用 *pl.*）窘迫，困境；危难

ignite ［ig'nait］ *v.* 点燃；（使）燃烧；（使）激动

【变】ignited ignited igniting ignites

【例】The 2011 research on the H5N1 influenza strain **ignited** a fierce ethical debate.

2011 年有关 H5N1 流感病菌类型的研究**引发**了激烈的伦理道德的争论。

【搭】ignite a fire 引发大火　ignite my interest in words 激发了我对文学的兴趣

【记】ignition *n.*（汽油引擎的）发火装置；着火，燃烧；点火，点燃

　　ignoble *a.* 卑鄙的；可耻的；出身低微的；地位低下的

　　ignominy *n.* 耻辱，污辱

　　ignitability *n.* 可燃性；可点燃性

ethical ['eθikl] *n.* 处方药　*a.* 伦理的；道德的；凭处方出售的

【例】The 2011 research on the H5N1 influenza strain ignited a fierce **ethical** debate.

　　　2011 年有关 H5N1 流感病菌类型的研究引发了激烈的伦理**道德的**争论。

【搭】ethical characteristic 道德特征　ethical education 伦理教育

【记】ethically *ad.* 伦理（学）上

　　ethics *n.* 伦理学；道德规范；伦理学著作；道德规范（ethic 的名词复数）；道德体系；行为准则；伦理学

词汇听写

1. _____　2. _____　3. _____

句子听写

2. Critics immediately voiced security concerns, raising fears that terrorists gaining access to the research could unleash a virulent, laboratory-grown strain and cause mass deaths.

　　批评者立刻表示安全问题令人担忧，他们的恐惧与日俱增，担心获得研究数据的恐怖分子可能会散播一种在实验室培养的致命的病菌，并导致大规模死亡。

critic ['kritik] 详细 *n.* 批评家，评论家；爱挑剔的人

【变】critics

【例】**Critics** immediately voiced security concerns, raising fears that terrorists gaining access to the research could unleash a virulent, laboratory-grown strain and cause mass deaths.

　　批评者立刻表示安全问题令人担忧，他们的恐惧与日俱增，担心获得研究数据的恐怖分子可能会散播一种在实验室培养的致命的病菌，并导致大规模死亡。

【记】critical *a.* 批评的，爱挑剔的；危险的，危急的；决定性的；［物］临界的

criticise *v.* 评论，批评

criticism *n.* 批评；审定，考证，校勘；苛求，［哲］批判主义；评论，评论文章

access [ˈækses] *n.* 进入；使用权；通路　*v.* 使用；存取；接近

【变】accessed　accessed　accessing　accesses

【例】Critics immediately voiced security concerns, raising fears that terrorists gaining **access** to the research could unleash a virulent, laboratory-grown strain and cause mass deaths.

　　批评者立刻表示安全问题令人担忧，他们的恐惧与日俱增，担心**获得**研究数据的恐怖分子可能会散播一种在实验室培养的致命的病菌，并导致大规模死亡。

【搭】access adit 巷道口　access board 搭板，跳板；便桥

【记】accessibility *n.* 易接近，可到达；学习资料利用率；可诣达性；可达性

accessible *a.* 易接近的；可理解的；易相处的；易感的

unleash [ʌnˈliːʃ] *v.* 发动；解开……的皮带；解除……的束缚；不受约束；自由自在；放荡不羁

【变】unleashed　unleashed　unleashing　unleashes

【例】Critics immediately voiced security concerns, raising fears that terrorists gaining access to the research could **unleash** a virulent, laboratory-grown strain and cause mass deaths.

　　批评者立刻表示安全问题令人担忧，他们的恐惧与日俱增，担心获得研究数据的恐怖分子可能会**散播**一种在实验室培养的致命的病菌，并导致大规模死亡。

【记】unless *conj.* 除非，如果不 *prep.* 除了，……除外

leash *n.* 拴猎狗的皮带 *v.* 用皮带系住

lease *n.* 租约；租契；租赁物；租赁权 *v.* 出租；租借

virulent ['virələnt] *a.* 剧毒的；恶性的；有恶意的

【例】Critics immediately voiced security concerns, raising fears that terrorists gaining access to the research could unleash a **virulent**, laboratory-grown strain and cause mass deaths.

批评者立刻表示安全问题令人担忧，他们的恐惧与日俱增，担心获得研究数据的恐怖分子可能会散播一种在实验室培养的**致命的**病菌，并导致大规模死亡。

【搭】virulent inflation 恶性通货膨胀

【记】virulently *ad.* 恶毒地，狠毒地

virus *n.* 病毒；病毒性疾病；毒素，毒害；[计算机科学] 计算机病毒

virulence *n.* 毒力，毒性，恶意

词汇听写

1. _____ 2. _____ 3. _____

句子听写

3. There is a hypothesis that the antioxidant flavanol, which is found in cocoa, helps cognition.

有一种假设，即被发现存在于可可中的抗氧化剂黄烷醇有助于认知。

hypothesis [hai'pɔθisis] *n.* 假设

【变】hypotheses

【例】There is a **hypothesis** that the antioxidant flavanol, which is found in cocoa, helps cognition.

有一种**假设**，即被发现存在于可可中的抗氧化剂黄烷醇有助于认知。

【搭】hypothesis testing 假设检验

【记】hypothesize *v.* 假设，假定，猜测

　　hypothetical *a.* 假设的，假定的；有前提的；爱猜想的；假想的

antioxidant [æntiˈɔksidnt] *n.* 抗氧化剂；硬化防止剂；防老化剂

【变】antioxidants

【例】There is a hypothesis that the **antioxidant** flavanol，which is found in cocoa，helps cognition.

　　　　有一种假设，即被发现存在于可可中的**抗氧化剂**黄烷醇有助于认知。

【搭】antioxidant ability 抗氧化能力

【记】oxidation *n.* 氧化

　　oxide *n.* ［化］氧化物

　　oxidized *v.* （使某物）氧化，（使某物）生锈

cocoa [ˈkəukəu] *n.* 可可粉；可可豆；可可饮料；深褐色

【变】cocoas

【例】There is a hypothesis that the antioxidant flavanol，which is found in **cocoa**，helps cognition.

　　　　有一种假设，即被发现存在于**可可**中的抗氧化剂黄烷醇有助于认知。

【搭】cocoa bean 可可豆　　cocoa cake 可可油饼

【记】coconut *n.* ［植］椰子；［植］椰肉

　　cocoon *n.* 茧，蚕茧 *v.* 把……紧紧包住

cognition [kɔgˈniʃn] *n.* 认识；知识；认识能力

【例】There is a hypothesis that the antioxidant flavanol，which is found in cocoa，helps **cognition**.

　　　　有一种假设，即被发现存在于可可中的抗氧化剂黄烷醇有助于认知。

【搭】process of cognition 认知过程　　affect cognition 影响认知能力

【记】cognitive *a.* 认知的；认识的

　　cognizant *a.* 察知的，认识（某事物）的

cognizance *n.* 认识，审理，认定

cognitional *a.* 认知的

词汇听写

1. _____ 2. _____ 3. _____

句子听写

Friday ··· «

1. Powder infant formula is not a sterile product. The WHO promotes breast feeding over the use of formula because breast milk provides children with key antibodies and better nutrition.

婴幼儿配方奶粉不是无菌产品。世界卫生组织提倡母乳喂养而不是配方奶粉喂养，正是因为母乳为孩子提供了关键的抗体和更好的营养。

formula [ˈfɔːmjulə] *n.* [数] 公式，准则；配方；婴儿食品

【变】formulas

【例】Powder infant **formula** is not a sterile product. The WHO promotes breast feeding over the use of formula because breast milk provides children with key antibodies and better nutrition.

婴幼儿**配方**奶粉不是无菌产品。世界卫生组织提倡母乳喂养而不是配方奶粉喂养，正是因为母乳为孩子提供了关键的抗体和更好的营养。

【搭】formula apportionment 按一定的公式分派费用等　formula calculation 配方计算

【记】formulaic *a.* （根据）公式的，用俗套话堆砌成的，刻板的

formulate *v.* 构想出，规划；确切地阐述；用公式表示

formulation *n.* 配方；构想，规划；公式化

sterile [ˈsteraɪl] *a.* 不育的；无菌的；贫瘠的；不毛的；枯燥乏味的

【例】Powder infant formula is not a **sterile** product. The WHO promotes breast feeding over the use of formula because breast milk provides children with key antibodies and better nutrition.

婴幼儿配方奶粉不是**无菌**产品。世界卫生组织提倡母乳喂养而不是配方奶粉喂养，正是因为母乳为孩子提供了关键的抗体和更好的营养。

【搭】sterile product 无菌产品　cold and sterile 阴冷，没有生气

【记】sterility *n.* 不毛；不孕；内容贫乏；不结果实

sterilize *v.* 消毒；使无菌；使失去生育能力；使不起作用

stern *a.* 严厉的，严峻的；坚定的，不动摇的；严肃的

antibody [ˈæntibɔdi] *n.* ［免疫］抗体

【变】antibodies

【例】Powder infant formula is not a sterile product. The WHO promotes breast feeding over the use of formula because breast milk provides children with key **antibodies** and better nutrition.

　　婴幼儿配方奶粉不是无菌产品。世界卫生组织提倡母乳喂养而不是配方奶粉喂养，正是因为母乳为孩子提供了关键的**抗体**和更好的营养。

【搭】antibody globulin 抗体球蛋白　antibody protein 抗体蛋白质

【记】antic *n.* 傻里傻气的举动；滑稽的动作，古怪的姿势 *a.* 古怪的，滑稽的；哗众取宠的

　　anti *n.* & *a.* 反对者，反对论者反对的

nutrition [njuˈtriʃn] *n.* 营养，营养学；营养品

【例】Powder infant formula is not a sterile product. The WHO promotes breast feeding over the use of formula because breast milk provides children with key antibodies and better **nutrition**.

　　婴幼儿配方奶粉不是无菌产品。世界卫生组织提倡母乳喂养而不是配方奶粉喂养，正是因为母乳为孩子提供了关键的抗体和更好的**营养**。

【搭】nutrition fat 消化吸收性脂肪　nutrition relationships 营养关系

【记】nutritional *a.* 营养的；滋养的；营养品的

　　nutritionally 在营养上

　　nutritionist *n.* 营养学家

词汇听写

1. ＿＿＿＿＿＿　　2. ＿＿＿＿＿＿　　3. ＿＿＿＿＿＿

句子听写

2. The periodic switch in magnetic polarity comes at the peak of each solar cycle when "the sun's inner magnetic dynamo re-organizes itself".

磁极的周期性改变发生在每个太阳活动周期的高峰期，那时，"太阳的内磁发电机在自我重组"。

periodic [ˌpiəriˈɔdik] *a.* 周期的；定期的

【例】The **periodic** switch in magnetic polarity comes at the peak of each solar cycle when "the sun's inner magnetic dynamo re-organizes itself".

　　磁极的**周期**性改变发生在每个太阳活动周期的高峰期，那时，"太阳的内磁发电机在自我重组"。

【搭】periodic accounting 期间会计核算　periodic change 周期变更

【记】periodical *n.* 期刊；杂志 *a.* 周期的，定期的；时常发生的；定期发行的，期刊的

　　periodically *ad.* 周期性地；定期地，偶尔地

　　period *n.* 时期；（一段）时间；学时；句号 *a.* 具有某个时代特征的；（关于）过去某一特定历史时期的

switch [switʃ] *n.* 开关；转换；鞭子　*v.* 转换；抽打；换防

【变】switched　switched　switching　switches

【例】The periodic **switch** in magnetic polarity comes at the peak of each solar cycle when "the sun's inner magnetic dynamo re-organizes itself".

　　磁极的周期性**改变**发生在每个太阳活动周期的高峰期，那时，"太阳的内磁发电机在自我重组"。

【记】switchback *n.* 在 Z 形路轨向原来的方向返驶，改变角度 *a.* 使用之字爬坡路线的

　　switchable *a.* 有开关控制的

magnetic [mægˈnetik] *a.* 地磁的；有磁性的；有吸引力的

【例】The periodic switch in **magnetic** polarity comes at the peak of each solar cycle when "the sun's inner magnetic dynamo re-organizes itself".

　　磁极的周期性改变发生在每个太阳活动周期的高峰期，那时，"太阳的内磁发电机在自我重组"。

【搭】magnetic acceleration 在磁场内的加速度　magnetic amplification 磁性放大

【记】magnetically *ad.* 有磁力地，有魅力地

　　magnetism *n.* 磁性，磁力；磁学；吸引力；催眠术

magnetize *v.* 使有磁性；使磁化；紧紧吸引；迷住

dynamo [ˈdainəməu] *n.* 发电机；精力充沛的人

【变】dynamos

【例】The periodic switch in magnetic polarity comes at the peak of each solar cycle when "the sun's inner magnetic **dynamo** re-organizes itself".

　　磁极的周期性改变发生在每个太阳活动周期的高峰期，那时，"太阳的内磁**发电机**在自我重组"。

【搭】dynamo bearing 发电机轴承　dynamo strap 发电机固定带

【记】dynastic *a.* 朝代的，王朝的

　　dynasty *n.* 王朝；朝代

　　dynamic *a.* 动态的；动力的，动力学的；精力充沛的；不断变化的

词汇听写

1. ＿＿＿＿＿＿＿＿　2. ＿＿＿＿＿＿＿＿　3. ＿＿＿＿＿＿＿＿

句子听写

3. IBM says the long-term goal is to "build a chip system with ten billion neurons, while consuming merely one kilowatt of power and occupying less than two liters of volume".

　　IBM 说他们长期的目标是"建立一个拥有 100 亿个神经元的芯片系统，而这个系统仅仅需要 1 千瓦的功率和占用不到两升的体积"。

chip [tʃip] *n.* [电子]芯片；筹码；碎片；(食物的) 小片；薄片

　　　　　v. 削，凿；削成碎片；剥落；碎裂

【变】chipped　chipped　chipping　chips

【例】IBM says the long-term goal is to "build a **chip** system with ten billion neurons, while consuming merely one kilowatt of power and occupying less than two liters of volume".

　　IBM 说他们长期的目标是"建立一个拥有 100 亿个神经元的**芯片系**统，而这个系统仅仅需要 1 千瓦的功率和占用不到两升的体积"。

【搭】chip away 拆掉，削掉，铲除；凿（敲）下碎片；逐步瓦解　chip density 基片密度

【记】chipboard *n.* 硬纸板，纸板；碎纸胶合板

neuron [ˈnjuərɔn] *n.* [解剖] 神经元，神经单位

【变】neurons

【例】IBM says the long-term goal is to "build a chip system with ten billion **neurons**, while consuming merely one kilowatt of power and occupying less than two liters of volume".

IBM 说他们长期的目标是"建立一个拥有 100 亿个**神经元**的芯片系统，而这个系统仅仅需要 1 千瓦的功率和占用不到两升的体积"。

【搭】neuron doctrine 神经元学说

【记】neurosis *n.* （医）神经机能病，神经衰弱症

neurotic *a.* 神经官能症的；神经质的；神经过敏的；极为焦虑的

neutral *a.* 中立的；（化学中）中性的；暗淡的；不带电的

volume [ˈvɔljuːm] *n.* 量；体积；卷；音量；大量；册　*a.* 大量的　*v.* 把……收集成卷　*v.* 成团卷起

【变】volumes

【例】IBM says the long-term goal is to "build a chip system with ten billion neurons, while consuming merely one kilowatt of power and occupying less than two liters of **volume**".

IBM 说他们长期的目标是"建立一个拥有 100 亿个神经元的芯片系统，而这个系统仅仅需要 1 千瓦的功率和占用不到两升的**体积**"。

【搭】volume adjuster 音量调整器　　volume calculation 容积计算

【记】voluminous *a.* 大的；多卷的；著作多的；宽松的

voluntarily *ad.* 志愿地；自动地，自发地

词汇听写

1. _____ 　　2. _____ 　　3. _____

句子听写

Saturday ·· ≪≪

1. Five years ago, they did not <u>tackle</u> problems of post-<u>traumatic</u> stress disorder, <u>acute</u> stress and <u>bereavement</u>.

五年前，他们没有面对过严重创伤后遗症、严重的压力症和丧亲之痛等问题。

---

tackle [ˈtækl] *n.* 滑车；装备；用具；扭倒　*v.* 扭倒；拦截抢球；处理；抓住；固定；与……交涉

【变】tackled　tackled　tackling　tackles

【例】Five years ago, they did not **tackle** problems of post-traumatic stress disorder, acute stress and bereavement.

五年前，他们没有**面对**过严重创伤后遗症、严重的压力症和丧亲之痛等问题。

【搭】tackle down（足球，橄榄球中）把对方弄倒　　tackle hook 提升钩，起重吊钩

【记】tacks *n.* 大头钉（tack 的名词复数）；平头钉；航向；方法

tacky *a.* 发黏的；俗气的；褴褛的；缺乏教养或风度的

---

traumatic [trɔːˈmætik] *n.* 外伤药　*a.* 外伤的；创伤的

【例】Five years ago, they did not tackle problems of post-**traumatic** stress disorder, acute stress and bereavement.

五年前，他们没有面对过严重**创伤**后遗症、严重的压力症和丧亲之痛等问题。

【搭】traumatic abscess 外伤性脓肿　　traumatic response 伤反应

【记】traumatize *v.* ［医］使受外伤；使受精神创伤

travail *n.* ［文］艰苦劳动；辛勤努力；痛苦；分娩的阵痛

---

acute [əˈkjuːt] *a.* 严重的，［医］急性的；敏锐的；激烈的；尖声的

【例】Five years ago, they did not tackle problems of post-traumatic stress disorder, **acute** stress and bereavement.

五年前，他们没有面对过严重创伤后遗症、**严重的**压力症和丧亲之

309

痛等问题。

【搭】acute abscess 急性脓肿　acute colitis 急性结肠炎

【记】acutely *ad.* 尖锐地；剧烈地

acuteness *n.* 敏锐，剧烈

acuity *n.* 尖锐，（疾病的）剧烈，（视力、才智等的）敏锐；敏度

bereavement [bi'ri:vmnt] *n.* 丧友，丧亲；丧失

【变】bereavements

【例】Five years ago, they did not tackle problems of post-traumatic stress disorder, acute stress and **bereavement**.

　　五年前，他们没有面对过严重创伤后遗症、严重的压力症和**丧亲之痛**等问题。

【记】bereave *v.* 使失去（希望、生命等）；（尤指死亡）使丧失（亲人、朋友等）；使孤寂；（废）抢走（财物）

beret *n.* 贝雷帽；[军]〈英〉军帽

词汇听写

1. _____　　2. _____　　3. _____

句子听写

2. Researchers found that after just one sleepless night, the brain's frontal lobe, which governs rational decision-making, was impaired. People craved unhealthy snacks and junk food when they were sleep deprived, and had less ability to rein in that impulse.

　　研究人员发现，仅仅一个不眠之夜过后，负责理性决策的大脑额叶就会受损。当人们被剥夺睡眠，他们会很渴望那些不健康的零食和垃圾食品，同时面对这种渴望、冲动时控制能力较弱。

govern ['gʌvn] *v.* 管理；支配；统治；控制

【变】governed　governed　governing　governs

【例】Researchers found that after just one sleepless night，the brain's frontal lobe，which **governs** rational decision-making，was impaired. People craved unhealthy snacks and junk food when they were sleep deprived，and had less ability to rein in that impulse.

研究人员发现，仅仅一个不眠之夜过后，**负责**理性决策的大脑额叶就会受损。当人们被剥夺睡眠，他们会很渴望那些不健康的零食和垃圾食品，同时面对这种渴望、冲动时控制能力较弱。

【记】governance *n.* 统治；管理；支配；统治方式

governess *n.* 女家庭教师；女统治者；女总督；保姆

impair [im'peə] *v.* 损害；削弱；减少

【变】impaired impaired impairing impairs

【例】Researchers found that after just one sleepless night，the brain's frontal lobe，which governs rational decision-making，was **impaired**. People craved unhealthy snacks and junk food when they were sleep deprived，and had less ability to rein in that impulse.

研究人员发现，仅仅一个不眠之夜过后，负责理性决策的大脑额叶就会**受损**。当人们被剥夺睡眠，他们会很渴望那些不健康的零食和垃圾食品，同时面对这种渴望、冲动时控制能力较弱。

【搭】impair our relations 有损我们的关系

【记】impairment *n.* 损害，损伤

impale *v.* 钉在尖桩上

impart *v.* 给予；告知，透露；传授

crave [kreiv] *v.* 渴望；恳求

【变】craved craved craving craves

【例】Researchers found that after just one sleepless night，the brain's frontal lobe，which governs rational decision-making，was impaired. People **craved** unhealthy snacks and junk food when they were sleep deprived，and had less ability to rein in that impulse.

研究人员发现，仅仅一个不眠之夜过后，负责理性决策的大脑额叶就会受损。当人们被剥夺睡眠，他们会很**渴望**那些不健康的零食和垃圾

食品，同时面对这种渴望、冲动时控制能力较弱。

【搭】crave for 渴望；期

【记】craven *a.* 懦弱的，胆小的 *ad.* 胆小地，懦弱地 *n.* 懦弱，胆小

crawl *v.* 爬行；缓慢行进；巴结

crab *n.* 蟹，蟹肉；阴虱；脾气乖戾的人；[植] 沙果，沙果树

rein [rein] *n.* **缰绳；驾驭；统治；支配** *v.* **控制；驾驭；勒住**

【变】reined reined reining reins

【例】Researchers found that after just one sleepless night, the brain's frontal lobe, which governs rational decision-making, was impaired. People craved unhealthy snacks and junk food when they were sleep deprived, and had less ability to **rein** in that impulse.

研究人员发现，仅仅一个不眠之夜过后，负责理性决策的大脑额叶就会受损。当人们被剥夺睡眠，他们会很渴望那些不健康的零食和垃圾食品，同时面对这种渴望、冲动时**控制**能力较弱。

【搭】rein back 勒（马）后退 rein leather 马具革

【记】reign *v.* 当政，统治；占主导地位

renal *a.* 肾脏的

词汇听写

1. _____ 2. _____ 3. _____

句子听写

3. 20-year-old Miley says despite her provocative videos and outfits, she's not sleazy — in fact, she declares herself one of the hardest-working young celebrities.

20 岁的麦莉说，尽管她的视频和着装性感，但她不是低俗的——事实上，她宣称自己是工作最努力的年轻名人之一。

provocative [prə'vɒkətiv] n. 刺激物，挑拨物；兴奋剂　a. 刺激的，挑拨的；气人的

【例】20-year-old Miley says despite her **provocative** videos and outfits，she's not sleazy — in fact，she declares herself one of the hardest-working young celebrities.

　　20 岁的麦莉说，尽管她的视频和着装**性感**，但她不是低俗的——事实上，她宣称自己是工作最努力的年轻名人之一。

【搭】provocative background 诱发环境

【记】provoke v. 激起，挑起；煽动；招致；触怒，使愤怒

outfit ['autfit] n. 机构；用具；全套装备　v. 配备；供应

【变】outfitted　outfitted　outfitting　outfits

【例】20-year-old Miley says despite her provocative videos and **outfits**，she's not sleazy — in fact，she declares herself one of the hardest-working young celebrities.

　　20 岁的麦莉说，尽管她的视频和**着装**性感，但她不是低俗的——事实上，她宣称自己是工作最努力的年轻名人之一。

【搭】outfit of equipment 装备总体

【记】outfitter n. 旅行用品商，运动用具商

　　outflank v. 翼侧包围

　　outfall n. 河口，排水口

sleazy ['sliːzi] a. 质地薄的；肮脏的；低级庸俗的；破烂的

【变】sleazier　sleaziest

【例】20-year-old Miley says despite her provocative videos and outfits，she's not **sleazy** — in fact，she declares herself one of the hardest-working young celebrities.

　　20 岁的麦莉说，尽管她的视频和着装性感，但她不是**低俗的**——事实上，她宣称自己是工作最努力的年轻名人之一。

【记】sleaze n. （俚）肮脏；污秽；破败；卑劣的人

　　sleazier a. 肮脏的，污秽的，破烂的（sleazy 的比较级）

　　sled n. 雪橇

celebrity [si'lebriti] *n.* 名人；名声

【变】celebrities

【例】20-year-old Miley says despite her provocative videos and outfits, she's not sleazy — in fact, she declares herself one of the hardest-working young **celebrities.**

　　20 岁的麦莉说，尽管她的视频和着装性感，但她不是低俗的——事实上，她宣称自己是工作最努力的年轻**名人**之一。

【记】celerity *n.* 迅速，敏捷

　　celery *n.* 芹菜；香芹粉；芹菜籽

词汇听写

1. _____　　2. _____　　3. _____

句子听写

Sunday ·· 《《《

1. For some, the outdoor movies are <u>reminiscent</u> of the drive-in theaters of their youths. Other fans say there is nothing like watching a movie on a <u>breezy</u> summer evening. Food trucks in the <u>vacant</u> lot <u>cater</u> to those who want something to eat before the show starts.

对于一些人来说，露天电影让他们回忆起年轻时代的路边电影。其他露天电影爱好者认为，在一个凉风习习的夏日傍晚看电影的感觉是无可比拟的。停在空地的食品卡车迎合了那些想要在演出开始前吃东西的观众。

reminiscent [remiˈnisnt] *n.* 回忆录作者；回忆者　*a.* 怀旧的，回忆往事的；耽于回想的

【例】For some, the outdoor movies are **reminiscent** of the drive-in theaters of their youths. Other fans say there is nothing like watching a movie on a breezy summer evening. Food trucks in the vacant lot cater to those who want something to eat before the show starts.

对于一些人来说，露天电影让他们**回忆**起年轻时代的路边电影。其他露天电影爱好者认为，在一个凉风习习的夏日傍晚看电影的感觉是无可比拟的。停在空地的食品卡车迎合了那些想要在演出开始前吃东西的观众。

【搭】reminiscent painting 怀旧风格的绘画

【记】reminiscence *n.* 旧事，回忆；回忆录

　　reminiscently *ad.* 回忆地，怀旧地

breezy [ˈbriːzi] *a.* 有微风的；轻松愉快的；通风好的；活泼的

【变】breezier　breeziest

【例】For some, the outdoor movies are reminiscent of the drive-in theaters of their youths. Other fans say there is nothing like watching a movie on a **breezy** summer evening. Food trucks in the vacant lot cater to those who want something to eat before the show starts.

对于一些人来说，露天电影让他们回忆起年轻时代的路边电影。其

他露天电影爱好者认为，在一个**凉风习习**的夏日傍晚看电影的感觉是无可比拟的。停在空地的食品卡车迎合了那些想要在演出开始前吃东西的观众。

【记】breeze *n.* 微风；轻而易举的事

breezily *ad.* 微风地，活泼轻松地

brevity *n.* 短暂；简洁

vacant [ˈveiknt] *a.* 空虚的；空的；空缺的；空闲的；茫然的

【例】For some, the outdoor movies are reminiscent of the drive-in theaters of their youths. Other fans say there is nothing like watching a movie on a breezy summer evening. Food trucks in the **vacant** lot cater to those who want something to eat before the show starts.

对于一些人来说，露天电影让他们回忆起年轻时代的路边电影。其他露天电影爱好者认为，在一个凉风习习的夏日傍晚看电影的感觉是无可比拟的。停在**空地**的食品卡车迎合了那些想要在演出开始前吃东西的观众。

【搭】vacant position 职位空缺　vacant terminal 空间端，空端

【记】vacantly *ad.* 神情茫然地

vacate *v.* 搬出；空出；取消；使撤退

vacation *n.* 假期，休假；[古] 空出，撤出，辞去 *v.* 度假

cater [ˈkeitə] *v.* 投合，迎合；满足需要；提供饮食及服务

【变】catered　catered　catering　caters

【例】For some, the outdoor movies are reminiscent of the drive-in theaters of their youths. Other fans say there is nothing like watching a movie on a breezy summer evening. Food trucks in the vacant lot **cater** to those who want something to eat before the show starts.

对于一些人来说，露天电影让他们回忆起年轻时代的路边电影。其他露天电影爱好者认为，在一个凉风习习的夏日傍晚看电影的感觉是无可比拟的。停在空地的食品卡车**迎合**了那些想要在演出开始前吃东西的观众。

【搭】cater for 提供饮食及服务；迎合　cater to 供应伙食，迎合；面向

【记】caterer *n.* （尤指职业的）酒席承办人，提供饮食及服务的人；筹办者

category *n.* 种类，类别；派别

categorical *a.* 绝对的，无条件的；分类的，按类别的；断言的；确信无疑的

词汇听写

1. _____ 2. _____ 3. _____

句子听写

2. New York's <u>multicultural</u> population is a <u>fertile</u> <u>medium</u> for new <u>fusions</u> in art and music.

　　　纽约人口的文化多元性对艺术和音乐的新的融合提供了肥沃的土壤。

multicultural [mʌltiˈkʌltʃrl] *a.* 多种文化的；融合或具有多种文化的

【例】New York's **multicultural** population is a fertile medium for new fusions in art and music.

　　　纽约人口的**文化多元性**对艺术和音乐的新的融合提供了肥沃的土壤。

【搭】multicultural education 多种文化教育

【记】multiculturalism *n.* 多元文化

multiculturalist 多元文化主义者

multiculturally *a.* 多种文化的，反映多种文化的，适合于多种文化的

fertile [ˈfɜːtail] *n.* 肥沃，多产　*a.* 富饶的，肥沃的；能生育的

【例】New York's multicultural population is a **fertile** medium for new fusions in art and music.

　　　纽约人口的文化多元性对艺术和音乐的新的融合提供了**肥沃的**土壤。

【搭】fertile absorber 再生物质，有效吸收剂　fertile land 肥沃的土壤

【记】fertility *n.* （土地的）肥沃；肥力；丰产；［生］繁殖力

fertilize *v.* 使肥沃；使受孕；施肥

fertilizing *v.* 施肥

medium [ˈmiːdiəm] *n.* 方法；媒体；媒介；中间物　*a.* 中间的，中等的；半熟的

【变】media　mediums

【例】New York's multicultural population is a fertile **medium** for new fusions in art and music.

　　纽约人口的文化多元性对艺术和音乐的新的融合提供了肥沃的**土壤**。

【搭】medium accelerator 中速促进剂　medium size 中号

【记】mediumistic *a.* 巫术的

　　mediumship *n.* 灵媒（或巫师）的能力（或功能、职业）

fusion [ˈfjuːʒn] *n.* 融合；熔化；熔接；融合物

【变】fusions

【例】New York's multicultural population is a fertile medium for new **fusions** in art and music.

　　纽约人口的文化多元性对艺术和音乐的新的**融合**提供了肥沃的土壤。

【搭】fusion alloying 熔配合金　fusion drilling 熔化钻眼法

【记】fuss *n.* 忙乱；大惊小怪；大惊小怪的人；争吵

　　fuse *n.* 保险丝；导火线；引信

　　fuselage *n.* [空]（飞机的）机身；火箭的外壳；弹体

词汇听写

1. _____　2. _____　3. _____

句子听写

3. Pakistani television is showing what many call its most controversial content yet in a ruthless quest for ratings: a talk-show host who gives away babies live on air.

　　巴基斯坦电视正在播放让很多人认为是最有争议的内容，他们认为电视台是在无情地追求收视率，播放的内容是脱口秀主持人通过电视节目

"送出" 婴儿。

ruthless [ˈruːθlis] *a.* 无情的，残忍的

【例】Pakistani television is showing what many call its most controversial content yet in a **ruthless** quest for ratings: a talk-show host who gives away babies live on air.

　　巴基斯坦电视正在播放让很多人认为是最有争议的内容，他们认为电视台是在**无情**地追求收视率，播放的内容是脱口秀主持人通过电视节目"送出"婴儿。

【记】ruthlessly *ad.* 无情地，冷酷地

　　ruthlessness *n.* 无情，冷酷

quest [kwest] *n.* 追求；寻找　*v.* 探索；追求；寻找

【变】quests

【例】Pakistani television is showing what many call its most controversial content yet in a ruthless **quest** for ratings: a talk-show host who gives away babies live on air.

　　巴基斯坦电视正在播放让很多人认为是最有争议的内容，他们认为电视台是在无情地**追求**收视率，播放的内容是脱口秀主持人通过电视节目"送出"婴儿。

【搭】quest about for 到处搜寻

【记】quester *n.* 探求者，追求者

　　question *n.* 问题；疑问；怀疑；议题

rating [ˈreitiŋ] *n.* 等级；等级评定；额定功率　*v.* 对……评价（rate 的 ing 形式）

【变】ratings

【例】Pakistani television is showing what many call its most controversial content yet in a ruthless quest for **ratings**: a talk-show host who gives away babies live on air.

　　巴基斯坦电视正在播放让很多人认为是最有争议的内容，他们认为电视台是在无情地追求**收视率**，播放的内容是脱口秀主持人通过电视节目"送出"婴儿。

【搭】rating curve 标定曲线，流量特性曲线，水位流量关系曲线　rating data 标定数据

【记】ratio *n.* 比，比率；比例；系数

ration *n.* 定量；配给量；口粮；合理的量，正常量

rational *a.* 神智清楚的；理性的；理智的；合理的

on air （无线电）广播的；送风期

【例】Pakistani television is showing what many call its most controversial content yet in a ruthless quest for ratings: a talk-show host who gives away babies live **on air**.

巴基斯坦电视正在播放让很多人认为是最有争议的内容，他们认为电视台是在无情地追求收视率，播放的内容是脱口秀主持人通过**电视**节目"送出"婴儿。

词汇听写

1. _____ 2. _____ 3. _____

句子听写

第9周

Monday ··· ≪

1. While the <u>charity</u> organization <u>scours</u> for <u>discarded</u> newborns, the host is also <u>appealing</u> for babies directly.

　　当慈善机构在四处寻找被抛弃的新生儿时，这个主持人则是直接向人们索要婴儿。

---

charity [ˈtʃæriti] *n.* 慈善；施舍；慈善团体；宽容；施舍物

【变】charities

【例】While the **charity** organization scours for discarded newborns, the host is also appealing for babies directly.

　　当**慈善**机构在四处寻找被抛弃的新生儿时，这个主持人则是直接向人们索要婴儿。

【搭】charity area 罚球区　charity dance 慈善舞会

【记】charlatan *n.* 冒充内行者，骗子

　　charmer *n.* 对异性有吸引力的人

---

scour [skau] *v.* 冲刷；擦亮；四处搜索；（用泻药）泻

【变】scoured　scoured　scouring　scours

【例】While the charity organization **scours** for discarded newborns, the host is also appealing for babies directly.

　　当慈善机构在**四处寻找**被抛弃的新生儿时，这个主持人则是直接向人们索要婴儿。

【搭】scour off 擦掉，洗去　scour prevention 防止冲刷

【记】scourer *n.* 洗擦者，洗刷物品

　　scourge *n.* 天灾，灾难；鞭子；苦难的根源

---

discard [diˈskɑːd] *n.* 抛弃；被丢弃的东西或人　*v.* 抛弃；放弃；丢弃

【变】discarded　discarded　discarding　discards

【例】While the charity organization scours for **discarded** newborns, the host is also appealing for babies directly.

当慈善机构在四处寻找被**抛弃**的新生儿时，这个主持人则是直接向人们索要婴儿。

【搭】discard solution 废液 discard tobacco 废烟丝

【记】discardable *a.* 可废弃的

discern *v.* 看出；理解，了解；识别，辨别

appeal for 恳求，请求；要求

【例】While the charity organization scours for discarded newborns, the host is also **appealing for** babies directly.

当慈善机构在四处寻找被抛弃的新生儿时，这个主持人则是直接向人们**索要**婴儿。

【搭】appeal board［法］上诉委员会 appeal to 诉诸武力；向……投诉；向……呼吁；对……有吸引力

词汇听写

1. _____ 2. _____ 3. _____

句子听写

2. The boy works in a local garment factory, loading bundles or doing embroidery, and earning roughly $10 a week. With little law enforcement, increasing unemployment and widespread poverty, it is hard to see how the young boy, and others like him, will have a different future.

这个男孩在当地的服装厂工作，装载包裹或做刺绣，收入约为每周10美元。由于相关法律很少被执行，失业不断增加，贫困蔓延，对于这个小男孩，以及类似的人，将很难有一个不同的未来。

garment［'ɡɑːmnt］*n.* 衣服，服装；外表，外观 *v.* 给……穿衣服

【变】garmented garmented garmenting garments

【例】The boy works in a local **garment** factory, loading bundles or doing embroidery, and earning roughly $10 a week. With little law enforcement, increasing unemployment and widespread poverty, it is hard to see how the young boy, and others like him, will have a different future.

　　这个男孩在当地的**服装**厂工作，装载包裹或做刺绣，收入约为每周 10 美元。由于相关法律很少被执行，失业不断增加，贫困蔓延，对于这个小男孩，以及类似的人，将很难有一个不同的未来。

【搭】garment bag 保护衣服用的塑胶套　garment tag 外表特征

【记】garage *n.* 车库；汽车修理站；飞机库

garbage *n.* 垃圾；脏东西；丢弃的食物；无用的数据

garner *v.* 获得；贮藏，积累 *n.* 谷仓

bundle [ˈbʌndl] *n.* 束；捆　*v.* 捆；匆忙离开

【变】bundled　bundled　bundling　bundles

【例】The boy works in a local garment factory, loading **bundles** or doing embroidery, and earning roughly $10 a week. With little law enforcement, increasing unemployment and widespread poverty, it is hard to see how the young boy, and others like him, will have a different future.

　　这个男孩在当地的服装厂工作，装载**包裹**或做刺绣，收入约为每周 10 美元。由于相关法律很少被执行，失业不断增加，贫困蔓延，对于这个小男孩，以及类似的人，将很难有一个不同的未来。

【搭】bundle away（使）匆匆离去　bundle buster 自动送进加热炉的装置

【记】bung *n.* 桶等的塞子 *v.* 桶孔堵

bun *n.* 圆形的小面包或点心；（女子的）圆发髻；酒宴，闹饮；〈英〉尾巴

embroidery [imˈbrɔidri] *n.* 刺绣；刺绣品；粉饰

【变】embroideries

【例】The boy works in a local garment factory, loading bundles or doing **embroidery**, and earning roughly $10 a week. With little law enforcement, increasing unemployment and widespread poverty, it is hard to see how the young boy, and others like him, will have a different future.

这个男孩在当地的服装厂工作，装载包裹或做**刺绣**，收入约为每周 10 美元。由于相关法律很少被执行，失业不断增加，贫困蔓延，对于这个小男孩，以及类似的人，将很难有一个不同的未来。

【搭】embroidery frame 绣花绷，刺绣绷子　embroidery machine 刺绣机，绣花机

【记】embroider v. 刺绣；在……上绣花；渲染

embroidering v.（在织物上）绣花（embroider 的现在分词）；刺绣；对……加以渲染（或修饰）；给……添枝加叶

embroil v. 使（自己或他人）卷入纠纷

---

enforcement [en'fɔːsmnt] *n.* 执行，实施；强制

【例】The boy works in a local garment factory, loading bundles or doing embroidery, and earning roughly ＄10 a week. With little law **enforcement**, increasing unemployment and widespread poverty, it is hard to see how the young boy, and others like him, will have a different future.

这个男孩在当地的服装厂工作，装载包裹或做刺绣，收入约为每周 10 美元。由于相关法律很少被**执行**，失业不断增加，贫困蔓延，对于这个小男孩，以及类似的人，将很难有一个不同的未来。

【搭】enforcement action 申请强制执行判决的诉讼　enforcement measures 强制措施

【记】enforce v. 强迫服从；实施，执行；加强

enforceable *a.* 可强行的，可强迫的，可实施的

enfold v. 围住……，抱紧……

词汇听写

1. _____　2. _____　3. _____

句子听写

3. We try to keep the time schedule pretty fixed so that the students get to know the pattern. We leave at 8:30 a. m. And return at 6 p. m. We figure it's best to keep the day fairly short.

我们尽量保持固定的时间表，让学生了解时间安排。我们上午 8 时 30 分离开，下午 6 点返回，我们认为出游的一天最好不要太长。

fix [fiks] *v.* 使固定；修理；安装；准备；注视　*n.* 困境；方位；贿赂

【例】We try to keep the time schedule pretty **fixed** so that the students get to know the pattern. We leave at 8:30 a. m. And return at 6 p. m. We figure it's best to keep the day fairly short.

　　我们尽量保持**固定**的时间表，让学生了解时间安排。我们上午 8 时 30 分离开，下午 6 点返回，我们认为出游的一天最好不要太长。

【搭】fix on 把……固定住；把……集中在……上；选定　fix with 用……维修；与（某人）商定（某事）；用（某种目光）看某人

【记】fixture *n.* （房屋等的）固定装置；［商］定期放款，定期存款

　　flag *n.* 旗；旗帜；信号旗；菖蒲

　　flake *n.* 小薄片，（尤指）碎片；火花；食品搁架

pattern ['pætn] *n.* 模式；图案；样品　*v.* 模仿；以图案装饰

【变】patterned　patterned　patterning　patterns

【例】We try to keep the time schedule pretty fixed so that the students get to know the **pattern.** We leave at 8:30 a. m. And return at 6 p. m. We figure it's best to keep the day fairly short.

　　我们尽量保持固定的时间表，让学生了解时间**安排**。我们上午 8 时 30 分离开，下午 6 点返回，我们认为出游的一天最好不要太长。

【搭】pattern airspeed 起落航线飞行速度　pattern color 图案颜色

【记】pause *n.* 暂时的停顿；犹豫；（诗中）节奏的停顿；［乐］延长号

　　pave *v.* 铺设；为……铺平道路；安

　　paw *n.* 爪子；手；〈俚〉笔迹

figure ['figə] *n.* 数字；人物；图形；价格；（人的）体形；画像　*v.* 计算；出现；扮演角色；描绘；象征

【变】figured　figured　figuring　figures

【例】We try to keep the time schedule pretty fixed so that the students get to know the pattern. We leave at 8:30 a. m. And return at 6 p. m. We **figure** it's best to keep the day fairly short.

我们尽量保持固定的时间表，让学生了解时间安排。我们上午 8 时 30 分离开，下午 6 点返回，我们**认为**出游的一天最好不要太长。

【搭】figure as 扮演……角色　figure out 计算出，解决；弄明白；合计

【记】file *v.* 提出（离婚诉讼或其他讼案）；把……归档；发稿，寄给报社

　　fill *v.* （使）充满，（使）装满

fairly [ˈfeəli] *ad.* **相当地；公平地；简直**

【变】more fairly　most fairly

【例】We try to keep the time schedule pretty fixed so that the students get to know the pattern. We leave at 8:30 a. m. And return at 6 p. m. We figure it's best to keep the day **fairly** short.

　　我们尽量保持固定的时间表，让学生了解时间安排。我们上午 8 时 30 分离开，下午 6 点返回，我们认为出游的一天**最好**不要太长。

【搭】fairly and squarely 光明正大地

【记】faith *n.* 信用，信任；宗教信仰；忠诚；宗教

　　faithful *a.* 忠实的；忠诚的；正确的

　　fake *v.* 伪造；篡改；对……做手脚；仿造

词汇听写

1. _____　2. _____　3. _____

句子听写

Tuesday ·· «

1. Alongside college and adult students, you can earn college credit in Harvard courses and explore subjects not <u>available</u> at your high school. You study with <u>distinguished</u> <u>faculty</u>, use state-of-the-art labs, and have access to the largest university library system in the world.

跟大学生和成人学生一起学习时,你可以获得哈佛大学的课程学分,并探索一些你高中所没有的课程。你可以与杰出的教师一起研究课题,使用的是最先进的实验室和世界上最大的图书馆系统。

> **alongside** [əˌlɔŋˈsaid] *ad.* 在……的侧面;在……旁边;与……并排
> *prep.* 在……旁边;横靠;傍着;并存的

【例】 **Alongside** college and adult students, you can earn college credit in Harvard courses and explore subjects not available at your high school. You study with distinguished faculty, use state-of-the-art labs, and have access to the largest university library system in the world.

跟大学生和成人学生**一起**学习时,你可以获得哈佛大学的课程学分,并探索一些你高中所没有的课程。你可以与杰出的教师一起研究课题,使用的是最先进的实验室和世界上最大的图书馆系统。

【搭】alongside delivery 船边交货

> **available** [əˈveiləbl] *a.* 可用的;有空的;可会见的;(戏票、车票等)有效的

【例】 Alongside college and adult students, you can earn college credit in Harvard courses and explore subjects not **available** at your high school. You study with distinguished faculty, use state-of-the-art labs, and have access to the largest university library system in the world.

跟大学生和成人学生一起学习时,你可以获得哈佛大学的课程学分,并探索一些你高中所没**有**的课程。你可以与杰出的教师一起研究课题,使用的是最先进的实验室和世界上最大的图书馆系统。

【搭】every available 每个能找到的　readily/freely available 容易得到的

distinguished [di'stiŋgwiʃt] *a.* 卓越的；著名的；受人尊敬的；显得重要的
　　　　　　　　　　　　　v. 辨别，区别（distinguish 的过去式和过去分
　　　　　　　　　　　　　词）；突出；区别（distinguish 的过去式）

【例】Alongside college and adult students，you can earn college credit in
Harvard courses and explore subjects not available at your high school.
You study with **distinguished** faculty，use state-of-the-art labs，and have
access to the largest university library system in the world.

　　跟大学生和成人学生一起学习时，你可以获得哈佛大学的课程学分，
并探索一些你高中所没有的课程。你可以与**杰出**的教师一起研究课题，
使用的是最先进的实验室和世界上最大的图书馆系统。

【搭】distinguish sb. /sth. from 分辨　distinguishing feature/mark 与众不同的
特征/标记

【记】distinguishable *a.* 易分辨出来的

　　distinguish *v.* 区别，辨别

faculty ['fæklti] *n.* 能力，才能；全体教职员；〈英〉（大学的）专科，系；
　　　　　　　　特权，特许

【变】faculties

【例】Alongside college and adult students，you can earn college credit in
Harvard courses and explore subjects not available at your high school.
You study with distinguished **faculty**，use state-of-the-art labs，and have
access to the largest university library system in the world.

　　跟大学生和成人学生一起学习时，你可以获得哈佛大学的课程学分，
并探索一些你高中所没有的课程。你可以与杰出的**教师**一起研究课题，
使用的是最先进的实验室和世界上最大的图书馆系统。

【搭】the faculty（大学的）全体教师　faculty for 擅长

词汇听写

1. ＿＿＿＿＿＿＿　　2. ＿＿＿＿＿＿＿　　3. ＿＿＿＿＿＿＿

句子听写

2. Saudi Arabia has offered Russia economic <u>incentives</u> including a major arms <u>deal</u> and a <u>pledge</u> not to challenge Russian gas <u>sales</u> if Moscow scales back support for Syrian President.

沙特阿拉伯为俄罗斯提供经济动力，包括重要军火的交易，并承诺如果莫斯科缩减对叙利亚总统的支持，他们也不为难俄罗斯天然气销售。

incentive [in'sentiv] *n.* 动机；刺激；诱因；鼓励

【变】incentives

【例】Saudi Arabia has offered Russia economic **incentives** including a major arms deal and a pledge not to challenge Russian gas sales if Moscow scales back support for Syrian President.

沙特阿拉伯为俄罗斯提供经济**动力**，包括重要军火的交易，并承诺如果莫斯科缩减对叙利亚总统的支持，他们也不为难俄罗斯天然气销售。

【搭】incentive force 鼓动力　incentive compensation 奖金

【记】inducement *n.* 诱导，劝诱；诱因，动机；［法］引言部分；刺激物

disincentive *a.* 妨碍活动的

deal [diːl] *v.* ［牌戏］分；分配；经营；施予；交易　*n.* （一笔）交易；许多；待遇；发牌

【变】dealt　dealt　dealing　deals

【例】Saudi Arabia has offered Russia economic incentives including a major arms **deal** and a pledge not to challenge Russian gas sales if Moscow scales back support for Syrian President.

沙特阿拉伯为俄罗斯提供经济动力，包括重要军火的**交易**，并承诺如果莫斯科缩减对叙利亚总统的支持，他们也不为难俄罗斯天然气销售。

【搭】a big deal（非正式）重要事件　a deal of 大量

【记】business *n.* 商业，交易；生意；事务；行业

commerce *n.* 商业；社交

pledge [pledʒ] *n.* 保证，誓言；［法］抵押权；公约；（表示友谊的）干杯
　　　　　　　　v. 使发誓，保证；典当，抵押；以誓言约束；向……祝酒

【变】pledged　pledged　pledging　pledges

【例】Saudi Arabia has offered Russia economic incentives including a major arms deal and a **pledge** not to challenge Russian gas sales if Moscow scales back support for Syrian President.

　　沙特阿拉伯为俄罗斯提供经济动力，包括重要军火的交易，并**承诺**如果莫斯科缩减对叙利亚总统的支持，他们也不为难俄罗斯天然气销售。

【搭】pledge of immovables 不动产抵押　　pledge of obligation 债权抵押
　　pledge oneself 保证，宣誓

【记】ensure *v.* 确保；担保获得（避免）；使（某人）获得；使安全
　　assure *v.* 向……保证；使……确信；〈英〉给……保险
　　guarantee *n.* 保证，担保；保证人，保证书；抵押品

scale [skeil] *n.* 规模；比例（尺）；鱼鳞；级别　　*v.* 测量；攀登；刮去……的鳞片

【变】scales　scaled　scaled　scaling　scales

【例】Saudi Arabia has offered Russia economic incentives including a major arms deal and a pledge not to challenge Russian gas sales if Moscow **scales** back support for Syrian President.

　　沙特阿拉伯为俄罗斯提供经济动力，包括重要军火的交易，并承诺如果莫斯科**缩减**对叙利亚总统的支持，他们也不为难俄罗斯天然气销售。

【搭】full-scale 全面的；极大限度的；照原物尺寸的　　large-scale 大规模的，大范围的；大比例尺的　　small-scale 小规模的；小型的；小比例尺的（地图）

【记】calibration *n.* 校准，标准化；刻度，标度；测量口径
　　gradation *n.* （从一事物到另一事物的）渐变；（事物划分的）阶段；等级；刻度
　　hierarchy *n.* ［计］分层，层次；等级制度；统治集团

词汇听写

1. ＿＿＿＿＿＿　　　2. ＿＿＿＿＿＿　　　3. ＿＿＿＿＿＿

句子听写

3. Elton John has been announced as the first <u>recipient</u> of the BRITs <u>Icon</u> Award. The six-time Grammy winner will be presented with the honor on September 2 during a <u>ceremony</u> <u>hosted</u> by British music industry trade organization BPI.

　　埃尔顿·约翰已经成为英国偶像奖的首位获得者。英国音乐行业贸易组织将于 9 月 2 日的仪式上向这位 6 次格莱美得主颁发这项荣誉。

recipient [ri'sipiənt] *n.* 接受者；容器；容纳者　*a.* 容易接受的；感受性强的

【变】recipients

【例】Elton John has been announced as the first **recipient** of the BRITs Icon Award. The six-time Grammy winner will be presented with the honor on September 2 during a ceremony hosted by British music industry trade organization BPI.

　　　埃尔顿·约翰已经成为英国偶像奖的首位**获得者**。英国音乐行业贸易组织将于 9 月 2 日的仪式上向这位 6 次格莱美得主颁发这项荣誉。

【搭】recipient cell 受体细胞　recipient dividend 股息领取人

【记】receiver *n.* 接受者，收款员；接收器；无限电接收机；（破产公司的）官方接管人

　　successor *n.* 接替的人或事物；继承人，继任者

icon ['aikɔn] *n.* 偶像，崇拜对象；图标，图符；[宗] 圣像；肖像

【变】icons

【例】Elton John has been announced as the first recipient of the BRITs **Icon** Award. The six-time Grammy winner will be presented with the honor on September 2 during a ceremony hosted by British music industry trade organization BPI.

　　　埃尔顿·约翰已经成为英国**偶像**奖的首位获得者。英国音乐行业贸易组织将于 9 月 2 日的仪式上向这位 6 次格莱美得主颁发这项荣誉。

【搭】icon file *n.* 图标文件

ceremony ['serəməni] *n.* 典礼，仪式；礼仪，礼节；虚礼，客气

【变】ceremonies

【例】Elton John has been announced as the first recipient of the BRITs Icon Award. The six-time Grammy winner will be presented with the honor on September 2 during a **ceremony** hosted by British music industry trade organization BPI.

埃尔顿·约翰已经成为英国偶像奖的首位获得者。英国音乐行业贸易组织将于9月2日的**仪式**上向这位6次格莱美得主颁发这项荣誉。

【搭】stand on ceremony 讲究礼节；拘礼　without ceremony 径直地，不打招呼地；不礼貌地

【记】solemnity *n.* 庄严；严肃；庄重；庄严的举止

custom *n.* 习惯，惯例；海关，关税；经常光顾

ritual *n.* （宗教等的）仪式；例行公事；典礼 *a.* 作为仪式的一部分的；礼节性的；例行公事的

---

host [həʊst] *n.* [计] 主机；主人，东道主；节目主持人；酒店业主

　　　　　　　 v. 当主人；主办宴会，主持节目；款待，做东

【变】hosted　hosted　hosting　hosts

【例】Elton John has been announced as the first recipient of the BRITs Icon Award. The six-time Grammy winner will be presented with the honor on September 2 during a ceremony **hosted** by British music industry trade organization BPI.

埃尔顿·约翰已经成为英国偶像奖的首位获得者。英国音乐行业贸易组织将于9月2日的仪式上向这位6次格莱美**得主**颁发这项荣誉。

【搭】host country 东道国；所在国　host city 主办城市

【记】flock *n.* 兽群，鸟群；群众；大量 *v.* 群集，成群结队而行

receptionist *n.* 接待员

quantity *n.* 量，数量；定量，大批；数目

词汇听写

1. ＿＿＿＿＿＿　　2. ＿＿＿＿＿＿　　3. ＿＿＿＿＿＿

句子听写

Wednesday ·· 《《

1. Astronomers have discovered a new exoplanet orbiting a sun-like star 57 light years away. The exoplanet is four times the size of Jupiter and can actually be seen by Earth-based telescopes.

天文学家已经发现了一个新的系外行星，该行星绕着离地球57光年远的一个类似太阳的恒星转动。系外行星是木星大小的四倍，其实，地面望远镜可以看到它。

astronomer [ə'strɔnəmə] *n.* 天文学者，天文学家

【变】astronomers

【例】**Astronomers** have discovered a new exoplanet orbiting a sun-like star 57 light years away. The exoplanet is four times the size of Jupiter and can actually be seen by Earth-based telescopes.

　　天文学家已经发现了一个新的系外行星，该行星绕着离地球57光年远的一个类似太阳的恒星转动。系外行星是木星大小的四倍，其实，地面望远镜可以看到它。

【记】stargazer *n.* 占星师，空想家，天文学家

　　astronaut *n.* 宇航员，太空人

exoplanet [ek'sɔpleinit] *n.* 外星球

【例】Astronomers have discovered a new **exoplanet** orbiting a sun-like star 57 light years away. The exoplanet is four times the size of Jupiter and can actually be seen by Earth-based telescopes.

　　天文学家已经发现了一个新的**系外行星**，该行星绕着离地球57光年远的一个类似太阳的恒星转动。系外行星是木星大小的四倍，其实，地面望远镜可以看到它。

orbit ['ɔːbit] *n.* 轨道；势力范围；眼眶；（人生的）旅程，生活过程
　　　　　　v. 在……轨道上运行，环绕轨道运行；盘旋

【变】orbited　orbited　orbiting　orbits

【例】Astronomers have discovered a new exoplanet **orbiting** a sun-like star 57 light years away. The exoplanet is four times the size of Jupiter and can actually be seen by Earth-based telescopes.

天文学家已经发现了一个新的系外行星，该行星**绕**着离地球 57 光年远的一个类似太阳的恒星**转动**。系外行星是木星大小的四倍，其实，地面望远镜可以看到它。

【搭】orbit attitude 航天器轨道飞行姿态　orbit centre 轨道中心　orbit circumference 轨道周长

【记】revolve *v.* 使旋转；反复考虑；使循环

orbital *a.* 轨道的；眼窝的

telescope [ˈteliskəup] *n.* 望远镜

【变】telescopes

【例】Astronomers have discovered a new exoplanet orbiting a sun-like star 57 light years away. The exoplanet is four times the size of Jupiter and can actually be seen by Earth-based **telescopes.**

天文学家已经发现了一个新的系外行星，该行星绕着离地球 57 光年远的一个类似太阳的恒星转动。系外行星是木星大小的四倍，其实，地面**望远镜**可以看到它。

【搭】telescope calipers 内径测微器　telescope collar 望远镜调整圈　telescope direct 正镜

【记】scope *n.* （处理、研究事务的）范围；眼界，见识；（活动或能力的）余地；广袤，地域

词汇听写

1. _____ 2. _____ 3. _____

句子听写

2. Collisions among asteroids and comets create a core, and when the mass of the core gets large enough, its gravity attracts gas and debris from the disk.

小行星和彗星之间的碰撞创建一个核心，当这个核心的质量变得足够

大时，它的引力将从外圈中吸引气体和碎片。

asteroid [ˈæstərɔid] n. [天] 小行星；海盘车；海星　a. 星状的

【变】asteroids

【例】Collisions among **asteroids** and comets create a core, and when the mass of the core gets large enough, its gravity attracts gas and debris from the disk.

小行星和彗星之间的碰撞创建一个核心，当这个核心的质量变得足够大时，它的引力将从外圈中吸引气体和碎片。

【搭】asteroid belt 小行星带

【记】astral a. 星形的；星际的

disastrous a. 灾难性的；损失惨重的；极坏的；悲惨的

comet [ˈkɔmit] n. [天] 彗星；孛

【例】Collisions among asteroids and **comets** create a core, and when the mass of the core gets large enough, its gravity attracts gas and debris from the disk.

小行星和**彗星**之间的碰撞创建一个核心，当这个核心的质量变得足够大时，它的引力将从外圈中吸引气体和碎片。

【搭】comet family 彗星族　comet formation（谱带）成彗星状（即拖尾）

comet phenomenon 彗尾现象

gravity [ˈɡrævəti] n. 重力；万有引力，地心引力；重要性，严重性；严肃，庄重

【例】Collisions among asteroids and comets create a core, and when the mass of the core gets large enough, its **gravity** attracts gas and debris from the disk.

小行星和彗星之间的碰撞创建一个核心，当这个核心的质量变得足够大时，它的**引力**将从外圈中吸引气体和碎片。

【搭】centre of gravity 重心　gravity battery 比重液电池，重力电池　gravity axis 重力（心）轴

【记】solemnity n. 庄严；庄重；庄严的举止

levity n. 欠考虑；不慎重；轻率；轻浮

debris [dəˈbriː] n. 碎片，残骸

【例】Collisions among asteroids and comets create a core, and when the mass of the core gets large enough, its gravity attracts gas and **debris** from the disk.

小行星和彗星之间的碰撞创建一个核心，当这个核心的质量变得足够大时，它的引力将从外圈中吸引气体和**碎片**。

【搭】debris avalanche 岩屑崩落　debris catcher room 爆片捕集室　debris flow 泥石流

【记】waste *n.* 浪费，白费，挥霍钱财；废料，废品，废物；荒地，荒芜

　　garbage *n.* 垃圾；脏东西；丢弃的食物；无用的数据

　　rubbish *n.* 垃圾；无意义的东西；废话；劣质的东西

词汇听写

1. ＿＿＿＿＿＿　　2. ＿＿＿＿＿＿　　3. ＿＿＿＿＿＿

句子听写

3. The Obama administration has overturned a U. S. trade panel's ban on imports of some Apple iPads and older iPhones into the United States, dealing a setback to Apple's rival, Samsung.

奥巴马政府已经推翻了美国的国际贸易委员会颁发的禁止一些苹果 iPad 和旧 iPhone 手机进入美国的禁令，目的是为了阻碍苹果的竞争对手，三星手机在美国的市场发展。

overturn [ˌəuvəˈtɜːn] *v.* （使）翻倒；使垮台，推翻；撤销（判决等）

【变】overturned　overturned　overturning　overturns

【例】The Obama administration has **overturned** a U. S. trade panel's ban on imports of some Apple iPads and older iPhones into the United States, dealing a setback to Apple's rival, Samsung.

奥巴马政府已经推翻了美国的国际贸易委员会颁发的禁止一些苹果 iPad 和旧 iPhone 手机进入美国的禁令，目的是为了阻碍苹果的竞争对手，三星手机在美国的市场发展。

【记】overcorrect *a.* 矫枉过正的

overwrought *a.* 神经紧张的，忧虑的，烦恼的

overcrowded *a.* 挤满的；过度拥挤的

panel ['pænl] *n.* 镶板；面；(门、墙等上面的) 嵌板；控制板　*v.* 选定 (陪审团)；把……分格；把……镶入框架内

【变】panelled/paneled　panelled/paneled　panelling/paneling　panels

【例】The Obama administration has overturned a U. S. trade **panel's** ban on imports of some Apple iPads and older iPhones into the United States, dealing a setback to Apple's rival, Samsung.

　　奥巴马政府已经推翻了美国的国际贸易**委员会**颁发的禁止一些苹果 iPad 和旧 iPhone 手机进入美国的禁令，目的是为了阻碍苹果的竞争对手，三星手机在美国的市场发展。

【搭】panel absorbent 薄板吸声体　panel absorber 板式吸声器，吸声板

panel bed 面板座，控制盘底座

【记】board *n.* 板；董事会；甲板；膳食

group *n.* 组，团体；群，批；(雕塑等的) 群像；(英美的) 空军大队

v. 使成群，集合

forum *n.* 论坛，讨论会，专题讨论节目；法庭

setback ['setbæk] *n.* 挫折；阻碍；退步；逆流

【例】The Obama administration has overturned a U. S. trade panel's ban on imports of some Apple iPads and older iPhones into the United States, dealing a **setback** to Apple's rival, Samsung.

　　奥巴马政府已经推翻了美国的国际贸易委员会颁发的禁止一些苹果 iPad 和旧 iPhone 手机进入美国的禁令，目的是为了**阻碍**苹果的竞争对手，三星手机在美国的市场发展。

【搭】setback force 后退力　setbacks in his career 他事业上的一些周折

【记】drawback *n.* 劣势；退税

tragedy *n.* 悲剧，惨剧；悲剧文学；悲剧理

misadventure *n.* 运气不佳的遭遇

disappointment *n.* 失望，扫兴；令人失望的行为 (人)

rival [ˈraivəl] *n.* 对手；竞争者　*v.* 与……竞争；比得上某人　*a.* 竞争的

【变】复数 rivals　rivaled/rivalled　rivaled/rivalled　rivaling/rivalling　rivals

【例】The Obama administration has overturned a U. S. trade panel's ban on imports of some Apple iPads and older iPhones into the United States, dealing a setback to Apple's **rival**, Samsung.

　　奥巴马政府已经推翻了美国的国际贸易委员会颁发的禁止一些苹果 iPad 和旧 iPhone 手机进入美国的禁令，目的是为了阻碍苹果的**竞争对手**，三星手机在美国的市场发展。

【搭】rival supply 竞争供给

【记】compete *v.* 竞赛；竞争；比得上；参加比赛（或竞赛）

　　contest *v.* 竞争，为……而奋争；辩驳

词汇听写

1. _____ 2. _____ 3. _____

句子听写

Thursday ·· ≪≪≪

1. Lifelike robotics are said to <u>elicit</u> feelings of fear, <u>disgust</u>, or dread in humans.

据说，栩栩如生的机器人会引起人们恐惧、厌恶或畏惧的感觉。

lifelike ['laiflaik] *a.* **活像真的，栩栩如生的；逼真；传神**

【例】Lifelike robotics are said to elicit feelings of fear, disgust, or dread in humans.

据说，栩栩如生的机器人会引起人们恐惧、厌恶或畏惧的感觉。

【记】pictorial *a.* 绘画的；有图片的；图画似的；形象化的 *n.* 画报；画刊；画页；图画邮票

vivid *a.* 生动的；（记忆、描述等）清晰的；（人的想象）丰富的；（光、颜色等）鲜艳的，耀眼的

graphic *a.* 图解的，用图表示的；用文字表示的；形象的，生动的

elicit [i'lisit] *v.* **引出，探出；诱出（回答等）**

【变】elicited　elicited　eliciting　elicits

【例】Lifelike robotics are said to elicit feelings of fear, disgust, or dread in humans.

据说，栩栩如生的机器人会引起人们恐惧、厌恶或畏惧的感觉。

【记】arouse *v.* 引起；唤醒；使行动起来

enkindle *v.* ［文］使（火焰）燃起；刺激；激发；煽起（感情、热情等）

evoke *v.* 产生，引起；唤起

disgust [dis'gʌst] *n.* **反感，厌恶，嫌恶 *v.* 使反感，厌恶**

【变】disgusted　disgusted　disgusting　disgusts

【例】Lifelike robotics are said to elicit feelings of fear, disgust, or dread in humans.

据说，栩栩如生的机器人会引起人们恐惧、厌恶或畏惧的感觉。

【搭】walk away in disgust 感到厌恶就走开了　to my disgust 让我恶心

【记】disgustedly *ad.* 厌烦地

revolt *v.* （使）厌恶 *v.* 反叛，背叛；厌恶

339

nauseate *v.* 使恶心，作呕

sicken *v.* 使生病；使厌恶，使恶心；患病

dread [dred] *v.* 害怕，担心；（古语）敬畏　*n.* 恐惧，畏惧；令人恐惧的
　　　　事物　*a.* 可怕的

【变】dreaded　dreaded　dreading　dreads

【例】Lifelike robotics are said to elicit feelings of fear, disgust, or **dread** in humans.
　　据说，栩栩如生的机器人会引起人们恐惧、厌恶或**畏惧**的感觉。

【搭】dread the grave 怕死　dread being sick 怕生病

【记】dead *a.* 死了的；完全的

　　deadly *a.* 极端的；致命的

词汇听写

1. _____　2. _____　3. _____

句子听写

2. Analysts had been predicting a fiery exchange between the two men, but Australian media said the tone of the debate had been far more cordial than expected.

　　分析师已经预测在这两个男人之间将出现一次激烈的辩论，但澳大利亚媒体说，辩论的基调已经比预期的要友好得多。

analyst ['ænəlist] *n.* 分析家，化验员；〈美〉精神病医师

【变】analysts

【例】**Analysts** had been predicting a fiery exchange between the two men, but Australian media said the tone of the debate had been far more cordial than expected.

　　分析师已经预测在这两个男人之间将出现一次激烈的辩论，但澳大利亚媒体说，辩论的基调已经比预期的要友好得多。

【搭】credit analyst 信用分析　defense analyst 防务分析家　economic analyst

经济分析家

fiery [ˈfaiəri] *a.* 激烈的；火似的；火热的；易燃烧的

【变】fierier　fieriest

【例】Analysts had been predicting a **fiery** exchange between the two men, but Australian media said the tone of the debate had been far more cordial than expected.

　　分析师已经预测在这两个男人之间将出现一次**激烈的**辩论，但澳大利亚媒体说，辩论的基调已经比预期的要友好得多。

【搭】fiery cross 血十字（古苏格兰高地人的氏族或部落聚众出战的信号）

　　fiery fracture 粗粒断口　fiery fermentation 激烈发酵

【记】ardent *a.* 热心的，炽热的；强烈的

　　fervent *a.* 热诚的，强烈的

　　fervid *a.* 充满激情的，热烈的

tone [təun] *n.* [语] 声调，语调　*v.* 定调；呈现某种色彩

【变】toned　toned　toning　tones

【例】Analysts had been predicting a fiery exchange between the two men, but Australian media said the **tone** of the debate had been far more cordial than expected.

　　分析师已经预测在这两个男人之间将出现一次激烈的辩论，但澳大利亚媒体说，辩论的**基调**已经比预期的要友好得多。

【搭】tone down 使温和一些　tone in with 调和　tone up 强化，有力

cordial [ˈkɔːdjəl] *a.* 热诚的；诚恳的；兴奋的

【变】cordials

【例】Analysts had been predicting a fiery exchange between the two men, but Australian media said the tone of the debate had been far more **cordial** than expected.

　　分析师已经预测在这两个男人之间将出现一次激烈的交流，但澳大利亚媒体说，辩论的基调已经比预期的要**友好**得多。

【记】cordially *ad.* 热情地

　　cordiality *n.* 热情

词汇听写

1. _____ 2. _____ 3. _____

句子听写

---

3. The two <u>candidates</u> also discussed climate concerns, with Mr. Rudd saying Australia's leader "will be doing a <u>disservice</u> to our kids and grandkids if we do not act", while Mr. Abbott said his <u>coalition</u> was committed to delivering the 5% reduction in carbon <u>emissions</u> it has already announced.

两位候选人还讨论了气候问题，陆克文说澳大利亚领导人"将对我们的子孙造成伤害，如果我们不采取行动"，而艾伯特先生说他的联盟已着手减少所公布数值的5%的碳排放量。

---

candidate [ˈkændidət] *n.* 报考者；申请求职者；攻读学位者

【变】candidates

【例】The two **candidates** also discussed climate concerns，with Mr. Rudd saying Australia's leader "will be doing a disservice to our kids and grandkids if we do not act"，while Mr. Abbott said his coalition was committed to delivering the 5％ reduction in carbon emissions it has already announced.

两位**候选人**还讨论了气候问题，陆克文说澳大利亚领导人"将对我们的子孙造成伤害，如果我们不采取行动"，而艾伯特先生说他的联盟已着手减少所公布数值的5％的碳排放量。

【搭】list of candidates 候选人名单　villes candidates 候选城市

disservice [disˈsəːvis] *n.* 伤害，虐待，不亲切的行为

【例】The two candidates also discussed climate concerns，with Mr. Rudd saying Australia's leader "will be doing a **disservice** to our kids and grandkids if we do not act"，while Mr. Abbott said his coalition was committed to delivering the 5％ reduction in carbon emissions it has already announced.

两位候选人还讨论了气候问题，陆克文说澳大利亚领导人"将对我们的子孙造成伤害，如果我们不采取行动"，而艾伯特先生说他的联盟已

着手减少所公布数值的 5％ 的碳排放量。

【记】service *n.* 服务，服侍；服务业；维修服务；服役 *v.* 检修，维修；向……提供服务；保养；满足需要

coalition [ˌkəuəˈliʃn] *n.* 结合体；联合；同盟；（两党或多党）联合政府

【变】coalitions

【例】The two candidates also discussed climate concerns, with Mr. Rudd saying Australia's leader "will be doing a disservice to our kids and grandkids if we do not act", while Mr. Abbott said his **coalition** was committed to delivering the 5％ reduction in carbon emissions it has already announced.

两位候选人还讨论了气候问题，陆克文说澳大利亚领导人"将对我们的子孙造成伤害，如果我们不采取行动"，而艾伯特先生说他的**联盟**已着手减少所公布数值的 5％ 的碳排放量。

【搭】minimum size of coalitions 最小规模联合　coalitionas of the willing 自愿联盟

emission [iˈmiʃn] *n.* 排放，辐射；排放物，散发物（尤指气体）；（书刊）发行，发布（通知）

【变】emissions

【例】The two candidates also discussed climate concerns, with Mr. Rudd saying Australia's leader "will be doing a disservice to our kids and grandkids if we do not act", while Mr. Abbott said his coalition was committed to delivering the 5％ reduction in carbon **emissions** it has already announced.

两位候选人还讨论了气候问题，陆克文说澳大利亚领导人"将对我们的子孙造成伤害，如果我们不采取行动"，而艾伯特先生说他的联盟已着手减少所公布数值的 5％ 的碳**排放**量。

【搭】emission taxes 排放税　global emissions 全球排放量

词汇听写

1. ＿＿＿＿＿＿＿　2. ＿＿＿＿＿＿＿　3. ＿＿＿＿＿＿＿

句子听写

Friday ·· ⋘

1. He said he was withdrawing "in the interests of ensuring that this matter does not distract from Labor's campaign for a fairer Australia".

他说，他退出是为了确保这件事情并不会转移工党建立一个更公平的澳大利亚的目标。

---

withdraw [wɪð'drɔː] *v.* 撤走；拿走；撤退；（从银行）取（钱）

【变】withdrew   withdrawn   withdrawing   withdraws

【例】He said he was **withdrawing** "in the interests of ensuring that this matter does not distract from Labor's campaign for a fairer Australia".

他说，他**退出**是为了确保这件事情并不会转移工党建立一个更公平的澳大利亚的运动。

【搭】withdraw a confession [法] 翻供   withdraw collar 分离环
withdraw deposit 提取存款；提款

---

ensure [in'ʃuə] *v.* 确保；担保获得（避免）；使（某人）获得；使安全

【变】ensured   ensured   ensuring   ensures

【例】He said he was withdrawing "in the interests of **ensuring** that this matter does not distract from Labor's campaign for a fairer Australia".

他说，他退出是为了**确保**这件事情并不会转移工党建立一个更公平的澳大利亚的运动。

【搭】ensure delivery 保证投送无误   ensure from 保护……免受危险
ensure to 保证给

【记】enclosure *n.* 圈占；围绕；附件
assure *v.* 确保

---

distract [di'strækt] *v.* 使分心；使混乱

【变】distracted   distracted   distracting   distracts

【例】He said he was withdrawing "in the interests of ensuring that this matter does not **distract** from Labor's campaign for a fairer Australia".

他说，他退出是为了确保这件事情并不会**转移**工党建立一个更公平的澳大利亚的运动。

【搭】distract from 转移；分散

【记】district *n.* 地区　*v.* 分区

　　distress *n.* 悲痛，不幸

　　distribute *v.* 分配，分布，分散

campaign [kæm'pein] *n.*　运动；竞选运动；战役；季节性竞赛　*v.* 参加
　　　　　　　　　　　　（发起）运动，参加竞选；参战，参加战役；作战

【变】campaigns

【例】He said he was withdrawing "in the interests of ensuring that this matter
does not distract from Labor's **campaign** for a fairer Australia".

　　　　他说，他退出是为了确保这件事情并不会转移工党建立一个更公平
的澳大利亚的**运动**。

【搭】advertising campaign 广告运动，广告战　public campaign 未付发票款

【记】battle *n.* 战争，争斗

　　war *n.* 战争的总称

　　struggle *n.* &*v.* 战斗，奋力斗争

词汇听写

1. _____ 2. _____ 3. _____

句子听写

2. Jason Dufner held his nerve to clinch his maiden major title with victory at the
US PGA Championship at Oak Hill.

　　詹森·杜夫纳第一次一举取得了在橡树山举行的美国 PGA 锦标赛的
胜利。

hold his nerve 面对紧张场面（局势）保持冷静

【例】Jason Dufner **held his nerve** to clinch his maiden major title with victory at
the US PGA Championship at Oak Hill.

詹森·杜夫纳第一次**一举**取得了在橡树山举行的美国 PGA 锦标赛的胜利。

【搭】nerve oneself 振作，鼓起勇气　nerve center 神经元，神经中枢　nerve growth factor 神经生长因子

clinch [klintʃ] *v.* （尤指两人）互相紧紧抱住；〈非正〉解决（争端、交易），达成（协议）；敲弯

【变】clinched　clinched　clinching　clinches

【例】Jason Dufner held his nerve to **clinch** his maiden major title with victory at the US PGA Championship at Oak Hill.

詹森·杜夫纳第一次一举取得了在橡树山举行的美国 PGA 锦标赛的胜利。

【搭】clinch an argument 作出最后的结论，使争论获得完全解决

clinch bolt 铆钉

【记】clutch *v.* & *n.* 抓紧

clinic *n.* 诊所；门诊部；临床实习课

maiden [ˈmeidn] *n.* 未婚女子；处女　*a.* 处女的，少女的；首次的，初次的；没有经验的

【变】maidens

【例】Jason Dufner held his nerve to clinch his **maiden** major title with victory at the US PGA Championship at Oak Hill.

詹森·杜夫纳**第一次**一举取得了在橡树山举行的美国 PGA 锦标赛的胜利。

【搭】weeping maidens 哭啼少女

seven fairy maidens 七仙女

championship [ˈtʃæmpiənʃip] *n.* 锦标赛；胜，冠军称号；拥护者（支持者，提倡者）的身份

【变】championships

【例】Jason Dufner held his nerve to clinch his maiden major title with victory at the US PGA **Championship** at Oak Hill.

詹森·杜夫纳一举拿下了在橡树山举行的美国 PGA 锦标赛的**胜利**。

【记】champion *n.* 冠军　*v.* 捍卫

backup *n.* 支持，后援；［计］备份文件

backing *n.* 支持；支持者；背衬

词汇听写

1. _____　2. _____　3. _____

句子听写

3. A malaria vaccine has shown promising results in early stage clinical trials, according to researchers.

据研究人员报告，一种疟疾疫苗在早期临床试验中已经显示出可喜的成果。

---

malaria [məˈleəriə] *n.* ［医］疟疾；瘴气

【例】A **malaria** vaccine has shown promising results in early stage clinical trials, according to researchers.

据研究人员报告，一种**疟疾**疫苗在早期临床试验中已经显示出可喜的成果。

【搭】malaria mosquito 疟蚊

【记】malarial *a.* 患疟疾的，毒气的

malarian *n.* ［医］疟疾；瘴气

malarious *a.* （患）疟疾的，（有）瘴气的

---

vaccine [ˈvæksiːn] *n.* 疫苗，痘苗　*a.* 痘苗的，疫苗的

【变】vaccines

【例】A malaria **vaccine** has shown promising results in early stage clinical trials, according to researchers.

据研究人员报告，一种疟疾**疫苗**在早期临床试验中已经显示出可喜的成果。

【搭】vaccine inoculation 疫苗接种，菌苗接种　　vaccine lymph 菌苗，疫苗

347

vaccine point 种痘针

【记】vaccinal *a.* 疫苗的

vaccinate *v.* 给……接种疫苗；注射疫苗，接种疫苗

vaccination *n.* ［医］种痘，接种；牛痘疤

promise [ˈprɔmis] *v.* 允诺，许诺；给人以……的指望或希望

【变】promised　promised　promising　promises

【例】A malaria vaccine has shown **promising** results in early stage clinical trials, according to researchers.

据研究人员报告，一种疟疾疫苗在早期临床试验中已经显示出**可喜**的成果。

【搭】promise oneself 指望　promise well 显示出成功的迹象，前景很好

【记】promiser *n.* 立约人，许诺者

promiscuity *n.* 混杂，混乱

clinical [ˈklinikl] *a.* 临床的；诊所的；冷静的；简陋的

【例】A malaria vaccine has shown promising results in early stage **clinical** trials, according to researchers.

据研究人员报告，一种疟疾疫苗在早期**临床**试验中已经显示出可喜的成果。

【搭】clinical analysis 临床分析　clinical death 临床死亡

【记】clinically *ad.* 冷静地，客观地

clinician *n.* 临床医生，门诊医师

词汇听写

1. ＿＿＿＿＿＿＿　2. ＿＿＿＿＿＿＿　3. ＿＿＿＿＿＿＿

句子听写

Saturday ·· ≪

1. It is hard to miss Tallinn's <u>multitude</u> of towers. Along with the city's <u>soaring</u> church <u>spires</u> and <u>distinctive</u> orange roofs, they are a key element of the Estonian capital's striking skyline.

很难错过塔林的众多塔，除了城市里教堂的尖顶和鲜明的橙色屋顶，数目众多的塔就是爱沙尼亚首都另一道重要的著名风景线。

multitude [ˈmʌltitjuːd] *n.* **大量，许多；大众，人群**

【变】multitudes

【例】It is hard to miss Tallinn's **multitude** of towers. Along with the city's soaring church spires and distinctive orange roofs, they are a key element of the Estonian capital's striking skyline.

很难错过塔林的**众多**塔，除了城市里教堂的尖顶和鲜明的橙色屋顶，数目众多的塔就是爱沙尼亚首都另一道重要的著名风景线。

【记】mumble *v.* 咕哝；抿着嘴嚼

mummified *v.* 成木乃伊状（mummify 的过去式和过去分词）；干瘪；使干瘪；使成木乃伊

soar [sɔː] *v.* **高飞；飞腾；猛增，剧增；高耸，屹立** *n.* **高飞；高涨；高飞范围；上升高度**

【变】soared soared soaring soars

【例】It is hard to miss Tallinn's multitude of towers. Along with the city's **soaring** church spires and distinctive orange roofs, they are a key element of the Estonian capital's striking skyline.

很难错过塔林的众多塔，除了城市里**教堂**的尖顶和鲜明的橙色屋顶，数目众多的塔就是爱沙尼亚首都另一道重要的著名风景线。

【记】soarer *n.* 滑翔机

soaring *a.* 高飞的，翱翔的；高耸的

spire [ˈspaiə] *n.* **螺旋；塔尖；尖塔；[动] 螺旋部，（软体动物的）螺塔** *v.* **给……装尖塔**

【变】spired spired spiring spires

【例】It is hard to miss Tallinn's multitude of towers. Along with the city's soaring church **spires** and distinctive orange roofs, they are a key element of the Estonian capital's striking skyline.

很难错过塔林的众多塔，除了城市里教堂的**尖顶**和鲜明的橙色屋顶，数目众多的塔就是爱沙尼亚首都另一道重要的著名风景线。

【搭】spire lamella 腕带

【记】spired v. （教堂的）塔尖，尖顶

spiry a. 尖端的，尖塔状的，螺旋状的

distinctive [di'stiŋktiv] a. **有特色的，与众不同的；区别的，鉴别性的；独特；特异**

【例】It is hard to miss Tallinn's multitude of towers. Along with the city's soaring church spires and **distinctive** orange roofs, they are a key element of the Estonian capital's striking skyline.

很难错过塔林的众多塔，除了城市里教堂的尖顶和**鲜明的**橙色屋顶，数目众多的塔就是爱沙尼亚首都另一道重要的著名风景线。

【搭】distinctive acoustic features 区别性声学特征　distinctive sound 区别性语音

【记】distinctively ad. 区别地，特殊地

distinctiveness n. 特殊性

distinctly ad. 明显地；无疑地；确实地；逼真地

词汇听写

1. ＿＿＿＿＿＿　2. ＿＿＿＿＿＿　3. ＿＿＿＿＿＿

句子听写

2. UK experts studied brain scans of 120 men and women, with half of those studied having autism. Experts said girls with the condition could be more stigmatised than boys — and it could be harder for them to be diagnosed at all.

英国专家研究了120名男性和女性的脑部扫描，他们中有一半是自闭症患者。专家说，女性自闭症患者可能会比男性自闭症患者更容易受屈

辱——并且她们的病症也更难以诊断。

scan [ˈskæn] v. & n. 扫描；细看，细查

【变】

【例】UK experts studied brain **scans** of 120 men and women, with half of those studied having autism. Experts said girls with the condition could be more stigmatised than boys — and it could be harder for them to be diagnosed at all.

英国专家研究了 120 名男性和女性的脑部**扫描**，他们中有一半是自闭症患者。专家说，女性自闭症患者可能会比男性自闭症患者更容易受屈辱——并且她们的病症也更难以诊断。

【搭】scanner disc 扫描盘　scan location 扫描地点　scanner recorder 扫描（器）记录器

【记】scanners n. 检测装置（scanner 的名词复数）；扫描设备

scantier a.（大小或数量）不足的，勉强够的

scantily ad. 缺乏地；不充足地；吝啬地；狭窄地

autism [ˈɔːtizəm] n. 孤独症，自我中心主义

【例】UK experts studied brain scans of 120 men and women, with half of those studied having **autism**. Experts said girls with the condition could be more stigmatised than boys — and it could be harder for them to be diagnosed at all.

英国专家研究了 120 名男性和女性的脑部扫描，他们中有一半是**自闭症患者**。专家说，女性自闭症患者可能会比男性自闭症患者更容易受屈辱——并且她们的病症也更难以诊断。

【记】autistic n.（专注自我而与现实隔绝的）孤独症患者（常指儿童），自闭症患者

stigmatize [ˈstigmətaiz] v. 使受耻辱，指责，污辱

【变】stigmatized　stigmatized　stigmatizing　stigmatizes

【例】UK experts studied brain scans of 120 men and women, with half of those studied having autism. Experts said girls with the condition could be more **stigmatised** than boys — and it could be harder for them to be diagnosed at all.

英国专家研究了 120 名男性和女性的脑部扫描，他们中有一半是自闭症患者。专家说，女性自闭症患者可能会比男性自闭症患者更容易受**屈**

辱——并且她们的病症也更难以诊断。

【搭】a stigmatized illness 一种见不得人的病

【记】stigmata *n.* 皮肤上的红斑，特征；耻辱的标记，瑕疵（ stigma 的名词复数）

stigma *n.* 耻辱，污名；烙印；（病的）特征

diagnose [ˈdaiəgnəuz] *v.* 诊断；判断

【变】diagnosed diagnosed diagnosing diagnoses

【例】UK experts studied brain scans of 120 men and women, with half of those studied having autism. Experts said girls with the condition could be more stigmatised than boys — and it could be harder for them to be **diagnosed** at all.

英国专家研究了 120 名男性和女性的脑部扫描，他们中有一半是自闭症患者。专家说，女性自闭症患者可能会比男性自闭症患者更容易受屈辱——并且她们的病症也更难以**诊断**。

【记】diagnosable *a.* [计] 可诊断的

diagnosis *n.* 诊断；诊断结论；判断；结论

diagnostic *a.* 诊断的，判断的 *n.* 诊断法，诊断结论

词汇听写

1. _____ 2. _____ 3. _____

句子听写

3. At the time, there were just a few companies who specialize in the creation of the generic images of places and things that are used to illustrate so many websites today.

当时，仅有少数几家公司专业于地方和事物的通用图像的创作，这些图像在今天已经被用于许多的网站。

specialize [ˈspeʃəlaiz] *v.* 专门从事；专攻；详细说明；特化

【变】specialized specialized specializing specializes

【例】At the time，there were just a few companies who **specialize** in the creation of the generic images of places and things that are used to illustrate so many websites today.

当时，仅有少数几家公司**专业**于地方和事物的通用图像的创作，这些图像在今天已经被用于许多的网站。

【搭】specialize in 专攻，精通，以······为专业；专修

【记】specialization *n.* 特别化；专门化；（意义的）限定

specialized *a.* 专门的；专业的；专用的

generic [dʒəˈnerik] *a.* 类的，属性的；一般的；不受商标保护的；[生] 属的，类的

【变】generics

【例】At the time，there were just a few companies who specialize in the creation of the **generic** images of places and things that are used to illustrate so many websites today.

当时，仅有少数几家公司专业于地方和事物的**通用**图像的创作，这些图像在今天已经被用于许多的网站。

【搭】generic category 种范畴　generic coefficient 种属系数

【记】generically *ad.* 一般地

generosity *n.* 慷慨，大方；宽容或慷慨的行为；丰富

generous *a.* 慷慨的，大方的；丰盛的；肥沃的；浓厚的

illustrate [ˈiləstreit] *v.* 说明；表明；给······加插图；（用示例、图画等）说明

【变】illustrated　illustrated　illustrating　illustrates

【例】At the time，there were just a few companies who specialize in the creation of the generic images of places and things that are used to **illustrate** so many websites today.

当时，仅有少数几家公司专业于地方和事物的通用图像的创作，这些图像在今天已经被**用于**许多的网站。

【记】illustration *n.* 说明；例证；图解；插图

illustrative *a.* 用作说明的，解说性的

353

illustrious *a.* 著名的；杰出的，卓越的；辉煌的；显赫

website ['websait] *n.* （环球网）的站点

【例】At the time，there were just a few companies who specialize in the creation of the generic images of places and things that are used to illustrate so many **websites** today.

当时，仅有少数几家公司专业于地方和事物的通用图像的创作，这些图像在今天已经被用于许多的**网站**。

【记】web space *n.* 网络空间

web *n.* 蜘蛛网，网状物

wedge *n.* 楔 *v.* 楔入；挤入

词汇听写

1. _____ 2. _____ 3. _____

句子听写

Sunday ·· ≪≪

1. Happy workers tend to be more productive, which makes it sensible to focus on making sure your staff are content.

快乐的工人往往能够更有生产力，所以，确保您的员工快乐是明智的。

tend [tend] *v.* 照料；护理；照管，管理；倾向（于），趋向（于）；伺侯，招待；关心；注意

【变】tended　tended　tending　tends

【例】Happy workers **tend** to be more productive, which makes it sensible to focus on making sure your staff are content.

快乐的工人**往往**能够更有生产力，所以，确保您的员工快乐是明智的。

【搭】tend on 照料，服侍，照管　tend shop 招待顾客

【记】tendency *n.* 倾向，趋势；意向

tendentious *a.*（指演说、文章等）宣传性的；有偏见的

tenderer *n.* 投标人

productive [prəˈdʌktiv] *a.* 富有成效的；多产的；生产性的；具有创造性的

【例】Happy workers tend to be more **productive**, which makes it sensible to focus on making sure your staff are content.

快乐的工人往往能够更有**生产力**，所以，确保您的员工快乐是明智的。

【搭】productive affix 派生词缀　productive assets 生产资产

【记】productivity *n.* 生产率，生产力；[经济学] 生产率

production *n.* 生产，制作；产品；产量；夸张的行动或形象，小题大做

products *n.* 乘积；（自然、化学或工业过程的）产物；产量；制品

sensible [ˈsensəbl] *a.* 明智的；合乎情理的；通情达理的；意识到的，能感觉到的

【变】more sensible　most sensible

【例】Happy workers tend to be more productive，which makes it **sensible** to focus on making sure your staff are content.

快乐的工人往往能够更有生产力，所以，确保您的员工快乐是**明智的**。

【搭】sensible horizon 感觉地平圈　　sensible heat 感热；显热

【记】sensibly *ad.* 明智地；理智地；能感觉得出来；切合实际地

sensitive *a.* 敏感的；感觉的；[仪] 灵敏的；易受影响的

sensitization *n.* 促进感受性，感光度之增强；激活

content [ˈkɔntent] *n.* 内容；（书等的）目录；满足　[kənˈtent] *a.* 满足的，满意的；愿意的；心甘情愿的　*v.* 使满足，使满意

【变】contented　contented　contenting　contents

【例】Happy workers tend to be more productive，which makes it sensible to focus on making sure your staff are **content.**

快乐的工人往往能够更有生产力，所以，确保您的员工**快乐**是明智的。

【搭】content by volume 单位体积含量　　content zero 零容度

【记】contact *v.* 联系

contend *v.* 争夺；竞争

context *n.* 上下文，语境

词汇听写

1. _____　2. _____　3. _____

句子听写

2. A transgender woman in Hong Kong, buzzing with nervous anticipation on the eve of her sex-reassignment surgery, keeps awake all night long.

在香港，一位想要改变性别的女人在变性手术前夕，对手术充满了紧张的期待，整夜无法入睡。

transgender [trænzˈdʒendə] *n.* 变性人

【变】transgenders

【例】A **transgender** woman in Hong Kong, buzzing with nervous anticipation on the eve of her sex-reassignment surgery, keeps awake all night long.

在香港，一位想要**改变性别的**女人在变性手术前夕，对手术充满了紧张的期待，整夜无法入睡。

【记】transgenic *a.* 基因改造的，基因被改变的

transgress *v.* 超越；越过；违反；违背

transgression *n.* 违反，违法，罪过

---

buzz [bʌz] *v.* 嗡嗡叫；低声谈；散布嗡嗡叫，发哼声；匆忙来去，奔忙 *n.* 嗡嗡声；电话；乱哄哄的说话声

【变】buzzed buzzed buzzing buzzs

【例】A transgender woman in Hong Kong, **buzzing** with nervous anticipation on the eve of her sex-reassignment surgery, keeps awake all night long.

在香港，一位想要改变性别的女人在变性手术前夕，对手术充满了紧张的期待，整夜无法入睡。

【搭】buzz about 闹哄哄地跑来跑去 buzz around 匆忙而紧张地行动，乱哄哄地跑来跑去

【记】buzzard *n.* 秃鹰

buzzer *n.* 蜂鸣器，嗡嗡作声的东西；〈口〉门铃；汽笛；〈俚〉信号兵

buzzsaw *n.* 圆锯

---

anticipation [ænˌtisiˈpeiʃn] *n.* 期待，希望；预期，预测，预感；［律］（信托财产收益的）预支

【变】anticipations

【例】A transgender woman in Hong Kong, buzzing with nervous **anticipation** on the eve of her sex-reassignment surgery, keeps awake all night long.

在香港，一位想要改变性别的女人在变性手术前夕，对手术充满了紧张的**期待**，整夜无法入睡。

【搭】anticipation of her arrival 惹得她的到来 anticipation mode 先行方式（形式）

【记】anticipatory *a.* 期待着的；提早发生的

anticlimax *n.* 突降法；虎头蛇尾；苍白无力的结尾；令人扫兴的结尾

antics *n.* 古怪、可笑的举动

assignment [əˈsainmənt] *n.* 分给，分配；任务，工作，（课外）作业；〈美〉任命；指定，委派

【变】assignments

【例】A transgender woman in Hong Kong, buzzing with nervous anticipation on the eve of her sex-re**assignment** surgery, keeps awake all night long.

　　在香港，一位想要改变性别的女人在变性手术前夕，对手术充满了紧张的期待，整夜无法入睡。

【搭】assignment card 作业卡片　assignment charge 转让费　assignment component 设定组件

【记】assign *v.* 分配；指派；指定；（作为说明或原因）提出

assignation *n.* 约会；幽会；分配；指派

assimilate *v.* 透彻理解；使吸收

词汇听写

1. _____ 2. _____ 3. _____

句子听写

3. The film's sympathetic portrayal of its protagonist stood out in the country where the vast majority of the population have scant understanding of transgender issues.

　　电影把主角描述成一个令人同情的角色，这在国内引起了轰动，因为这个国家的绝大多数人口对变性问题都缺乏了解。

sympathetic [ˌsimpəˈθetik] *a.* 同情的，有同情心的；赞同的；相投合的，称心的

【例】The film's **sympathetic** portrayal of its protagonist stood out in the country where the vast majority of the population have scant understanding of transgender issues.

电影把主角描述成一个令人**同情的**角色，这在国内引起了轰动，因为这个国家的绝大多数人口对变性问题都缺乏了解。

【搭】sympathetic atrophy 交感性萎缩　　sympathetic chain 交感（神经）干

【记】sympathetically *ad.* 悲怜地，富有同情心地

sympathies *n.* 同情，支持；同情（心）（sympathy 的名词复数）；（感情上的）支持；意气相投

sympathize *v.* 同情，怜悯；共鸣，同感；支持，赞成；安慰

portrayal [pɔːˈtreiəl] *n.* **画像，肖像；描述，描写；叙述**

【变】portrayals

【例】The film's sympathetic **portrayal** of its protagonist stood out in the country where the vast majority of the population have scant understanding of transgender issues.

　　电影把主角**描述**成一个令人同情的角色，这在国内引起了轰动，因为这个国家的绝大多数人口对变性问题都缺乏了解。

【记】portrayed *v.* 画像（portray 的过去式和过去分词）；描述；描画

ports *n.* 港口（port 的名词复数）；（事情的）意义；（计算机与其他设备的）接口；（船、飞机等的）左舷

protagonist [prəˈtæɡənist] *n.* **（戏剧的）主角；（故事的）主人公；现实事件（尤指冲突和争端的）主要参与者；领导者**

【变】protagonists

【例】The film's sympathetic portrayal of its **protagonist** stood out in the country where the vast majority of the population have scant understanding of transgender issues.

　　电影把**主角**描述成一个令人同情的角色，这在国内引起了轰动，因为这个国家的绝大多数人口对变性问题都缺乏了解。

【记】protean *a.* 多变的，易变的，变化多端的

protect *v.* 保护，保卫；贸易保护；备款以支付

toniest *a.* 高贵的，时髦的

scant [skænt] *a.* **不足的；缺乏的；将近的；吝啬的　　*v.* 限制；节省；吝惜**

【变】Scanted　scanted　scanting　scants　scanter　scantest

【例】The film's sympathetic portrayal of its protagonist stood out in the country where the vast majority of the population have **scant** understanding of transgender issues.

电影把主角描述成一个令人同情的角色，这在国内引起了轰动，因为这个国家的绝大多数人口对变性问题都**缺乏**了解。

【搭】scant of breath 呼吸困难

【记】scantly *ad.* 缺乏地，仅仅

scandal *n* 丑闻，丑事，丢脸的事件，耻辱；流言蜚语；诽谤

scantily *ad.* 缺乏地；不充足地；吝啬地；狭窄地

词汇听写

1. _____   2. _____   3. _____

句子听写

第10周

1. Crucially, micro movies create an <u>outlet</u> for directors that largely <u>bypasses</u> the strict film <u>censorship</u> of the state and avoids studio domination and substantial commercial <u>restraints</u>.

最重要的是，微电影为导演创造了一个平台，这个平台在很大程度上绕过了国家严格的电影审查制度，避免了电影制片厂的垄断和主要的商业限制。

outlet [ˈautlet] *n.* 出口，出路；批发商店；排水口，通风口；发泄（情感）的方法

【变】outlets

【例】Crucially, micro movies create an **outlet** for directors that largely bypasses the strict film censorship of the state and avoids studio domination and substantial commercial restraints.

最重要的是，微电影为导演创造了一个**平台**，这个平台在很大程度上绕过了国家严格的电影审查制度，避免了电影制片厂的垄断和主要的商业限制。

【搭】outlet angle 出口角 outlet box 出线盒

【记】outline *n.* 梗概，提纲，草稿，要点，主要原则；轮廓，轮廓线

outlive *v.* 比……长寿；度过……而健在

out *v.* 使熄灭；揭露；驱逐 *a.* 外面的；出局的；下台的；外围的 *n.* 不流行；出局

bypass [ˈbaipɑːs] *n.* 旁道，支路；迂回管道；[电] 分路迂徊；[医] 导管 *v.* 疏通；忽视；管道运输

【变】bypassed bypassed bypassing bypasses

【例】Crucially, micro movies create an outlet for directors that largely **bypasses** the strict film censorship of the state and avoids studio domination and substantial commercial restraints.

　　最重要的是，微电影为导演创造了一个平台，这个平台在很大程度上**绕过**了国家严格的电影审查制度，避免了电影制片厂的垄断和主要的商业限制。

【搭】take the bypass 走旁道　　bypass condenser 旁路电容器

【记】bypath *n.* 小路，私道

　　byproduct *n.* 副产品；意外结果，副作用

censorship ['sensəʃip] *n.* 审查制度；审查机构；审察员的职权；［心］潜意识中的抑制力

【例】Crucially, micro movies create an outlet for directors that largely bypasses the strict film **censorship** of the state and avoids studio domination and substantial commercial restraints.

　　最重要的是，微电影为导演创造了一个平台，这个平台在很大程度上绕过了国家严格的电影**审查**制度，避免了电影制片厂的垄断和主要的商业限制。

【记】censor *n.* 监察官，检查员；（牛津大学等的）学监 *v.* 审查，检查；审查（书刊等）

　　censorious *a.* 苛评的，吹毛求疵的

　　censure *n.* & *v.* 指责，谴责；责备；斥责

restraint [ri'streint] *n.* 抑制；控制，限制；拘束

【变】restraints

【例】Crucially, micro movies create an outlet for directors that largely bypasses the strict film censorship of the state and avoids studio domination and substantial commercial **restraints**.

　　最重要的是，微电影为导演创造了一个平台，这个平台在很大程度上绕过了国家严格的电影审查制度，避免了电影制片厂的垄断和主要的商业**限制**。

【搭】absence of restraint 无约束　　continual restraint 一直受到约束　　restraint moment 约束力矩

【记】restrain *v.* 抑制，压抑；限定，限制；制止；监禁

restrict *v.* 限制，限定；约束，束缚

词汇听写

1. _____ 2. _____ 3. _____

句子听写

2. The doctor says it is v̲i̲t̲a̲l̲ that chest c̲o̲m̲p̲r̲e̲s̲s̲i̲o̲n̲s̲ occur at the right rate and force and that patients are not over-ventilated. So, it's important for people to learn how to do Cardiopulmonary r̲e̲s̲u̲s̲c̲i̲t̲a̲t̲i̲o̲n̲ (CPR).

医生说，以正确的速度和力度进行胸外按压是非常重要的，患者不会因为力度过大而导致过度换气，所以学会如何做心肺复苏很关键。

vital ['vaitl] *a.* 维持生命所必需的；至关重要的；生死攸关的；生气勃勃的

【变】more vital　most vital

【例】The doctor says it is **vital** that chest compressions occur at the right rate and force and that patients are not over-ventilated. So，it's important for people to learn how to do Cardiopulmonary resuscitation (CPR).

医生说，以正确的速度和力度进行胸外按压是**非常重要的**，患者不会因为力度过大而导致过度换气，所以学会如何做心肺复苏很关键。

【搭】vital information 重要情报　vital organ 要害部位　vital dye 活体染料

【记】vitally *ad.* 充满活力地；极其，绝对致命地

vitamin *n.* 维生素；维他命

vitiate *v.* （使）削弱；（使）破坏；（使）损害；（使）无效

compression [kəm'preʃn] *n.* 压缩，压紧，浓缩，紧缩；加压，压抑；（表现的）简练

【例】The doctor says it is vital that chest **compressions** occur at the right rate and force and that patients are not over-ventilated. So，it's important for people to learn how to do Cardiopulmonary resuscitation (CPR).

医生说，以正确的速度和力度进行胸外**按压**是非常重要的，患者不

会因为力度过大而导致过度换气，所以学会如何做心肺复苏很关键。

【搭】compression annealing 压缩熟炼，压缩退火　compression area 受压面积，压缩区

【记】compressor *n.* 压气机，压缩机

compress *v.* 压紧；压缩；精简 *n.* 止血敷布；打包机

comprise *v.* 包含，包括；由……组成；由……构成

ventilate ['ventileit] *v.* 使通风；通风；公开；公开讨论

【变】ventilated　ventilated　ventilating　ventilates

【例】The doctor says it is vital that chest compressions occur at the right rate and force and that patients are not over-**ventilated.** So，it's important for people to learn how to do Cardiopulmonary resuscitation（CPR）.

医生说，以正确的速度和力度进行胸外按压是非常重要的，患者不会因为力度过大而导致过度**换气**，所以学会如何做心肺复苏很关键。

【记】ventilation *n.* 空气流通；通风设备；通风方法；公开讨论

ventilator *n.* 通风设备；通风机；气窗；负责通风的人

ventral *a.* 腹的，腹部的，腹侧的 *n.* 腹鳍

resuscitation [ri‚sʌsi'teiʃn] *n.* 恢复知觉，苏醒

【例】The doctor says it is vital that chest compressions occur at the right rate and force and that patients are not over-ventilated. So，it'simportant for people to learn how to do Cardiopulmonary **resuscitation**（CPR）.

医生说，以正确的速度和力度进行胸外按压是非常重要的，患者不会因为力度过大而导致过度换气，所以学会如何做心肺**复苏**很关键。

【记】resuscitate *v.* 使复苏；使复兴

retail *n.* 零售 *v.* 零售；零卖；转述；传播

词汇听写

1. _____　2. _____　3. _____

句子听写

3. Cooling <u>therapy</u> is changing everything. Whereas Carol's <u>seizures</u> and low brain activity would once have been seen as unambiguously bad signs, such <u>symptoms</u> may be <u>compatible</u> with a good recovery.

冷却疗法正在改变一切。然而，卡罗尔病情的发作和大脑活动不足都曾经被明确地认为是坏预兆，这些症状通过好的治疗法可以得到缓解。

therapy [ˈθerəpi] *n.* 治疗，疗法，疗效；心理治疗；治疗力

【变】therapies

【例】Cooling **therapy** is changing everything. Whereas Carol's seizures and low brain activity would once have been seen as unambiguously bad signs, such symptoms may be compatible with a good recovery.

冷却**疗法**正在改变一切。然而，卡罗尔病情的发作和大脑活动不足都曾经被明确地认为是坏预兆，这些症状通过好的治疗法可以得到缓解。

【搭】therapy dose 治疗剂量，药用量

【记】therapist *n.* 治疗专家，特定疗法技师

therapeutic *a.* 治疗（学）的，疗法的；有益于健康的

thereby *ad.* 由此，从而；在那附近

seizure [ˈsiːʒə] *n.* 没收；夺取；捕捉；突然发作

【变】seizures

【例】Cooling therapy is changing everything. Whereas Carol's **seizures** and low brain activity would once have been seen as unambiguously bad signs, such symptoms may be compatible with a good recovery.

冷却疗法正在改变一切。然而，卡罗尔病情的**发作**和大脑活动不足都曾经被明确地认为是坏预兆，这些症状通过好的治疗法可以得到缓解。

【搭】seizure notes 擒获私运货物单　seizure of assets 扣押财产

【记】seize *v.* 抓住；逮捕；捉拿；俘获

seine *n.* （捕鱼用）围网 *v.* 用围网捕鱼

seismic *a.* 地震的；由地震引起的；震撼世界的

symptom [ˈsimptəm] *n.*　症状；征兆

【变】symptoms

【例】Cooling therapy is changing everything. Whereas Carol's seizures and low brain activity would once have been seen as unambiguously bad signs, such **symptoms** may be compatible with a good recovery.

　　冷却疗法正在改变一切。然而，卡罗尔病情的发作和大脑活动不足都曾经被明确地认为是坏预兆，这些**症状**通过好的治疗法可以得到缓解。

【搭】symptom complex 症候群

【记】symptomatic *a.* 有症状的；症候的；根据症状的

symphathetic *a.* 同情的，有同情心的；相投合的，称心的

sympathizer *n.* 同情者；同感者；支持者；赞助者

compatible [kəmˈpætəbl] *a.* 兼容的，相容的；和谐的，协调的；[生] 亲
和的；可以并存的，能共处的

【例】Cooling therapy is changing everything. Whereas Carol's seizures and low brain activity would once have been seen as unambiguously bad signs, such symptoms may be **compatible** with a good recovery.

　　冷却疗法正在改变一切。然而，卡罗尔病情的发作和大脑活动不足都曾经被明确地认为是坏预兆，这些症状通过好的治疗法可以得到缓解。

【搭】compatible circuit 兼容电路　compatible class 兼容类

【记】compatriot *n.* 同胞；同国人 *a.* 同国人的；同胞的

compatibility *n.* 适合；互换性；通用性；和睦相处

compel *v.* 强迫，迫使；强制发生，使不得不

词汇听写

1. _____　2. _____　3. _____

句子听写

Tuesday ·· ≪≪

1. In this syndrome, the <u>swelling</u> and pressure in a <u>restricted</u> space limits blood flow and causes <u>localised</u> <u>tissue</u> and nerve damage.

这种综合症的表现是，在有限的空间里，膨胀和压力会限制血液流动，并导致局部组织和神经损伤。

swell [swel] *v.* 增强；肿胀；膨胀；充满（激情）　　*n.* 汹涌；重要人士；（尤指身体部位）凸起的形状；声音渐强

【变】swelled　swelled　swelling　swells

【例】In this syndrome, the **swelling** and pressure in a restricted space limits blood flow and causes localised tissue and nerve damage.

这种综合症的表现是，在有限的空间里，**膨胀**和压力会限制血液流动，并导致局部组织和神经损伤。

【搭】swell box 风琴的音响调节箱　　swell diameter 膨胀直径

【记】swelter *n.* 热得难受，闷热

swear *v.* 发誓；咒骂 *n.* 发誓，宣誓；咒骂

sweat *v.* 流汗，渗出；发酵；做苦工；烦恼，焦急

restrict [rɪtˈstrɪkt] *v.* 限制，限定；约束，束缚

【变】restricted　restricted　restricting　restricts

【例】In this syndrome, the swelling and pressure in a **restricted** space limits blood flow and causes localised tissue and nerve damage.

这种综合症的表现是，在**有限的**空间里，膨胀和压力会限制血液流动，并导致局部组织和神经损伤。

【搭】restrict sales 限制销售

【记】restriction *n.* 限制，限定；拘束，束缚；管制

restructure *v.* 重建；调整；重组

restrain *v.* 抑制，压抑；限制；制止；监禁

localise [ˈləʊkəlaɪz] *v.* 使局部化，使具有地方色彩

【例】In this syndrome, the swelling and pressure in a restricted space limits blood flow and causes **localised** tissue and nerve damage.

这种综合症的表现是，在有限的空间里，膨胀和压力会限制血液流动，并导致局部组织和神经损伤。

【记】localities *n.* （出事的）位置，地区，地点

localily *n.* 位置；地区；产地

tissue ['tiʃuː] *n.* 薄纸，棉纸；[生] 组织；一套

【变】tissues

【例】In this syndrome, the swelling and pressure in a restricted space limits blood flow and causes localised **tissue** and nerve damage.

这种综合症的表现是，在有限的空间里，膨胀和压力会限制血液流动，并导致局部**组织**和神经损伤。

【搭】tissue ballots 用薄纸制成的投票纸 tissue bundle 用玻璃纸包装的包

【记】issue *v.* 发行，发表，颁布

pursue *n.* 追赶；从事

词汇听写

1. _____ 2. _____ 3. _____

句子听写

2. And the trainer trend hasn't slacked. I bought two pairs of the original black and white without the least hesitation when they first debuted.

训练鞋的流行趋势并没有丝毫减退。首发时，我就毫不犹豫买了两双黑白色的训练鞋。

trend [trend] *n.* 走向；趋向；时尚，时髦 *v.* 倾向；趋势

【变】trended trended trending trends

【例】And the trainer **trend** hasn't slacked. I bought two pairs of the original black and white without the least hesitation when they first debuted.

训练鞋的流行**趋势**并没有丝毫减退。首发时，我就毫不犹豫买了两

双黑白色的训练鞋。

【搭】trend analysis 趋势分析　　trend extrapolation 趋势线外推（法）

【记】trench *n.* 沟，渠；战壕

trendy *a.* 时髦的，赶时髦的，追随时髦的 *n.* 时髦人物，赶时髦的人；领导时尚的人

trendier *a.* 时髦的，赶时髦的，追随时髦的

slack［slæk］*a.* 松（弛）的；清淡的；不活跃的；懈怠的　*v.* 懈怠；偷懒；减速；放松

【变】slacked　slacked　slacking　slacks

【例】And the trainer trend hasn't **slacked.** I bought two pairs of the original black and white without the least hesitation when they first debuted.

训练鞋的流行趋势并没有丝毫减退。首发时，我就毫不犹豫买了两双黑白色的训练鞋。

【搭】slack action 列车冲动　　slack adjuster block 缓冲调整块

【记】slack-jawed *a.* 发呆的，目瞪口呆的

slacker *n.*〈非正〉逃避工作的人，偷懒的人；懒鬼

slacken *v.*（使）放慢；（使）放松、松懈、松弛；（使）减弱

original［əˈridʒənl］*a.* 原始的；独创的；最初的；新颖的

【变】originals　original arbitration award

【例】And the trainer trend hasn't slacked. I bought two pairs of the **original** black and white without the least hesitation when they first debuted.

训练鞋的流行趋势并没有丝毫减退。首发时，我就毫不犹豫买了两双黑白色的训练鞋。

【搭】original recording 原声录音

【记】originality *n.* 独创性，独到之处；新颖

originally *ad.* 起初，独出心裁地

originate *v.* 引起；创始，创作；开始，发生；发明

hesitation［ˌheziˈteiʃn］*n.* 犹豫；踌躇；含糊

【变】hesitations

【例】And the trainer trend hasn't slacked. I bought two pairs of the original black and white without the least **hesitation** when they first debuted.

　　训练鞋的流行趋势并没有丝毫减退。首发时，我就毫不**犹豫**买了两双黑白色的训练鞋。

【记】hesitate *v.* 犹豫，踌躇；不愿；支吾；停顿 *v.* 对……犹豫；不情愿

　　hessian *n.* 粗麻布

---

debut ['deibju:] *n.* 初次露面，初次表演，首次出场，处女秀　*v.* 初次表演，初次登台

【变】debuts　debuted　debuted　debuting　debuts

【例】And the trainer trend hasn't slacked. I bought two pairs of the original black and white without the least hesitation when they first **debuted**.

　　训练鞋的流行趋势并没有丝毫减退。首发时，我就毫不犹豫买了两双黑白色的训练鞋。

【记】debug *v.* 拆除窃听器；排除故障

　　debunk *v.* 揭穿真相，暴露

　　debutante *n.* 初进社交界的上流社会年轻女子

词汇听写

1. _____　2. _____　3. _____

句子听写

---

3. But I suspect that a lot of women are looking for ways to integrate their kids into the identities they worked so hard to forge in all those years before they got pregnant.

　　但我怀疑，很多女性正在寻找各种方式，让她们的孩子融入到她们怀孕前努力工作换来的身份阶层。

---

suspect [sə'spekt] *v.* 猜疑（是）；怀疑，不信任；怀疑……有罪
　　　　　　　　　　　 n. 嫌疑犯

【变】suspected　suspected　suspecting　suspects

【例】But I **suspect** that a lot of women are looking for ways to integrate their kids into the identities they worked so hard to forge in all those years before they got pregnant.

但我**怀疑**，很多女性正在寻找各种方式，让她们的孩子融入到她们怀孕前努力工作换来的身份阶层。

【搭】suspect of 怀疑　suspect patient 疑似症患者，可疑病人

【记】suspend *v.* 暂停；延缓；暂停；悬浮

---

integrate [ˈintigreit] *v.* 使一体化；使整合；使完整；使结合成为整体

【变】integrated　integrated　integrating　integrates

【例】But I suspect that a lot of women are looking for ways to **integrate** their kids into the identities they worked so hard to forge in all those years before they got pregnant.

但我怀疑，很多女性正在寻找各种方式，让她们的孩子**融入**到她们怀孕前努力工作换来的身份阶层。

【搭】integrate with（使）与……结合在一起

【记】integration *n.* 结合；整合；一体化；（不同肤色、种族、宗教信仰等的人的）混合

integral *a.* 完整的；积分的；必须的

integrities *n.* 正直（integrity 的名词复数）；完整；[计] 保存；健全

---

forge [fɔːdʒ] *n.* 锻造车间；熔铁炉，锻铁炉；铁匠铺，铁匠工场

【变】forged　forged　forging　forges

【例】But I suspect that a lot of women are looking for ways to integrate their kids into the identities they worked so hard to **forge** in all those years before they got pregnant.

但我怀疑，很多女性正在寻找各种方式，让她们的孩子融入到她们怀孕前努力工作换来的身份阶层。

【搭】forge ahead 稳步前进，突然加速前进；开拓进取　forge bar 锻制棒材

【记】forger *n.*（钱、文件等的）伪造者

forgery *n.* 伪造；伪造罪；伪造物；伪造签字

pregnant [ˈpreɡnənt] *a.* 怀孕的；孕育着……的；富于想象的；富于成果的

【例】But I suspect that a lot of women are looking for ways to integrate their kids into the identities they worked so hard to forge in all those years before they got **pregnant.**

　　但我怀疑，很多女性正在寻找各种方式，让她们的孩子融入到她们**怀孕**前努力工作换来的身份阶层。

【搭】pregnant pause 意味深长的停顿　　pregnant silence *n.* 耐人寻味的沉默

【记】pregnancy *n.* 怀孕，妊娠；丰富，多产；意义深长

　　preheat *v.* 预热

　　dominant *a.* 统治的

词汇听写

1. ＿＿＿＿＿＿＿　　2. ＿＿＿＿＿＿＿　　3. ＿＿＿＿＿＿＿

句子听写

Wednesday ··· «

1. The Duchess's exquisite wedding gown converted even the most cynical of critics with its elegance and credentials.

公爵夫人精致的婚纱礼服因其优雅与高档成为批评家们指责最多的批判目标。

exquisite [ik'skwizit] *a.* 精致的；细腻的；优美的；剧烈的

【变】more exquisite　most exquisite

【例】The Duchess's **exquisite** wedding gown converted even the most cynical of critics with its elegance and credentials.

公爵夫人**精致的**婚纱礼服因其优雅与高档成为批评家们指责最多的批判目标。

【记】exquisitely *ad.* 精致地；强烈地；异常地

exceedingly *ad.* 极端地，非常

convert [kən'vəːt] *v.* （使）转变；使皈依；兑换，换算；侵占　*v.* 经过转变；被改变；[橄榄球] 触地得分后得附加分

【变】converted　converted　converting　converts

【例】The Duchess's exquisite wedding gown **converted** even the most cynical of critics with its elegance and credentials.

公爵夫人精致的婚纱礼服因其优雅与高档**成为**批评家们指责最多的批判目标。

【搭】convert a penalty kick 罚中　convert instruction 变符号指令

【记】converter *n.* 变压器，变频器；冶炼钢炉，吹风转炉；使转变（改变信仰）的人

convertible *a.* 可改变的；可变换的；（货币）可以自由兑换的；（汽车等）有折篷的 *n.* 敞篷

convertibility *n.* 可改变性，可变化性

cynical ['sinikl] *a.* 怀疑的；愤世嫉俗的；冷嘲的；见利忘义的

【例】The Duchess's exquisite wedding gown converted even the most **cynical** of critics with its elegance and credentials.

公爵夫人精致的婚纱礼服因其优雅与高档成为批评家们指责最多的批判目标。

【记】cynically *ad.* 爱嘲笑地，冷笑地

cynicism *n.* 讥笑，讥讽的言词；玩世不恭；犬儒哲学

cynics *n.* 愤世嫉俗者，玩世不恭的人；犬儒主义者

---

credential [krə'denʃl] *n.* 外交使节所递的国书，信任状；文凭 *v.* 提供证明书

【例】The Duchess's exquisite wedding gown converted even the most cynical of critics with its elegance and **credentials**.

公爵夫人精致的婚纱礼服因其优雅与高档成为批评家们指责最多的批判目标。

【记】credibility *n.* 可靠性，可信性；确实性

credible *a.* 可信的，可靠的；（因看似可能成功而）可接受的

credit *n.* 信誉，信用；[金融] 贷款；荣誉；学分

词汇听写

1. _____ 2. _____ 3. _____

句子听写

2. The police made dramatic swoops last month, raiding dozens of premises and arresting six people as part of a massive bust on a suspected art forgery ring.

上个月，警方进行了一次大搜捕，突袭了几十个处所，并逮捕了六人，这次行动是针对一个涉嫌艺术伪造团体的重大抓捕行动的一部分。

---

swoop [swu:p] *v.* （鹰）俯冲，猛冲；突然扑向

【变】swooped swooped swooping swoops

【例】The police made dramatic **swoops** last month, raiding dozens of premises and arresting six people as part of a massive bust on a suspected art forgery ring.

上个月，警方进行了一次大搜捕，突袭了几十个处所，并逮捕了六

人，这次行动是针对一个涉嫌艺术伪造团体的重大抓捕行动的一部分。

【搭】swoop down on 猛扑向

【记】swop n. 交换

swoon v. & n. ［文］昏厥，昏倒

sword n. 剑，刀；武力，战争；兵权，权力

raid ［reid］ n. （骑兵队等的）急袭，突击，（军舰等的）游击；劫夺，突然查抄，围捕

【变】raided　raided　raiding　raids

【例】The police made dramatic swoops last month, **raiding** dozens of premises and arresting six people as part of a massive bust on a suspected art forgery ring.

上个月，警方进行了一次大搜捕，**突袭**了几十个处所，并逮捕了六人，这次行动是针对一个涉嫌艺术伪造团体的重大抓捕行动的一部分。

【搭】raid the market 扰乱市场

【记】raider n. 袭击者；扰乱者；进行突袭的舰队、飞机等

rail n. 围栏；轨道，钢轨；扶手 v. 责备；抱怨；责骂

railcard n. 火车优惠购票卡

premise ［'premis］ n. 前提；（pl.）房屋；（pl.）（合同、契约用语）上述各点；（逻辑学中的）前提

【变】premises

【例】The police made dramatic swoops last month, raiding dozens of **premises** and arresting six people as part of a massive bust on a suspected art forgery ring.

上个月，警方进行了一次大搜捕，突袭了几十个**处所**，并逮捕了六人，这次行动是针对一个涉嫌艺术伪造团体的重大抓捕行动的一部分。

【记】premiss n. ［法］前提

premium n. 费用，额外费用；保险费；奖赏，奖励；（商品定价、贷款利息等以外的）加价

premier n. 总理；首相

forgery ［'fɔːdʒəri］ n. 伪造；伪造罪；伪造物；伪造签字

【变】forgeries

【例】The police made dramatic swoops last month, raiding dozens of premises and arresting six people as part of a massive bust on a suspected art **forgery** ring.

上个月，警方进行了一次大搜捕，突袭了几十个处所，并逮捕了六人，这次行动是针对一个涉嫌艺术**伪造**团体的重大抓捕行动的一部分。

【搭】forgery bond 伪造保证保险

【记】forger *n.* （钱、文件等的）伪造者

forge *v.* 锻造；伪造；艰苦干成；努力加强

forget *v.* 忘却；忽略，疏忽；遗落；忘掉

词汇听写

1. _____ 2. _____ 3. _____

句子听写

3. This commanding and supremely elegant skyscraper is, beyond doubt, one of the world's most revered buildings.

毋庸置疑，这幢威严的、优雅的摩天楼，是世界上最受崇敬的建筑之一。

command [kə'mɑːnd] *n.* 命令，指挥；司令部，指挥部；[计] 指令；控制力 *v.* 指挥，控制，命令；应得，值得

【变】commanded commanded commanding commands

【例】This and supremely elegant skyscraper is, beyond doubt, one of the world's most revered buildings.

毋庸置疑，这幢、优雅的摩天楼，是世界上最受崇敬的建筑之一。

【搭】command airplane 长机，指挥机 command bit 命令位

【记】commandant *n.* 司令官；指挥官；〈美〉（陆军军官学校的）校长

commandeer *v.* 征用；强占

commandment *n.* 戒条

skyscraper ['skaɪskreɪpə] *n.* 摩天大楼，超高层大楼；特别高的东西

【变】skyscrapers

【例】This commanding and supremely elegant **skyscraper** is, beyond doubt, one of the world's most revered buildings.

毋庸置疑，这幢威严的、优雅的**摩天楼**，是世界上最受崇敬的建筑之一。

【记】scrapers *n.* 刮刀；刮的人；平土机；铲土机

scrapheap *n.* 废料堆，废物堆

scrap *n.* 废料；残余物；小片；吵架

beyond doubt 毫无疑问，无疑地，不容怀疑；确凿不移

【例】This commanding and supremely elegant skyscraper is, **beyond doubt**, one of the world's most revered buildings.

毋庸置疑，这幢威严的、优雅的摩天楼，是世界上最受崇敬的建筑之一。

【记】beyond reach 够不到

beyond words 可意会不可言传

beyond control 无法控制

beyond belief 难以置信

revere [ri'viə] *v.* 崇敬；尊崇；敬畏

【变】revered revered revering reveres

【例】This commanding and supremely elegant skyscraper is, beyond doubt, one of the world's most **revered** buildings.

毋庸置疑，这幢威严的、优雅的摩天楼，是世界上最受**崇敬**的建筑之一。

【记】reverberate *v.* 回响；弹回；反射

reveal *v.* 显露；揭露；泄露；［神］启示

severe *a.* 严峻的；剧烈的

词汇听写

1. _____ 2. _____ 3. _____

句子听写

Thursday ··· ⋘

1. Profitable, polished, efficient and as elegant and as popular as ever, the Empire State Building fully deserves its place in the pantheon of the world's greatest buildings.

创造利润的、完美的、高效的、优雅的，和以往一样受欢迎的帝国大厦完全称得上是世界上最伟大建筑中的神殿级建筑。

profitable [ˈprɔfitəbl] *a.* 有利可图的，有益的；可赚钱的，合算的

【例】**Profitable**, polished, efficient and as elegant and as popular as ever, the Empire State Building fully deserves its place in the pantheon of the world's greatest buildings.

创造利润的、完美的、高效的、优雅的，和以往一样受欢迎的帝国大厦完全称得上是世界上最伟大建筑中的神殿级建筑。

【搭】profitable field of investment 有利的投资场所　profitable projects 可赚钱的项目

【记】profit *n.* 收益，得益；利润；红利；净值利润率

proficiency *n.* 熟练，精通，娴熟

proficient *a.* 精通的，熟练的

polish [ˈpɔliʃ] *v.* （使）光滑，擦亮；修正；文饰；（涂蜡等）打光滑；使（人、举止、仪表等）变得优雅

【变】polished　polished　polishing　polishes

【例】Profitable, **polished** efficient and as elegant and as popular as ever, the Empire State Building fully deserves its place in the pantheon of the world's greatest buildings.

创造利润的、**完美的**、高效的、优雅的，和以往一样受欢迎的帝国大厦完全称得上是世界上最伟大建筑中的神殿级建筑。

【搭】polish attack 抛光浸蚀　polish away 擦去

【记】polite *a.* 有礼貌的；有教养的，文雅的；上流社会的

political *a.* 政治的；政党的；对政治有兴趣的；争权夺利的

politic *a.* （计划、言行）考虑周到的；有见识的；谨慎的；慎重的

deserve [di'zə:v] *v.* 应受；应得；值得

【变】deserved　deserved　deserving　deserves

【例】Profitable, polished, efficient and as elegant and as popular as ever, the Empire State Building fully **deserves** its place in the pantheon of the world's greatest buildings.

　　创造利润的、完美的、高效的、优雅的，和以往一样受欢迎的帝国大厦**完全称得上**是世界上最伟大建筑中的神殿级建筑。

【搭】deserve a beating 该挨打　deserve a corner 应受罚

【记】deservedly *ad.* 应得地，当然地

　　desiccate *v.* 弄干，使脱水；使失水

pantheon ['pænθiən] *n.* 万神庙；（一国或一民族信奉的）众神；名流；伟人

【变】pantheons

【例】Profitable, polished, efficient and as elegant and as popular as ever, the Empire State Building fully deserves its place in the **pantheon** of the world's greatest buildings.

　　创造利润的、完美的、高效的、优雅的，和以往一样受欢迎的帝国大厦完全称得上是世界上最伟大建筑中的**神殿级**建筑。

【记】panther *n.* 豹，黑豹；美洲豹

　　pantheism *n.* 泛神论

　　panties *n.* （妇女或儿童的）短衬裤；童裤，女裤

词汇听写

1. ＿＿＿＿＿＿　　2. ＿＿＿＿＿＿　　3. ＿＿＿＿＿＿

句子听写

2. Make sure you have well worn boots, a sturdy tent, a warm sleeping bag, a reliable cooking stove, and an emergency communication device like a satellite phone or a personal locator beacon.

　　确保你有双合脚好穿的靴子、一个牢固的帐篷、一个温暖的睡袋、一个可靠的灶具和应急通信设备，如卫星电话或个人定位信标。

well worn 好穿的，合身的

【例】Make sure you have **well worn** boots, a sturdy tent, a warm sleeping bag, a reliable cooking stove, and an emergency communication device like a satellite phone or a personal locator beacon.

　　确保你有双合脚**好穿的**靴子、一个牢固的帐篷、一个温暖的睡袋、一个可靠的灶具和应急通信设备，如卫星电话或个人定位信标。

sturdy ['stəːdi] *a.* 强壮的，健全的；坚固的，耐用的；坚定的；精力充沛的

【变】sturdier　sturdiest

【例】Make sure you have well worn boots, a **sturdy** tent, a warm sleeping bag, a reliable cooking stove, and an emergency communication device like a satellite phone or a personal locator beacon.

　　确保你有双合脚好穿的靴子、一个**牢固的**帐篷、一个温暖的睡袋、一个可靠的灶具和应急通信设备，如卫星电话或个人定位信标。

【搭】sturdy man 壮汉

【记】sturdily *ad.* 坚强地，刚强地，坚毅地

　　sturgeon *n.* 鲟

　　stutter *v.* 结结巴巴地说；不顺畅的工作，时断时续地移动

reliable [ri'laiəbl] *a.* 可靠的；可信赖的；真实可信的　*n.* 可靠的人

【变】more reliable　most reliable

【例】Make sure you have well worn boots, a sturdy tent, a warm sleeping bag, a **reliable** cooking stove, and an emergency communication device like a satellite phone or a personal locator beacon.

　　确保你有双合脚好穿的靴子、一个牢固的帐篷、一个温暖的睡袋、一个**可靠的**灶具和应急通信设备，如卫星电话或个人定位信标。

【搭】reliable account 可靠账户　reliable friend 可靠的朋友

【记】reliability *n.* 可靠，可信赖

　　reliably *ad.* 可靠地，确实地

device [dɪˈvaɪs] *n.* 装置，设备；方法；策略；手段

【变】devices

【例】Make sure you have well worn boots, a sturdy tent, a warm sleeping bag, a reliable cooking stove, and an emergency communication **device** like a satellite phone or a personal locator beacon.

　　确保你有双合脚好穿的靴子、一个牢固的帐篷、一个温暖的睡袋、一个可靠的灶具和应急通信**设备**，如卫星电话或个人定位信标。

【搭】device address 设备地址　　device availability 设备利用率

【记】devil *n.* 魔鬼；家伙；淘气鬼；冒失鬼

　　deviance *n.* 偏常，异常，异常行为

　　deviant *n.* 不正常的人，异常的人

词汇听写

1. ＿＿＿＿＿＿＿＿　2. ＿＿＿＿＿＿＿＿　3. ＿＿＿＿＿＿＿＿

句子听写

3. Whether you seek outdoor adventure or quiet reflection, the majesty of the American West shines through at these heavenly retreats.

　　无论您是寻求户外冒险或安静思考，美国西部都会让这些神圣的静养地闪耀着庄严。

adventure [ədˈventʃə] *n.* 冒险活动；冒险经历；奇遇

【变】adventures

【例】Whether you seek outdoor **adventure** or quiet reflection, the majesty of the American West shines through at these heavenly retreats.

　　无论您是寻求户外**冒险**或安静思考，美国西部都会让这些神圣的静养地闪耀着庄严。

【搭】adventure experience 冒险经历　　adventure film 惊险影片

【记】adventurer *n.* 探险家，冒险家；投机商人

adventurism *n.* （外交、政治等方面的）冒险主义

adventurous *a.* 爱冒险的；大胆的；危险的

reflection [riˈflekʃn] *n.* 反映；（关于某课题的）思考；（声、光、热等的）反射；映像

【变】reflections

【例】Whether you seek outdoor adventure or quiet **reflection**, the majesty of the American West shines through at these heavenly retreats.

无论您是寻求户外冒险或安静**思考**，美国西部都会让这些神圣的静养地闪耀着庄严。

【搭】reflection altimeter 反射测高计 reflection arcs 反射线

【记】reflect *v.* 反射（光、热、声或影像）；考虑

reflective *a.* 反射的，反映的；反省性的；（指人、心情等）深思熟虑的；（指物体表面）反光的

reflector *n.* 反射器，反射光（热、声音）的物体 *v.* 加工某物使之反射光线；在……上装反射器

majesty [ˈmædʒəsti] *n.* 主权，统治权；陛下，王权；庄严，雄伟；光轮中的耶稣（圣母、上帝）圣像

【变】majesties

【例】Whether you seek outdoor adventure or quiet reflection, the **majesty** of the American West shines through at these heavenly retreats.

无论您是寻求户外冒险或安静思考，美国西部都会让这些神圣的静养地闪耀着**庄严**。

【记】majestic *a.* 宏伟的；壮丽的；庄重的；磅礴的

majestically *ad.* 雄伟地；庄重地；威严地；崇高地

major *a.* 主要的；重要的；大调的；主修的（课程）

retreat [riˈtriːt] *v.* 撤退，后退；撤销，作罢；（眼睛等）凹进；[航] 向后倾斜 *n.* 撤回；静居处

【变】retreated retreated retreating retreats

【例】Whether you seek outdoor adventure or quiet reflection, the majesty of the American West shines through at these heavenly **retreats**.

无论您是寻求户外冒险或安静思考，美国西部都会让这些神圣的**静养地**闪耀着庄严。

【搭】retreat from 从……撤退；避开……

【记】retrench v. 紧缩开支

　　retrial n. 再审，复审

　　retrieval n. 收回，挽回；检索

词汇听写

1. _____　2. _____　3. _____

句子听写

Friday ·································· ≪

1. In New York City, the hot dog is as <u>iconic</u> as the yellow taxi. For locals, one <u>bite</u> triggers memories of sand-strewn lunches on the beaches or the smell of just-cut grass and <u>yeasty</u> beer at a summer baseball game.

在纽约市，热狗和黄色出租车一样都是标志性的东西。对于本地人，咬一口热狗就让他们回忆起海滩上洒落了一些沙子的午餐，或夏天棒球比赛场上新割草坪的青草香和啤酒的酵母香。

iconic [aiˈkɔnik] *a.* 符号的；图标的；图符的；偶像的

【例】In New York City, the hot dog is as **iconic** as the yellow taxi. For locals, one bite triggers memories of sand-strewn lunches on the beaches or the smell of just-cut grass and yeasty beer at a summer baseball game.

在纽约市，热狗和黄色出租车一样都是**标志性的**东西。对于本地人，咬一口热狗就让他们回忆起海滩上洒落了一些沙子的午餐，或夏天棒球比赛场上新割草坪的青草香和啤酒的酵母香。

【搭】iconic element 图像成分　iconic memory 映像记忆

【记】iconographic *a.* 肖像的；肖像学的；图像材料的；图示法的象征
　　icon *n.* 偶像，崇拜对象；图标，图符；[宗] 圣像；肖像

bite [bait] *v.* 咬；叮　*n.* 咬；咬伤；疼痛；受骗

【变】bites　bit　bitten　bitting　bites

【例】In New York City, the hot dog is as iconic as the yellow taxi. For locals, one **bite** triggers memories of sand-strewn lunches on the beaches or the smell of just-cut grass and yeasty beer at a summer baseball game.

在纽约市，热狗和黄色出租车一样都是标志性的东西。对于本地人，**咬**一口热狗就让他们回忆起海滩上洒落了一些沙子的午餐，或夏天棒球比赛场上新割草坪的青草香和啤酒的酵母香。

【搭】bite a file 白费力，徒劳无功，白费力气（来自猫想咬锉的寓言）　bite at 向……咬去；向……叫骂；上当

【记】bitmap *n.* 位图

bitt *n.* 缆柱 *v.* 系于缆柱

bitty *a.* 片段的，细短的，支离破碎的

strewn [struːn] *v.* 撒在……上（strew 的过去分词）；散落于　*a.* 散播的

【例】In New York City, the hot dog is as iconic as the yellow taxi. For locals, one bite triggers memories of sand-**strewn** lunches on the beaches or the smell of just-cut grass and yeasty beer at a summer baseball game.

　　在纽约市，热狗和黄色出租车一样都是标志性的东西。对于本地人，咬一口热狗就让他们回忆起海滩上**洒落**了一些沙子的午餐，或夏天棒球比赛场上新割草坪的青草香和啤酒的酵母香。

【记】strew *v.* 撒在……上；散落于；点缀；撒满

streak *v.* 快速移动；加上条纹 *v.* 使布满条纹

streaky *a.* 有斑点的，有条纹的，容易变的

yeasty [ˈjiːsti] *a.* 动荡的；有酵母的

【例】In New York City, the hot dog is as iconic as the yellow taxi. For locals, one bite triggers memories of sand-strewn lunches on the beaches or the smell of just-cut grass and **yeasty** beer at a summer baseball game.

　　在纽约市，热狗和黄色出租车一样都是标志性的东西。对于本地人，咬一口热狗就让他们回忆起海滩上洒落了一些沙子的午餐，或夏天棒球比赛场上新割草坪的青草香和啤酒的**酵母**香。

【记】yeast *n.* 酵母；酵母粉；动乱 *v.* 发酵

yell *v.* 叫喊，大声叫；叫喊着说

yard *n.* 院子，场地；码

yearly *a.* 每年的

词汇听写

1. ＿＿＿＿＿＿＿＿　　2. ＿＿＿＿＿＿＿＿　　3. ＿＿＿＿＿＿＿＿

句子听写

2. A hot dog is a frankfurter-style <u>sausage</u> that is made of <u>ground</u> pork, beef or a combination of the two, <u>flavoured</u> with garlic, mustard, nutmeg and other spices, gut-encased, then cured, smoked and cooked.

热狗是一种法兰克福香肠，由绞碎的猪肉、牛肉（或猪牛肉一起绞碎）制成，使用大蒜、芥末、肉豆蔻和其他调味品，包裹后加工储藏，再进行烟熏烹饪。

sausage [ˈsɔsidʒ] *n.* 香肠，腊肠

【变】sausages

【例】A hot dog is a frankfurter-style **sausage** that is made of ground pork, beef or a combination of the two, flavoured with garlic, mustard, nutmeg and other spices, gut-encased, then cured, smoked and cooked.

熱狗是一种法兰克福**香肠**，由绞碎的猪肉、牛肉（或猪牛肉一起绞碎）制成，使用大蒜、芥末、肉豆蔻和其他调味品，包裹后加工储藏，再进行烟熏烹饪。

【搭】sausage cage 熏（香）肠架　sausage cross cutter 香肠切片机

【记】savage *a.* 未开化的；野蛮的；凶猛的；残忍的

savagely *ad.* 野蛮地；残忍地；粗野地；凶猛地

ground [graund] *n.* 地面，土地；基础；范围；阵地，战场　*v.* (grind 的过去式和过去分词) 磨碎的；嚼碎的

【变】grounded　grounded　grounding　grounds

【例】A hot dog is a frankfurter-style sausage that is made of **ground** pork, beef or a combination of the two, flavoured with garlic, mustard, nutmeg and other spices, gut-encased, then cured, smoked and cooked.

熱狗是一种法兰克福香肠，由**绞碎**的猪肉、牛肉（或猪牛肉一起绞碎）制成，使用大蒜、芥末、肉豆蔻和其他调味品，包裹后加工储藏，再进行烟熏烹饪。

【搭】be ground using traditional methods 用传统方法磨制　ground alert 戒备状态，进入戒备状态的信号

【记】groan *v.* 呻吟；发牢骚；抱怨

flavour ['fleivə] *n.* 风味，情趣；味，滋味；香味，气味　*v.* 给……添风味；给……增加香气；给……调味

【变】flavoured　flavoured　flavouring　flavours

【例】A hot dog is a frankfurter-style sausage that is made of ground pork, beef or a combination of the two, **flavoured** with garlic, mustard, nutmeg and other spices, gut-encased, then cured, smoked and cooked.

　　热狗是一种法兰克福香肠，由绞碎的猪肉、牛肉（或猪牛肉一起绞碎）制成，使用大蒜、芥末、肉豆蔻和其他**调味**品，包裹后加工储藏，再进行烟熏烹饪。

【搭】flavour additive 香味添加剂　flavour enhancer 香味增强剂，风味增强剂，鲜味增强剂（如味精等）

【记】flavourless *a.* 无味的，无滋味的
　　flavoursome *a.* 味道浓郁的；有滋味的；有味道
　　flawed *a.* 有缺点的；有缺陷的；错误的

encase [in'keis] *v.* 包装；围绕；把……装箱

【变】encased　encased　encasing　encases

【例】A hot dog is a frankfurter-style sausage that is made of ground pork, beef or a combination of the two, flavoured with garlic, mustard, nutmeg and other spices, gut-**encased**, then cured, smoked and cooked.

　　热狗是一种法兰克福香肠，由绞碎的猪肉、牛肉（或猪牛肉一起绞碎）制成，使用大蒜、芥末、肉豆蔻和其他调味品，**包裹**后加工储藏，再进行烟熏烹饪。

【记】encasement *n.* 装箱，套
　　enchant *v.* 使心醉，使迷惑；用魔法迷惑

词汇听写

1. _____　2. _____　3. _____

句子听写

3. Around the time a <u>bald</u> eagle turns 3-years-old, it will pick a <u>mate</u>. The new couple might fly off separately after raising their <u>offspring</u>, but every year in mating season, they will meet back up to <u>renew</u> the relationship.

　　秃鹰满 3 岁左右时，它会选择一个伴侣。在养育了后代之后，他们可能会各自飞离，但每年交配季节时，他们将会再次相会，重新开始。

bald [bɔːld] *a.* 秃头的；单调的，枯燥的；光秃的；赤裸裸的，毫无掩饰的

【变】balder　baldest

【例】Around the time a **bald** eagle turns 3-years-old, it will pick a mate. The new couple might fly off separately after raising their offspring, but every year in mating season, they will meet back up to renew the relationship.

　　秃鹰满 3 岁左右时，它会选择一个伴侣。在养育了后代之后，他们可能会各自飞离，但每年交配季节时，他们将会再次相会，重新开始。

【搭】bald coot 骨顶鸟　bald head 秃头

【记】balder *a.* 秃头的（bald 的比较级）；明显的；简单的；赤裸裸的

baldly *ad.* 坦率地

bold *a.* 明显的；勇敢的

mate [meit] *n.* （工人间的）伙伴，同事，老兄；配偶（男女任何一方），[航海]（商船的）大副，驾驶员

【变】mates

【例】Around the time a bald eagle turns 3-years-old, it will pick a **mate.** The new couple might fly off separately after raising their offspring, but every year in mating season, they will meet back up to renew the relationship.

　　秃鹰满 3 岁左右时，它会选择一个**伴侣**。在养育了后代之后，他们可能会各自飞离，但每年交配季节时，他们将会再次相会，重新开始。

【搭】mate account 对应科目　mate up 使配对

【记】material *n.* 材料，原料；素材；布，织物；适当人选

materialism *n.* 唯物主义；唯物论；实利主义，物质主义；[艺] 写实主义

offspring ['ɔfspriŋ] *n.* 后代，子孙；产物，结果；（动物的）崽；幼苗

【变】offspring

【例】Around the time a bald eagle turns 3-years-old，it will pick a mate. The new couple might fly off separately after raising their **offspring**，but every year in mating season，they will meet back up to renew the relationship.

　　秃鹰满 3 岁左右时，它会选择一个伴侣。在养育了**后代**之后，他们可能会各自飞离，但每年交配季节时，他们将会再次相会，重新开始。

【记】offstage *n.* 舞台内部，舞台后面

often *ad.* 常常；经常；时常；再三

spring *n.* 春季；泉水，小溪；弹簧，弹性；跳跃

renew [riˈnjuː] *v.* **重新开始；使更新；使恢复；补充**

【变】renewed　renewed　renewing　renews

【例】Around the time a bald eagle turns 3-years-old，it will pick a mate. The new couple might fly off separately after raising their offspring，but every year in mating season，they will meet back up to **renew** the relationship.

　　秃鹰满 3 岁左右时，它会选择一个伴侣。在养育了后代之后，他们可能会各自飞离，但每年交配季节时，他们将会再次相会，**重新**开始。

【搭】renew business relations 恢复业务往来　renew cartridge 换滤芯

【记】renewable *a.* 可继续的，可续订的；可更新的；可再生的；可翻新的

renewal *n.* 重建，重生；革新；合同的续订

renounce *v.* 放弃，抛弃；拒绝，否认；宣布与……决裂

词汇听写

1. ＿＿＿＿＿＿＿　2. ＿＿＿＿＿＿＿　3. ＿＿＿＿＿＿＿

句子听写

Saturday ·· **《《**

1. The commitment problem is particularly acute in the United States, in part because of the way people in the country measure the trait. For the most part, US corporate culture still values the number of hours spent at work which can be written in the contract.

　　承诺这个问题在美国尤为突出，部分是因为美国人对其颇为重视，但主要还是因为美国的企业文化仍然重视花在工作上的时间量，而这点可以在合同中进行明文规定。

commitment [kəˈmitmənt] *n.* 承诺，许诺；委任，委托；致力，献身；承担义务

【变】commitments

【例】The **commitment** problem is particularly acute in the United States, in part because of the way people in the country measure the trait. For the most part, US corporate culture still values the number of hours spent at work which can be written in the contract.

　　承诺这个问题在美国尤为突出，部分是因为美国人对其颇为重视，但主要还是因为美国的企业文化仍然重视花在工作上的时间量，而这点可以在合同中进行明文规定。

【搭】commitment authority 承诺（授）权　commitment value 约定价值

【记】commit *v.* 犯罪，做错事；把……托付给

commitee *n.* 委员会

commodity *n.* 商品，物品

common *a.* 共同的

acute [əˈkjut] *a.* 尖锐的；敏感的；严重的，剧烈的；[医] 急性的

【例】The commitment problem is particularly **acute** in the United States, in part because of the way people in the country measure the trait. For the most part, US corporate culture still values the number of hours spent at work which can be written in the contract.

承诺这个问题在美国尤为**突出**，部分是因为美国人对其颇为重视，但主要还是因为美国的企业文化仍然重视花在工作上的时间量，而这点可以在合同中进行明文规定。

【搭】acute abscess 急性脓肿　acute accent 重音符

【记】acutely *ad.* 尖锐地；剧烈地

acuteness *n.* 敏锐，剧烈

acuity *n.* 尖锐，（疾病的）剧烈，（视力、才智等的）敏锐；敏度

trait [treit] *n.* **特点，特性；少许**

【变】traits

【例】The commitment problem is particularly acute in the United States，in part because of the way people in the country measure the **trait**. For the most part，US corporate culture still values the number of hours spent at work which can be written in the contract.

承诺这个问题在美国尤为突出，部分是因为美国人对其颇为重视，但主要还是因为美国的企业文化仍然重视花在工作上的时间量，而这点可以在合同中进行明文规定。

【搭】human trait 人类的特性　dominant trait 最主要的特点　personality traits 人格特征

【记】trail *v.* 跟踪，追踪；拖沓而行

trailer *v.* 用拖车运 *v.* 乘拖带式居住车旅行

trace *v.* 跟踪；追溯，探索

corporate [ˈkɔːpərət] *a.* **法人的，团体的，社团的；公司的，总体国家的**

【例】The commitment problem is particularly acute in the United States，in part because of the way people in the country measure the trait. For the most part，US **corporate** culture still values the number of hours spent at work which can be written in the contract.

承诺这个问题在美国尤为突出，部分是因为美国人对其颇为重视，但主要还是因为美国的**企业**文化仍然重视花在工作上的时间量，而这点可以在合同中进行明文规定。

【搭】corporate accounting 公司会计 corporate income 公司收入，法人收入

【记】corporation *n.* 公司；法人；社团，团体

corporatism *n.* 组合主义，社团主义

corporatist *n.* 组合主义者，社团主义者

词汇听写

1. _____ 2. _____ 3. _____

句子听写

2. The designer's new <u>collection</u> featured all manner of '<u>feminine</u>' detail. What made it <u>intriguing</u>, though, was the fact that the attitude of the clothes was so incontrovertibly <u>masculine</u>.

设计师的新系列以"女性"化为特征。但是，让人疑惑的是，新系列衣服的风格是如此的阳刚。

collection [kəˈlekʃn] *n.* 收集，采集；征收；收藏品；募捐

【变】collections

【例】The designer's new **collection** featured all manner of 'feminine' detail. What made it intriguing, though, was the fact that the attitude of the clothes was so incontrovertibly masculine.

设计师的新**系列**以"女性"化为特征。但是，让人疑惑的是，新系列衣服的风格是如此的阳刚。

【搭】collection agency 为其他公司代收欠款的公司　collection of deposits 取得存款

【记】collective *a.* 集体的；共同的；集合的；集体主义的

collectively *ad.* 全体地，共同地

collectivism *n.* 集体主义

feminine [ˈfemənin] *a.* 有女性气质的；女子气的；[语] 阴性的；阴柔的

【变】feminines

【例】The designer's new collection featured all manner of '**feminine**' detail. What made it intriguing, though, was the fact that the attitude of the clothes was so incontrovertibly masculine.

设计师的新系列以"**女性**"化为特征。但是，让人疑惑的是，新系列衣服的风格是如此的阳刚。

【搭】feminine belongings 女性用品

【记】femininity *n*. 女性气质；娇弱，温柔；妇女的总称

feminism *n*. 女权主义；争取女权的运动

feminist *n*. 男女平等主义者，女权扩张论者

intrigue [in'tri:g] *n*. 密谋，阴谋；私通　*v*. 耍阴谋；激起……的好奇心

【变】intrigued　intrigued　intriguing　intrigues

【例】The designer's new collection featured all manner of 'feminine' detail. What made it **intriguing**, though, was the fact that the attitude of the clothes was so incontrovertibly masculine.

设计师的新系列以"**女性**"化为特征。但是，**让人疑惑**的是，新系列衣服的风格是如此的阳刚。

【搭】intrigue against 与……密谋反对……　intrigue with 与……私通

【记】intricacy *n*. 错综复杂；（因复杂而产生的）难以理解；（*pl.*）错综复杂的事物

intricately *ad*. 杂乱地，复杂地；难懂地

intricate *a*. 错综复杂的；难理解的；曲折的

masculine ['mæskjəlin] *a*. 男子气概的；阳性的，雄性的；男性化的，像男人的　*n*. [语] 阳性；阳性词；男性

【变】more masculine　most masculine

【例】The designer's new collection featured all manner of 'feminine' detail. What made it intriguing, though, was the fact that the attitude of the clothes was so incontrovertibly **masculine**.

设计师的新系列以"**女性**"化为特征。但是，让人疑惑的是，新系列衣服的风格是如此的**阳刚**。

【搭】masculine belongings 男性用品　masculine voice 男性化的声音

【记】masculinity *n*. 男性；男子气概

masculinize *v*. 使男子化（尤指使女人具有男子特征），使（雌性）雄性化

词汇听写

1. _____　2. _____　3. _____

句子听写

3. Brazilian Sports Minister said the pace of construction must be accelerated if the venues are to be ready by this December. Only one of the six stadiums under construction is on schedule.

　　巴西体育部长说，如果场馆都需要在今年 12 月建成，建设步伐必须加快。正在建设中的 6 个场馆中，只有一个是按计划进行。

> **pace** [peis] *n.* 一步；长度单位；步幅，步调；快步　*v.* 踱步，走来走去；步测；调整步调

【变】paced　paced　pacing　paces

【例】Brazilian Sports Minister said the **pace** of construction must be accelerated if the venues are to be ready by this December. Only one of the six stadiums under construction is on schedule.

　　巴西体育部长说，如果场馆都需要在今年 12 月建成，建设**步伐**必须加快。正在建设中的 6 个场馆中，只有一个是按计划进行。

【搭】brisk pace 轻快的步伐　　pace of change 变革的步伐

【记】pacemaker *n.* 领跑者；带头人；标兵；起搏器

　　pacesetter *n.* 步调调整者，先导者

> **accelerate** [ək'seləreit] *v.* (使) 加快，(使) 增速；催促；促进；速度增加

【变】accelerated　accelerated　accelerating　accelerates

【例】Brazilian Sports Minister said the pace of construction must be **accelerated** if the venues are to be ready by this December. Only one of the six stadiums under construction is on schedule.

　　巴西体育部长说，如果场馆都需要在今年 12 月建成，建设步伐必须**加快**。正在建设中的 6 个场馆中，只有一个是按计划进行。

【搭】growth will accelerate to 增长会加快到　　accelerate away from 加速驶离

【记】accelerative *a.* 加速的，催促的

　　acceleration *n.* 加速；[物] 加速度；加速升级；(优秀学生的) 跳级

　　accelerator *n.* 加速器；催速剂

　　decelerate *v.* 减速

venue [ˈvenjuː] *n.* 犯罪地点，案发地点；会场；（尤指）体育比赛场所；审判地

【变】venues

【例】Brazilian Sports Minister said the pace of construction must be accelerated if the **venues** are to be ready by this December. Only one of the six stadiums under construction is on schedule.

　　巴西体育部长说，如果**场馆**都需要在今年 12 月建成，建设步伐必须加快。正在建设中的 6 个场馆中，只有一个是按计划进行。

【搭】Olympic venue 奥林匹克会场　　a dispute over the venue 关于举办地点发生的争论

【记】Venus *n.* 金星，太白星；维纳斯（爱与美的女神）；美女

　　veracity *n.* 诚实，真实

on schedule [ɔn ˈʃedjuːl] 按时间表，准时；如期；正点；按计划

【例】Brazilian Sports Minister said the pace of construction must be accelerated if the venues are to be ready by this December. Only one of the six stadiums under construction is **on schedule.**

　　巴西体育部长说，如果场馆都需要在今年 12 月建成，建设步伐必须加快。正在建设中的 6 个场馆中，只有一个是**按计划**进行。

【搭】arrive on schedule 准点到达　　hectic schedules 日程安排得很紧

　　behind schedule 比计划时间晚

【记】scare *v. & n.* 惊恐，恐慌

　　scene *n.* 景象，景色

　　scheme *v. & n.* 计划；阴谋

　　scholar *n.* 学者

词汇听写

1. _____　　2. _____　　3. _____

句子听写

Sunday ·· 》》》

1. US mortgage rates are hovering near record lows, prompting many to jump into the housing market. In the rush to buy, first-time home buyers are finding themselves caught unaware by additional fees.

　　美国抵押贷款利率在创纪录的低点附近徘徊，促使许多人跳进住房市场。在抢购潮中，首次购房者发现自己面对着许多之前不知道的额外费用。

mortgage [ˈmɔːɡidʒ] *n.* 抵押；抵押单据，抵押证明；抵押权，债权
v. 抵押

【变】mortgaged　mortgaged　mortgaging　mortgages

【例】US **mortgage** rates are hovering near record lows, prompting many to jump into the housing market. In the rush to buy, first-time home buyers are finding themselves caught unaware by additional fees.

　　美国**抵押**贷款利率在创纪录的低点附近徘徊，促使许多人跳进住房市场。在抢购潮中，首次购房者发现自己面对着许多之前不知道的额外费用。

【搭】mortgage assets 抵押资产　mortgage bank 抵押银行

【记】mortician *n.* 殡仪业者

mortification *n.* 屈辱；羞愧

mortify *v.* 使受辱；克制；抑制（肉体、情感等）

hover [ˈhɒvə] *v.* 盘旋；徘徊；犹豫　*n.* 徘徊；盘旋

【变】hovered　hovered　hovering　hovers

【例】US mortgage rates are **hovering** near record lows, prompting many to jump into the housing market. In the rush to buy, first-time home buyers are finding themselves caught unaware by additional fees.

　　美国抵押贷款利率在创纪录的低点附近**徘徊**，促使许多人跳进住房市场。在抢购潮中，首次购房者发现自己面对着许多之前不知道的额外费用。

【搭】hover round the table 围着桌子走来走去　hover overhead 头顶盘旋

【记】hovercraft *n.* 气垫船

hovered *v.* 鸟，靠近（某事物）；（人）徘徊；犹豫

prompt [prɔmpt] *a.* 敏捷的；迅速的；立刻的；[商] 即期付款的　*v.* 指点；促进；激起，唤起　*n.* 刺激物；提示；付款期限

【变】prompted　prompted　prompting　prompts

【例】US mortgage rates are hovering near record lows, **prompting** many to jump into the housing market. In the rush to buy, first-time home buyers are finding themselves caught unaware by additional fees.

　　美国抵押贷款利率在创纪录的低点附近徘徊，**促使许多人跳进住房市场**。在抢购潮中，首次购房者发现自己面对着许多之前不知道的额外费用。

【搭】prompt attention 从速办理　prompt book 台词提示本

【记】promptly *ad.* 敏捷地；迅速地；立即地；毫不迟疑地

prom *n.* 正式舞会

promenade *n.* 散步，闲逛；走廊；舞会 *v.* 漫步；骑马

additional [ə'diʃənl] *a.* 额外的，附加的；另外的，追加的；补充；外加

【例】US mortgage rates are hovering near record lows, prompting many to jump into the housing market. In the rush to buy, first-time home buyers are finding themselves caught unaware by **additional** fees.

　　美国抵押贷款利率在创纪录的低点附近徘徊，促使许多人跳进住房市场。在抢购潮中，首次购房者发现自己面对着许多之前不知道的**额外费用**。

【搭】additional advance 追加垫款　additional allocation 增拨

【记】additionally *ad.* 此外

additions *n.* 加；增加；增加的人或事物；新增产品

additive *n.* 添加剂；添加物；[数] 加法 *a.* 附加的；[化] 加成的，加和的；[数] 加法的

词汇听写

1. _____　2. _____　3. _____

397

句子听写

2. A grand jury on Thursday indicted two students from the neighboring country on obstruction of justice charges, alleging they helped hide evidence related to the April Boston marathon bombing.

上周四一个大陪审团起诉从邻国来的两名学生妨碍司法，指控他们隐藏了与4月波士顿马拉松轰炸案相关的证据。

jury ['dʒuəri] *n.* 陪审团;（展览会，竞赛等的）全体评审员; 舆论的裁决; 评判委员会 *a.* 应急的;〔航〕（船上）应急用的; 暂时的

【变】juries

【例】A grand **jury** on Thursday indicted two students from the neighboring country on obstruction of justice charges, alleging they helped hide evidence related to the April Boston marathon bombing.

上周四一个大陪审团起诉从邻国来的两名学生妨碍司法，指控他们隐藏了与4月波士顿马拉松轰炸案相关的证据。

【搭】jury box 陪审（团）席 jury system 陪审制度

【记】panel *n.* 镶板; 面;（门、墙等上面的）嵌板; 控制板

forum *n.* 论坛，讨论会，专题讨论节目

indict [in'dait] *v.* 〔法〕控告，起诉; 告发

【变】indicted indicted indicting indicts

【例】A grand jury on Thursday **indicted** two students from the neighboring country on obstruction of justice charges, alleging they helped hide evidence related to the April Boston marathon bombing.

上周四一个大陪审团起诉从邻国来的两名学生妨碍司法，指控他们隐藏了与4月波士顿马拉松轰炸案相关的证据。

obstruction [əb'strʌkʃn] *n.* 障碍物;阻碍的行为或例子;阻碍，受阻;妨碍议事

【变】obstructions

【例】A grand jury on Thursday indicted two students from the neighboring country on **obstruction** of justice charges, alleging they helped hide evidence related to the April Boston marathon bombing.

　　上周四一个大陪审团起诉从邻国来的两名学生**妨碍**司法，指控他们隐藏了与 4 月波士顿马拉松轰炸案相关的证据。

【搭】obstruction beacon 障碍物信标　　obstruction buoy 障碍物浮标，沉船浮筒

obstruction marker 障碍标志板，障碍标志器

alleging [əˈledʒiŋ] *v.* **断言，宣称，辩解（** allege **的现在分词）**

【例】A grand jury on Thursday indicted two students from the neighboring country on obstruction of justice charges, **alleging** they helped hide evidence related to the April Boston marathon bombing.

　　上周四一个大陪审团起诉从邻国来的两名学生妨碍司法，**指控**他们隐藏了与 4 月波士顿马拉松轰炸案相关的证据。

词汇听写

1. _____ 2. _____ 3. _____

句子听写

3. The moist water of the earth is exhausted by evaporation and the pesticide cannot degrade.

　　土地中的水分全被蒸发光了，所以杀虫剂无法分解。

moist [mɔist] *a.* **潮湿的；微湿的；多雨的；含泪的**

【例】The **moist** water of the earth is exhausted by evaporation and the pesticide cannot degrade.

　　土地中的水分全被蒸发光了，所以杀虫剂无法分解。

【搭】moist chamber 保湿室　　moist soil 湿地

【记】moistly *ad.* 潮湿地，湿性地，含泪地

moistness *n.* 湿

moisten *v.* （使）变得潮湿，变得湿润

exhaust [igˈzɔːst] *v.* **用尽，耗尽；使精疲力尽；排出；彻底探讨**

【变】exhausted　exhausted　exhausting　exhausts

【例】The moist water of the earth is **exhausted** by evaporation and the pesticide cannot degrade.

土地中的水分全被蒸发光了，所以杀虫剂无法分解。

【搭】physically exhaust oneself 耗尽自己的体力　exhaust pipe 排气管
exhaust fumes 排废气

【记】exhausted *a.* 耗尽的，疲惫的
exhibit *v.* 展出，陈列 *n.* 展出，展览（会）

evaporation [iˌvæpəˈreiʃən] *n.* 蒸发，发散；消失；汽化；蒸发法

【例】The moist water of the earth is exhausted by **evaporation** and the pesticide cannot degrade.

土地中的水分全被蒸发光了，所以杀虫剂无法分解。

【搭】evaporation surface 蒸发面　high evaporation 高度蒸发　evaporation boiler 蒸发锅

【记】evaporate *v.* 蒸发，挥发；沉淀；发射；消失
vapor *n.* 水汽，蒸汽
evaporated *a.* 浓缩的，脱水的，蒸发干燥的

degrade [diˈgreid] *v.* 降低，贬低；使降级；降低……身份；使丢脸

【变】degraded　degraded　degrading　degrades

【例】The moist water of the earth is exhausted by evaporation and the pesticide cannot **degrade**.

土地中的水分全被蒸发光了，所以杀虫剂无法分解。

【搭】degrades someone 降低某人　degrade with age 随着年龄的增长而退化

【记】degrading *a.* 可耻的，不名誉的
graduation *n.* 毕业（典礼）；刻度

词汇听写

1. _____　2. _____　3. _____

句子听写